Applause for Eric

WHAT GOES UP

THE UNCENSORED HISTORY OF MODERN WALL STREET AS TOLD BY THE BANKERS, BROKERS, CEOs, AND SCOUNDRELS WHO MADE IT HAPPEN

"Wall Street from the inside. . . . An engaging history of how Wall Street came to be what it is today."

— Dave Kansas, *Wall Street Journal*

"The story hums along, like a conversation among street-smart uncles who've imbibed too much brandy. . . . A rare mix of breadth and immediacy." — Bloomberg.com

"Eric Weiner shows a knack for getting Wall Street types to let their hair down. . . . An engaging narrative that's hard to put down."

— Harvard Business School Working Knowledge

"I liked the book's immediacy and candidness. Eric Weiner digs deep to peel back the complex layers comprising modern Wall Street, letting the key figures speak for themselves. He weaves their takes into a fascinating narrative of frank, no-holds-barred discussion of Wall Street. . . . A delightful change from the usual business histories."

— Steve Powers, *Houston Chronicle*

"Entertaining. . . . Bracing, informative, and always interesting reading."
— *Kirkus Reviews*

"Delightfully different."
— Celia Johnson, *Fort Worth Star-Telegram*

"An excellent book. . . . Weiner intrigues and entertains us with his lively twentieth-century tales of modern Wall Street."
— Mary Whaley, *Booklist*

"Weiner ably covers the high and low points of modern Wall Street. . . . An easy introduction to some of the major events that have shaped the modern financial world."
— Gerald J. Russello, *New York Sun*

"A good, easy-to-read history of Wall Street. . . . Hearing what the players actually said, unfiltered, gives the events immediacy — and makes the book fun to read."
— Steven T. Gold, *Kiplinger's*

"Illuminating. . . . Weiner provides an insider's perspective on Wall Street. . . . For those in the industry — and perhaps those with a stake in the stock market, too — Weiner's book is a sharp, informative history from the people who shaped Wall Street's bottom line."
— *Publishers Weekly*

WHAT GOES UP

WHAT GOES UP

**THE UNCENSORED HISTORY
OF MODERN WALL STREET
AS TOLD BY THE BANKERS, BROKERS, CEOs,
AND SCOUNDRELS WHO MADE IT HAPPEN**

Eric J. Weiner

BACK BAY BOOKS
Little, Brown and Company
New York Boston London

Back Bay Books / Little, Brown and Company
Hachette Book Group USA
237 Park Avenue, New York, NY 10017
Visit our Web site at www.HachetteBookGroupUSA.com

Originally published in hardcover by Little, Brown and Company, September 2005
First Back Bay paperback edition, July 2007

The author is grateful for permission to include excerpts from the following previously copyrighted material: *The Seven Fat Years.* Reprinted by permission of Harold Ober Associates Incorporated. First published in *The New Yorker,* 1955. Copyright © 1955 by John Brooks. Copyright renewed 1983 by John Brooks; from *The Money Managers,* edited by Gilbert Edmund Kaplan and Chris Welles, copyright © 1969 by Institutional Investor Systems, Inc. Used by permission of Random House, Inc.; excerpts from *The Way It Was: An Oral History of Finance 1967–1987* by Institutional Investor, Inc. Copyright © 1988 by Institutional Investor, Inc. Reprinted by permission of HarperCollins Publishers Inc. William Morrow.

Library of Congress Cataloging-in-Publication Data

Weiner, Eric J.
What goes up : the uncensored history of modern Wall Street as told by the bankers, brokers, CEOs, and scoundrels who made it happen / by Eric J. Weiner. — 1st ed.
p. cm.
Includes bibliographical references and index.
HC ISBN: 0-316-92966-2 / 978-0-316-92966-0
PB ISBN: 0-316-06637-0 / 978-0-316-06637-2
1. Wall Street — History. 2. New York Stock Exchange — History. I. Title.
HG4572.W37 2005
332.64'273'09 — dc22

2005000151

10 9 8 7 6 5 4 3 2 1

Q-MART

Designed by Meryl Sussman Levavi
Printed in the United States of America

For my mother,
Carol Anne Weiner

"The public be damned.

I am working for my stockholders."

— William H. Vanderbilt, president of
the New York Central Railroad, 1882

CONTENTS

PART TWO

PART THREE

WHAT GOES UP

PROLOGUE

It all started in May 1792, under a buttonwood tree near the southern tip of Manhattan Island. There, a group of post–Revolutionary War merchants and traders established a formal exchange for the buying and selling of stocks and bonds of emerging companies. This bold step meant that there now would be a formal structure for raising money in what was quickly becoming the new nation's financial capital. For years, these traders and merchants had conducted their affairs informally on a one-mile thoroughfare that ran alongside a wooden barricade that the Dutch governor Peter Stuyvesant had erected centuries earlier to protect his village of settlers from the local Indian tribes. This road was called, simply, Wall Street.

These informal trades had resulted in the development of a less sophisticated version of existing financial exchanges in European cities like London and Antwerp. But this new market was so unstructured that it was vulnerable to manipulation by auctioneers and brokers looking to take advantage of customers by fixing prices. The Buttonwood Agreement, forged at the site of what today is 68 Wall Street, established the rules for a formal exchange where stocks and bonds could be bought and sold without manipulation. The market would have set hours when there would be continuous trading and prices could adjust accordingly. The traders also agreed that they would accept a set commission in their dealings with each other. Dealers who did not sign the agreement would be charged a higher rate for their business. And with that act of anticompetitive collusion, New York had the makings of its first formal stock exchange.

As primitive as it was, the arrangement worked fine for a couple of decades. Then came the War of 1812, which roiled the financial markets and spurred the dealers who had signed the Buttonwood Agreement to further structure their market. In 1817, they held a series of meetings, the result of which was the formation of the first organized stock exchange in the United States, the New York Stock and Exchange Board. In 1863, the organization would change its name to the New York Stock Exchange. But regardless of what they called it, the mystique of Wall Street began with the creation of this institution.

Throughout the nineteenth century, as Wall Street grew, more people turned to lower Manhattan when they needed to raise capital. The Street financed the building of the railroads and the creation of just about every major American industry imaginable, including the steamship, steel, oil, electrical power, telephone, and automobile industries. Along the way, it also saw its share of scoundrels. The Civil War era gave rise to dastardly speculators like Jay Gould, Jim Fisk, and Henry Clews, who made millions of dollars by cornering the market in different commodities and securities. Robber barons — including Andrew Carnegie, Cornelius Vanderbilt, and John D. Rockefeller — were able to put together massive corporate empires, and amass enormous fortunes, with financing arranged on the Street. And by the turn of the twentieth century, the power of Wall Street's financiers grew to the point that during the panic of 1907 four bankers — led by John Pierpont Morgan of J. P. Morgan and Company, and including Jacob Schiff of Kuhn Loeb, George Baker of First National Bank, and James Stillman of the National City Bank — were called on to rescue the entire banking system and prop up the New York Stock Exchange. At a meeting in New York with George Cortelyou, the treasury secretary under President Theodore Roosevelt, they quickly put together a $25 million finance package to keep the markets liquid and secure the financial system.

But for all the stories about power brokers, swashbuckling traders, and high-stakes financial intrigue, the fact is that during most of its early history, Wall Street in general was completely remote from the rest of the country. Financial information for the public was sparse, if it existed at all. Indeed, until 1896, when Charles Dow of the *Wall Street Journal* introduced the Dow Jones Industrial Average, it wasn't even possible to track the daily progress of the stock market as a whole. To most of Main Street America, Wall Street was an exclusive, rarefied club for a select group of rich and powerful men and a few others who someday hoped to become rich and powerful men. It was something to be looked upon with a degree of scorn, if at all. And for the most part, Wall Street didn't concern itself with the public's opinion, one way or the other. The insular culture of the Wall Street investment-banking partnerships prized privacy and secrecy above all else. The attitude of the financiers was, the fewer people who were interested in their affairs, the better.

For Wall Street, the eye-opener came in 1917, when the government announced it was selling tax-free Liberty Bonds to fund the war effort, and average Americans eagerly snapped them up as a show of patriotism and to capture the tax-free profits. From 1917 to 1919, the government issued $21.5 billion of these bonds and millions of individuals, many of whom had never invested before in their lives, signed up. To some people on Wall Street, including a young broker named Charlie Merrill, this was a sign that there was a whole new world of potential customers out there on Main Street that could be tapped for business.

Of course, not everybody was so laissez-faire about the power Wall Street's bankers were wielding. On September 16, 1920, right around lunchtime, a bomb packed inside a horse-drawn cart exploded underneath a window of the J. P. Morgan and Company headquarters at 23 Wall Street. More than thirty people were killed and several hundred were wounded in the blast, which caused damage of more than $2 million, a sum that would be worth nearly $20 million today. Witnesses described an eerie two seconds of silence on Wall Street, followed by a shower of glass from the windows above that were blown open. Although the culprits were never caught, police at the time believed it was the work of Italian anarchists or Communists. Either way, they missed their target: J. P. Morgan Jr., who by this time was head of his father's bank, was traveling in Europe when the incident took place.

The attack had little lasting impact on the collective imagination of the investing public. Throughout the 1920s interest rates stayed low, and that more than anything helped the stock market to climb; as any Wall Street pro will tell you, in a low-interest-rate environment investors naturally will look for the higher returns found in the more risky stock market. In addition, new technologies, radio in particular, were bringing into the market speculative investors looking to catch onto the next hot thing. Factories in the United States were mass-producing products like automobiles and telephones at a seemingly miraculous pace. Wall Street still largely remained a game for the elite, as less than 2 percent of the population owned stocks in the 1920s, but that 2 percent witnessed quite a run while it lasted. From 1925 to 1928, the stock market gained 200 percent. At the end, many investors were buying stocks on margin, which is borrowing money from a bank to buy securities. Others were investing in vehicles called investment trusts, which were designed to be early forms of mutual funds but turned out to be nothing more than fraud schemes. It was a classic speculative mania, and it could not last.

Although the 1929 stock-market crash is blamed for the Great Depression, the reality is the Depression started several months before, in August 1929. But late October 1929 is the point that most people consider to be the unofficial start of the most dismal economic period in American history. Over a series of weeks in October and November 1929, the Dow Jones Industrial Average was sliced in half. Millions and millions of dollars were lost in the market. Across the country, banks, securities firms, and insurance companies collapsed because of financial problems. And whatever goodwill the public had built up toward Wall Street was gone.

Naturally, after surveying the wreckage from the disaster, regulators stepped in and decided that reforms were needed on Wall Street. A slew of new laws and regulations were passed to protect Main Street from the manipulations of the Street's financiers. Two of those rules would come into play in later years. One was Regulation Q, which was established by the Federal Reserve Board in 1933 to limit the amount of money that banks could pay in interest to their customers. The theory was that the banks had paid too much in interest while competing for deposits, and that's why they'd gotten into trouble.

Among the other new rules that Wall Street had to contend with was the Glass-Steagall Act of 1933. The main purpose of this law was to formally divide commercial banks, which accepted deposits and made loans to people and businesses, and investment banks, which underwrote, bought, and sold securities, such as stocks and bonds. Banks that did both, and there were a considerable number of those on Wall Street at the time, would have to choose whether they wanted to be a commercial or an investment bank. The logic was that since commercial banks would hold the deposits of ordinary Americans they could not be allowed to put their capital in jeopardy by underwriting securities and operating in the risky environment of Wall Street. If there was a single target of the Glass-Steagall Act it was the mighty J. P. Morgan and Company. Most of the partners stayed with the old firm, which remained a commercial bank, though six partners, led by Henry S. Morgan, the grandson of J. P. Morgan, and Harold Stanley, split off to form the investment bank Morgan Stanley.

But despite the legal crackdown and Wall Street name shuffling, the 1929 stock-market crash and the Great Depression had had a devastating psychological effect on Main Street America. From now on there would be a deep and abiding cynicism on the part of the public toward Wall Street. The modicum of trust that had developed during the 1920s bull market was shattered. And it would take some time for healing and a concerted effort on the part of someone on Wall Street to bring it back.

CHAPTER 1

GOOD TIME CHARLIE

If you had to name the one person in the last hundred years who was most responsible for bringing individual investors to Wall Street, your list of candidates would have to begin with Charlie Merrill. Merrill and his firm, Merrill Lynch, probably did more than anyone to sell the stock market to America in the first half of the twentieth century. Considering Wall Street's traditional insular culture, it's hardly surprising that its first great democratizer was a true outsider. Merrill had none of the family connections and breeding that defined the upper crust of the financial world. His background was in grocery stores, and he brought many of those retail concepts to Wall Street through Merrill Lynch.

Charlie Merrill and his partner, Edmund Lynch, formed Merrill Lynch in 1914. They made a fortune for themselves and their customers through the Roaring Twenties by investing in the chain stores, like Safeway and McCrory, that were sprouting up around the country. These were the growth stocks of the day, and they were shunned by Wall Street's old guard, as personified by Morgan Stanley and Kuhn Loeb. But Merrill and Lynch didn't care. They kept on pitching stocks that others ignored and built a fairly substantial business with branches in Chicago, Detroit, and Los Angeles connected to the home office on Wall Street through a Teletype wire. Things were looking good.

But then, in 1928, Charlie Merrill became pessimistic about the stock market and his business. And here's where his story really begins.

EDWIN PERKINS (financial historian and author of *Wall Street to Main Street: Charlie Merrill and Middle Class Investors*):

In March of 1928, Charlie Merrill started to have some serious doubts about the market. He sent out letters to his customers telling how he felt. Of course, the people he had the hardest time convincing were Eddie Lynch and his partners. They thought it was one of those "new eras," like we heard about not too long ago. But Merrill got quite cautious and he sent letters to all their customers, not necessarily saying sell, but saying that now might not be a great time to be buying stocks on margin [with borrowed money]. And he urged the people with margin accounts to sell off some of their securities and pay off their debts.

CHARLIE MERRILL (cofounder and former chairman of Merrill Lynch and Company):

The advice we have given important corporations can be followed to advantage by all classes of investors. We do not urge that you sell securities indiscriminately, but we do advise, in no uncertain terms, that you lighten your obligations, or better still, pay them off entirely. Many fine reputations have been built up in this era of extraordinary prosperity, which will not stand the acid test when troublesome times are here. Take advantage of the present high prices and put your own financial house in order.

EDWIN PERKINS:

That was his feeling in early 1928. By 1929, he became even more convinced that this was true. In his letters he would quite often cite reports coming out of the Federal Reserve Bank saying that things were getting a little exuberant, sort of like when [Fed chairman Alan] Greenspan said that there was "irrational exuberance" in the market in the 1990s. I think

Merrill was saying the same thing in 1929. He took it to heart. But the rest of his partners did not. At one point in 1929, Lynch went on vacation in Europe and gave Merrill power of attorney over his stocks, and Merrill sold every single one of them. Lynch wasn't happy about that at all, but later it turned out he was lucky that Merrill did that.

After the crash, Charlie Merrill and Eddie Lynch decided to downscale. Lynch was pretty certain he was ready to cash in his chips. He pretty much dropped out entirely. In the meantime, they sold their retail business, the branches that existed, to E. A. Pierce, which was around as sort of a regional brokerage chain. But it wasn't a total sale, because Merrill Lynch invested a million or so dollars in that firm. They, in a sense, became silent partners. And they kept the Merrill Lynch office on a skeleton staff in New York. They didn't look for new business, but when any of the bonds from the old business came through and needed to be financed, they'd handle it. There wasn't much business, but that's the way it was for the rest of Wall Street in the 1930s. Charlie, meanwhile, continued as a private investor, but he really focused most of his attention on Safeway and the chain stores he owned.

ROBERT NEWBURGER (executive director of the New York Stock Exchange Alliance of Floor Brokers and member of the exchange since 1940):

When I came to Wall Street [in 1933] Merrill Lynch was E. A. Pierce and Company. Ed Pierce had the office at 40 Wall Street, and E. A. Pierce had more branch offices than anyone else, about five more than Bache and Company. Both of them had their main offices at 40 Wall Street, oddly enough. Ed Pierce came to work at about six o'clock every morning and stayed there until late at night. He was a real shirtsleeve fellow, and he built up quite a business.

EDWIN PERKINS:

Like many other brokerage houses on Wall Street, E. A. Pierce fell on hard times through the 1930s. By 1939 it was facing dissolution. Pierce and Win Smith [a former Merrill Lynch executive who went to E. A.

Pierce] were looking around to see who they could merge with. What Smith decided to do was try to convince Merrill to come back into the business. He showed him how with certain economies of scale here and there the company could be salvaged.

ROBERT MAGOWAN (former Merrill Lynch executive and Charlie Merrill's son-in-law):

Merrill was getting bored about 1940 after sitting on his ass for ten years. It looked like an opportunity, the only one left, and he had all the money.

EDWIN PERKINS:

The other thing I think that might've helped that decision was the death of Eddie Lynch. He died in 1938. And Lynch and Merrill had had some conflicts in the twenties and Merrill wasn't too eager to go through that again. But Smith convinced Merrill that if he could come in and put up some money, he could be the single senior partner. He could make all the major strategic decisions. That appealed to Merrill. So he decided to come back into the business in 1940. You really could say that the modern era of Wall Street began right there.

WINTHROP SMITH JR. (former Merrill Lynch executive vice president and son of former chairman Winthrop Smith Sr.):

To be successful in business you have to realize that a great time to do something often is when nobody else thinks it's a great time. The contrarian usually is a step ahead. When you look at this industry back then, nobody wanted to get in and a lot of people wanted to get out. The world looked terrible in 1939. We hadn't really emerged yet from the Depression and Europe was at war. Why would you want to take a risk at that time?

JOE NOCERA (financial journalist and author of *A Piece of the Action*):

Win Smith said, "The firm is about to fold. Please come and save it." That's the perfect kind of appeal to a guy like Charlie Merrill because being the savior and the center of attention is exactly what he craved.

WINTHROP SMITH JR.:

It really did take Merrill a while to warm to the concept. A fellow by the name of Ted Braun was very important in all this. He was a consultant who had worked with Merrill in California during his Safeway days and ended up being a consultant to Nelson Rockefeller and others. Braun did some market research that convinced Merrill — and reinforced my father's conviction — that out of the adversity that was happening there was a real opportunity to do something different.

JOE NOCERA:

What made Charlie Merrill different from the rest of his contemporaries on Wall Street was, he had a populist instinct. That's what he brought to the table right from the start. Charlie Merrill did not grow up wealthy. He was a poor boy, basically. He had to drop out of college for a while because his father was this sort of itinerant doctor who went broke. So he had to go out and make some money to pay for classes. Through a variety of circumstances he ended up on Wall Street basically as a kid. And even though he evolved into this extremely rich and powerful financier, he always stressed that the little guy could do this too, which was a foreign notion in the early part of the twentieth century.

DONALD REGAN (former Merrill Lynch chairman, treasury secretary, and White House chief of staff):

How do you take the mystery out of finance? How can you explain this business to somebody else so the curtain parts for him, too? "Take the mystery out of finance!" It's what Merrill kept advocating.

JAMES MERRILL (poet, author, and son of Charlie Merrill):

My father despised secrecy. Demystification had been the key to his own great success: no more mumbo jumbo from Harvard men in paneled rooms; let the stock market's workings henceforth be intelligible even to the small investor.

WINTHROP SMITH JR.:

There was a famous Roper Survey in 1939 that showed most people in this country thought livestock was traded on the New York Stock Exchange, not stocks and bonds. In fact, most people didn't know the difference between a stock and a bond. There was a real lack of information. And the truth is, until the SEC [Securities and Exchange Commission] was formed in 1933 the little guy didn't get a break.

There wasn't a transparent system. There wasn't a system of checks and balances. You had poor understanding and frankly not a good environment for the individual to participate. You also had Wall Street firms that were run very poorly and very unprofitably. But even though times were tough, Charlie Merrill could see that there would be a great need to recapitalize the United States in the near future to fuel the coming growth after the war. The individual investor could be a fundamental part of that growth. But what was needed was education. People were going to have to understand how to invest. There was going to have to be a different approach. The clients' interests had to be served, not the firm's interests, or this would never work.

There also was an understanding that firms were going to have to be run differently. A lot of the principles Charlie Merrill learned from Safeway and the chain stores were brought to Merrill Lynch. It's a high-volume, low-margin business that has to be run like a business, not a club. If you looked at a lot of the Wall Street firms in 1940, like J. P. Morgan, they operated in palaces with mahogany walls and stuffed leather sofas. Merrill said most of the business is done by telephone so you don't need mahogany walls and leather sofas. You had to run the business efficiently. The whole idea of sales per square foot was a merchandising principle that Charlie brought to this firm. The other thing was advertising, which Wall Street firms never did. Charlie brought advertising to Wall Street. He did everything from print advertising to sending people out across the country in wagons and setting up shop in places like Williamsport, Pennsylvania.

DONALD REGAN:

Charlie Merrill was against the establishment on Wall Street from the time he started. Remember that Merrill and Eddie Lynch originally were known as "the boy bandits" of Wall Street. Why? Because they cut prices, did things differently than anyone else. They went after the chain stores for business. It may seem funny now, but chain stores were controversial back then. I remember in my high school days at Cambridge Latin in the 1930s one of the major topics of the debating team was: "Resolved: Chain Stores Should Be Abolished." Individual towns couldn't stand having a major store — a Kroger or Safeway or A&P — on Main Street.

But this was Merrill's background. He backed J. C. Penney. He backed Newbury. He was a good friend of Frank Woolworth. When he came back to Wall Street in 1940, after he left in '29, he wanted to do the same thing at Merrill Lynch that he did at Safeway.

EDWIN PERKINS:

Merrill had all this experience from the chain stores that he invested in. So on a strategic basis, he decided to apply some of the lessons he learned from the retail business to what he was doing on Wall Street. He took his salesmen off commissions and paid them a salary, which was revolutionary. He said the interests of the customer MUST come first, with MUST in capital letters. And when he looked at it, the first thing he really had to do was educate his customer.

CHARLIE MERRILL:

It was probably the biggest job of mass education that's ever confronted any business at any time in the history of this country.

JOE NOCERA:

It wasn't just that Charlie Merrill's ideas permeated the firm. His whole larger-than-life personality dominated the place. Charlie Merrill was the sort of person who had to be at the center of any room he entered. He was a small man but he dominated a conversation, expecting you to hang on his every word. He also wanted you to accept his word as the received wisdom from the gods. He was a fabled womanizer and a remote figure to his children. Like many driven, successful people he was a mass of contradictions, ornery but generous, that kind of thing. He loved to party and drink, consuming huge quantities of martinis as he spun his stories. And he was that way from the very beginning. He met his partner Eddie Lynch because the two of them liked to crash debutante parties together when they were young men.

DONALD REGAN:

Charlie Merrill was a great ladies' man. He had four wives and about sixteen mistresses. And he was a great bridge player. He could be very disarming. Small in stature — I don't think he stood taller than five foot seven — white hair and soft complexion. He had sort of a droll sense of humor. He was quiet and very soft-spoken with a gentle southern accent. But he had a hell of a temper. Rub the guy the wrong way and you saw the fur fly. And Charlie had a will of iron. There was one way of doing things — his way or no way.

WINTHROP SMITH JR.:

I was really young when I met Charlie Merrill, maybe six or seven. I remember that even though he was a small man in size he actually was a very large person when you met him. He had this enormous personality. Even at that young age I could see that he was a very colorful character, completely different from any of my father's other friends. I remember he had this great smile and a way of carrying himself that drew you to him. My father, on the other hand, was a New England Yankee, very unassuming, very modest, very unpretentious. He was quite the opposite of Charlie. But I think those opposing traits helped cement their relationship as it developed. In some ways they were the better parts of each other.

DONALD REGAN:

After Merrill had his first heart attack in 1944 he basically retreated from running the firm full-time. In those days heart attacks were much more serious than they are today, so he had to quiet down, be the guy who operated from a distance. He'd come to the office seldom but he always knew what was going on. Win became his eyes and ears at the firm. The relationship was symbiotic and worked extremely well. Merrill was the idea man while Win's job was execution.

WILLIAM SCHREYER (former Merrill Lynch chairman):

Mr. Merrill had all the externals, a genius and all that. Mr. Smith was a guy who could analyze things, didn't shoot from the hip. He was very thoughtful and made good decisions. By the end Mr. Merrill had such bad heart disease that he very rarely came into the office. Mr. Smith was the guy that made things happen, beautifully.

LOUIS ENGEL (Merrill Lynch's first advertising director):

Win Smith was the only man who, after Charlie Merrill had his heart attack, could have held this thing together. He was an incredible man. He was absolutely one of the most quiet, unassuming men you've ever met in your life. In those early days the partners came from all these different firms. They still had their old ties, their old loyalties, and their particular buddies down the hall. But it was Win Smith who welded this thing together and made it one organization.

WINTHROP SMITH SR. (former chairman of Merrill Lynch):

In some ways Charlie's absence was an advantage. He had a better perspective on what was happening to the business as a whole, and to our firm in particular, than he might have had had he been actually participating in the day-to-day events.

ROBERT BALDWIN (former Morgan Stanley chairman):

Morgan Stanley did not advertise. We didn't have any public customers. We just didn't do it. Our standing came from people knowing who we were and what we were already, without advertisement. It worked very well for quite a while. Now, Merrill Lynch, they advertised.

JOE NOCERA:

A guy by the name of Lou Engel created perhaps the most famous financial ad in history. It ran in 1948 in the *New York Times*. Basically, it was a one-page instruction manual on the stock market called "What Everybody Ought to Know About This Stock and Bond Business." If you look at it today it's unreadable — just a mess of words. But at the time it was a sensation.

WILLIAM SCHREYER:

I remember the first time I saw that ad. I was taking the subway down to work in the morning — first thing I used to do with my paycheck was get two weeks' worth of dimes so I could get back and forth to the office from my apartment uptown — and I opened up the paper and there that ad was. I was jammed in there, holding on, and having no luck in trying to read the thing. I thought, "Jeez, this is way too long for anyone to pay any attention to. I wonder why they did that." Turns out I was wrong.

WINTHROP SMITH JR.:

I think this was the first time you really saw anything like that on Wall Street. A firm was reaching out to explain to normal investors how the business worked because it wanted their business. A lot of folks at the time really thought it was gauche for Wall Street firms to do things like advertise.

ROBERT BALDWIN:

The other firms, without exception, were brokerage firms. They'd give the guys a phone, have them follow the tape, and pitch ideas to clients.

WINTHROP SMITH JR.:

My father and Charlie Merrill started Wall Street's first training program in the 1940s. It's another thing that just wasn't done on Wall Street at the time, and another reason some firms snickered at us back then. But today it's a given that you have to train your employees. Out of those training classes we've gotten some of our most important leaders, including Don Regan, who was in our first training class.

DONALD REGAN:

December 1945 — I interviewed with somebody in the personnel department of the main office, which was then at 70 Pine Street. I was living in Washington, D.C., where I was married and where my first two children were born. After an extensive interview going over my background — a modest upbringing in Cambridge, Harvard undergraduate on a scholarship, an unfinished stint at Harvard Law School, five and a half years in the Marine Corps during World War II where I served as a major — this guy asked me, "What else can you bring to this firm?"

I said, "I don't understand the question. I've already told you my background." So he said, "Do you have any other specialties, something that might appeal to the firm?"

I thought about that for a minute. Then I said, "I only have one specialty now. I kill people. If you want people killed I've been doing that for five and a half years and I've gotten pretty good at it. Otherwise I could use some training." He was surprised. "Mr. Regan, I'm not sure that we need that particular ability here at Merrill Lynch."

In February they offered me a position in the new training school, which was starting in March 1946. At that time nobody else on Wall Street had a training program. Everyone used the old apprentice system, in which someone known to a partner in the firm by blood relationship or by being a relative of a client or something of that nature was taken on as an apprentice and brought up through the firm. It was not a formal training program. Merrill's was the first of the formal training programs where you were specifically trained in financial principles. They basically sent you to school for a quick degree in economics and finance. And then after you finished your courses you did not stay in New York. Instead, you migrated to a branch office to start building a business. Often you went back to the branch office that sent you in, because the branch office managers were encouraged to take men from their communities and send them on to the training school. Then they'd get them back as account executives, or what today they call financial consultants, FCs.

I think everybody in my training class was an ex-GI except for one guy who had been deferred for health reasons. And it was mostly officers. This was deliberate on the part of Charlie Merrill and Win Smith. They realized there was this cadre of people coming out of the service who needed jobs. They would be young, ambitious, and trained by colleges and the military.

They thought this was just the pool from which they should operate in order to train people to be financial advisers. Merrill knew this because he had been in the military himself. He was in World War I as an artillery captain.

JOE NOCERA:

Don Regan was a sterling example of the culture Merrill developed. For many years if you were Irish and a former marine you had a leg up at Merrill Lynch. It was like being a German Jew at Goldman Sachs or Skull and Bones at Morgan Stanley. But Merrill's culture was much more of a hustling culture than the rest of Wall Street. You were a salesman and you had to make your numbers; if not, there would be trouble. This wasn't cushy "white shoe" investment banking. The Wall Street establishment looked at Merrill Lynch as a lower form of life. But all Merrill cared about was building an army of brokers to preach the gospel of the stock market to the common man.

DONALD REGAN:

The military mentality works on Wall Street because if you put the order and discipline of the military into the world of finance it takes away a bit of the chaos that is normal in finance. You take the New York Stock Exchange or a trading room. You can have absolute chaos there if somebody is not guiding it and making certain that things are organized and controlled. I think the military learns that by necessity. In the heat of combat you've got to have control or you'll have utter chaos. You'll lose what you're there for, which is victory. If you lose control of the New York Stock Exchange or a trading room you will lose a lot of what finance is all about, the safety of money. Although a person who's too rigid doesn't succeed in finance either. You also have to be creative. That's what they tried to teach you as you progressed at Merrill Lynch.

BERNARD HEROLD (fifty-year Wall Street veteran and founder of Bernard Herold and Company):

If you ever want to get a job on Wall Street here are the magic words:

if you give me a chance, I can make you money. It's not, I can make money — it's I can make *you* money. That's what's always been most important in this business.

JOE NOCERA:

The one place where Merrill Lynch missed out in reaching Main Street was mutual funds. Charlie Merrill hated mutual funds. In the 1930s there was a scandal where college kids went door-to-door selling people these things called investment trusts that eventually had all kinds of problems. Some of them were Ponzi schemes and others simply didn't deliver what they promised. These investment trusts really were the forerunners of mutual funds, and as mutual funds developed Merrill linked them to all the wrongdoing that had gone on in the twenties. He truly thought they were bad for his clients. So even as mutual funds became popular again in the 1950s — when increasing numbers of ordinary people started turning to mutual funds as the way they wanted to touch the stock market — Charlie Merrill harbored this enormous prejudice against them. He wouldn't have anything to do with them.

WILLIAM SCHREYER:

Charlie would just pound his fist on the desk and say, "Mutual funds — they're evil!"

WINTHROP SMITH JR.:

The reason was, Charlie Merrill didn't believe that mutual funds were structured in a way that was in the best interests of the individual investor. He thought a portfolio of well-chosen stocks and bonds was the most efficient way to earn a return on your money. Our entire top-management team felt that way and there was no chance of persuading them otherwise, though a few people, particularly Don Regan, tried.

DONALD REGAN:

When we got into the subject of teaching women about finance I could see that mutual funds were made for that type of client. I used to argue about this all the time with my boss, Bob Magowan, though I never had the nerve to talk about this stuff with Merrill. Merrill was a merchandiser. He believed in packaging things. He didn't believe in loose coffee, he believed in a package of the stuff. What's the difference between a package of stocks and a package of coffee or walnuts? It was stupid, but they wouldn't go for it.

Finally, in 1949, I spent months working over a paper on why Merrill Lynch should be in mutual funds. It was pretty long when I started, but I managed to cut it down to a couple of pages. I remember Merrill was staying out in Southampton and Win Smith was visiting over the weekend. Bob Magowan also had a house out there not too far from Merrill's. He was going out that weekend, so I gave him the paper and said, "Put this in your briefcase. When you see Charlie and Win you'll be talking about the business, going over where we're headed. I think the 1950s is the time for us to get into the mutual fund business and this paper explains why. Please talk about it with them."

He said, "You'll never get it past them." And I said, "Please show them this paper and see what they say."

So Monday rolled around and I heard Magowan's heels clicking down the hall. He never wore rubber heels, always leather heels, and he clicked down the hallway into his office. When I went in to see him I remember Bob was all cheery, telling me about his tennis game. I could've cared less. Finally I said, "What happened?" He didn't know what I was talking about. So I said, "What happened with the mutual funds paper?"

"Oh that. I spoke to Win about it and Win talked to Charlie. Charlie didn't like it, so Win didn't like it. I figured I'd go along with them."

I said, "Goddamn! Shot down by the father, the son, and the Holy Ghost." That was it. Merrill Lynch was not going to get involved with mutual funds as long as any of them were alive and in charge. The ban lasted until 1968, when I became president.

EDWIN PERKINS:

Charlie Merrill died on October 6, 1956. He basically had been having heart trouble for a long time. He did agree to some experimental treatment where he had to drink this radioactive material, and it seemed to work miracles for him for a while, and he was able to keep up his pretty active social schedule. But at the end there, he really started to give out. He got weaker and weaker, and finally his body just succumbed to the disease.

The company he left was in great shape, though. It was still hitting high points. Volumes were picking up, prices were going up, and Merrill was in a commanding position to take advantage of it. They were way ahead of the pack on the brokerage side, and they were starting to make inroads on the investment-banking side. You'd have to say that the firm had fulfilled all of Charlie Merrill's dreams and hopes when he came back to the business in 1940.

By the time Charlie Merrill died, the firm he'd resurrected was one of the most powerful forces on Wall Street in terms of distributing securities — nobody did that better than Merrill Lynch. Merrill left a firm that was Wall Street's only truly national brokerage house, with nearly 6,000 employees in more than 120 offices around the country. Its $83.5 million in revenues made it the largest firm in the securities industry. At the time, Merrill Lynch was responsible for 20 percent of the volume in small trades of fewer than 100 shares on the New York Stock Exchange and 12 percent of the volume in larger trades. None of its competitors was even close. And with Win Smith in charge, Merrill could rest assured that his firm would continue in his image for some time. In fact, although Wall Street in the twenty-first century is a vastly more complicated place than it was when Charlie Merrill agreed to rejoin the business in 1940, there are still remnants of what he was trying to create today in just about every other major player in financial services.

Still, Merrill's missionary instinct was hardly bringing people to the stock market in droves. In 1953, more than a decade after he returned to Wall Street, there were only 6.5 million individual investors in the United States, accounting for just 4 percent of the population. By 1959, the number of individual investors would nearly double to 12.5 million, which shows that things were picking up — but not nearly as fast as they would later on.

CHAPTER 2

WHITE SHOES

To find the polar opposite of Merrill Lynch on Wall Street in the 1950s, you need not look beyond 2 Wall Street, across the street from Trinity Church, where Morgan Stanley was holding court. It was just a tiny firm in terms of capital, with only $7.5 million total. It had roughly two dozen partners and maybe a hundred employees. But it was the most esteemed investment bank on Wall Street, and it held enormous sway throughout the financial community.

The firm essentially was created by congressional mandate as a result of the Glass-Steagall Act of 1933. The law, passed during the Great Depression, was designed to break up the money trust, the interconnected web of Wall Street banks that was blamed in part for the stock-market crash of 1929. What Glass-Steagall did was make it illegal for commercial banks that made loans and accepted deposits to engage in the securities business, buying, selling, and issuing stocks and bonds. For the mighty J. P. Morgan bank and its powerful Philadelphia affiliate Drexel and Company, that meant one thing: the house would have to be divided.

Morgan Stanley was founded in September 1935 by Henry S. Morgan, who was known as Harry and was the son of Jack Morgan, the younger son of J. P. Morgan, and Harold Stanley, a former partner at the J. P. Morgan bank. They were joined by William Ewing, who also was a Morgan partner; Drexel partners Perry Hall and E. H. York; and John M. Young and A. N. Jones, both of whom worked at the J. P. Morgan bank. At the time, the move was seen as a way for the J. P. Morgan bank to legally get around the Glass-Steagall Act. Morgan Stanley immediately assumed all of J. P. Morgan's investment-banking clients and a powerful stature on Wall Street.

The center of activity at Morgan Stanley in the 1950s was known as "the platform," the area where the partners sat behind the same distinguished roll-top desks used at the old J. P. Morgan bank. From the platform, Morgan Stanley's partners charted the course for corporate America's growth plans. It was a small game at that time, but they controlled it. Of course, in time, the game would grow to become something much larger than the partners had ever envisioned. And when that happened, their grip would start to slip.

ROBERT BALDWIN (former Morgan Stanley chairman):

Harry Morgan sort of represented the Morgan name, which had great éclat at that time. Harold Stanley was a man of unquestioned integrity. They set the tone for the firm. There were a lot of people who said, I want to do business with Harold Stanley's firm. With all of us, the relationships were much, much more personal than they are today. Today, people put their issues up for bids and the best price wins. I know we beat ourselves to death trying to get the best price for people. But it's a different world. The relationships were much more intimate, and your customer was less concerned about a couple of pennies here or there.

JOE NOCERA (financial journalist and author):

Frankly, if you were an investment banker in the 1940s and 1950s you didn't have to work that hard. Firms had client relationships that went back for generations and the bankers basically inherited lists of clients.

JACK HYLAND (former Morgan Stanley partner):

I remember walking through the platform, which was the main partners' floor, when I joined the firm. The carpets were threadbare but on top sat these ominously impressive rolltop desks, mahogany wood with big crinkly roll tops. Of course, the partners worked at those desks so the roll tops usually were open and you'd see the black leather desktops covered with papers and files. In the far corner was Mr. Morgan's office, which also served as the partners' meeting room. The idea behind the platform area was that anyone could stand up and instantly talk to all the other partners about anything that was relevant in the marketplace.

A single phone call from one of those rolltop desks on the platform could raise $100 million or $200 million. There weren't too many places like that on Wall Street, or in the world for that matter. Now this area was not opulent. This was an investment-banking business that had made it through the Depression and the Second World War. The capital markets had just started to open up, but there had never been a feeling of luxury or spending for the surroundings. Everybody always had an eye toward the possibility that the balloon would go down. Whatever could be outsourced, was. If the rugs were old they were just as good as new ones. And there was this notion that it would be offensive to the clients if you tried to be too fancy in your surroundings, because they would see how your money was spent. So it was very low-key.

ROBERT BALDWIN:

When our firm was formed it had $7.5 million in capital, and I think $5 million of it came from senior partners at J. P. Morgan. Only $2.5 million came from Harold Stanley and Harry Morgan. In 1941, when we changed from a corporation to a partnership so we could join the New York Stock Exchange, our capital still was $7.5 million. When we finally incorporated back again in June of 1970, our capital still was $7.5 million. That was part of the old attitude that you didn't want to have too much capital.

RICHARD FISHER (former Morgan Stanley chairman):

The thing that I remember most about that office was bonus time at the end of the year. The whole firm would gather on the platform and Henry Morgan, who was still *the* presence, would come out of his office and walk down the hall. All of us, everyone in the firm, would be standing there waiting for him. He would say whatever he wanted to say about the year and tell us that the bonuses would be distributed at the end of the day. He'd always finish with, "Save it for a rainy day." This also was part of the tradition. Then we'd all go back and sit there, waiting for the checks to be handed out and wondering if the rainy day would come.

ROBERT BALDWIN:

From the start, Morgan Stanley got its clients from the old J. P. Morgan bank. That's pretty much the way it worked. After Glass-Steagall divided us, our firm took care of the investment-banking needs of those clients, and J. P. Morgan took care of their commercial-banking needs. In the 1930s and 1940s, the financial markets were very limited. Morgan Stanley did not do business with institutions. It didn't have any individual customers. It didn't do research. And it wouldn't even sell common stocks, because stocks were too risky. Morgan Stanley did bonds.

JOE NOCERA:

You didn't have to do much to be moderately good at that. This was the age of the three-martini lunch and Wall Street was full of those kinds of characters. To get one of these cushy jobs you had to graduate from the right school, have the proper background, and hope that one of the firms tapped you on the shoulder and said, "Come with us." Otherwise you probably couldn't just become an investment banker. A few people broke into the business, but not many. It really was like a secret society.

FRED WHITTEMORE (former Morgan Stanley partner in charge of syndicate operations):

We grew up in an era when basically it was womb to tomb. If you polished up the handle on the big front door, didn't make a lot of mistakes and weren't dumb, you could eventually expect to have a good career at Morgan Stanley.

I came here from Dartmouth, and Dartmouth was an outsider. This was a Harvard, Princeton, Yale place. Sumner Emerson, one of our partners, thought it was a great thing to get some Dartmouth people in here because it was diversification. Understand that this was *the* firm with *the* traditions and history. It was pinstriped suits and all that stuff. When I started, if Harry Morgan or Perry Hall or any of the original partners saw you in the elevator without a hat on they would say, "Don't we pay you enough to wear a hat?"

There are certain old Wall Street habits that don't exist anymore. For instance, if you were in an elevator with a woman south of Canal Street you never took your hat off, but north of Canal Street you did. It was a man's world down there. Hudson Lemko and these other Morgan Stanley partners all wore straw hats in the summer. If they commuted by ferryboat to Hoboken to go to Princeton on Labor Day, they would throw their hats into the water and wear their fedoras on Monday. It was fedoras in the winter and straw hats in the summer. People forget how we were, and it's just as well. John Kennedy may not have been the greatest president in the world, but at least he had a full head of hair. He got rid of hats.

JOHN WHITEHEAD (former co-senior partner of Goldman Sachs):

Wall Street always has been conscious of projecting the right image. I remember the first summer that I was at Goldman Sachs, in 1947, it was really hot. And I was walking around in a wool suit, so even if I took my jacket off and loosened my tie I was still hot. Finally I said, "I just can't take it. I'm going to have to get a lighter suit."

So that weekend I went out and bought a lovely seersucker suit, blue and white striped, quite dashing. On Monday morning I came in wearing my seersucker suit and straw hat, because nobody went hatless on Wall Street in those days, summer or winter. I walked into the building, into the elevator, and behind me came Walter Sachs, who then was one of the two senior partners, a very distinguished gentleman with a white beard. I was quite in awe of him. He looked at me and said, "Good morning, young man. Do you work at Goldman Sachs?" I sort of raised myself up in pride and said, "Why yes, sir, I do."

And so he said, "In that case, go home right now and change your pajamas." Unlike what probably would've happened today under similar circumstance, I did exactly as he said. That seersucker suit sat in my closet for a long time, unworn.

RICHARD FISHER:

To be honest, Wall Street was such a closed environment that it wasn't even a popular career choice when I was at Harvard Business School. In fact, investment banking was about the worst-paying job available to us. I started at Morgan Stanley at $5,800 a year. It was the lowest offer I had, the Morgan Stanley offer, but the others were within $200. I'm sure my classmates who went to Procter and Gamble started at $9,000 a year.

I remember the placement director at Harvard Business School called me into his office one day and said that he understood from some of the finance faculty members that I was thinking about Morgan Stanley. He didn't think Morgan Stanley was such a great idea for me. I thought that was interesting; after all, he was the placement director. So I said, "Why not?" And this is exactly what he told me: "It takes three things to succeed at Morgan Stanley: blood, money, and brains. At best you've got one of them."

ROBERT BALDWIN (former Morgan Stanley chairman):

Frank Petito's father was a night laborer down at a steel company in Trenton, New Jersey. My family was from a modest background. My father was an electrical engineer at Bell Labs. We had any number of people like this throughout the firm. As time went on, it was purely based on ability, who moved up, and so forth. So "white shoe" was mostly a derisive term. And I think that the press really ended up using it more than anyone.

RICHARD FISHER:

The term "white shoe" refers to white bucks, the shoes that were the rage for the upper classes after the war. You had to have a pair of white bucks if you were going to make it in that society. I guess the "white shoe" Wall Street firms were supposed to be filled with guys who wore white bucks. So you would hear "white shoe." You would hear the word WASP. You would hear all these things. But they weren't true.

FRED WHITTEMORE:

What "white shoe" really meant, and I'm being bluntly honest here, was that Morgan Stanley wasn't a part of the great Jewish community on Wall Street. It was sort of the standard by which things *should be* done, rather than necessarily how they *are* done.

Sure, there were Morgan Stanley partners like Frank Petito who weren't silver-spooners, if you know what I mean. But I'll say this: you wouldn't exactly feel sorry for a partner back then. John Young was a real character. He was one of these guys who made up his mind about life once and never thought about it ever again. Traveling with him was an experience. He would take you to some store and say, "This is the best place to buy toothbrushes. They have the natural bristles, which are the best, you know. Buy twenty." Then he would grab twenty for himself and twenty for you to buy. He didn't care about the price. These were the best. But he didn't offer to pay for your toothbrushes either. Then we'd walk down the street and he'd say, "This is where you buy your linen underwear." And I'd say, "But Mr. Young, I don't wear linen underwear." "Well, you should."

John Young always stayed at the Ritz because that's where you stayed. He made me pay a few extra hundred dollars every time we left so that they would make sure he got the proper treatment the next time he came. These were the old-world rules of how you travel. He kept a steamer trunk at Claridges and the Ritz with an alpaca coat he didn't want to take, a special bottle of brandy, a few other things, tennis racket, golf clubs, and so on. That's the way the game was played back then, and John Young and some of the other guys around here definitely played the game.

Harold Stanley, with his wonderful shock of gray hair, had a style about him. When he was running the firm if you didn't wear a jacket on the platform you were sent back to your office to get one whether you were a partner or not. Go into the Morgan Stanley offices now. No one wears a jacket. If you used a four-letter word or told a dirty story in Mr. Stanley's presence in the office you were sent out of the room. I don't care who you were. Mr. Stanley lived in a world that the others all respected.

ROBERT BALDWIN:

Okay. General Motors has about 88 million shares of common stock outstanding — 88,513,817 to be exact. Its current price on the New York Stock Exchange is not quite $100 a share. The corporation wants to raise $325 million or so for additional plant needs. So they've decided to do it by issuing 4,380,683 new shares and giving each of their stockholders rights to buy one new share for every 20 shares held, at a price below the going market price. The subscription price hasn't been decided on yet . . . but let's say for the sake of argument that it will be around $75 or $80. Since that's below the current price [for General Motors stock], the rights, which have to be mailed out to stockholders, will have cash value. If the stockholders don't want, or are unable, to exercise their rights to subscribe for their additional stock, they can sell the rights to other people, who will then either exercise them or try to resell them at a profit themselves. Either way, General Motors eventually sells its new stock and gets the money it needs.

Fair enough. Now, where does Morgan Stanley come in? Well, the point is that raising corporate funds this way involves risk. Suppose — knock on wood — that during the subscription period the stock market goes blooey for some reason or another, and the price of General Motors stock goes down below our hypothetical offering price. Then the rights become worthless, the new stock won't be subscribed for, and the issue turns out to be a failure. So General Motors pays Morgan Stanley to take that risk. For a fee, Morgan Stanley underwrites the entire issue; that is, it agrees to buy up any stock that isn't subscribed for. By the way, when I've been saying "Morgan Stanley" what I've actually meant is a syndicate of 330 investment-banking firms — coast-to-coast — headed by us. No one firm can assume the whole risk. The syndicate, you see, would be out about $4.33 million for every dollar the market price of the stock dropped below the offering price. You can't imagine what effect that would have on any single underwriter.

JOHN WHITEHEAD:

When there was an underwriting coming we would work for a few days on it, and then we would meet in Walter Sachs's office to decide what Goldman Sachs thought the price of the bond should be. Then Walter Sachs would go to the meeting at Morgan Stanley, whose bidding group we were in, and I've been told that he rarely had the courage to even speak up at the pricing meeting. Basically, we took what we got. But at least we did the work so he was well-prepared if called on.

RICHARD FISHER:

All the national wirehouses [brokerages whose branches were connected by Teletype wire], with Merrill being the obvious one, would come to Morgan Stanley, mainly to Bob Baldwin, Fred Whittemore, and their predecessors in the syndicate department, and bow and scrape. And it wasn't just Merrill and the other wirehouses. There were regional firms that had to do the same thing, like Rhineholt and Gardner out in St. Louis, Howard Weil in New Orleans, Shuman Agnew in San Francisco, and Crowell Weeden in Los Angeles. These are names that are gone now, but at the time they were important names in their communities. They all needed the merchandise because they weren't originators of anything. So they needed us because that's what we did. We originated the stock and bond offerings that they would sell to their customers. Of course, we also worked hard at having good relationships with them because underwritings go both ways. There would be times when we really needed their help to get something distributed. That's how it worked.

ROBERT BALDWIN:

The reason for the syndicate is to spread the risk. I spent many a night studying who'd done the best job on a recent issue.

FRED WHITTEMORE:

Morgan Stanley's strength was based on the fact that we had eleven of the top twenty companies in the Fortune 500 as clients. No one else had more than three or four. Since we were originating all this good business we expected to be treated differently. That's where the term "bulge bracket" came in.

ROBERT BALDWIN:

The brackets were all about your standing on Wall Street. Some people were in the major bracket because of their name and some were in there because of their performance.

FRED WHITTEMORE:

When offerings are completed on Wall Street you usually publish a tombstone ad in the newspaper listing the company and all the underwriters in the syndicate. The bulge bracket was the first group of underwriters listed in the ad.

For a while the bulge bracket was Morgan Stanley, First Boston, Kuhn Loeb, and Dillon Read. In the early days, Kuhn Loeb and Dillon Read represented a lot of origination power, but that faded over a period of time. By the midsixties they were hanging on to their reputation rather than asserting themselves. Salomon, Goldman, and Merrill Lynch were clearly evolving as stronger firms, and they eventually became members of the bulge bracket. Of course, there were other positions that filled out the syndicate. There was the major bracket, the submajor bracket, and a mezzanine bracket that developed over the years. Then there was the first regional bracket, second regional, and all the rest of that.

JOHN WEINBERG (former co-senior partner at Goldman Sachs):

The bulge bracket was Morgan Stanley, Dillon Read, First Boston, and Kuhn Loeb. They had the big clients. Morgan Stanley took all of J. P. Morgan's old clients, so they were the godfathers of the industry. There wasn't much we could do about that. So what we decided to do was just keep plugging along, focus on doing quality work as a team, and start competing for business. The guts of it is earning a relationship with a company, and that's what we tried to develop. The guys at Morgan Stanley did it on the golf courses, and all that kind of stuff. We didn't go in for any of that. We worked on the professionalism of what we did and the way we did business. We cared about our business and we cared about our clients. That's why clients came to us, and that's why we got more business than anyone else once Wall Street became competitive.

Through the postwar period, Morgan Stanley maintained its standing as Wall Street's most prominent investment bank. The bull market of the late 1950s created enormous demand for new financings, and many of the firm's clients brought new issues to market to keep pace with the booming economy. But as the 1960s started to evolve, it became clear to a few executives at Morgan Stanley, particularly Robert Baldwin, and to some of the younger guys coming up in the firm, like Richard Fisher, that Morgan Stanley and the rest of the bulge bracket needed to change its attitude about a lot of things if it was going to survive the competition from growing firms like Merrill Lynch, Goldman Sachs, Lehman Brothers, and Salomon Brothers.

At that point Morgan Stanley basically was just an underwriter of stock and bond issues. It couldn't distribute stocks and bonds, because it didn't have a bunch of brokers to sell the stuff. It didn't have an army of traders to move the blocks of stock that were starting to hit the market, so taking positions wasn't easy. And it didn't have a pile of permanent capital to build its business because the partnership structure enabled the partners to withdraw their capital every year. So planning for the future was difficult because the partners never knew how much money they'd actually have to work with. There were clear challenges on the table. The question for Morgan Stanley and the rest of the bulge bracket partnerships was: what are you going to do about it?

CHAPTER 3

"OUR CROWD"

JUDITH RAMSEY EHRLICH (coauthor of *The New Crowd*):

At the turn of the century the world of finance really revolved around a single axis. On one pole you had J. P. Morgan of J. P. Morgan and Company, and on the other you had Jacob Schiff of the very august German-Jewish firm of Kuhn, Loeb and Company. These two men, Morgan and Schiff, ran the two most powerful investment banks in the country, and the rivalry between them intensified as they continued to grow. None of the other investment banks had their financial clout. They helped finance the building of America's railroads, the creation of mammoth industries like steel and oil, and the arming of world powers. In a sense they came to symbolize the two sides of Wall Street, the dominant Protestant establishment and the wealthy German-Jewish "Our Crowd."

This was a split that had existed among the rich in America ever since the Civil War, and, though it wasn't openly acknowledged, had at its root a pronounced anti-Semitism. The capital controlled by the Our Crowd bankers enabled them to invest their firms' money and their own money in industry, and to participate in the important underwriting syndicates with the Gentile banking firms. But they weren't made partners at these Gentile firms, or in most cases even hired by them. And they weren't socially accepted by the Morgans, the Astors, and the other reigning dynasties in New York City.

In response, the wealthy German Jews formed their own society, which became known as Our Crowd. The most well-known Our Crowd families were the Seligmans, Lehmans, Goldmans, Sachses, Warburgs, Schiffs, and Loebs of Salomon Loeb. They made vast fortunes and were celebrated for their philanthropy, public service, and patronage of the arts. So these families were linked not only by business interests but also by inbreeding.

ROBERT BERNHARD (former partner at Lehman Brothers and Salomon Brothers):

I have a typical Our Crowd background. By looking at me you can see how we were all interrelated through Wall Street. I am the great-grandson of Mayer Lehman, one of the founders of Lehman Brothers, grandson of Arthur Lehman. Arthur had three daughters. My mother, Dorothy, was the oldest. Her husband was Richard Bernhard, and he was a partner at Wertheim and Company, which was a lesser firm but still powerful in its own right. The middle sister, Helen, married Ben Buttenwieser, a partner at Kuhn Loeb, probably the leading Our Crowd investment bank at the time. The youngest daughter was Frances, who was known as "Peter," and she married John Loeb, the head of Loeb Rhoades. So even before I was born there were tentacles in all these investment-banking firms on Wall Street. That's the way it was in those days. When they talk about how *relationships* were important, that's what they mean.

STEPHEN BIRMINGHAM (novelist and author of *"Our Crowd"*):

I got the phrase "our crowd" from a novel called *Red Damask* written by a woman named Emanie Sachs. She was married to Walter Sachs of Goldman Sachs. I think the book was published in the late twenties. She used the phrase "our crowd" here and there throughout the book to describe this Upper East Side of New York Jewish world that extended to Elberon, New Jersey. And I actually think that "our crowd" was a term they used without even being aware that they were using it.

When I handed in my book and called it *"Our Crowd,"* my publisher didn't like the title at all. They wanted to call it *The Jewish Grand Dukes,* which I thought was a terrible title. So they said, how about *Many Mansions*? And I said, "My God, that's the wrong Testament." I had to fight hard to keep it *"Our Crowd."* Anyway, when the book first came out, Mrs. John Loeb Sr. called me. She'd been one of the people who helped me with the research. And she said, "I haven't read the book yet, Steve, but I think it's got the silliest title. Nobody in our crowd ever called ourselves 'our crowd.'" I think it's an apt title.

DAVID SCHIFF (great-grandson of Kuhn Loeb founder Jacob Schiff and former partner at Kuhn Loeb and Lehman Brothers):

I had almost no awareness of the whole Our Crowd thing when I was growing up. My father [former Kuhn Loeb chairman John Schiff] was not terribly involved with the Jewish community. Many of the Jewish descendants in the early 1900s, Otto Kahn and Morti Schiff and others, had distanced themselves to some degree from their religion and sought to assimilate more, whether for better or for worse, and I think there's something to be said on both sides of that coin. John Schiff was not a religious man. He went to temple once a year. He never took me to anything Jewish at all, and I was raised by a Christian mother, so I was Episcopalian. In terms of my Jewish identity, that's something I've sought out more as an adult. Obviously, to Jews, I'm not a Jew. But at the same time, they accept me in a certain way because of my heritage.

ROBERT BERNHARD:

There were two cliques on Wall Street. There was the Jewish clique and the Presbyterian, or WASP, clique. We knew each other, but we didn't really mix. It wasn't because of race or religion specifically — it's just the way it was. I remember when I got out of business school — Harvard Business School — I thought I'd go to work at Wertheim because that's where my father was. But Mr. Klingenstein [Wertheim cofounder Joseph Klingenstein] didn't want competition for his son, so he suggested that I look elsewhere. My then father-in-law set up a meeting with First Boston, which were the bankers for his family's business, American Optical. I had a lovely meeting with somebody over at First Boston, who ended by saying, "I think you should go to Lehman Brothers because, you know, we don't hire Jews." That was a statement of fact in 1953. It wasn't an anti-Semitic remark, and I wasn't offended by it. If you were young and Jewish and wanted to go into the investment-banking business, you worked at Lehman Brothers, Loeb Rhoades, Kuhn Loeb, or Goldman Sachs. And if you were Gentile you went to First Boston, Morgan Stanley, Dillon Read, et cetera.

RICHARD FISHER (former Morgan Stanley chairman):

Of course, there were Jewish people who worked at Morgan Stanley. But this was all part of the myth that wasn't true. It used to annoy me when somebody would ask, "How many Jews do you have?" I really didn't know. I had a few colleagues who I knew were Jewish because they told me they were. And there were some people I knew were Jewish because of their names. But I couldn't tell you how many Jews worked at Morgan Stanley. It wasn't important one way or the other.

JOHN WEINBERG (former co-senior partner at Goldman Sachs and son of former Goldman Sachs senior partner Sidney Weinberg):

When I joined the firm nobody gave a damn about your religion, Jewish or otherwise. The Jewish element was a nonfactor. When I was growing up I didn't know any of the Lehmans or anything like that. It was very removed from my experience as a child. My father wasn't a member of Our Crowd, and we had no interest in it.

ROBERT BALDWIN (former Morgan Stanley chairman):

The Jewish firms would tell capable Jewish workers, "Don't go to Morgan Stanley. They won't make you a partner." Finally, a fellow by the name of Lewis Bernard came along, and he became our youngest partner at the time and our first Jewish partner. He was talking to us and talking to Goldman Sachs, and they said, "Don't go to Morgan Stanley, they won't make you a partner."

Well, I went over to [former Goldman Sachs senior partner] Gus Levy and I said, "Damn you, Gus, you say we're discriminatory. How can we make a Jewish person a partner if you keep telling them not to come to us?" Gus shut up, and we made [Bernard] a partner.

JUDITH RAMSEY EHRLICH:

Between 1880 and the mid-1920s more than 2.5 million Jews poured into the United States. They came primarily from Russia and eastern Europe, fleeing the pogroms and other forms of persecution. They settled mainly in the urban areas of the East, particularly in New York City. Compared to the German Jews who arrived thirty years earlier, they had a far more difficult time fitting in because they were poor and uneducated and there were so many of them.

The German-Jewish financiers looked down on the new Jewish immigrants as aliens. They didn't want to fraternize with the eastern European Jews because they felt such an association could be harmful to them socially and economically. Still, they had good values so they set up a vast network of philanthropic agencies and a wide range of services to help the new arrivals find homes and jobs and adjust to their new surroundings. However, even as these new Jews began to make their way in New York, the Our Crowd financiers continued to focus on the differences. Since they were not one of them, they were not part of Our Crowd. It was carried over into the business world as well. It was very hard for any of these new Jews to get hired by one of the Our Crowd banking houses, especially on the investment-banking side of the businesses. These were tightly knit groups, with partnerships descending to sons, sons-in-law, and nephews. When they did take in a non-family member it was most likely to be a Christian with an established reputation rather than a black-shoe, white-stocking type of Jew from Brooklyn.

THOMAS E. DEWEY JR. (former Kuhn Loeb partner and son of former New York governor Thomas E. Dewey):

At Kuhn Loeb there wasn't much of an emphasis on religion, per se. Most people on Wall Street wanted to get as far away as they could from religion. I think [Kuhn Loeb senior partner] John Schiff and [Kuhn Loeb managing partner] Freddy Warburg would make a point of coming to work on Jewish holidays just to show that they weren't really that way. And I think that probably half the partnership was Christian. But it is true that a lot of the Jewish-owned and Jewish-led big companies and medium-sized companies would come to KL for investment-banking services rather than going to Morgan Stanley. We took Uris Brothers public. We took Dreyfus public. We did Inland Steel, which was run by the Bloch family — I think they were the only major Jewish-owned firm in the steel industry. So the Jewish connection was important on the client side. On the partner side, it was much more important to have the *right* kind of person. In that respect, religion didn't matter at all.

Of course, this attitude of who was the right kind of person extended to Wall Street firms as well. For example, when I was deciding what investment bank I wanted to pursue, my father said he would disown me if I went to work for Goldman because of the stink that was still there from the Depression. Goldman had a couple of mutual funds, they might have been closed-end funds, and during the Depression they went belly-up very badly. It cost a lot of people an awful lot of money and their reputation had not completely rebounded at that point. Salomon Brothers wasn't even in the business; they were bond traders. Merrill Lynch wasn't in the business either; they were stockbrokers. Lehman Brothers was somewhere in between. They very definitely were in the investment-banking business, but they weren't in Kuhn Loeb's league yet. Before the Depression, Lehman and Goldman had been the underwriters of the retail and merchandising trade. But that was considered inferior business on Wall Street; it wasn't "real America" the way the major industrial firms were, you know.

JOHN WHITEHEAD (former co-senior partner at Goldman Sachs):

During my first years at Goldman Sachs, the only person who ever produced any investment-banking business was Sidney Weinberg. I don't believe that anybody else brought in a public offering or a private placement or any kind of investment-banking business except for Sidney Weinberg. He knew everybody. He was the best-known businessman in America, and when someone wanted to deal with an investment banker they tried to get an appointment to come see Sidney Weinberg. He didn't do much traveling; everybody came to him. The trouble is, Sidney's relationships were so strong that when he eventually left the firm there was a hole. We had to find other ways to build the business.

JOHN WEINBERG:

My father was the only man here who brought in any business, period. He was a giant in the industry, one of the great investment bankers of all time, at least that's what they say. But he knew everyone and had contacts everywhere, and he advised presidents and politicians as well as corporate executives, so he really had wide-ranging interests. He was a remarkable man. He was small; he stood just about five foot four. His mother died when he was about nine years old, and his father married another woman who hated my father. So at age ten he said, "To hell with this. I'm leaving." And he moved over to the Y and lived there. From there he managed to do all this, largely with street smarts. Of all the men I've ever met, I've never met anyone who was smart like my father.

JOHN WHITEHEAD:

Sidney was very protective of the business he had developed. He didn't like to share it. I remember one time he got very mad at me because Henry Ford had called me instead of him. I said, "But I didn't call him. I'd never call him without you knowing about it. He called me." And he said, "Well, I don't want you talking to my clients."

After Sidney, Gus Levy took over the firm. Gus was your typical trader — short-term was this morning and long-term was this afternoon. That's how Gus viewed the business. Every day you tried to take in more money than you spent.

JOHN WEINBERG:

Gus Levy really was the guy who originated the whole idea of block trading. When he started, the blocks were very small. So he'd go to guys on the floor of the stock exchange and say, "Why don't we go joint venture on this, and we'll take part of your block." But eventually the blocks got so huge that they were bigger than anyone on the floor could handle. And that's when he set up the block-trading operation and put in place the distribution system to do it. It was something to see, boy. They could sell half a million or a million shares in a few hours sometimes, which was unheard-of at the time.

WILLIAM (BILLY) SALOMON (former Salomon Brothers senior partner):

Salomon Brothers wasn't really in the same business as the Morgan Stanleys and Kuhn Loebs, the investment banks that were underwriting the major industrial firms. We weren't even in the same business as Goldman Sachs, really. At that time we were a market-maker in the bond business. Originally, the firm was exclusively focused on money markets and short-term securities. Then we did commercial paper, banker's acceptances, and things of that ilk. We gradually got into the bond business, which was a very dull area. The major underwriters of securities each had their own major industrial companies and utilities that they handled, and they didn't have to compete for customers. So the only thing we could do was make markets in securities that people wanted to trade. We didn't have enough contacts in industry, but by making good markets we could get customers because people would come to us if we offered them a better price.

Here's the way our business worked. Say Equitable Life wanted to sell a million Treasuries. They would go to their favorite investment bank and say, "Sell them for me." Then the investment bank would put together a syndicate to distribute the bonds. What we did was buy the bonds for our own account at a negotiated price, and then hope to sell them to somebody else for a profit. So we became risktakers by necessity from an early point. This was the only way we could compete. If you were a member of the well-known clubs and went to Princeton, Yale, and Harvard you could sit back and your friends would give you business. We were not in that position, so we had to trade and compete.

RICHARD FISHER:

The truth is, at first it was difficult for us to attract talented Jewish traders because of the Morgan Stanley image. But one of the things you come to realize in this business is that traders are oriented solely to performance. They quickly forget whether you're female, Jewish, green, from Mars, whatever. They don't care because none of it lasts very long in a trading environment. Once we got some seriously talented traders in here it stopped being an issue completely.

DONALD REGAN (former Merrill Lynch chairman):

Over the years I've asked myself the question "What makes a trader?" There is no answer to that. Some say that the guy who has instincts at the craps table in Vegas makes the best trader. Others say traders are good for a while and then they go sour. Still others say it's a person with a very reasoned, disciplined approach, sharp and shrewd.

When I was head of trading I decided to find out. We took eight people — four college graduates, four non-college graduates. I wanted arithmetic skills and a mix of cultures, some Catholics, some Jews, and some WASPs. I wanted to see who makes the best traders. A lot of people said the best trading houses were Jewish, others said the Irish were better. Nobody knew. Mike Meehan on the floor of the stock exchange was a well-known Irish-type trader, but some pointed to the Jewish houses like Salomon and Goldman as having the best traders. So we mixed them all up and you know what? We never found out. I got taken off the job after three years so my experiment ended abruptly. But it was fascinating to watch. Never did find out, though, what makes the best trader.

JOHN GUTFREUND (former Salomon Brothers chairman):

Wall Street had always been a place where the trading firms were for the immigrants and the nouveau riche, as opposed to the banking firms, which were more white shoe. Keep in mind that Wall Street was coming out of a long, tough period. From the Depression in the early thirties to the fifties, Wall Street wasn't exactly a place of prestige for people to go unless their family had money or relationships in the business. America at that point was a Protestant country and New York was the scene where the immigrants arrived and did their business. The establishment was overwhelmingly Protestant and my recollection is that Jews and Catholics were not in the social hierarchy at that point in our social history.

When I arrived in 1953, Wall Street was very staid and conservative, not dominated by genius. Innovation was not exactly the product. The New York Stock Exchange was prestigious and each firm that was a member had to have a seat or two. This was even before the emergence of Merrill as a popularizer of investing. Most people I think considered Wall Street a gambling game, and they wanted to keep their savings in savings banks, which paid very low rates of interest in those days.

Although competition was familiar to Salomon it wasn't necessarily a hallmark of Wall Street. On the trading side of the business, there was competition for the institutions — the lenders and investors — and Salomon competed on price rather than social panache or relationships. Whether it was the Chase Bank or Morgan Guaranty or Metropolitan Life or the Equitable, they listened to the best bid and best offer.

ROBERT BERNHARD:

In those days there were usually one or two underwritings per week. That's for all of Wall Street, not just one firm. This was the early 1950s and the business was pretty sleepy. The major underwriters were Morgan Stanley, Kuhn Loeb, First Boston, and Dillon Read. That was the bulge bracket. Anybody who was asked into the underwriting syndicates always took whatever piece they were asked to take and didn't put up much of a fight. It was a very collegial atmosphere. It wasn't until the 1960s that the volume began to pick up, the size of underwritings began to pick up, and people began to concentrate on their own deals maybe to the detriment of somebody else's. Then the syndicate departments became really professional. Prior to that, the guy in the syndicate department usually was a WASP who played good golf and had a lot of friends.

As the market began to pick up in the 1960s and Wall Street started to grow, the rivalry between Lehman Brothers and Kuhn Loeb flip-flopped. Once Kuhn Loeb was the mightiest Our Crowd investment bank and Lehman Brothers was in the second tier, nipping at its heels. But while John Schiff tried to run Kuhn Loeb as if the year was still 1900 and his grandfather Jacob was in charge, Lehman Brothers senior partner Bobbie Lehman pushed his firm to the forefront of Wall Street's increasingly competitive environment.

THOMAS E. DEWEY JR.:

Kuhn Loeb didn't really choose to compete with people. We had our clientele, and as Otto Kahn said, we had our show window. People knew our address and if they wished to do business with us they could come, presumably on bended knee, and see if Kuhn Loeb and Company would do their business. A remarkable number of clients went back to the early twentieth century. I'll give you the example of Eastern Airlines. When General Motors acquired North American Aviation in the early 1930s, North American owned Eastern Airlines, which was a fledgling airline as they all were in those days. The antitrust department forced North American Aviation to sell Eastern before it would bless the takeover by General Motors. Now, the pioneer investment bankers in the airline business were Bill and Charlie Harding of Smith Barney, both delightful guys. But, of course, in 1935 Smith Barney didn't have any money, like most of the Wall Street firms. Kuhn Loeb always had money, so they came in and said, "Let's do this fifty-fifty." The two firms bought Eastern Airlines. That's another way of getting clients. Eventually they sold it to the public, but the relationship remained. Obviously, we handled Eastern Airlines' investment-banking assignments from then on.

But there were only so many Eastern Airlines out there, and as the market got more competitive we had to go out and hustle for clients. Many Kuhn Loeb partners simply didn't have the stomach for that.

We lost a lot of ground once Wall Street adopted a competitive stance. The rules of the game had changed, but we were still playing by the old rules. If you do that for too long, eventually you find that you're out of the game.

ROBERT BALDWIN:

Kuhn Loeb, I'll never understand what happened there. They just didn't take the steps necessary to survive. The whole firm fell apart and they really opened up the door for some of the other firms to do well.

WARREN HELLMAN (former Lehman Brothers partner):

When I got to Lehman Brothers, we weren't quite Kuhn Loeb, in the sense that Kuhn Loeb was probably one step up the Jewish establishment ladder. It was a very eclectic place. Bobbie Lehman was sort of the Sun God and everybody revolved around him. It was a very competitive place, but probably more internally competitive than it should've been.

JUDITH RAMSEY EHRLICH:

Bobbie Lehman was one of the last great members of Our Crowd. In the 1960s, Lehman Brothers was one of the most powerful firms on the Street, and Bobbie Lehman had run the family firm for the better part of four decades as his personal fiefdom. He enjoyed all the privileges and social acceptability of great wealth. You could say that he really lived in baronial splendor. His wealth was dazzling. He had an extremely important art collection that included paintings by El Greco, Renoir, Rembrandt, and other masters and was worth some hundred million dollars. Many of these paintings hung in the Lehman headquarters, so the partners were constantly reminded of just how rich he was. He also had incredible business and political contacts at a time when that was all it took to be a baron of finance. He was close to the Whitneys and the Harrimans and of course to his own family.

ANDY SAGE (former Lehman Brothers partner):

Bobbie Lehman was it. It was his firm. He was God. Nobody else mattered at Lehman Brothers. He was a good guy, but he didn't know stock from livestock. A technician he wasn't. But it didn't matter. He was sort of slight of build and he had probably the smallest office in the place — you wouldn't put your dog in there. He was in a hovel. It had a tiny sofa because that was all they could squeeze in there and this little desk. To this day I don't know why. That was just his thing. He had a tiny office. He was very generous and nice, but really tough at times. And he was really great to me.

BOB RUBIN (former Lehman Brothers partner):

Lehman Brothers was Bobbie Lehman, and Bobbie Lehman was Lehman Brothers, among other things. He was a patrician who incidentally was the driving force at Lehman Brothers. He was not an investment banker. He was a personality. He was dignified. He had the highest ethics you could think of. But he was a very modest, self-effacing person. He had the smallest office of any of the partners at Lehman when I got there. His personality dominated the firm. He let other people run the firm, but if it ever came down to a serious decision, it was his decision.

ANDY SAGE:

The other thing Bobbie did that was different was in those days the old firms were either all Jewish or not at all. Kuhn Loeb and Goldman were Jewish, Morgan Stanley and First Boston were not, no way. Bobbie's vision was that from a business point of view we should be both. If we could do that we'd have a much bigger crack at doing all the business. And it worked, more than anything else that he did. He peopled the firm with all kinds of people with different kinds of education.

WARREN HELLMAN:

Lehman was a very small firm. I think it had nineteen partners when I got there. It was a very white-shoe establishment. The partners were a lot of people from Century Country Club [a Jewish club in Westchester County], but also a lot of people from Piping Rock [a Long Island golf club that was restricted].

ROBERT BERNHARD:

Bobbie Lehman ran Lehman Brothers like a virtuoso piano player. He had a number of extremely bright, talented, competitive men as partners — and he played them one against the other. One day you thought you were in the know, the next day you found out you weren't. The partnership agreement was very simple: Bobbie Lehman was partner of the first part and everybody else was partner of the second part. Bobbie Lehman could fire anybody with or without cause whatsoever, if he wanted to. He was both respected and feared.

WARREN HELLMAN:

The business was different in those days — if you were a Lehman client most other firms would lay off until it was clear that you were disgusted with us or vice versa. Wall Street was nowhere near as competitive as it is today. But if it was a new piece of business, Bobbie Lehman was intensely competitive. He was very political, in the sense that those who he liked got rewarded. And whether you were liked often had to do with whether you were producing. That's why I'd say it was internally competitive, quite political. He used his favors to play people off each other. And by his favors I mean, "Warren, you'll own 6 percent next year."

JUDITH RAMSEY EHRLICH:

Working at Lehman Brothers was like belonging to one of the most exclusive, elegant men's clubs in America. The boardroom had a limestone fireplace and hearth that had carvings. There were leaded casement windows that were embellished with Wall Street motifs. The partners would sit in the grand partners' room, which was paneled in a dark, rich English oak, with antique silver chandeliers hanging from the ceiling. The Georgian-style partners' dining room had been decorated by the noted society designer Sister Parrish, and it featured another antique chandelier and a Sheridan table that seated ten. The kitchen was managed by the former chef of the famed Pavillon restaurant and it was renowned for its fine food, with a wine list that would have rivaled any restaurant in the country at that point. In the morning when the partners arrived, the waiters, who were dressed in white linen jackets, would serve them coffee, teas, and pastry. The partners also enjoyed the privilege of a private gym, a masseur, and a plentiful supply of Havana cigars.

PETER SOLOMON (former Lehman Brothers partner):

The gym was a small place on the eleventh floor used principally by two people: Warren Hellman, who used to try to commit suicide by running around and hanging upside down and doing all these things he continues to do; and Joe Thomas, another important senior partner, who used to go up there and drink. He would drink, get massages, use oxygen because he had terrible emphysema, and smoke cigars at the same time.

WARREN HELLMAN:

The partners, a lot of them not having had enough to drink at lunch, after a long day of, say, nine thirty until five thirty would go up to the "health club" and get a massage. It basically was a room with a masseur and chairs. They'd have a few more drinks and smoke their cigars. It was a fairly repulsive way to be. The reason they built a gym was I started working out in that room and more than a few partners complained that somebody was up in the health club sweating.

ROBERT BERNHARD:

We had a really good chef at Lehman Brothers, but that fit with the style of the place. When I first became a partner, Lehman was very different from any other firm on Wall Street. For example, at Salomon Brothers lunch was served from noon to two — you came in whenever you were ready to come in, there usually were partners sitting around the table, you chatted and that was that. But this was not the case at Lehman Brothers, where lunch was a ceremony. Every day at one o'clock Robert Lehman walked into the partners' dining room. Oftentimes he had somebody of note who he had brought down with him for lunch. So it could be Jake Javits on one hand, Sam Goldwyn on the other hand, and maybe Armand Hammer on another hand, but it was always *somebody*. Then the other partners would come in. You sat around this big table. There was Bobbie at the head with his guest to the right and the other partners filled in on down with the junior partners all the way at the end. And then, always right at one o'clock, lunch was served. They didn't give you a menu or anything. It was soup, main course, and dessert — every day. When I first got there these were serious, heavy meals, like cream soup, meat and potatoes, salad, cheese, apple pie. It really could kill you.

ANDY SAGE:

I went up to 215 pounds from 160 just from going to the dining room and having those big meals, and then going home and having a big supper at night.

WARREN HELLMAN:

You had a martini before lunch and sherry with lunch. It wasn't considered good form not to drink, and since I don't I was more than once warned that this wasn't a way for advancement.

PETER SOLOMON:

The dining room was the center of activity. But the partners of Lehman were very bad investors, and you could lose more money listening to their ideas than any group of people. They had an unerring sense of disaster.

By the mid-1960s Our Crowd basically was dead on Wall Street. Lehman Brothers was in ascendance and would remain a power on Wall Street for as long as its dynamic partners could stand the sight of one another. The Jewish trading houses, Salomon Brothers and Goldman Sachs, also were thriving and starting to grow in stature. But the once-mighty old-line German-Jewish partnerships like Kuhn Loeb and Loeb Rhoades clearly were in decline. Within a decade, those names and many others would be wiped from the Wall Street landscape.

CHAPTER 4

INTRINSIC VALUE

The long history of financial markets is littered with get-rich-quick schemes, plans to cash in by speculating on the prices of certain commodities and securities. From the Dutch tulip-bulb mania in the seventeenth century to the frenzy for Internet stocks in the late twentieth century, people have sought to cash in on the hot investing idea of the day. But prior to the mid-twentieth century, what was lacking from the investing canon was an explanation of how to understand the financial markets as a place where money could be left as a long-term investment. Coming out of the Depression, Americans for the most part were skeptical of Wall Street, viewing the financial markets as casinos where you rolled the dice and hoped to escape with your shirt still on. As the stock market began to heat up in the 1950s, more people started to notice that anyone could make a lot of money with the right stock. The trouble was, nobody could explain how to pick the right stock without getting the proverbial lucky tip from a rich uncle. Nobody, that is, except Benjamin Graham, a Wall Street money manager and professor at Columbia University.

With his two landmark books, Security Analysis, *published in 1934 and coauthored with his teaching partner David Dodd, and* The Intelligent Investor, *published in 1949, Ben Graham set the ground rules for what came to be known as "value investing." Simply put, the idea of value investing is that each company has an intrinsic value that can be quantified through analysis and is separate from the company's market value, or stock price. The goal of value investing is to reduce the inherent risk of Wall Street — that an investor could lose all his money — by buying stocks only when the intrinsic value of the company is higher than the market value, on the assumption that eventually the stock price will rise to reflect its true worth.*

Graham put his value-investing ideas to work at a small brokerage operation called Graham-Newman Corporation, which he owned with his partner, Jerry Newman. Both Graham and Newman were children of the Depression, and they didn't want to lose whatever capital they had accumulated. So their firm invested only in situations that they deemed safe. Since there were only so many stocks that met Graham's strict value-investing criteria, they also devised arbitrage trades that essentially could be considered riskless. Arbitrage is a trading strategy where investors try to capitalize on price discrepancies in different securities or in different markets. For example, if gold is selling for $425 an ounce in Zurich and $420 an ounce in Singapore, you could buy gold in Singapore, sell it in Zurich, and take home a profit of $5 for each ounce of gold you bought and sold. That's called arbitrage.

For Graham-Newman, arbitraging different securities was useful as a value-investing technique because it could reduce the risk in a transaction by mitigating the potential loss if the price of a stock went down rather than up. Say for $100 you can buy one share of IBM and for $1,000 you can buy an IBM convertible bond, a bond that converts into 10 IBM shares and also pays interest. Obviously, if you think $100 is a cheap price for IBM's stock, the convertible bond is a particularly good value because you have the interest from the bond and the potential that the stock price could be higher when the bond converts to 10 IBM shares. So Graham-Newman would buy the bond and — understanding that the price of IBM also could fall — simultaneously "sell short" IBM shares. Short selling is Wall Street's primary technique for betting against a stock. An investor borrows a certain number of shares from a brokerage house's *inventory and then immediately sells the shares in the open market. For the trade to work out, the price of the stock needs to fall so the investor can buy back the shares at a lower price, return the borrowed shares to the brokerage house, and pocket the difference. Graham-Newman used short selling primarily as an effective hedging tool. In buying the IBM convertible bond Graham-Newman was essentially "long" the stock, meaning they were betting its price would rise. So by simultaneously shorting IBM they had some downside protection in case IBM tanked, while still being able to benefit from the bond's return. That was the kind of arbitrage trade Graham-Newman liked. It wasn't enormously profitable because the short and long IBM positions would cancel each other out to a certain extent, but it was safe—and if the strategy was deployed often enough it could provide steady capital growth.*

Still, more than playing the market, Graham's main love was teaching, which he did in addition to running Graham-Newman. Through his classes at Columbia and the New York Institute of Finance, Graham developed a loyal following of devotees and true believers who thought that his ideas on value investing unlocked a secret door to understanding how the markets worked. Like disciples, Graham's students fanned out across the country, spreading the gospel of buying low and selling high. Many went on to highly successful careers as portfolio managers and Wall Street investors, but none is more famous than Graham's ultimate protégé, perhaps the greatest investor in the history of the modern financial markets: Warren Buffett.

IRVING KAHN (chairman of the value-investing firm Kahn Brothers and Company, former analyst at Graham-Newman, and longtime friend and colleague of Benjamin Graham):

Ben Graham's father died when he was young, and his two brothers didn't have his ability, so he supported them and their mother. He got a scholarship from Columbia, and he wanted to teach there, but he couldn't because they paid such poor salaries. So he came to Wall Street.

TOM KNAPP (noted value investor, former head of Tweedy Browne Company, and former analyst at Graham-Newman):

When Ben graduated from Columbia, he was offered three professorships — one was in economics, one was in math, and one was in classics. He had all the attributes of a genius. He taught himself to read ancient Greek and Latin languages so he could study the famous philosophers. And he had a phenomenal memory. He remembered everything he read, and if he particularly liked something, he'd memorize the whole page — in Greek — and repeat it. He had an absolutely incredible mind.

Interestingly, Ben had a great reputation at Columbia for being a smart guy, and so when he decided to go to work on Wall Street he applied to several of the large firms. But they all turned him down. His belief was that it was because he was Jewish. These were the old New England–type firms, and that's the way it was in those days. He finally got a job with a firm, and eventually he started his own firm, Graham-Newman. But it always stuck with him.

IRVING KAHN:

His first real job was with a firm called Newburger, Henderson and Loeb Brokerage, a Philadelphia firm with a New York branch. Eventually he and a friend from high school, a man by the name of Jerome Newman, started their own firm called Graham-Newman. Ben started to correctly analyze the stock market and individual companies from the point of view of risk avoidance. He devised riskless transactions, of which there are few.

TOM KNAPP:

Ben was hurt during the Depression. So he wanted to have things riskless. Riskless! Of course, nothing's completely riskless, but there can be a wide range of value above the cost.

WALTER SCHLOSS (noted value investor, founder and former chairman of Walter and Edwin Schloss Associates, and former analyst at Graham-Newman):

They would do these arbitrages, as we called them, where we'd buy certain bonds in bankrupt companies that were selling for very little and sell off the stock, which was at a higher price comparatively. They did this a lot with the railroads — I remember Missouri Pacific particularly.

There were a number of stocks selling for below working capital in the 1930s and 1940s. There were a lot of companies like that. My job really was to find those stocks that were selling for below working capital and figure out how many shares to buy. The fund was so small that they bought in very small quantities. They had been so hurt by the Depression that they became very careful. Graham did not want to lose money, and he couldn't lose money the way he was investing.

ROGER LOWENSTEIN (financial journalist, Buffett biographer, and director of value-investing company Sequoia Fund):

Arbitrage is a fancy-sounding word, but it really takes place in any transaction. Every time you buy a stock, you're arbitraging the price of the company now versus the value that you believe is inherent in the company. A bankruptcy, a liquidation, these are just the trigger events that crystallize the situation. So in that sense Graham's brand of arbitrage can be seen as easy money.

IRVING KAHN:

Even though he worked on Wall Street, Ben's mind always was more on his ideas and teaching than making money. I think that's why he started his course at Columbia. I know that's how I met him. I wanted to go to graduate school, and I couldn't afford to. But I could work on Wall Street. In 1929, when the market closed at three in the afternoon, I could get on the subway and be up at Columbia in forty minutes. In fact, that's how I met Ben Graham. He initiated a class for the first time in the late afternoon. Other people like me who were working during the day could leave by three fifteen. That's how he got some fairly prominent guys, like partners at Goldman Sachs or other people who later became well-known, who also were trying to learn the business.

WALTER SCHLOSS:

I took a course with Ben on security analysis at the New York Stock Exchange Institute, which is now called the New York Institute of Finance, and a few years later I took another course on advanced security analysis. You had a lot of very smart people taking his courses on value investing — Gus Levy, who became the head of Goldman Sachs, took his classes, and people like that.

IRVING KAHN:

I would come to him and I would say, "Ben, I think we should buy this for Graham-Newman." He'd say, "What are the earnings?" I'd say, "Two dollars." He'd say, "For five years?" It's very important because people always want to talk about this year, but he wanted you to go back four more years to see whether that earnings power was stable and if it was likely to continue.

"How much do they owe?" That was another thing he wanted to know. If they had big debt they might be called out on their stock. They might be forced into a decision that they didn't want to make. They might be unable to buy out a competitor, which could be the best thing to do.

You have to separate out what you can analyze and what you can only talk about. I can agree on what a great leader [former General Electric chairman] Jack Welch is. But I can't tell you that the price of GE times the number of shares outstanding less the debt and so forth is going to prove to be a good price.

CHARLES BRANDES (founder of Ben Graham–style value-investing firm Brandes Investment Partners):

One of Graham's great lessons is that you've got to stay away from the stock market for a majority of the time. You can't get confused between investing and speculating. People speculate by worrying about short-term price movements rather than relying on the wealth-producing capability of the business. And investing is what we do.

ROBERT OLSTEIN (chairman of Olstein Financial Alert Fund and former high-net-worth broker for Smith Barney):

There are two kinds of investing that I know of. The first is paying attention to the value of a company and having some method of valuing it. That's what I do. And then there's what I call momentum investing, or psychological investing, which is trying to predict the behavior of crowds. The reality is that for the most part the crowd dominates the market, and if you can predict the behavior of the crowd with any degree of regularity, you're going to have good performance because the crowd determines prices in the short term. That being said, a value investor, or an investor who pays attention to values, says, "Here's what the crowd is saying. What are they seeing?" Sometimes the crowd is seeing exactly the right thing. But sometimes the crowd is only seeing temporary phenomena and missing the real value of a company. When you look for deviations between the perceptions of crowds and long-term reality, that, to me, is value investing.

ROGER LOWENSTEIN:

There were a lot of smart people who were drawn to Ben Graham and his classes. But I think he really started to reach people when he published *The Intelligent Investor* in 1949. I know that's how he reached Warren Buffett. At the time, Buffett was a young man just getting interested in Wall Street, and like many people he'd been searching for a system. If you read the financial papers, every day there's a new system. Buy the ten cheapest Dow stocks. Buy them when they're ahead of their "daily moving average." Buy them on alternating Tuesdays after the Cubs have won. There are as many systems as there are investors, but very few of them have anything to do with what the securities are worth.

The Intelligent Investor spoke to Warren and others because it did two things: one, it emphasized that owning a share of stock actually is owning a piece of a business, so you shouldn't want to pay more for that share than you would if you were buying the whole business; and two, it presented an enormously useful and pleasing parable of how to deal with Wall Street. In that book Graham says that if you're investing in the stock market you should imagine that you're really a partner with a very temperamental person named Mr. Market. Some days he comes in and he's extremely optimistic, wants to buy out your half, and is willing to pay any price. So you should sell to him. But on other days he comes in and he's just terribly depressed and he feels that the business you're partners in is going nowhere, so he wants to sell his half for whatever you'll give him. So you should buy it from him. And then on many days he's neither up nor down, but the good thing is you don't have to transact with him at all because he'll come back the next day and make you another offer. The only thing you don't want to do is, if your partner Mr. Market comes in and is depressed, you don't want to get depressed yourself. Or if your partner comes in and is wildly enthusiastic, you don't want to get caught up in it too. It's really a wonderful way of thinking about the stock market.

WARREN BUFFETT (Berkshire Hathaway chairman):

I read the first edition of this book when I was nineteen. I thought then that it was the best book about investing ever written. I still think it is.

ANDY KILPATRICK (stockbroker, longtime Berkshire Hathaway shareholder, and author of a self-published, 1,500-page biography of Warren Buffett):

When Buffett graduated from the University of Nebraska he applied to the Harvard Business School but was rejected because he was too young. He applied at nineteen, so that was a stretch. But he was rejected and it sort of stung. Then he read *The Intelligent Investor* and saw that this guy Ben Graham was teaching at Columbia. So he went to Columbia and had the top academic record in the business school.

TOM KNAPP:

After graduating from Columbia I went to work with some guys who went to the Harvard Business School, but I wasn't very happy there because their methods were very different from what I'd been taught by Graham and Dodd. The Harvard Business School teaches a very macroeconomic view of the market. If you think that the economy is going to be good for automobiles, then you take a look at automobile companies, and so forth. The price of the stock didn't seem to make much of a difference. They were looking more at what the economic outlook was for the particular industry.

ANDY KILPATRICK:

You can't underestimate the kind of impact Ben Graham has had on Buffett. He's said, "Ben Graham was my God." He was struck by his personality and he felt that value investing was really the only rational way to look at investments. What is it really worth? Can you buy it at fifty cents on the dollar? That's the rational way to look at things, not with tips, or graphs and charts.

WALTER SCHLOSS:

I met Warren Buffett because of Ben Graham. What happened was, when companies have problems they often like to have their annual meetings in cities and states where there aren't too many stockholders. Marshall Wells was a wholesaler up in Minneapolis that had some problems, and they had their annual meeting in Jersey City. I was at Graham-Newman at the time, and I went to Jersey City because we had stock in Marshall Wells, which was selling for below working capital. And wouldn't you know it, Warren Buffett was there. He was a student at Columbia at the time, but he had evidently read Graham-Newman's reports, saw that Marshall Wells was interesting, and bought some of the stock. We struck up an acquaintance and hit it off nicely.

TOM KNAPP:

I never met anyone who had more of an aptitude for value investing than Buffett. He has the most unbelievable memory. He could tell you the balance sheet of practically every company listed on the New York Stock Exchange at that time. He was way beyond what most people were doing.

IRVING KAHN:

Warren was, and is, an extremely good judge of people. He could meet you, you could give him a wonderful deal, and after you left the room he'd say, "I'll never put a dime in that man's business because I don't like the way he reacts." Or he could like you very much. He always had a very unusual sense of people.

ROGER LOWENSTEIN:

When Buffett graduated from Columbia, Graham and his father both advised him not to go to Wall Street, which seems pretty funny when you think about that now. Graham thought the market was too high and he wanted him to wait until it came down to a lower level. Buffett's father agreed. Buffett said in the 1980s that if he'd listened to them he'd still be waiting. That's a lesson as well. Just imagine if he'd gone into sales and risen to become a regional vice president at Woolworths. That really would've been a shame for the rest of us.

IRVING KAHN:

After he graduated, Buffett came to Ben, but he wouldn't hire him. He said he didn't have enough experience. But Buffett kept after him. One day he said to Ben, "Mr. Graham, I'll work for you for nothing." He meant it, you know. He knew that Ben was such a smart man.

TOM KNAPP:

Warren did offer to work for Graham for free, that's absolutely true. But everyone at Graham-Newman was Jewish, from the top right down to the bottom. This was because Graham remembered how hard it was for a Jewish guy to get a job when he was trying to come to Wall Street. So Warren came in and offered to work for free. But Ben wasn't about to break his philosophy on hiring. He told Warren no. And Warren went back to Omaha.

ROGER LOWENSTEIN:

Graham didn't want Buffett to come to Wall Street to work for him because he wanted to save the positions in his firm for Jews, who had a hard time finding work on Wall Street. So Buffett went to work for his father for a little bit, and then he came back East to work for Graham.

IRVING KAHN:

Warren is really very different from Ben. Ben was never driven to be rich, although he ended rich. He was very charitable and very much of a teacher and a leader. Buffett is concentrating on controlling as much as he can.

ROGER LOWENSTEIN:

Graham was more conservative than Buffett. And I think Buffett was actually making more money off his own investments than from anything he was doing for Graham. He was just devouring the stock exchange at that time. There wasn't a balance sheet out there that he wasn't aware of. He would read through annual reports the way you or I would read through the phone book. At some point there was no one he could work for, even his hero. He was going to have to be turned loose.

IRVING KAHN:

At the end of the Graham-Newman partnership in 1956 they decided to liquidate. They'd made enough money. They gave me back my $104 for each share that I had bought. And I calculated that I had received dividends each year of 20 percent from the profits.

WALTER SCHLOSS:

By the time Graham decided to close the business he was about sixty-two and he wanted to go out to California. He didn't want to have responsibility and had enough money. So he went out there and folded the partnership.

TOM KNAPP:

Graham decided to retire, and Warren decided, after Graham decided to retire, to go back to Omaha and start his own partnership. That left [Graham's original partner] Jerry and [his son] Mickey Newman, who I think felt at that point it would be advisable to liquidate.

ROGER LOWENSTEIN:

When Buffett went back to Omaha the second time, he started his own partnership, which he modeled after Graham-Newman. It was a private partnership, and he was doing the same operations. But Buffett's returns were out of this world.

ROBERT SOENER (retired stockbroker in Omaha, Nebraska, and longtime friend of and investor with Warren Buffett):

I met Warren Buffett in the early 1950s. I was working as a stockbroker in Omaha at the time, and he just walked in the office one day. Talk about a red-letter day for me. He's seven years younger than I am, and at that time he was going to school at the University of Nebraska and doing business with our office in Lincoln. So we started talking, and he asked me for a few quotes. He asked me what the price of Studebaker Packard was, and I told him that. And he said, "I'm short the stock." I was just a rookie at that point, but I looked at this young whippersnapper and said, "You can't buy stocks. You're too young." And he said, "I have it in my sister's name." That put me down in my place right away.

Our friendship grew, and when he eventually went to Columbia University we corresponded. Then, when he got back home, he was working for his father, who operated an over-the-counter house in Omaha. Warren was selling stocks of his choice to clients, and he realized that he was making $45 or $50 in commission and the customers were making several thousand dollars. So he said, "I'd like to participate in that." I think that's where the idea for the partnership came from.

RICHARD HOLLAND (retired advertising executive in Omaha, Nebraska, and longtime friend of and investor with Warren Buffett):

I was relatively young, in my late twenties, when I started doing some investing. But I was just investing in the typical way. I knew somebody who was a broker who would give me some advice on a certain stock, and I'd buy it. I remember one was Columbia Gas. That's the way I invested. I didn't do badly, but I didn't do well either.

Then a group of us got together and formed an investing club. Basically, it was twelve or thirteen people who didn't know their ass from apple butter when it came to investing. Everybody had his own ideas, but it was all very speculative. "I'm sure this stock is going to go up." Or, "This company's got a great future." In the very beginning we hit on one that was just like that, a thing called Steep Rock Iron Mines. It was about $2 or $3 a share, and it went to about $14 or $15 a share in less than a year. We thought we were marvelous. But after that I don't think we ever hit one again. We had all kinds of arguments about what was a good idea and what was bad, but at no time did anyone ever bring up the idea of value investing, of looking at what these companies were really worth and then buying stocks based on their price. It was always some speculative idea about how this was a good stock with real prospects and it would go up.

I began to hear more and more about this idea of value investing, and I began to listen more and more. I went to lunch with Warren a couple of times, and I didn't realize then that he would not ask me to invest with him. He wanted you to ask him if you could invest with him. This was a partnership, and he had this thing where he did not want to be aggressive in seeking money. So I was too damn dumb to ask if I could invest with him.

But the thing that Warren always talked to me about was the idea of looking at the value of a company and buying stocks that were undervalued. He told me to read *The Intelligent Investor.* I've always said to my children, "I don't care if you read the whole damn book, but at least read the first six or seven chapters, because it changed my life." I realized suddenly that there was a way of investing that had a certainty about it if you could hang on long enough. If you could properly value an undervalued investment and then had the discipline to hang on, you would be rewarded eventually. The book gave several examples of this, how the market doesn't believe in a stock or isn't interested in a stock, and suddenly it reaches a point where the price of the stock is significantly below the company's true asset value. That's the time to buy it and safely go to sleep at night, not worry. God, that was a bigger revelation to me than almost anything I'd ever read. Up until that point I'd had a very different kind of orientation, and I didn't even know it.

ROBERT SOENER:

In order to spread the word about his new partnership, Warren thought it would be a good idea to teach classes, noncredit investment classes, at the University of Omaha. He asked me to teach the first four weeks of the ten-week course and then he would take over. He got a lot of people interested, of course, because they liked what they heard from him about his philosophy on investing, and he seemed to be quite honest. We had a class with just "regular people." And we had another class with professional people, doctors and lawyers. And we had an afternoon class for the wives of the doctors and lawyers, which I enjoyed most thoroughly. These people had "adult money" in those days, which wasn't the case with me. In fact, I was enjoying the class I was teaching because I was making more money from teaching than I was in the brokerage business.

TOM KNAPP:

I always thought Warren had a very good rapport with audiences. I visited him a couple of times out in Omaha and he was teaching an investment course, sort of a night course that he had. I was very impressed with the way he could handle the whole thing.

LELAND OLSON (retired doctor in Omaha, Nebraska, and longtime friend of and investor with Warren Buffett):

I was buying stocks on my own, but I didn't really have any money. I was in my early thirties and I realized that I needed training and help if I was going to invest in the stock market. And that's how I met Warren Buffett. He was teaching a night course at what at the time was the University of Omaha, but what is now called the University of Nebraska at Omaha. He had a night course going and I took it. In fact, I took it twice because I was so impressed with his teaching.

He was only twenty-seven years old at that time, but he was so clear on how he evaluated stocks using the Graham technique. He was a value investor. And he evaluated not only the stock, but the background of it. I remember he was interested in a company that was based in Kansas City, and rather than just sit around and read reports, he went out to Kansas City to see what the company was doing. That impressed me very much.

RICHARD HOLLAND:

All the talk among the people who invested, all the stories in the financial press at that time, invariably were about prospects. They were about somebody finding a gold mine, all kinds of schemes of invention and discovery. There was never any real discussion of how much this stuff was worth. The big stock of the day back then was IBM. There's no doubt about it that people made fortunes on it, and afterward everybody was looking around for the next IBM. But that's not the way to invest.

LELAND OLSON:

After I took the course twice he was very friendly. We're talking about fifteen, twenty people in the class with us, so it was a small group and he got to know us and we got to know him. At that point in time he offered his advice, saying that he had an investment vehicle. What he did was, he would offer yearly a portfolio that he had put together, and that's how I got started. That went on from the late fifties until 1970 when he discontinued the operation.

ROBERT SOENER:

So, my dad passed away in 1952 and left $21,000 to my mother. We were fooling around with AT&T, and when Warren opened up his partnership I suggested to my mother that we take $15,000 and put it with Buffett. He was going to pay 6 percent a year, and she needed that to pay her rent, which was $70 a month. So I said, "Mom, this will take care of the rent money." She asked me, "Can we trust him?" And I said that I thought we could. So that's what we did. She took the 6 percent out the rest of her life, and she lived to be ninety-six years old. By the end she was paying $3,200 a month in a nursing home. The $70 a month she was trying to obtain years ago had grown, but she could afford it because of Buffett. [Without him,] there's no way on God's green earth that I was going to be able to afford that, and neither would she. A little later I also came across some bonus money and put it with him, and that's how we got started as investors with Warren. It's just been a godsend for us.

RICHARD HOLLAND:

Around 1961, I convinced my wife, who had a little money, to put some with Warren. I think about that a lot, because if I'd failed at that and given her bad advice I would've been in trouble. Then, a little later, I went through the trouble of borrowing on my life insurance to put some of my own money with Warren. Over the years we gradually put in more because he just kept doing better and better. It was a real Goin' Gussie. And then Warren and I became personal friends. We played bridge together, we played golf together, we played tennis and table tennis — God, we played everything. My wife got Warren interested in buying his house in Southern California, and Susan Buffett became one of my wife's better friends. We were very close to them during that time, and have been good friends ever since. So we never sold it. Even after he folded the partnership, we held onto Berkshire until beginning sometime in the nineties. It's just been phenomenal. One time not too long ago I said to Warren, "You know, I want to thank you for all you've done for me." And Warren said, "Hell, Dick, I didn't do anything for you. You never sold."

I think I get along with Warren because we have a similar outlook. We lead very simple lives. We don't have mansions or fancy cars or all the paraphernalia. We've lived in the same house now for forty-seven years. Warren's lived in the same house for thirty or forty years now. There's a certain similarity to Buffett investors. They are like that. You don't see a Buffett investor being very conspicuous. In the early days I went to all the partnership meetings, and I've got to say, looking at those guys you'd never guess that these were some of the richest people around. There were two old ladies, friends of [value investor and Buffett friend] Sandy Gottesman, who lived out on Long Island. There was an old guy who was the head of a school up in Vermont. There were some families here in Omaha who were early investors. But if you hung around these people you never had any idea that they were worth a pile of money. The impression I've had is that this is the kind of person who is attracted to Warren. I've never met a Buffett investor who flaunted it.

ROGER LOWENSTEIN:

If you had to characterize the Buffett Partnership, you'd have to look at something like the '27 Yankees with Ruth and Gehrig. If you could freeze-frame a moment in time in investing and say, "This is it, fellas," Warren Buffett's investment partnership would have to be it. I don't know if there's ever been an investing engine like it. It went for thirteen years. It never had a down year. It never had a single year in which it trailed the stock market. It returned on average 27 percent a year, and the margin over the Dow was just a herculean amount. The guy never had a down year. There was apparently no risk. By the way, he was continually saying, "This can't go on. There's no way it can last." By 1968, the market was in a state of froth and speculation not unlike the late 1990s, and Buffett sent out a warning to his investors saying, "I can't find anything. I'm not going to play the speculative game. If I can do 5 percent I'll consider myself lucky. You're probably better off somewhere else." Blah, blah, blah. He earned 57 percent that year, which was way ahead of the average.

WALTER SCHLOSS:

In 1969 the market was much too high. Look at any of his partnership letters from that time and he's saying that there isn't anything to buy.

TOM KNAPP:

I don't remember exactly the year, but in the late 1960s Warren consistently said that the good buys were shrinking. It was getting much harder to find good values. I think that really was the reason he folded the partnership.

ROGER LOWENSTEIN:

He folded because as the market went higher and higher there were fewer and fewer stocks that on a Ben Graham basis were trading for what they were worth. So he did what nobody does. He quit with a perfectly unblemished record. He'd long since closed the fund. Lord knows how much he could've brought in if he'd opened it, to his own enrichment. But that wasn't what he was interested in. And so when he looked at the market in 1968 and 1969, he said, "I don't understand this market, and I'm not going to play a game I don't understand."

RICHARD HOLLAND:

When Warren folded the partnership in 1970 he paid everybody in kind. We got our share of Berkshire Hathaway, which was a Massachusetts textile mill he'd bought in the 1960s, our share of cash, and there were five or six other things that the partnership held that he also distributed to his investors. I think there were even some bonds. And what he told us was that if we didn't like any of our distributions, he would buy them from us. But I wasn't about to sell any of it to anyone.

LELAND OLSON:

He called each of us in and had a conference with us separately. By that time I had put my mother's account with him and my account with him. And he called me in and said the advice for Mother, who was a widow and needed income, was a portfolio he'd built of stocks that were paying good dividends and bonds with good yields. For me, he chose his Berkshire Hathaway stock, which I think was worth $45 a share at the time, and he invested in some bonds for me. So I decided to stay with him, and I've been with him ever since.

Of course, Warren Buffett wasn't done with Wall Street when he folded his partnership. He just moved on to bigger targets, using his Berkshire Hathaway stock as his vehicle. In time, Buffett would expand Ben Graham's ideas, and apply the tenets of value investing to buying entire companies. Today, Berkshire Hathaway is one of the few successful diversified conglomerates in the world. Its holdings run the gamut, from a mammoth insurance empire to a Nebraska furniture store. Berkshire Hathaway "A" shares, which represent the same ownership level as the original Berkshire Hathaway stock the Buffett Partnership received at a value of around $45 a share in 1970, trade for more than $85,000. And Warren Buffett is arguably the most respected investor in the world.

CHAPTER 5

BLACKBALLED

With the stock market climbing in the late 1950s and early 1960s new partnerships started springing up to challenge the establishment powers and capture the growth of the securities business as a potent bull market exploded into what became known as the "go-go years." In particular, the new firm Donaldson, Lufkin and Jenrette had attracted a lot of attention with its dedication to in-depth research on companies that most Wall Street firms didn't bother to cover. In DLJ's successful wake, a slew of new firms followed. One of them was Carter, Berlind, Potoma and Weill. The partners were young, primarily Jewish guys from Brooklyn and Long Island — true outsiders in the clubby world of Wall Street. Arthur Carter was the clear leader of the group, and Roger Berlind served as his cerebral counterweight. Peter Potoma was considered the best salesman of the bunch. The fourth partner was quieter than the others and showed little interest in anything other than building his personal business with his own clients. His name was Sandy Weill. Though nobody could see it then, from these humble beginnings, Weill would grow to become the biggest banker in the business.

JUDITH RAMSEY EHRLICH (coauthor of *The New Crowd*):

As strange as this may seem today, when Sandy Weill first joined the business in the 1950s he lacked the background, credentials, and style to get a job as an investment banker at one of the Our Crowd firms like Lehman Brothers or Kuhn, Loeb. He was not one of them. He was the wrong kind of Jew. He'd grown up in Bensonhurst, Brooklyn.

Despite the fact that these days Sandy sometimes talks about his past as if it was a rags-to-riches story, he actually grew up in a moderately comfortable middle-class family. He spent his childhood in his parents' three-story house in Brooklyn with some other close relatives living nearby. His father, who ran a small garment-manufacturing business, actually moved the family to Florida for two years because he thought his business might do better there. Weill didn't adjust well to the move and his grades suffered. Two years later the family returned to Brooklyn and Sandy was enrolled in the Peekskill Military Academy, which was a private school. This more regimented environment somehow gave him the structure he needed. He tried harder and therefore did better. He managed to graduate third in his class and was accepted by both Harvard and Cornell. He attended Cornell. Initially he had planned to study metallurgical engineering and then go into business with his father, who at that time had given up manufacturing clothing and was importing steel. Sandy did poorly academically and in fact would've flunked out if there hadn't been a special program that gave students like him a second chance in another department. So he opted to major in government and his grades improved.

In June of his senior year at Cornell, Weill was getting ready to marry Joan Mosher and his prospects were unimpressive to say the least. Earlier that year Sandy's father had left his mother for a younger woman. This was a shattering experience for Sandy.

SANDY WEILL (former Citigroup chairman):

It was a turning point in my life. I felt I had to stand up on my own from then on.

JUDITH RAMSEY EHRLICH:

After trying to reconcile his feelings about his parents' divorce, Sandy failed to complete a required course at college and he couldn't graduate with his class. As a result, Joan's parents tried to persuade her not to marry him. They didn't want a son-in-law without a diploma and with no prospects. Given the way that Weill's father had behaved, Joan's father cautioned her, saying, "The apple doesn't fall far from the tree." However, Joan was determined to marry Sandy, and when her parents were faced with the inevitable they offered the young couple a choice — a large wedding or money. Well, they took the cash.

After getting married, Sandy took a job delivering commercial directories. At the time Joan was completing her senior year at Brooklyn College and working as a substitute teacher. She was earning more money than he was. Sometimes when he had nothing to do, Weill would hang out at Times Square and play amusement-arcade games. One day in Times Square he passed by a branch office of Bache, and he was attracted by all the activity.

SANDY WEILL:

It was very exciting to me, but I really had no idea what I was looking at. I remember thinking that if I had $10,000 I could probably buy every stock I'd ever want to buy.

JUDITH RAMSEY EHRLICH:

Realizing that he needed training, Weill tried to enter a broker-training program at Bache, as well as at Merrill Lynch and Harris Upham. But he was rejected by all three houses. So as he saw it, he had no money and no connections to get ahead on Wall Street. Finally, Bear Stearns hired him as a $35-a-week runner, which meant that he was still a delivery boy or messenger, but instead of lugging directories he was delivering bundles of securities around the financial district.

DAN CORWIN (former partner at Burnham and Company):

[Sandy] had such terrible clothes when he showed up here that we were worried he couldn't make a good impression on potential clients. So a few of us got together a few hundred dollars to buy him a couple of suits and some shirts.

JUDITH RAMSEY EHRLICH:

Eventually he demanded a shot at being a broker. He told his boss that if his request was turned down he'd enlist in the air force.

SANDY WEILL:

I think they realized I was the only guy in there with a college degree. All the other runners were over sixty-five and on Social Security.

JUDITH RAMSEY EHRLICH:

Weill was able to take advantage of some of the people he knew in Brooklyn, and they became his first customers. Soon he was earning enough money to move with Joan into their own apartment. By this time Joan was pregnant and up until then they'd been spending their time shuttling between their two sets of parents, spending some time at one home and then moving over to the other. Now they finally had a home of their own.

At the same time Weill was trying to climb the ladder on Wall Street, he also was forging the most significant professional relationship of his life — his friendship with his neighbor in an East Rockaway apartment complex, Arthur Carter.

JUDITH RAMSEY EHRLICH:

Arthur Carter lived across the hall from the Weills in Rockaway, and he had only recently gone to work for Lehman Brothers. He was the son of an Internal Revenue Service agent, and he had dreamed of becoming a concert pianist. He did a stint with a U.S. Coast Guard base and then caught the same Wall Street fever Weill had. So he returned to school for an MBA. That meant he was better equipped for Wall Street than Weill was.

ARTHUR CARTER (cofounder of Carter, Berlind and Weill):

Sandy and I became friends sometime before he was hired at Burnham and Company. Both of us had apartments, our first apartments, on the same floor on Atlantic Avenue in East Rockaway, Queens, when we were first married. Sandy at the time was a stockbroker at Bear Stearns and I was at Lehman Brothers. We commuted to Manhattan together every day. It turned out we both had little boys and our wives became friends. Our families shared a beach cabana in the summer. Through all that we became close friends.

JUDITH RAMSEY EHRLICH:

As Weill and Carter became more experienced Wall Street players, they began to talk about starting their own securities firm. At first Sandy just thought this idea was too ambitious. He wanted to succeed, but his goals in those days were quite simple. He once told me, and I remember this very clearly, that he considered the purchase of a deep fryer as an extremely significant acquisition. He also yearned for a Kodak slide projector so he could display pictures of his family.

ARTHUR CARTER:

We both talked about starting our own firm over a long period of time. We both knew the concerns with doing it. We had very little capital and there was always this question of "Where is the business going to come from?" Our plan was to focus on three things: the private-account business, where individuals with their own brokerage businesses — like Roger Berlind and Sandy — would fund the day-to-day operations with their commissions; the institutional brokerage business, which would take a while to get going; and underwritings, which was an area of some expertise for me because I had been at Lehman.

This was not an ordinary decision by any stretch of the imagination, but it was done. In the sixties the establishment started to crack in some ways, creating more opportunities for the young guys. This wasn't happening just on Wall Street; it was happening across a vast cultural horizon, you might say. But on Wall Street it resulted in some younger guys breaking off from the establishment and starting their own successful firms.

RICHARD JENRETTE (cofounder of Donaldson, Lufkin and Jenrette):

When we started DLJ in 1960 we were the first new firm on Wall Street since 1932. I remember someone I worked with at Brown Brothers said to me, "Dick, you're crazy. Don't you know there have been no new firms since 1932?" But I am a contrarian, so the idea appealed to me.

Basically I'd always been very impressed with Bill Donaldson and Dan Lufkin, who I'd known since our days at Harvard Business School, as bright, articulate young fellows. They seemed to know everybody around town. They had all the right connections. I mean, they were Yale blood, Skull and Bones, all that. So a lot of doors were open to us that weren't necessarily open to others, if you know what I mean. In my mind, if there was anyone to go into business with, it was those two.

ARTHUR CARTER:

I mean Milbank Tweed — a classic old-line white-shoe law firm — put money into DLJ. We didn't have anything like that. We did it with nothing more than the small amount of capital that we could put into the firm ourselves.

RICHARD JENRETTE:

To be honest, we didn't feel that we were taking an awful risk because we were young, we weren't giving up very big salaries, and we didn't have wives or children yet. And I guess we all had parents, so if all else failed we could fall back on the safety net of the family. It all seemed so easy for us. Under Dan's plan we were going to raise enough money to tide us over a couple of years so we could survive on low overhead. You know, I credit Lufkin with much of the idea for getting it started. From there things just sort of fell into place pretty quickly. It didn't take us long to become respected players. As for the other young guys who followed us, the Sandy Weills and the rest, well, I think you'll find they had a tougher go of it right out of the gate than we did. They had to work for their contacts and connections. We already had ours.

DAN LUFKIN (cofounder and former chief executive of Donaldson, Lufkin and Jenrette):

I took our idea of starting a new brokerage firm based on researching and trading in shares of these growing young companies to all the heads of the establishment investment banks at that time — Sidney Weinberg and Gus Levy at Goldman Sachs, Bobbie Lehman at Lehman Brothers, André Meyer at Lazard, Percy Stewart at Kuhn Loeb, Billy Salomon at Salomon Brothers, John Loeb at Loeb Rhoades, and a few others that I can't think of right now. And they all told me the same thing: How old are you, twenty-six? What are you, crazy? You're going to compete with Lehman Brothers and Loeb Rhoades? You can't do it. This business is based on trust and you need time to create that trust.

They turned out to be totally wrong. Many of these companies were the blue chips of the future. There was a growing number of us younger guys who were interested in these companies, people like Jerry Tsai and Ned Johnson [of Fidelity] and the other go-go fund managers. So that's where we sought to do business, providing good, thoughtful research on companies that were out of the mainstream. See, back then brokerage commissions on the New York Stock Exchange were fixed. If you bought a share of stock you paid a commission that was established by the New York Stock Exchange — you couldn't negotiate a lower rate if you wanted to. But as a customer you could direct a portion of your commission payments to another firm.

So commissions became the currency of Wall Street, called soft dollars. As mutual fund sales took off in the 1960s, the fund world would direct its commissions to the firms that were selling its shares and to the firms that were providing quality research. The business grew almost immediately. I'm serious — we never had a losing month. We added people, we added services, and we kept growing. Eventually we started positioning block trades for some of our institutional customers, who had been going to Goldman Sachs and Salomon Brothers for that service. Then, over time, we started to get a little investment-banking business from the developing companies we were covering. And that's how we built the company. It was a classic American free-enterprise story. Before we knew it, we were major players on Wall Street, full-fledged members of the club.

ARTHUR CARTER:

Now Sandy and I knew we couldn't go into this business alone; we'd need at least one other partner. So after we seriously discussed starting this firm I called my friend Roger Berlind, who was working as a broker at Eastman Dillon Union Securities, to see what he thought about joining us. Roger and I grew up in the same town, Woodmere, Long Island. I knew Roger and his family very well from the time we were eleven or twelve years old. In fact, his mother took French lessons from my mother. We stayed in contact over the years, particularly since we both were on Wall Street.

When I called Roger he said, "I've been talking to Peter Potoma, who's here with me at Eastman Dillon, about starting a firm. So I'd have to bring him in to talk to you and Sandy." We thought that Roger would be a good third piece because we didn't have much capital and we needed the business to be slightly more diversified. So we met with Peter and Roger and decided it would be a good fit.

ROGER BERLIND (cofounder of Carter, Berlind and Weill):

The firm originally was called Carter, Berlind, Potoma and Weill. I remember we were primarily concerned with making as much money as we could right away. We pooled all our resources — every penny that each of us had or could borrow went into this company. It was a total of about $250,000. That bought us a seat on the New York Stock Exchange with just enough left over to have the regulatory capital necessary, something like $150,000, and rent the small office that the four of us sat in.

ARTHUR CARTER:

It was a very simplistic business structure. The first thing we had to do was find a firm to clear through. Back then very few firms handled their own clearing business [the recording and processing of trades]. Since we were just starting out, we knew we had to find someone who would clear our trades for us. This was an issue because we had no real meaningful business. Each of the partners other than me had his own brokerage business that he had brought to the firm, but it was a very modest amount. So we had to sell some clearing firm on the idea that this modest number was a worthwhile thing for them to pursue because it would grow into a larger number down the road.

We went to see several firms, Eastman Dillon, Loeb Rhoades, and Burnham and Company. Loeb Rhoades turned us down and Eastman Dillon didn't really have the kind of clearing operation we were looking for. Burnham didn't have much of a clearing operation either, but they were starting to do more and more business. Sandy had been at Burnham, so he and I went to see I. W. "Tubby" Burnham, the chairman of the firm. To our surprise he said yes. Not only did he agree to clear for us, but he also furnished our offices, paid the rent, and paid for everything, all the expenses. That was part of the deal. We had a revenue-sharing arrangement, which is how he made his money back.

JUDITH RAMSEY EHRLICH:

Donaldson, Lufkin and Jenrette had opened for business six months earlier, and at that time they sold the Street on this idea of the "research boutique." Their main claim was that a stock's future could be predicted through securities analysis, a far more glamorous term for what Wall Street traditionally called statistics. This was a brilliant sales tool that was picked up quickly by the financial community. It helped other small firms, like Carter, Berlind, Potoma and Weill, attract the attention of institutional investors, such as pension funds and insurance companies.

ROGER BERLIND:

Our first office was at 37 Wall Street. God, it was small. It was basically one room with a very small room in the back that we called "the conference room." We were all equal partners in the firm and we were all generalists. We had five desks in the main room, four for the partners and one for the secretary-receptionist–everything else. Of course, we outgrew that office very quickly and moved to 60 Broad Street. There we began hiring a lot of people in research and sales.

From a personality standpoint I would say that Arthur Carter was the real driving force of the firm when we started. Arthur was always stimulating intellectually. He was primarily interested in developing the corporate-finance business, which is what he had done at Lehman Brothers. I sort of started us in the institutional business because I went up to Boston and came back with a big mutual fund account, which was crazy. You know, who'd believe it? I also was handling the individual accounts I'd brought with me. Sandy had his own accounts and he brought in a number of small corporate clients that ultimately became our underwritings — small companies for a small firm. I'd say he brought in more small corporate clients than any of us in the beginning. Sandy — I don't quite know how to describe him. He was very tape oriented, securities oriented. He wanted to make money in the stock market and he watched the tape very carefully. Peter Potoma was a big business doer. We knew we had a core of business with Peter. He also was a very good friend of mine from Eastman Dillon, very funny and witty.

JUDITH RAMSEY EHRLICH:

Peter Potoma was a savvy stockbroker who took it upon himself to teach Sandy the finer points of the business. Weill was still the same insecure retail broker — he'd sleep badly on the night before he had to go to make a presentation to a client, things like that. Potoma came from more humble origins than Sandy; his father had been an Italian immigrant steelworker. But Potoma had come up in the world. He earned his way into Harvard Law School, then quit after two years and married a wealthy woman. Like Weill's former associates at Bear Stearns, Potoma didn't think Weill made a good appearance with clients. So he persuaded him to buy a three-piece suit and gave him a hat and an umbrella so he'd look older than twenty-seven.

ROGER BERLIND:

This seemed like such an exciting, entrepreneurial thing to do — so dangerous. That was attractive to me. I thought we had a good combination of bright young people and that we could make a go of it, if such a thing was possible. In fact, we proved to be quite successful on our own terms right off the bat. Of course, that still meant we personally made no money. I think we gave ourselves salaries of $10,000 a year. Everything else stayed in the firm so we could pay back our debt and start building our company. It turned out that people wanted to work for us because there weren't many attractive places to go to work where there was this sense of ebullience and intellectual creativity.

JUDITH RAMSEY EHRLICH:

In the winter of 1962 the partners learned from the surveillance office of the New York Stock Exchange that Potoma faced suspension for "free-riding," which essentially meant buying stock on the way up without paying for it and then selling the stock before paying. The partners took over the stock-exchange seat, forced Potoma's resignation, and dropped his name a month before the exchange gave him the one-year suspension.

ROGER BERLIND:

Peter had so much promise — he was our biggest producer of commissions when we started out — but unfortunately he had a very sad life. After we were in business for about a year he started drinking a lot and would disappear for days at a time. His wife complained to us that this firm was a very competitive environment and Peter couldn't handle it. I don't think we were responsible for how his life spiraled downward, but we were another problem. I think he also had a couple of bad friends from law school who didn't help matters. Then he overtraded in his wife's account and got into trouble with the New York Stock Exchange. We had to let him go. Subsequently he was suspended by the SEC. I remember I read about that on my honeymoon.

ARTHUR CARTER:

Six months before Peter was suspended by the New York Stock Exchange I had gotten an indication that the exchange was not happy with something he had done and that something bad was going to happen to him. So I went to Roger and Sandy and said, "I think we should change the name of the firm from Carter, Berlind, Potoma and Weill, to Carter, Berlind and Weill, because if he gets suspended we'd be better off not having our name associated with him." By the time the news that Peter had been suspended hit the Dow tape our firm was known as Carter, Berlind and Weill. Officially, we had nothing to do with him.

After Potoma's departure, Carter, Berlind and Weill started bringing in other talented young people to help them build the firm. One of their first key hires came in 1963, a glib, lanky man named Arthur Levitt Jr., the son of New York State comptroller Arthur Levitt Sr. And the other significant addition to the Carter, Berlind and Weill team was Marshall Cogan, who was several years younger than the others.

ARTHUR LEVITT JR. (former partner at Carter, Berlind and Weill):

I never thought I would work on Wall Street. I started life off as a drama critic for the *Berkshire Eagle*. Then I went to work for *Life* magazine in Cincinnati and came back to New York to work for *Time* magazine. In 1959, when I was making $12,000 a year, I received an offer to go to work for a cattle company in Kansas City, Missouri, for $25,000. I accepted that offer and for the next few years I bought and sold herds of breeding cattle and ranch land with people who were very well-to-do and could afford those investments. That experience taught me a great deal about investments and how to deal with people making investment decisions.

Around 1963, one of my customers who bought a herd of cattle told me his son-in-law was starting a brokerage firm. He said if I could sell cattle I could probably sell stocks. He asked if I would be interested in joining and I said, "Sure." So I went down and met Arthur Carter, who headed the firm of Carter, Berlind and Weill. They offered me a job, but I decided that if I was going to go to Wall Street I wanted to go with a well-known firm rather than a peanut firm. I read about the firm of H. Hentz and decided that they were big enough to sustain me. So I went out to Chicago to be interviewed by one of their executives, who turned me down because he didn't think I could sell. So I cast my lot with the only firm that would offer me a job, Carter, Berlind and Weill.

ARTHUR CARTER:

I thought Arthur was a very attractive guy as soon as I met him. He was a fellow who had gone to Williams, a Phi Beta Kappa, a hardworking guy. I liked him very much. He met with Roger and Sandy, and after we talked about it a bit we decided to bring him in as a junior partner. Arthur didn't have any Wall Street experience, but he knew a lot of the players. He was very instrumental in getting us into syndicates by schmoozing the other firms. He probably did more than anyone to get us into the syndicate business.

ROGER BERLIND:

Arthur's family background was appealing to me, certainly. Arthur Levitt Sr. was a well-known and enormously respected man. As I remember, he got more votes as New York State comptroller than the governor. And young Arthur had a lot of his father's qualities in terms of rigorous behavior and strict attention to correct dealings. We were very impressed with him and happy when he decided to join up.

MARSHALL COGAN (former partner at Carter, Berlind and Weill):

I wanted to work at one of the Our Crowd investment banks, but not one of them accepted me. I remember I took these tests that clearly indicated that I should be an entrepreneur and would not be symmetrical with the ideological makeups of the people they were recruiting. I always try to see things, not as they are, but as they could be. I've never been particularly impressed by authority, which I guess wouldn't make me a good fit for one of those old-line investment banks.

JUDITH RAMSEY EHRLICH:

Marshall Cogan came from Boston. He was younger than the others, and he was the only one in the group who'd always wanted a career on Wall

Street. His academic credentials were impeccable. He had a bachelor's degree from Harvard and an MBA from the Harvard Graduate School of Business. Nonetheless, he was rejected by Goldman Sachs and Lehman Brothers because, as he told me years later, "I was too brash and fat."

MARSHALL COGAN:

I remember I was working at a small firm called Orvis Brothers, which was controlled by the Rockefeller family, and I wrote a report on a company called Purolator Products, which made oil filters for cars. The report focused on how money could be made using information based on the automotive aftermarket rather than making judgments based on original equipment sales. My idea was, you eliminated the cyclicality in the decision process by looking at the aftermarket prices for auto parts. Shortly after I wrote the report somebody from Carter, Berlind and Weill, I believe it was Arthur Carter, read it and contacted me.

I interviewed with Carter in a room not as big as this. I was intrigued with him and continue to think to this day that he's got just a stellar mind. I then met the other partners, Roger Berlind, Sandy Weill, and Arthur Levitt. I immediately had a great respect for Roger Berlind and Arthur Levitt, which also continues to this day. After several discussions with Arthur Carter, he offered me a job. I remember he said, "I'm going to give you enough rope so you can go hang yourself. But you can also swing with it. It's up to you." I'll never forget that, even after thirty-five years.

So I took the job and started working at Carter, Berlind and Weill. Style and design were not a hallmark, but this was a group of the brightest people I've ever dealt with. When I joined, Arthur Carter clearly was the leader of the firm; the rest of the partners were junior to him. Arthur has a very refined intellect with a killer sense of judgment. Roger Berlind was a savant, a very thoughtful, conceptual man who had a passion for patience and was a wonderful writer. I believe he played an integral role in the beginning of the company. Sandy Weill was relatively indifferent. For five or six years his role was limited or modest at best, quite frankly. When I showed up he had no business. He was selling retail securities and he had done a couple of transactions. Someone had to pay the secretaries and Sandy became the administrative partner. Arthur Levitt's principal role was that of building a syndicate business for a firm that had no historical tradition. Despite that he put together syndicate relationships for us.

ARTHUR CARTER:

In the 1960s the institutions — the mutual funds, pension funds, and insurance companies — were becoming an increasingly important part of the business. It was becoming clear that you wouldn't survive on a few rich clients and the scraps of underwritings Morgan Stanley threw your way. You needed to have access to the institutional market, which was what Marshall did for us.

MARSHALL COGAN:

My job was securities analyst and salesperson. At that time Carter, Berlind and Weill mainly did retail brokerage. What I didn't know was that at that time Carter, Berlind and Weill mainly did retail brokerage in the "Five Towns," the Jewish communities on Long Island's South Shore. They were a small brokerage firm selling ideas of rather nondescript companies to retail individuals.

Now I came from Boston and had no idea what the Five Towns was or was not. But I immediately noticed the institutionalization of the market. Having grown up in Boston, where much of the mutual fund industry is based, I said to the partners, "You shouldn't bring these ideas to the butcher, the baker, and the candlestick maker." That's who their clients were — these individual accounts were responsible for 98 percent of the revenue. I said, "We should call on the institutions."

ARTHUR CARTER:

Marshall also started developing relationships with some of the major players on Wall Street at the time, Charlie Bludhorn in particular. Bludhorn, who ran Gulf and Western, was very significant to our firm because he was a major industrial conglomerateur. Here's a perfect example of how we were cracking the establishment, because in the old days all of Bludhorn's business would have gone to one of the big old-line firms. But instead he utilized us, basically because he liked Marshall. In time, he became a very significant account for us. Then his account brought other conglomerating accounts to us. That was the kind of business we were looking for.

ROGER BERLIND:

Have you met Marshall? He's a hell of a salesman. He would go out and make presentations to institutional accounts and started generating a considerable amount of business for the firm from the institutions. I'd say he changed our firm by simply increasing the scale of what we were doing. Our business was pretty small before he showed up. Now we were players, and that was exciting. It was clear to us that we were on the cusp of doing some important things. You never would have convinced me that was going to be the case when we started out just five years earlier.

CHAPTER 6

GO-GO BOYS

Today, it's basically accepted as gospel that mutual funds are the most popular way for individual investors to own a diversified portfolio of stocks or bonds and receive professional advice without doing all the trading and research required to buy all these different securities. But throughout the early history of mutual funds, this was not the case. In the 1920s, some mutual funds gained a reputation on Wall Street as speculative investments, and when many went belly-up after the '29 crash they were revealed to be frauds. This is the reason given for Charlie Merrill's refusal to allow Merrill Lynch to enter the fund business.

Merrill's decision opened up the door for a small mutual firm in Boston called Fidelity to dominate the business. Fidelity was started in 1943 as a single fund managed by a lawyer named Edward C. Johnson II, who was known as "Mr. Johnson" to anyone who ever worked for him. That Fidelity was based in Boston rather than New York was hardly surprising, since there had long been a mutual fund industry in New England that was separate in attitude and temperament from its Wall Street cousins. These were small pools of capital that were managed conservatively with the single goal of preserving the money for future generations. But that style didn't make much sense to Mr. Johnson, who believed the goal of investing was to increase your holdings, not just preserve them. In time, he would set about changing the way the mutual fund industry did business.

ROGER SERVISON (executive vice president of Fidelity Investments):

Boston was the home of some of the great early wealth in this country. But by the turn of the century a lot of that wealth was being passed on to second and third generations, and many of the businesses where that wealth had been created, mostly shipping businesses, were disappearing. So now the families were living off the wealth their parents and grandparents had created, and by the second or third generation they needed people who could manage it for them. Since they already were rich enough to live extremely comfortably they were looking for a fairly conservative capital-preservation approach to managing the money.

On a gut level I think the Yankee tradition of frugality and conservatism appealed to these old-line New England families. That's why they didn't send their money to New York. New York was much more of a merchant environment, much more of a freewheeling environment. New York was Wall Street. So these wealthy families ignored Wall Street and instead went to the law firms at home in Boston, where they felt they could get a conservative, prudent, trusted person to manage their money. Later many of these law firms evolved into money-management firms. All those traditions of risk-averse fiduciary money management really were founded in Boston largely because that's what the clients were looking for.

Mutual funds emerged from here because as these families passed money down through the generations it was spread out into smaller and smaller chunks. So suddenly what a family originally could manage as one large pool of capital would now have ten or twenty different owners. Eventually somebody suggested that these families commingle their funds so they could be managed more efficiently for smaller and smaller holdings. And that's what spawned the mutual fund as we know it today.

JACK BOGLE (founder of Vanguard Group, president of Bogle Markets Research Center, and former chairman of Wellington Management):

I think 70 percent of the mutual fund business was based up in Boston in the 1950s. The Boston trustee was sort of a national icon. They were known for prudence and fiduciary duty. It was Justice Samuel Putnam, clearly a Bostonian, who made the original "prudent man" decision [the legal foundation for professional investment management].

Mutual funds came about because some lawyers were looking over trust estates, and they basically decided to manage the estates as well as doing the tax and estate work. Many of the early mutual funds were structured trusts, and they could get favorable tax treatment in Massachusetts. Pennsylvania was not hospitable at all to mutual funds. The Keystone Funds, a huge organization at that time that is now gone, moved from its home in Pennsylvania to Boston to take advantage of the favorable tax treatment.

JOE NOCERA (financial journalist and author):

Now Edward C. Johnson II — or Mr. Johnson, as he was forever known at Fidelity — was a lawyer who happened to love the stock market. He wasn't brought up in the traditional mutual fund universe; he was completely new to it. In 1943, he was given the chance to buy an inconsequential fund called Fidelity Fund, which held about $3 million at the time. He jumped at the chance.

When Johnson took over Fidelity Fund he couldn't bear the thought that all it would do was preserve capital. That wasn't what was fun about the stock market to him. What Johnson liked about the stock market was finding stocks that won, that beat the market. And that's what he turned Fidelity Fund into — a fund that wanted to beat the market. Over time it became clear that there were a lot of people who liked this idea, and those people began to gravitate to Fidelity. So Johnson started a second fund and a third fund, eventually winding up with about a half dozen.

EDWARD C. JOHNSON II (founder of Fidelity Investments):

We didn't want to feel that we were married to a stock when we bought it. You might say that we preferred to think of the relationship to it as a "compassionate marriage." But that doesn't go quite far enough, either. Possibly now and again we liked to have a "liaison" — or even, very occasionally, "a couple of nights together."

PETER LYNCH (Fidelity Investments executive vice president and former manager of Fidelity's Magellan Fund):

I remember Mr. Johnson had this expression: "Wives you're stuck with, but stocks you trade." That was in an era when people bought stocks for protection and safety, and even if something was overpriced they just held on forever. Relative to other people he had more of a capital-appreciation viewpoint. If you find a better stock than the one you're holding, sell your position and buy the better stock. He didn't have a preservation-of-capital mentality. It was about making money.

MARSHALL COGAN (former partner at Carter, Berlind and Weill):

Edward C. Johnson II was the Abraham Lincoln of mutual funds.

JOE NOCERA:

But Mr. Johnson's real radical innovations for the mutual fund industry began in 1952, when he hired Jerry Tsai as a stock analyst.

JERRY TSAI (founder of Manhattan Fund and original manager of Fidelity Capital Fund):

I was born in 1929 in Shanghai. In the old days Shanghai was divided into seven sections based on nationalities. I was living in the French section, but I went to school in the British section. During World War II China was broken up into two — Japan occupied the southeast portion and Chungking was the wartime capital. My father was in that area working as a district manager for the Ford Motor Company. But my family stayed in Shanghai. So we were split up. The country was split up and my family was split up.

My mother, with just a high-school education, decided that she could make enough money to support us by trading. She was probably the only woman around at that time buying and selling stocks, bonds, gold, silver, anything. I have no idea how she knew about all this stuff; I was very young. But she was doing very well. We continued to have servants and kept a high standard of living. My father was completely separated from the family so all this was provided by my mother. She was just terrific, all that with just a high-school education.

Education was a priority for my family. My two grandfathers were educated in the United States and then returned to China. My father also was sent to study in the United States when he was seventeen. He went to the University of Michigan and then got a job with the Ford Motor Company. About a year or so later he was transferred back to Shanghai and gradually worked his way up from there. One of my grandfathers was a Methodist and my family was very connected to religion, so after the war, in 1947, they sent me to Wesleyan University in Middletown, Connecticut, a nice Methodist college. Talk about culture shock. You know Shanghai at that time was a major city. It had five to six million people. There I was, seventeen years old, in Middletown, Connecticut, where there was one main street, a Woolworths, a Montgomery Ward, and that was it. It was a big adjustment from Shanghai to Middletown, Connecticut, let me tell you.

At the end of the semester I said, forget this, I'm going to Boston. Boston also was a lot smaller than Shanghai, but at least it was a growing community. I knew there were lots of Chinese students in Boston. Plenty of Broadway shows opened in Boston. Lots of stores had branches in Boston. It was a very nice place to be, not like Middletown. So I transferred to Boston University. In 1949 I graduated with a bachelor's degree and a master's degree in economics.

I had several jobs after graduating from Boston University — I was a trainee in a textile company, I was a statistician for Blue Cross — and in 1951 I was hired as a junior securities analyst at Bache and Company, a wirehouse in New York. But after about a year I decided that the brokerage business was not for me. Over the summer of 1952 I was in Boston on vacation, staying with my wife's family because she was pregnant and we didn't have enough money to go anyplace else. One day I was talking to their neighbor, telling him how I wasn't happy at Bache. He said he had a friend who was head of research at Scudder, Stevens and Clark, a money-management firm. He offered to set up an appointment with this man, Mr. Wiese.

So a few days later I went to see Mr. Wiese. He talked to me for over an hour. At the end he said, "Unfortunately, we don't have an opening here right now. But give me a local number in case I need to reach you." The next morning at about ten thirty I got a call from this man who said, "Hello, Jerry. This is Edward C. Johnson II." Now, I didn't know too much about mutual funds and I certainly didn't know who he was. So, young and stupid, I asked him, "What do you do, Mr. Johnson?" And he said, "I am what you would call the chairman and president of Fidelity Funds." Then he said a few things about mutual funds and told me how he was an old friend of Mr. Wiese. He said, "Mr. Wiese said he met a young man who appears to be very smart and he asked me to call you. Would you like to come in and talk?"

I went to see him the next day. It was the strangest interview I've ever had. After a few minutes of chitchat he said, "What makes you tick?" You know, he asked me if I liked the stock market and all that stuff, but what he really wanted to know was *why* I liked the stock market. I remember I said something like, "It's interesting. Things are changing all the time. And whether you're black, white, Chinese, or Italian, if you buy General Motors and the stock goes up you make money. It doesn't matter who or what you are." I think that tickled him. At the end of an hour or so he asked me if I'd like to work there. I said yes, and he said how about a month from now? That was it. A month later I joined Fidelity.

JOE NOCERA:

Before Edward C. Johnson II and Jerry Tsai came along mutual funds were managed by committee. For a fund to buy or sell a stock a committee meeting had to be held where a vote was taken on each investment decision. And these committees often met just a few times a year, so portfolios didn't turn over all that much. It certainly wasn't like today, when fund managers dart in and out of stock positions in the course of a single trading session. In the old days, if you changed your fund by 10 percent in a year you were considered a big risktaker. The way Mr. Johnson changed this was by giving one man, Jerry Tsai, his own fund to run. By handing over the task of managing a fund to a single person you could move much faster. You didn't have to sit around waiting for a meeting to respond to fluctuations in the market.

JOHN NEFF (former manager of Windsor Fund for Wellington Management):

Investment committees were cumbersome, and their ideas tended to reflect what already had happened in the marketplace instead of what was going to happen in the marketplace.

ROBERT POZEN (chairman of MFS Investment Management, former president of Fidelity Management and Research, and author of *The Mutual Fund Business*):

Management by committee, where a committee formally votes on an approval, is pretty inconsistent with a fast-moving market. There needs to be accountability, and putting one manager in charge of a fund puts that accountability on that manager.

JERRY TSAI:

Mr. Johnson single-handedly changed the mutual fund business. When I joined Fidelity it was a small bunch of people. I was employee number eighteen. We were managing less than $200 million. Can you believe it? It's over $800 billion today. Mr. Johnson was president, chairman, portfolio manager, and treasurer, too.

Now, Mr. Johnson was a lawyer, and at law firms you create your own responsibilities. Early on I remember I went to Mr. Johnson and said, "I've been here three months and nobody's told me what to do." So he asked what I had been doing. I said I'd been reading Standard and Poor's guides and stuff like that. And I'll never forget what he told me: "This place is like a law firm. We don't tell anybody what to do. Now you go back to your office and think about what you should do to be helpful to this company." For the next fourteen years he didn't tell me what to do.

EDWARD C. JOHNSON II:

We want a man with an instinctive sense of value, an artist. Investing is like any art. We don't want the theoretical man with a lot of words, the so-called intellectual. We like the young man who will come in and not have ideas that are too firm and counter to our own. This doesn't mean we don't want a high level of difference of opinion; we thrive on it. I love prima donnas. They blow off steam and then go off and do something artistic again.

JERRY TSAI:

I started at Fidelity as a junior analyst and quickly earned more responsibilities. Within a few years I was the head of research. Then in 1958 I went to Mr. Johnson and said I needed to talk to him about something important. I asked if I could visit his home on Cape Cod that weekend because I wanted his undivided attention. He said, "It's a long ride, but go ahead." So I drove a couple of hours on a Saturday out to his home on the Cape to show him a memo describing the formation of a new Fidelity fund.

I remember he looked at that memo and said, "You want us to buy growth stocks? What's a growth stock? You mean you don't want to buy General Motors and U.S. Steel and Standard Oil of New Jersey?" I said no, I thought this new fund should buy Texas Instruments, Polaroid, Avon, and IBM, consumer-related companies in industries that were growing and not cyclical like aluminum, chemicals, or oil. He asked how much money the fund needed, and I said it would need the regular SEC seed money, $100,000. At which time he handed me back my memo and said, "Here's your $100,000 and your rope. Go ahead, hang yourself with it." I took it. And that was the start of Fidelity Capital Fund, in 1958.

This fund was completely different from what anyone else was doing at the time. He told me, "Jerry, investing is an art, not a science. You're the portfolio manager. Give me a list of stocks you want to buy at first, no more than twenty. But you're the portfolio manager alone. Two people cannot play the violin at the same time." And that's how I became the first portfolio manager. Mr. Johnson said, "You buy and sell what you want, when you want."

PETER LYNCH:

I think what appeals to a young person about the culture Mr. Johnson created at Fidelity starting back with Jerry Tsai, and it's still true today, is that often when you're young you do a lot of work but somebody above you has to check it, and then somebody above him has to look at it, and so on. So when it comes time to figure out how you're doing it's somebody else's opinion that counts. As a portfolio manager or analyst you get a lot of responsibility and your success is measurable. You say, this stock is going up, and if you're right it's a good feeling. You don't have to worry about somebody else's judgments of your accomplishments. To a lot of people around here that's very comforting.

EDWARD C. JOHNSON II:

You want an environment where people can develop their talents to the greatest extent. How do you do that? It's just one word: attitude. You want the greatest degree of laissez-faire without chaos. Children know you love them and that you're always there and otherwise you leave them alone and that's it. That's the way it is here, too, I think. What you want to do is get away from an organization and create an organism. Separate cells working together in something completely natural and unplanned.

ROGER CLINTON (former Fidelity fund manager):

The freedom here does create anxiety. And I think this is exactly the intent. It's cruel and frustrating at times. It's very much like Darwinism. There are some people who might be more efficient if they had more guidance, but they have to develop in a different way to survive here. All of us might be happier, but the question is, what is most important? Mr. Johnson thinks it's the development of the individual. He thinks that every little bit of structure you add takes something away from the human being.

JOE NOCERA:

Johnson couldn't have timed his decision to give Tsai his own fund any better. This was the beginning of the whole phenomenon called go-go investing. Postwar America's first real bull market ran from about 1951 to its top in 1966, with some interruptions in between. But what we think of as the real frenzy of "the go-go years" happened afterward, from 1967 to 1969.

JACK BOGLE:

Mutual funds were still relatively small in the 1960s. The real story at that time, in terms of institutionalization, was the pension funds. Behind the scenes the big pension plans were beginning to become a force in investing, too. The General Motors pension plan began in the early 1950s, and that was America's first pension plan. From there you really have the beginning of the institutionalization of the market, where you have this disintermediation of investing through pension plans and mutual funds. But the mutual fund industry was still very small, holding only 1 or 2 percent of stocks. So even when it doubled over a few years it was still a fairly small part of the overall scheme of things.

JOE NOCERA:

The 1960s was the era of the conglomerates, when guys like Charlie Bludhorn at Gulf and Western and Harold Geneen at ITT and James Ling at LTV were just buying and selling, wheeling and dealing. And developing technology companies like Xerox and Polaroid were taking off. The papers became captivated with all the excitement and stocks started to soar. People began to think that these conglomerates were new forms of corporations that could defy the market's historic principles. Folks all around Wall Street were talking about how technology companies like Xerox had unlimited futures. You had a frenzy where a lot of people got very excited and felt they needed to be in on the action. That's what go-go investing was all about.

BERNARD HEROLD (fifty-year Wall Street veteran and founder of Bernard Herold and Company):

You want to know how Jerry Tsai bought stuff? If a stock was selling for $50 and Jerry bought it, if it went down to $45 he bought more, and then if it went down to $40 he bought more. He was perpetually dollar-cost averaging. There was a group of guys that I sponsored — I paid for their goddamn lunches — who met in a restaurant in the East Fifties uptown that had a private room. They would sit in there and decide what stocks they wanted to sell, and then they'd feed them to Jerry Tsai because he would go out and buy them in huge quantities.

JERRY TSAI:

I never fight the tape. I look at charts every day on certain stocks. If I like the fundamentals and the charts look correct then I might decide to buy twice as many shares as I'd planned. But if the chart is bad I'll sell half the stock without asking a question. My theory is: if the chart looks bad somebody else knows something that I may not know today, but that I probably will know later when it's too late. So a simple theory of money management is, if you find a story that's right and the chart is right, buy more than you normally would. But when the fundamentals are good and the chart is bad, sell half and don't ask any questions. Then do your homework right away, check your story, and see what you want to do with the other half.

EDWARD C. JOHNSON II:

It was a beautiful thing to watch his reactions. What grace, what timing — glorious! Why, if he had been on the New York Stock Exchange floor he'd have become its number-one trader in no time.

JERRY TSAI:

Fidelity Capital Fund was successful almost immediately. In 1958, that's the year we started, we were up 58 percent.

JOE NOCERA:

Obviously, with the numbers Tsai put up right away it wasn't long before the public and press took notice of what was happening at Fidelity. Every year Tsai ran Fidelity Capital it was near the top of the industry in terms of its annual gain. Once, in 1962, he got caught in a market downdraft, but he recovered with such astonishing speed that his fund gained 68 percent in the next three months. He was amazing and people were starting to pay attention.

JOHN NEFF:

I started managing the Windsor Fund in 1964, which was right at the heart of the era of the go-go funds. I called them adrenaline funds, which if you think about it is a pretty apt description. Over that period, from 1964 to '69, I was about six hundred basis points [six percentage points] better than the S&P 500 annually and I still wasn't getting any attention. The fund was $75 million and it grew to about $100 million, and I had a decent following because I went out in the hustings and talked to boardrooms across America. But everyone was focused on these go-go funds and wasn't really interested in what I was doing.

MARSHALL COGAN:

I had a particular advantage with the mutual funds because when I went to Harvard Business School many of my classmates wanted to go to work in the mutual fund business. I could communicate with these people in their language. In fact, I give a great deal of credit for the success of Carter, Berlind and Weill to Ned Johnson, whose father then was the owner and controlling shareholder of the Fidelity Group of mutual funds. At that time Ned was running a fund and Jerry Tsai was running a fund. It was fashionable in those days to deal only with Jerry Tsai because he received all the attention in the media. I was a philosophy and history major at Harvard, and at some unusual event I met Ned's father. I remember we spent some time together and at one point Mr. Johnson Sr. said, "Marshall, owning securities is as much about philosophy, poetry, and history as it is about numbers." That impressed me very much.

Now, this was during the go-go years and, as I said, everyone was seeking Jerry Tsai's business. I decided to develop a relationship with Ned

Johnson because the Johnson family owned the funds, not Jerry Tsai, and I liked Mr. Johnson. I then became very fond of Ned. He had a brilliant mind and I had an easy communication with him. I would always provide provocative ideas in a provocative way to him. Over time Fidelity began doing business of scale through Carter, Berlind and Weill. Since Fidelity then was in many ways more important than it is today — it's still vital today, but then Fidelity was *it* in the mutual fund business — everyone else in Boston began to follow them to our doorstep.

JOE NOCERA:

You can't underestimate what the idea of having one person run a fund did to the psychology of trading. The rise of the single mutual fund manager basically brought about this idea of instinctive trading. A guy like Jerry Tsai did his research and knew his stuff, but then he had to pull the trigger. There wasn't a vote and you didn't listen to dissenting voices. You listened to your gut. If this was what you felt, you did it. That's why they called Jerry Tsai and the rest of the fund managers that followed him gunslingers. They were shooting, and they were shaking up the system. In the counterculture-obsessed world of the 1960s, the go-go fund managers were seen as outlaws on Wall Street. And they developed their own cult of personality.

FRED ALGER (portfolio manager and founder of Fred Alger Management):

We really owe [Jerry Tsai] a lot. He was a pioneer. He created the idea of intensive money management and he showed the way for all of us.

JOE NOCERA:

This development of portfolio managers as personalities brings up another point about Johnson's decision to let one man run a fund — he created a system that was tailor-made for press coverage. Here's how it works: You give a guy responsibility for a fund. He starts to have fantastic performance. People start to talk about him. The fund gets a buzz and more money starts to flow in. All of a sudden *Newsweek* and *Business Week* are knocking at the guy's door. Journalism, particularly business journalism, needs personalities to make the stories interesting. Journalists need human beings who they can write about and talk about in some heroic fashion. So the stories were: "He's turning over his portfolio. He's beating the market. He's a gunslinger, by God!"

JACK BOGLE:

I actually merged Wellington with a go-go fund group from Boston. It was the stupidest thing you could ever imagine. So young, so callow, so cocksure of oneself, and totally unwilling to listen to the lessons of history — it was probably one of the worst decisions anyone in the mutual fund industry has ever made. We got Ivest, which was the go-go fund we wanted to acquire. We got a pension business. We got four managers who we thought were brilliant, though it's hard to say that in retrospect.

We were all caught up in the investment fad of the times. We launched Explorer Fund to capture the new-concept stocks. I remember we were in a meeting and one of the sales guys said, "Tell me the truth, what kind of rate of return do you think Explorer Fund can earn over the long run?" And one of the managers said 25 percent. I almost fell out of my chair, because that means money doubles every three years. At that point I started to think that maybe I had made a mistake.

JOE NOCERA:

People who actually were pretty obscure figures just a few years earlier suddenly were captivating, powerful personalities in the 1960s. And it wasn't just Jerry Tsai, who became the personification of go-go investing. There were a slew of guys who followed in his wake and were beating the market — Fred Carr at Enterprise Fund, Fred Alger at Security Equity Fund, and of course Howard Stein at Dreyfus. The whole mutual fund thing took on a life of its own, to the point where a lot of people who never cared about stocks or bonds were interested in the market all of a sudden.

JERRY TSAI:

Mr. Johnson was a fairly conservative guy. He never wanted to talk to the press. He always felt that they would misquote him or something, so he didn't want to have anything to do with them. At Fidelity we never had a public relations firm. Any publicity we got was just created by the press. Mr. Johnson wouldn't talk and I almost never gave interviews. Reporters just wrote about me and said whatever they wanted to say, good or bad. And I can say this from experience: the trouble with getting a little bit of good publicity is, when something goes wrong they love to kill you on the way down. The media like to build things up so they can tear them down.

JOE NOCERA:

Looking back, I think most of the air of mystery that Tsai had basically came from his refusal to talk about his childhood in Shanghai with the press. The attitudes in this country toward the Far East were very different back then, and people weren't nearly as sensitive to those kinds of racial issues. So they called him things like "inscrutable."

JOHN JAKOBSON (member of the New York Stock Exchange since 1955):

Jerry Tsai dominated the market. I'm not going to tell you what his nicknames were, but he was a man with nicknames.

JERRY TSAI:

All that stuff about my race was ridiculous. It was just some guys looking for things to write about, whether they were true or not. But that's the media.

Tsai put up with the stereotyping and racial insensitivity because he generally got glowing press from reporters who were amazed at the results he was putting up. Indeed, Tsai thought he was doing well enough that one day he might be able to run Fidelity. But then he noticed that somebody was blocking his way: Edward C. Johnson III, known to everyone as Ned.

JERRY TSAI:

I met Ned Johnson in 1957. I was head of research at Fidelity and Mr. Johnson called me one day and said, "I need your assistance. I'd like Ned to join the firm and I need you to train him." When he came in we worked together for a while and I helped him get his bearings in the business a little bit. Then in 1961, a few years after we started Fidelity Capital Fund, we launched another fund called Fidelity Trend Fund. Mr. Johnson decided to make Ned the portfolio manager of Fidelity Trend Fund. He did quite well with it and there was a healthy competition between us. But we were friends, always. I was one of his ushers when he got married, one of six ushers at Ned Johnson's wedding. So I don't know that I would call it a rivalry.

NED JOHNSON (Fidelity Investments chairman):

Jerry started out with me as a teacher, and we ended up as competing portfolio managers. I always thought he was an excellent teacher. I learned a great deal about the stock market from him. He had then, and has today, an extraordinary energy. At that time, there wasn't a company listed on the New York Stock Exchange that he didn't know the quarterly earnings of and a projection for.

JOE NOCERA:

Jerry Tsai got all the acclaim and press attention at Fidelity, but I think you'll find that the dirty little secret is if you tally up the results Ned Johnson comes out ahead. Look it up. From 1961 until 1965, Ned's Fidelity Trend Fund actually outperformed Tsai's Fidelity Capital Fund.

JERRY TSAI:

Want to know why I left Fidelity? I finished playing golf with Mr. Johnson on a Saturday in June 1964. It was around six thirty in the evening. So he said, "Jerry, you've been here a long time now, maybe twelve, thirteen years. Next Thursday I'm going to make you president of this company." I said okay. I mean, that sounded good. Then on Monday morning at nine thirty he called me and said, "I don't think I can do that yet . . . because of family." I'm being very careful here, and you can interpret this however you want to interpret it. I said that was okay, and he told me that maybe in six months it would happen. But six months later nothing had happened. From that point on I never discussed the subject with him again — not once.

Now 1965 was a bull-market year so our funds in general were doing very well. I said to myself that if there ever was a good time for me to leave, this was it. It was the summer, a year after my conversation with Mr. Johnson, and I decided that in the fall I would leave Fidelity and go to New York to start a new fund. I didn't want to be in anyone's shadow, you know. So I left. If he'd made me president of Fidelity Funds I would still be there today. Well, maybe not today, but I would have stayed a lot longer. Some people have said that an era ended on the day I left Fidelity. I don't know about that. They've done pretty well without me.

EDWARD C. JOHNSON II:

We start off with the assumption that when you get somebody good and he pays off in a big way it's difficult to hold him. When he goes off, believe it or not, this is a strengthening thing. Besides, a star is at his best on the way up. Somebody leaving to go after a glamorous future is the best possible incentive for the men here.

JERRY TSAI:

We were at the height of the bull market and lots of brokers knew that I was managing a hot fund. They knew my name. It was a very good time to start. We filed for $25 million. Truthfully, I did expect to get more than $25 million, but I wasn't sure if it would be $50 million, $60 million, or $70 million. No way did I expect it to be more than $100 million. When we finished we were at $270 million — can you believe that? It's equal to about $3.5 billion today. It was the largest fund underwriting in the history of the world at that time, February 1966.

MARSHALL COGAN:

Wall Street had never seen anything like the demand for Jerry Tsai's Manhattan Fund. For a while there he was the most sought-after man in New York. It was like those old E. F. Hutton commercials. When people heard that Tsai was buying something they were all ears. Just the idea that he was interested in a stock could send its price soaring. Rumors were flying all over the place. That popularity actually became a curse for him because he couldn't do anything without attracting an enormous amount of attention.

RICHARD JENRETTE (cofounder of Donaldson, Lufkin and Jenrette):

"Tsai is buying!" God, we used to hear that all the time. Someone would come running into the office screaming that Jerry Tsai was buying this or that, and you could just sit there and watch the numbers go on the stock ticker. Of course, half the time I'm sure the rumor was complete garbage, but that didn't seem to matter. If there was a perception that Tsai was buying something, there were people on Wall Street who wanted to be there too.

JERRY TSAI:

That kind of thing always happens. It's no different than it was when Peter Lynch became so popular. If Peter Lynch was buying something and everybody thought he was smart, lots of people would buy the same stock he was buying simply because he was buying it. It didn't just happen to me, it happened to lots of people. Peter Lynch is buying this. George Soros is buying that. Warren Buffett, all these guys go through it.

JOE NOCERA:

Tsai set up his fund like his old Fidelity Capital Fund, filled it with all his favorite glamour stocks. To capitalize on his enormous popularity, the Manhattan Fund set fees that were egregiously high — an 8.5 percent upfront commission called a "load" in the mutual fund business, as well as a stiff management fee. No one cared. There were a number of other funds with track records every bit as good as Tsai's. It didn't matter. Jerry Tsai was the mutual fund manager everybody wanted, the man with the golden touch. His fund opened for business in 1966 and it had about 125,000 shareholders and $270 million under management. Within two years it had around 225,000 shareholders and held about $525 million.

Of course, that's when Tsai lost his golden touch. In truth, it wasn't exactly his fault. He couldn't have picked a worse moment to start a new fund. The first month Manhattan Fund was in operation, February 1966, the Dow hit its all-time high of just about 1,000. Then it started to drop, and by October it had fallen 250 points. After that, the market fluctuated up and down until it began its slow march down into the 1970s. This was not a great time to be in the investment business.

JACK BOGLE:

Jerry Tsai did this huge offering for the Manhattan Fund, and within a few years it became the worst-performing fund in America. He of course made a fortune for himself, which is very typical of the business. The managers make fortunes and the buyers get their heads handed to them.

JERRY TSAI:

By the end of 1967, the glamour stocks were way ahead of themselves; they had become way overpriced. The charts kept telling us they were not the most desirable areas, but we were too dumb to realize it. I didn't do anything about it.

JOE NOCERA:

In 1968, the roof caved in for the Manhattan Fund. It wasn't that Tsai did anything differently; it's just that the market finally caught up with him. Tsai invested as he always had. He still made these dramatic moves, still bought and sold huge blocks of stock. But it wasn't working. In the spring of 1968, Tsai missed out on a market rally, and by July the Manhattan Fund had lost nearly 7 percent of its value while the Dow gained 5 percent, and it was the sixth-worst performer among the three hundred largest funds in the world. What a public relations nightmare. Shareholders, who once clamored to get into the fund, now wanted to kill him.

JERRY TSAI:

In 1968, Tsai Management and Research was sold to CNA Financial, a giant insurance company that wanted to be in the money-management business and wanted to use my name to help them do it. I didn't want to be in the mutual fund business anymore. Their stock was cheap and they came to me with an offer, which was very high. Really, they paid me a ridiculous price. And for us to exchange Tsai Management stock for CNA stock at a very low price was great for liquidity; it increased the value of the company. It made sense to me.

So we sold the company and I went on the board and executive committee of CNA. I was their largest stockholder; obviously, I had a lot of responsibilities. That's when the people at CNA asked me to give up the daily responsibility for managing the Manhattan Fund. What did I do? I brought in two guys to be portfolio managers and split the fund in half. I don't want to use their names because what I'm about to tell you would be a smear on them. But I actually talked them into joining me. I even personally went to the bank and cosigned a note for $250,000 for each of them to put back into Manhattan Fund. I wanted them to own $250,000 worth of the fund to give them a real incentive.

Now, this may sound like an excuse, but they were very bad. That's the only way I can put it. So at the end of the year, year and a half, whatever it was, I fired both of them, redeemed part of the mutual funds, and personally took the loss. But nobody's interested in telling that story.

JOE NOCERA:

Economically, the reason for the market's tumble was simple: guns and butter. Lyndon Johnson was trying to finance the Vietnam War and his social programs without adding new taxes. Deficits became part of the lingo and inflation started to happen. Things on Wall Street got to the point where the market was supported by fifty stocks, known as the Nifty Fifty, which wasn't sustainable. The new technology revolution didn't represent a new stock-market paradigm, as some had suggested. And the industrial conglomerates faltered. They'd started out as a good idea because it looked as if you could protect yourself from hard times in one sector by having something else in another sector that was doing well. But it didn't work out that way. If you try to gin up your numbers by going on acquisition sprees the law of numbers eventually catches up with you. You can't grow fast enough to keep up and things spiral out of control.

There always are these moments that should tell you when the market has reached a top. Unfortunately, they're only obvious in retrospect. Looking back, Jerry Tsai's departure from Fidelity in 1965 to start his own fund should have been a very clear sign of a top. The market was overheated and people were way too excited about stocks. Then, within a few years, the market completely collapsed on itself. All the stuff that had worked for Tsai in the past — the constant trading, the portfolio turnover, the buying into the glamour stocks of the day, the Polaroids and Xeroxes and ITTs — crashed in on him. It was just a disaster.

JERRY TSAI:

The worst part of all this is I think lots of people remember '68, but not too many remember '66 anymore. That's always felt terrible, really lousy. It was a bad year.

So the go-go years were over, killed along with the bull market that raged through the midsixties. Nobody shed a tear for the death of the gunslingers, and the press, which was so focused on chronicling Tsai's rise and fall, missed the larger picture entirely. Sure, the market got caught up in a period of wild euphoria, and many inexperienced investors got hurt in the process. But the period also offered a glimpse of the future. Mutual funds and other investment vehicles no longer would be run strictly for the purpose of preserving capital. Now they would live and die by their performance. For most investors this was a radical change in philosophy, and ultimately it was a change for the better.

As for Tsai himself, he left CNA a very wealthy man but he still was looking for something to do. He started buying companies. Through a series of mergers in the 1970s and 1980s he would transform American Can into the financial-services powerhouse Primerica, even adding the well-known brokerage firm Smith Barney to the fold in early 1987. And once again, Tsai would find himself in the middle of a runaway bull market.

CHAPTER 7

POWER TO THE PEOPLE

The late 1960s were a period of upheaval. Across the country societal traditions were being turned upside down. So it could hardly be considered surprising that on Wall Street the financial community's old-world ways were under seige. For instance, after the New York Stock Exchange had operated for centuries as a gentlemen's club, its sexist traditions were being questioned by Muriel Siebert, who wanted to become its first female member.

But beyond the cultural issues, the real impact of the changing times was felt on the business side of Wall Street. As mutual funds and pension plans grew in influence during the go-go years, volume at the New York Stock Exchange exploded, pushing the limits of Wall Street's antiquated record-keeping systems. The old-line partnership structure that had served the securities industry so well for so long suddenly became a burden because the firms did not have the capital to invest in their businesses and improve their operations. When brokerage firms started to go out of business because they couldn't handle the pressure, it became clear that something had to give. Wall Street was going to have to go public.

PETER LOW (member of the New York Stock Exchange since 1963 and former floor broker):

The sixties were very interesting. It was a wild, wild time. We had the Vietnam War, which obviously captivated everyone's attention. There was a lot of turmoil, a lot of anger, throughout the country. And since the stock exchange and the whole financial district are seen as the bastion of capitalism, we were a target for protesters who wanted to get some attention. There were protests down here; some even turned violent.

Mostly we saw the war play out on the floor of the stock exchange. A rumor would start that there'd been a moratorium on bombing, and the defense stocks would sell off. Or there would be a rumor that bombing resumed, and the defense stocks would rally and others would fall. People were betting on which companies would do better if there was war or if there was peace. You almost felt guilty that guys were dying in Vietnam and here we were speculating on the news, but that's been this business forever. It's mean. If news breaks out that there's a drug epidemic, Wall Street asks, "Who makes the needles?"

But the war really wasn't the reason that things were tense around here. The stock exchange was going through a lot of changes too, and people were scared about whether the business was going to survive, as crazy as that may seem. Obviously, everything we went through back then was necessary if we were going to remain the dominant stock exchange. But that didn't make it any easier at the time. This isn't a place that likes change. The floor hadn't changed all that much from when I was a kid.

JERRY GENTILELLA (barber at the New York Stock Exchange since 1963):

I've seen a lot of changes, you know? I was hired here in April 1963. There were seven barbers and we were pretty busy. People wore their hair very short in those days, very neat. Our customers would come in maybe every week or ten days. But then the Beatles came up with the long hair and they all started growing their hair. Naturally, we started to lose some business. Suddenly people were coming every two weeks, or three weeks, or once every month.

PETER LOW:

When I was fourteen, fifteen years old, before I went to camp my father insisted that I work, which was very good training. He was a member on the floor of the New York Stock Exchange so he got me a job as a runner for the brokerage house that he cleared through. This was in the 1950s, before all the electronic trading, so what a runner would do in that day and age was carry securities to be delivered to different brokerage firms and banks. That's how they cleared — they physically delivered the securities from place to place. I had to be bonded, fully insured. I remember the first week I started I was extraordinarily enthusiastic, and the other runners were older retired postmen or cops or transit workers. And one guy pulled me aside and said, "Hey kid, don't come back so fast. You're making us all look bad. Go to the park, take a break, read the paper. There's no reason to come back in fifteen minutes."

ROBERT NEWBURGER (executive director of the New York Stock Exchange Alliance of Floor Brokers and member of the exchange since 1940):

On the floor of the New York Stock Exchange back then you didn't have to be particularly good to be successful. You didn't have to be particularly bright. Young kids coming out of Harvard, Princeton, Yale, or wherever, their father would buy them a seat [making them a member of the New York Stock Exchange] and they'd go on the floor. There were two major odd-lot firms [firms that sold very small orders] and these kids would become associate brokers for the odd-lot firms. From there they'd build a business. And in those days, with no brains and no creative thinking, the average income was $50,000 a year. I'm talking about what would now correspond to $500,000 a year. So when one of these young fellows would first come on the floor, all the clerks would gather around on the side and holler out, "Too dumb to be a doctor or a lawyer, his old man bought him a seat."

PETER LOW:

For many people, a seat on the New York Stock Exchange, which is what a membership is called, was a very lucrative proposition. But I'll use this analogy: A bat in Ted Williams's hands and a bat in my hands are two different things. A balance sheet in Warren Buffett's hands and a balance sheet in my hands are two different things. A seat on the exchange was like that — some people knew what to do with it and some couldn't seem to get it. Being successful on the floor of the stock exchange is more about having a knack for it than anything else. It's not brilliance or rocket science. It's if you have it, you have it.

ROBERT NEWBURGER:

When anyone came onto the floor for the first time he got something of a hazing. They'd put ink pads on your telephone receiver and you'd go home with a purple ear. Or if it was a rainy day and you brought an umbrella, they'd rip up a bunch of paper and stick it inside so when you opened up your umbrella you'd get a confetti shower. It was all good-natured because the business was so easy. On the floor we were executors of orders. You didn't try to do anyone in. There was none of that because sooner or later you'd meet that guy again. People who did that didn't last very long. The idea was to take a little, leave a little, and don't bust up the game. There were no geniuses down there.

ROY SMITH (finance professor at New York University and former partner at Goldman Sachs):

Wall Street had been a pretty inactive place in the thirties and forties, and it wasn't really until the end of the fifties that it began to revive. You had the reregulation of the thirties, then the war and the postwar period, and it just took a long time to get going.

PETER LOW:

Most trades were 100 and 200 shares back then. I was on the floor for six months before I was given the responsibility of handling an order over 500 shares. A very big order was 2,500 shares.

ROY SMITH:

There was kind of a bull-market bubble in the late fifties and early sixties, and that revived Wall Street a lot. But what it was doing, really, was reviving a partnership structure that was antiquated and old-fashioned. It had worked for many years because it was suited to this sort of small, intimate industry that Wall Street was. But as you can imagine, such a structure just couldn't bear the weight of a ten-fold increase in volume and everything else that was going on. So it was only a matter of time before some changes occurred.

BERNARD HEROLD (fifty-year Wall Street veteran and founder of Bernard Herold and Company):

There were a lot of stupid guys who didn't know how to run a business. It was a pretty wild time. They didn't know what the hell they were doing. There were a lot of lousy firms. There are very few firms from that day that still exist under their own names today. Sometimes changes come and the only thing you can do is adapt or die — and this was one of those times.

The first major change the New York Stock Exchange experienced in the late 1960s was cultural. In 1967, the exchange got its first female member, Muriel Siebert.

MURIEL SIEBERT (founder and chairman of Muriel Siebert and Company):

I really wanted to be at a major firm. I was tired of being at places with eight, ten people. It was limiting. I was doing well, don't misunderstand me, but it was limiting. But I could not become a partner at a major firm. I couldn't even get paid for the business I was doing at a major firm because they wouldn't have a woman.

BERNARD HEROLD:

W. E. Hutton hired one woman as a salesman. I'll never forget, one of my clients came in and she was sitting a few desks away from me. After listening to her talk on the phone for a little while he said, "What is she selling — dresses?" Women for the most part didn't have any experience or any knowledge about the business.

Now, Mickie Siebert was a tough son of a bitch. She could handle it.

MURIEL SIEBERT:

So one day I was talking to Jerry [Tsai] about this. I said, "Jerry, what large firm can I go to where I'll get credit for my business?" And he told me, "Don't be ridiculous. You'll never find it. Go buy a seat [on the New York Stock Exchange] and work for yourself." I said, "Don't you be ridiculous." But he said, "I don't think there's a law against it."

And he was right.

JERRY TSAI (founder of Manhattan Fund and original manager of Fidelity Capital Fund):

We were doing some business with Muriel at Manhattan Fund. I was talking to her one day, and I said, "Mickie, why don't you buy a seat on the stock exchange? I don't think it's illegal or anything. And you'll be the first female stock-exchange member." She thought about it and said, "You know, that's not a bad idea."

You see, I believe that you should never be afraid to be the first at anything. Tradition doesn't mean much to me. If you only believe in tradition, you'll never try something new.

PETER LOW:

I don't know why we didn't have any female members — tradition, I guess. It's not as if women weren't allowed on the floor of the exchange. During World War II women took the place of men, not as brokers but as what we call squads, or basically pages. They'd carry the messages from the brokers in the crowd back to the booth, where they can be relayed up to the firm and ultimately to the customer. Then, when the war was over and the men came back, I guess it went back to the way it was.

JENNIFER WILLIAMS (New York Stock Exchange floor broker for Griswold Company):

Wall Street is typically an environment that most people would say is probably twenty or thirty years behind the rest of society in terms of gender equality, feminism, things like that. To this day there aren't that many women at the New York Stock Exchange — I know there are only fifty or so women floor brokers.

MURIEL SIEBERT:

So I decided to do it. Well, the establishment was not happy with me. When you break a tradition that's 170 years old, not everyone's going to love you. That's the difference between the group today and the group that was. I will tell you that they didn't want me, but I joined a group where your word was your bond, and you would go broke before you broke your word. That is not the case today. So tradition does cut both ways.

But as I said, the establishment was not happy with me. They told me there was no ladies' room. I didn't know that there was a ladies' room on the floor for two and a half years. One day, long after I'd become a member, I went down to the floor to do a block. I knew the specialist pretty well, and I said, "I'll see you in a few minutes, Frank. I'm going upstairs."

He said, "Why are you going upstairs?"

And I said, "I've got to go to the john."

He said, "What?" In the middle of the trading day he took me by the hand, walked me across the floor, and showed me where there was a ladies' room left over from the Korean War when they had women clerks. But nobody told me about it.

PETER LOW:

My daughter worked on the floor when she was in college, and my son worked on the floor when he was in college. And I have to say it was a much different feeling having a son on the floor than a daughter. I felt a lot more protective of her. The floor can be a tough place, a chauvinistic place. It's less so now, but it still has that dynamic. A woman would sometimes come on the floor as a guest, a woman who you wouldn't give a second glance on the subway, and she would get an inordinate amount of attention just because she was a woman closeted in a men's environment.

MURIEL SIEBERT:

The exchange also made me jump through some extra hoops. I had a relationship with J. P. Morgan. I did business with them, and my personal account was there. And they said they'd make me a loan so I could buy the seat. I was going to put down $145,000 and they were going to lend me $300,000. They made these kinds of loans all the time. But the stock exchange wanted a letter from the bank saying that, "in the event the stock exchange accepts the bid card from Muriel Siebert, the bank will make the loan."

J. P. Morgan said, "We've never had to write such a letter before. Get the seat, we'll give you the loan." But that wasn't good enough for the exchange.

After a while it was clear I was not going to get the letter. So I went to see a friend of mine at the Chase Manhattan Bank. I also did business with Chase, and when I told my friend there about what was happening, that day they gave me the letter. Then, with the letter in hand, I got my seat.

The exchange had never asked for that letter from a man before, but now I met all their requirements. They didn't have a choice. I will say that the guys at Chase later told me that they had a bet going around the bank that they'd never have to make the loan. But they did. I got my seat. And the rest, as they say, is history.

PETER LOW:

Mickie Siebert joining the exchange probably was more controversial in the press than it was on the floor of the stock exchange. She wasn't that active really. I do remember that one time she put together a massive trade, 400,000 shares or something like that, and we were pretty impressed. But other than that, I think she was accepted and everyone moved on.

ROY SMITH:

I don't think Wall Street was thought to be a place where women worked. There were all sorts of reasons why. It was an all-boys club; the stock exchange was always a male environment. It's kind of the way the marines were never thought to be a place where women would work. That changed with other social pressures. But I never really thought that letting Mickie Siebert buy a seat changed anything. That was not a watershed event.

Now, what you could consider a watershed event was the paperwork problem that crushed a lot of brokerage firms in the late 1960s. There was real panic at the stock exchange and among the retail firms about that. Many of these old partnerships went out of business in the late sixties and early seventies simply because they couldn't keep up with their paperwork.

DONALD REGAN (former Merrill Lynch chairman):

By the late 1960s, Wall Street was living hand-to-mouth. Basically, you had partnerships where at the end of every year they split up the kitty and started out fresh with a zero balance sheet. When a partner died his money went out of the firm unless his widow or heirs decided to leave part in on a limited capacity. So you were never really sure what your capital position was going to be.

You burn up capital quickly if you keep expanding and adding staff, because for every salesperson you add you also have to take on at least one in operations or administration. So Wall Street was adding people, which meant more salaries and benefits — the government was becoming much more insistent on health plans, Social Security costs were going up, and things of that nature. So every time you expanded you got this added baggage coming along with you. If you had a downturn you wouldn't have profits. What would you rely on then?

DONALD MARRON (former PaineWebber chairman):

By and large Wall Street wasn't computerized back then, so nobody could keep up with the flood of paperwork. The stock market had to close one day a week and take off an hour on the rest of the days just so we could try to put together the paper trail, making sure that all the trades matched. It's hard to imagine now, but our trading hours were limited because of paperwork. At that time it was a very people-intensive business without a high degree of automation. If you got behind the curve it could be highly problematic. Needless to say, by the end of the sixties there were lots of firms behind the curve.

ROBERT NEWBURGER:

With the advent of mutual funds the size of orders at the stock exchange just exploded. Jerry Tsai, Jack Dreyfus, these guys really changed our business. Mutual funds brought a lot of people into the market who wouldn't have been there otherwise. Small shop owners, farmers, teachers — these people had never been interested in stocks before, but suddenly they were starting to buy mutual funds. It seemed safer because somebody else was making the decisions for them. Don't forget, the wealth of the country was growing and a lot of things were happening. People had to do something with the money they were making, so some turned to mutual funds. Not too many people, mind you, because in the 1960s mutual funds still were pretty small compared to where they are today. But they were exposing more people to the stock market.

PETER LOW:

By 1969 volume had exploded to the point where the industry could not handle the paper. What we would do is close on Wednesdays and for a period of time close every day at 2:00 p.m., just to catch up with the paperwork.

DONALD REGAN:

People took delivery of their own certificates back in those days. Since then we've gone to a certificateless society, but at the time if you bought 100 shares of IBM you actually got a paper certificate saying so. Securities firms were inundated with paperwork keeping track of all those goddamn certificates. Suddenly Wall Street couldn't deliver your certificates because the firm didn't know about your trade or they didn't know when it was coming through. So the records at IBM's agent, which was some bank in New York, wouldn't jibe with the records of the brokers. The brokers down on the floor of the stock exchange had errors with the specialists. It created a hell of a mess.

WICK SIMMONS (former partner at Hayden Stone and great-grandson of Hayden Stone cofounder Galen Stone):

In the late sixties people like Jerry Tsai came along and popularized the idea of people investing in mutual funds. What that did was increase the public's awareness of owning equities. You can't underestimate how important the attention Jerry got was to Wall Street, because it created a way for a whole new group of people to enter the market. From that time on, we've gone from a country where one in five people owned stock, directly or indirectly, to one in two owning stock, directly or indirectly.

So the increased interest in mutual funds brought more and more people to the stock market. And what it did was tax the processing capabilities of Wall Street. In those days, for instance, although we were new users of the computer, all our systems did not talk to one another. At Hayden Stone — which was just like Merrill Lynch and Bache and Company, the two biggest firms in the industry then — we had what we called a wire where all of our orders were carried. We switched those orders to the floor and returned those orders for execution. And then at the end of the day we had to dump all those orders onto paper and resubmit them on a new computing system. We used Univac for the front end and IBM for the back end, and we had to dump them, retype them, keypunch them, verify them, and then put them into the back-office system in order to get the whole thing up and ready by the next morning so everybody would know what his margin and account status was. We just simply couldn't keep up.

In 1967, 1968, what have you, we literally shut down the stock market early every day and didn't open on Wednesdays every once in a while. We simply couldn't process the volume that we had, but we all had to keep up. Hayden Stone not only lost complete control of its processing systems, but we really didn't know what we owned at the end of the day. In those days, when you didn't know what you owned you took those securities, delivered them to somebody else, and hoped you got paid for them. So we had what we called in those days "suspense accounts," which held everything that you couldn't identify whether you bought or sold during the day. You had to put up reserves against these suspense accounts, and those reserves ate into your profitability significantly.

DONALD REGAN:

The stock exchange was frantically trying to keep up. They had no insurance, there was no such thing as an insurance program, and they passed the hat. The way to help out a firm that was in trouble was to have somebody take it over. That's when Sandy Weill and a lot of the others were grabbing up failed firms. It had just gotten completely out of hand. Some firms had to be taken over or they would just have gone under. I remember the guy at E. F. Hutton kept taking over firms even though he was as badly off as anybody. He just kept adding on bulk in an attempt to wring out production from a few more brokers. But what he really was doing was adding to their woes. F. I. Dupont did that and they had to be saved by Ross Perot. Walston did the same thing and they disappeared. There were so many firms then that don't exist now simply because of poor planning.

ROBERT NEWBURGER:

My firm, Newberger Loeb, went under in 1969. It was the paper crunch. We were a by-hand operation; we had no computers. We tried to install a system right in the middle of the crisis, but it was a mess. As a result we couldn't hire any decent people. If certain receipts didn't match the securities that we had in the vault, they'd put the securities in the wastebasket when it was time to go home. So stock that should've been delivered someplace never got there, checks that should've gone to another place went somewhere else.

We went completely under and out of business. Nobody was saving us. My brother and I by that time were the only two senior partners remaining in the general partnership, owing several million dollars. We didn't have it. I was wiped out completely — lost every penny I had because I was always happy to put my capital back into Newberger Loeb. I owned 25 percent of it and I lost every penny. Thank God we had an apartment in New York and a home in Quiogue [in the Hamptons on Long Island], both of which fortunately were in my wife's name. As long as she was willing to tolerate me, I had a place to live.

I got myself a job with a small regional firm that had an idle seat, but I never got back to where I was because I was a reasonably wealthy man before Newberger Loeb went under. I went from that to zilch. Also, there were so many judgments out against me that I couldn't even have a bank account. I'd get my check cashed by the firm that handled our clearing and I'd buy money orders. I did this for twenty years until the statute of limitations ran out.

But I had very good friends who helped me get through. A couple of friends on the floor came up to me and said, "Bob, here's $25,000 to tide you over. Pay it back when and if you can." These were my competitors on the floor — competitors! In many ways it really is a wonderful culture here. I paid it all back, of course, much quicker than they'd expected.

PETER LOW:

It happened to a lot of people I knew. I had friends at Goodbody who lost their capital and lost their seats on the exchange. If you want to know why Wall Street went public, there you have it. The partnership structure wasn't built to withstand the growth of the business and these guys were not about to sit around with their capital at risk.

DONALD REGAN:

The paper-crunch period of the late sixties and early seventies killed the partnerships. It also showed the frailty of individual capital in a firm, whether it be in the form of stock or a partnership arrangement. You needed real permanent capital and the ability to go to the public for it. We were practicing that, advocating that everybody else go to the public for capital. Why not Wall Street? My word is my bond? Bullshit.

ROY SMITH:

The partnerships were largely a creation of the New York Stock Exchange, which at one time had a rule that you had to be a partnership if you wanted to be a member. But once Donaldson, Lufkin and Jenrette decided to challenge that, it really fell apart.

JOHN JAKOBSON (member of the New York Stock Exchange since 1955):

The exchange didn't want any member firm to go public because the idea was that partnerships promoted more financial responsibility than the corporate structure, which limited liability. It was all about promoting this idea of safety and security. It's the same reason that in the old days they used to build banks to look like fortresses. I live on the Upper West Side and there are some banks there that take up a whole block. It was all done to promote the idea that your money is safe in there. Now, the guy inside could be a crook and funneling your money out the back door, but it's what's out front that matters.

RICHARD JENRETTE (cofounder and former chairman of Donaldson, Lufkin and Jenrette):

I give Bill Donaldson credit for first bringing up the idea that we should think about going public. In 1959, when we were originally putting together our partnership, we didn't have any money ourselves. I had to borrow from friends what I put up, and the others were about as badly off. To round it out, we found ten of our former classmates who put up the rest of the capital we needed. It was really difficult raising the money, and at that time Bill Donaldson predicted that one day New York Stock Exchange member firms would be publicly owned. Think about it for a second — it didn't make any sense that the New York Stock Exchange was telling corporations that being publicly traded was good for them, but not for us.

DAN LUFKIN (cofounder and former chief executive of Donaldson, Lufkin and Jenrette):

When we were starting our firm we took a look at the landscape on Wall Street and saw an opportunity in research. As a customer, if you went to the establishment investment banks at the time — Kuhn Loeb or Lehman Brothers or Brown Brothers or even Merrill Lynch — you could find information on General Motors, Coca-Cola, Procter and Gamble, and IBM. The research wasn't very good, mostly basic statistics, but at least it was there. But nobody was dealing with the younger, smaller, newer companies that were developing technology or breaking into new markets. You didn't see any research on Haloid Xerox or Avon or Diebold or Dun and Bradstreet or American Photocopy or Alcon Laboratories.

WILLIAM DONALDSON (chairman of the Securities and Exchange Commission, former New York Stock Exchange chairman, and cofounder of Donaldson, Lufkin and Jenrette):

Our basic concept was that the ranks of institutional investors were growing and they were going to need more than statistical research. They were going to need qualitative judgments, particularly in an area that we thought was attractive in 1959: small companies.

DAN LUFKIN:

I was elected to the stock exchange's board of governors in 1969. You don't get much more establishment than that, you know. But once we got into the club and took a look around, we realized some major changes were needed if any of us were going to survive much longer.

Under the partnership structure that was dominant on Wall Street, a firm's capital was fixed, meaning it was the partners' money and as each partner retired he gradually withdrew his capital by selling back his stock in the firm at book value. So you had a situation where the actual amount of money the partnerships had to build their businesses changed every year. Partners were pressured to keep their capital in the firm as long as possible because the removal of any money was a serious imposition. It was totally ass-backward and impossible to plan for anything. And then things got out of control in the paper crunch.

What happened was, we had so much volume coming in during the middle to late sixties that the back offices of many Wall Street firms were overwhelmed. These back offices were geared to a different era when this was a cottage industry. They weren't prepared for the exponential growth we were experiencing. As a result, many firms ran into net-capital violations. Now net-capital requirements were a severe issue, checked by the exchange every day at three o'clock. If you were in violation it meant the equity in your firm could not support the debt you'd run up. Once you were in violation of the exchange's net-capital requirements you had to fix your business fast, but there was no way to get new capital under the partnership structure. So the whole thing became a vicious circle, and finally it got ugly and emotional. Some of the larger firms merged to survive; the smaller ones simply folded. It was a disaster that we were determined to avoid at DLJ, which is basically what drove us to the decision that we needed to have a publicly traded stock regardless of the exchange's rules.

I'll never forget the reaction I got at the meeting where I told them our plans. It was pretty nasty, old men screaming, "Who the hell do you think you are?" Felix Rohatyn compared me to Judas Iscariot. They felt that I was forsaking the rules and traditions of the exchange and forcing their hand, which of course I was. But I also was right. I remember that night there was a dinner for the governors of the exchange, and nobody would speak to me. I was standing by myself and people turned their back on me. Finally Gus Levy came up to me and said, "I don't agree with what you did, I don't agree with how you did it, and I don't agree with why you feel this way. But I'll tell you this, I admire your guts for coming to this dinner."

ROY SMITH:

I think Donaldson, Lufkin's decision to go public was controversial because it just didn't seem necessary. It wasn't exactly clear that they were doing this for reasons other than being self-promotional. If you know those guys, they're all self-promotional, particularly Donaldson. So it felt as if these upstart people were challenging the stock exchange, which didn't need a challenge at that time, saying that they were going to incorporate and go public, contrary to the rules of the exchange. They lobbied for it and convinced the exchange that they should be allowed to do it. Meanwhile, the stock exchange was getting a lot of pressure from the government and its institutional clients for having fixed commission rates and this clublike attitude where everybody had to do things the old-fashioned way. So the stock exchange wanted to be seen as more modern, and that opened the door to Donaldson, Lufkin's initial public offering.

RICHARD JENRETTE:

At the time people said we were a stalking horse for Merrill Lynch because they decided to go public shortly after we did. But that wasn't true. We never talked to them. We suspected, and it was rumored, that they were champing at the bit to go public, but nobody on Wall Street wanted them to do it because they were already too powerful. They were a logical choice because they were the only truly national firm, they had a brand name, and they had a real need for capital with all their varied interests. So we suspected that Merrill Lynch would support us, while the Lazards and Morgan Stanleys would not.

DON REGAN:

Those bastards stole my thunder!

ROY SMITH:

Very soon after Donaldson, Lufkin went public, Merrill Lynch went public, and that did change things. It changed things a lot. For one, we began to realize that all the partners of Merrill Lynch were able to cash out and go home with their money much sooner than anyone had ever figured. They were able to do it at a good price and the institutional capital came in to replace them. So they were able to expand their business in a variety of ways, and all of a sudden this idea of going public started to look very different.

ROBERT NEWBURGER:

Here's the parallel: Where does a bear sleep? Wherever it wants. The rule at the stock exchange was no corporations, only general partnerships, and it had never been questioned. But once Donaldson, Lufkin started making noise about wanting to go public, the bear decided to sleep over there. They said they were going to do it, and we all knew it was a matter of time before it happened. Sure, people were pissed about it and wanted to fight it. Just as nature abhors a vacuum, so too does human nature instinctively resist change. But deep down I think we knew there wasn't much anyone could do when it came down to it. It was an inevitable change, and probably one that we needed.

On April 9, 1970, DLJ sold 800,000 shares to the public at $15 apiece, which was substantially lower than the price it had originally hoped for. DLJ couldn't even support the $15 IPO price; within months the stock had tanked to roughly $5, and it didn't rebound for some time. Still, DLJ did provide the impetus for Wall Street to go public. Shortly afterward, brokerage firms like Merrill Lynch, Bache, and several others would follow DLJ into the public markets with IPOs of their own. Whether the timing was right or not, Wall Street finally was seeing the light.

CHAPTER 8

CORNED BEEF WITH LETTUCE

As the late sixties heated up, conditions at the fledgling firm of Carter, Berlind and Weill were rapidly coming to a boil. The problem within the partnership came down to a difference of opinion on where the firm should be headed. Arthur Carter, the group's undisputed leader, wanted to pursue a strategy similar to the classic British merchant banks, where the firm would take ownership positions in companies that they could control as investments. Meanwhile, the other partners saw no reason to abandon their growing strength in retail brokerage. So when Carter, Berlind and Weill advised the young Long Island entrepreneur Saul Steinberg in his 1968 takeover of Reliance Insurance of Philadelphia, the conflict finally came to a head.

SAUL STEINBERG (former chairman of Reliance Insurance and founder of Leaseco):

In a lot of ways my takeover of Reliance Insurance probably was the beginning of the end for Arthur Carter at Carter, Berlind and Weill. It's funny — I hadn't really thought about it that way before.

ARTHUR CARTER (cofounder of Carter, Berlind and Weill):

In the late 1960s we were very much involved in the insurance industry. Our institutional brokerage accounts bought a lot of insurance stocks and we followed them closely. It was clear to us that there were real opportunities to acquire some of these insurance companies at attractive prices. Many of them had good book values, good balance sheets, and excessive surplus — what we used to call "surplus surplus." This was extra capital that was unnecessary for the operations of the insurance business, surplus above and beyond, so to speak. So there were cash and equity and assets inside these companies that could be used for other things outside the insurance business.

The other key characteristic of these insurance companies was that no one controlled them. In other words, there was no family that you had to answer to because they owned most or all of the firm's stock. These were large independent-stock companies: Continental Insurance, National General, Great American Insurance, Reliance, companies like that. So it became a natural thing for us to think about the possibilities of doing mergers and acquisitions where some of the conglomerates or financial entrepreneurs of the time would acquire some of these insurance companies. In our eyes the most logical candidate to emerge as a takeover target was Reliance, because our institutional clients owned a *very* significant percentage of that stock. It became our first big takeover idea.

When we started looking for someone to take over Reliance we targeted everyone. But they all turned us down. Larry Tisch, Charlie Bludhorn, Jimmy Ling, Meshulam Riklis, Steve Ross — we literally went through an M&A All-Star team from the 1960s and not one of them was interested. To them insurance wasn't sexy. Insurance was boring.

The last guy we went to was Saul Steinberg.

MARSHALL COGAN (former partner at Carter, Berlind and Weill):

Saul Steinberg's takeover of Reliance was the result of the extraordinary intellect of a fellow named Ed Netter. Edwin Netter was a rather quirky individual. Today he would be called a geek, a brilliant geek. He was an analyst at Carter, Berlind and Weill, and for some reason in the late

1960s he became fascinated with the excess capital in the insurance industry. It was a concept that made sense to me. So based on Ed Netter's research we started buying these insurance stocks for our clients. There was Reliance, Great America, and several others.

Eventually Saul Steinberg saw that report and became interested in taking over one of these insurance companies. Saul was a pudgy Jewish guy from Long Island who had conceived of a successful business leasing computers. But he knew that business wouldn't last and he wanted to use the high equity valuation of his leasing company to get solid, long-term value. A quality insurance company had a big book value, it didn't have excess goodwill, it had a wonderful, balanced business. Meanwhile, it was possible that the Leaseco business could disappear eventually. Saul was bright enough to see this and want to do something about it.

So we talked to Saul about the report and our ideas, and developed a strategy for him. When we looked at it we noticed that for some reason I, along with another partner at the firm, had placed about 60 percent of Reliance's stock with our institutional clients. That was an extraordinary number. Basically, we controlled the company at that point. We were able to apply the institutional pressure to steer Reliance to Saul.

SAUL STEINBERG:

There were a number of firms that we looked at, but in the end I picked Reliance because they had a great chief executive in the property-and-casualty business, A. Addison Roberts, Bill Roberts from Virginia. He was a lawyer, not from the property-and-casualty business himself.

Bill Roberts was very much against this deal at first. He told me he would never go for it, having somebody like me running an old-line company like Reliance. But he also could see that the world was changing. There wasn't much he could do. We were inevitable. I was prepared to go hostile if I had to, but it wasn't necessary because we had already won over their board.

Getting Roberts on board was tough. We met several times, Roberts and I. Eventually I convinced him that our interests were aligned. My proposal was that the management of Reliance would continue to manage the insurance business and we would run the noninsurance part. Over time, whoever was the better manager would run the whole business. There would be no guarantees for anybody.

MARSHALL COGAN:

As the deal was closing, Arthur Carter correctly saw that we should have been doing it for ourselves. He told me that Carter, Berlind and Weill should have taken over Reliance as a vehicle for merchant banking and leveraged buyouts, buying stakes in companies and taking them over to make a profit. That's what he wanted us to do, take over Reliance instead of Saul Steinberg.

Arthur and I had a disagreement on this. We had negotiated a transaction with Saul Steinberg. I had shaken hands on it. On Wall Street your word is your bond, with some exceptions. But I felt I could not go back on my word here. He was intellectually right, but we had a moral obligation. It was an intense battle between Arthur and myself. Arthur was the senior partner, but I was the producer.

Eventually I prevailed. Steinberg ended up taking over Reliance and we ended up accepting our $750,000 fee. In principle I thought Arthur was right, but I wanted us to keep our word. After that he became very focused on doing takeovers and changing Carter, Berlind and Weill from a retail brokerage firm into a merchant-banking or leveraged-buyout firm.

SAUL STEINBERG:

Merchant banking was on the minds of all the guys at Carter, Berlind and Weill at the time. I think a lot of people around Wall Street, myself included, were beginning to come to this conclusion. LBOs were on the horizon and the conglomerateurs were getting lots of attention. I remember Sandy said something to me about it just as we were getting ready to close the acquisition. He said, "On Monday, if you finish this deal, you'll get a business and we'll have to start all over again."

JUDITH RAMSEY EHRLICH (coauthor of *The New Crowd*):

When Steinberg acquired Reliance, Carter decided that he too was ready to move on to bigger things, either by starting a company of his own or by restructuring Carter, Berlind and Weill. Now Sandy Weill had no idea that anything was wrong. He told me he was stunned when Arthur Levitt and Marshall Cogan told him in confidence that Carter had been making plans to reshape the firm to his own design. Apparently Carter had grown tired of the brokerage business and wanted to turn the firm into a merchant bank that provided advice and capital to companies in exchange for a share of ownership. Carter also planned to cut Weill's and Berlind's shares of the profits to low levels, perhaps 1 percent, because he felt they weren't pulling their own weight.

Weill felt betrayed. He had considered Carter among his closest friends. Levitt pressed the others to unite against Carter since all of them would be vulnerable if Carter succeeded in reducing an officer's share. Weill was torn. He knew his own role in the firm was being challenged, but he worried about whether he could manage without Carter.

ROGER BERLIND (cofounder of Carter, Berlind and Weill):

There was a philosophical difference within the firm that came to a head. Arthur Carter really wanted us to be a merchant bank. He wanted to move the firm in that direction. But when the rest of us really thought about it we weren't comfortable going there.

Then there also was the matter of Arthur wanting to break up the equal-partner arrangement we'd had since the beginning of the firm. Sandy, Arthur, and I had incorporated Carter, Berlind and Weill as equals. The truth is the equal partnership probably should have been broken up, just not the way Arthur wanted to do it. He wanted to be the number-one guy and demote Sandy and me — and eventually everyone else. So that obviously broke up the partnership because he had to leave once we found out what his plans were.

MARSHALL COGAN:

Arthur felt, and I'm not going to say correctly or incorrectly, that Sandy in particular didn't deserve the share of the firm he had. This was based on six, seven years when Sandy was really a nonparticipant in building the business. So what he wanted to do was reduce the stake held by Sandy and Roger to nothing and promote Arthur Levitt, who also was a partner in the firm, and me in their places. Then he wanted us to move ahead with plans to focus on takeovers rather than brokerage.

I felt that Sandy and Roger were the original partners and what Arthur [Carter] wanted to do was wrong as a matter of corporate philosophy, even though I would be the beneficiary. I just felt it was wrong. But Arthur's attitude was that the past was not indicative of the future. For more than five years there had been a lack of contribution, from Sandy in particular, and he wanted to do something about it.

JUDITH RAMSEY EHRLICH:

The firm of Carter, Berlind and Weill held a board meeting on the morning of September 10, 1968. The atmosphere was extremely tense. Carter announced that he wanted the title and authority of chief executive officer, and he wanted to reshuffle the stock-ownership percentages, elevating Cogan and Levitt and reducing Weill and Berlind. Levitt, Weill, Cogan, and Berlind then called for a recess and weighed their options. Weill learned that Carter had actually filed the papers to set up a holding company without the knowledge and consent of all the officers, and that revelation left him devastated.

Levitt admitted to the group that he'd known about Carter's plan for some time but couldn't tell them. Levitt later told me that he said, "If we confront him and let him stay at the firm, he'll act like a wounded animal who'll come back to kill us. I'm not going to stick around if we let him stay." Weill agreed and said, "He's left us no choice. But let's give him some time, a few months' grace." Still, Levitt was adamant. "He's got to be out today."

When the meeting was reconvened, Carter was asked to resign on the spot. He refused and said he wanted to consult an attorney. The partners replied, "Either resign today, or we'll fire you." Carter resigned and walked out. Afterward they met with their attorney, Ken Bialkin, at the offices of Willkie Farr and Gallagher, and talked until two in the morning, ironing out all the details of Carter's departure.

MARSHALL COGAN:

I would say what influenced me most in all this was Arthur Levitt. Arthur's position was about responsibility to your colleagues, which I agreed with. I wanted to keep everybody within the firm. Despite what Arthur Carter was saying, I thought Sandy was smart and everybody would have his day in the sun eventually. I didn't feel that anyone should be demoted. Levitt and I owned less of a stake in the firm, so I thought we should be given more and everything should be adjusted pro rata.

Obviously, when Weill and Berlind became aware of what Arthur Carter wanted to do, they called a vote and asked for him to leave the company. They had the majority of shares, but I was the swing. At that point I probably influenced more than half of the firm's revenue because of the institutional clients I controlled. So my ownership stake in the firm was insignificant, but if I left there would be a problem. My influence was disproportionate to my equity.

Although the press release we put out announcing Arthur's departure said it was a "friendly" parting, I wouldn't categorize it like that at all. It was a very difficult time. In retrospect, I think those events in September 1968 had a big impact on the way Sandy viewed his life. It made him much more focused on survival than he had been before.

ARTHUR CARTER:

That's absolutely incorrect. It did not happen that way. I left the firm after almost ten years because I saw a great opportunity, or what I thought was a great opportunity, to raise money and do a series of leveraged buyouts. I told my partners that I was going to go ahead and do this. Maybe — with the benefit of hindsight — I should have let the firm participate with me. But I left the firm and really branched out on my own. I was really concerned that I couldn't do it under the umbrella of the firm. That was basically the fundamental issue. I'm sure people thought other things and wanted to present it other ways — all that played a role. But these are the facts.

SANDY WEILL (cofounder of Carter, Berlind and Weill):

We did what we had to do. But something was lost.

JUDITH RAMSEY EHRLICH:

Immediately after Carter left, Weill really was in a state of shock. He couldn't concentrate on his work. He had a wife and two children at home to support, all his assets were tied up in the company, and he wasn't sure the firm could succeed without Carter. He was thirty-five and still very insecure.

MARSHALL COGAN:

You have to understand that Arthur Carter was our intellectual and strategic muscle. So it wasn't a comfortable feeling to be in the firm on our own without Arthur. After he left, Carter wanted me to join him in a venture. Looking back, I should have gone with him. In the combination of the way he saw things and the way I conceptualized things we could have created a dynamic entity. But I stayed because I had great confidence in the integrity of Roger Berlind and Arthur Levitt. I had brought in many people to the firm and I just felt it was not appropriate to hurt my colleagues like that. I wasn't dealing from self-interest on that one.

We named the new firm Cogan, Berlind, Weill and Levitt. Since my institutional clients were essential to the new firm, I said, "If you want me to stay and nothing to change, this firm had the letter 'C' first and now I want that 'C' to be Cogan." It was the only thing I asked for.

ROGER BERLIND:

When Arthur Carter left we changed the firm's name to Cogan, Berlind, Weill and Levitt. Why? For euphony reasons. Cogan, Berlind, Weill and Levitt sounded like Carter, Berlind and Weill, so it sounded as if nothing had happened.

We handed out the titles just as haphazardly. Chairman, vice chairman, president — nobody cared. The only title that mattered was chief executive officer, and I was the first CEO of Cogan, Berlind, Weill and Levitt. There were a variety of reasons for that. Each of my partners I'm sure had a different take on why I should be CEO. Of course, I thought I could run the company best. But in reality I think I was the least-threatening partner to the other three. We had become a very competitive shop and I retained the partnership sense of style. I always wanted to debrief everybody thoroughly before making a decision, whereas some of my other partners would have done that a little differently. So they were most comfortable having me in the CEO's slot. We did very well for quite a while operating like that.

ARTHUR LEVITT JR. (former partner at Cogan, Berlind, Weill and Levitt):

We all had the same salaries and the same ownership interests. We decided on the titles this way: whoever had his name first in Cogan, Berlind, Weill and Levitt would choose his title last, and whoever had his name last had his first choice of titles. I chose first and became president. Sandy chose to be chairman. Roger chose to be CEO and Marshall became executive vice president. CEO was the only title that mattered. I don't think we would have allowed anyone but Roger to be CEO. We all wanted the CEO to be the person who threatened us least, which was Roger.

SANDY WEILL:

Whoever had brought in the most business the week before had the strongest voice of influence.

ROGER BERLIND:

So we unveiled the new firm on Wall Street and we immediately got this ridiculous nickname, Corned Beef With Lettuce for Cogan, Berlind, Weill and Levitt. I guess it was supposed to be a knock on the firm. Everybody on Wall Street did that. People did whatever they could to denigrate another firm in a joking way. But Corned Beef With Lettuce didn't make much sense to me because you never ate lettuce with corned beef. That sounds kind of disgusting. Eventually we shortened the name of the firm to CBWL, but that didn't stop people from calling us Corned Beef With Lettuce. I'll never understand it.

MARSHALL COGAN:

Corned Beef With Lettuce was an anti-Semitic slur. We were shaking the roots of Morgan Stanley, Dillon Read, and First Boston. We were challenging Goldman Sachs, Lehman, and Salomon. The establishment was becoming scared of us and they resorted to stupid nicknames to try to put us down.

PETER COHEN (analyst for Cogan, Berlind, Weill and Levitt):

When I came to the firm it was basically a bunch of guys trying to figure out how to build a business on Wall Street. Cogan was the partner all the younger guys looked to because he was really the driving force. Sandy Weill was very much in the background in those days. He was very laid-back — sort of "the partner in charge of second-guessing." He wasn't really a frontline guy, at least not to those of us who were out there on the front lines all the time. Marshall Cogan was the rainmaker, moving and shaking and pushing us all the time. Roger Berlind had the responsibility for operations and the back office. And Arthur Levitt was a client guy, bringing in clients and trying to fit them in somewhere.

PETER BERNSTEIN (head of asset management for Cogan, Berlind, Weill and Levitt):

Sandy was a very quiet, withdrawn kind of guy. He didn't have natural charm the way Arthur Levitt did and some of the other guys over there did.

PETER COHEN:

Based on sheer ambition and ego, it quickly became obvious that the two leading characters in the firm were going to be Marshall and Sandy. Roger and Arthur just didn't have the inclination to take over the way those two did. There was one partners' office that was across the front of the GM Building on the thirty-fourth floor. Marshall was at one end and Sandy was at the other with Roger and Arthur in between. All these guys were so secretive with each other — they didn't want the others to know what they were up to. So they'd be ducking under their desks all the time while they talked on the phone, trying to do all this stuff in secret.

FRANK ZARB (former executive vice president at Cogan, Berlind, Weill and Levitt):

The firm's structure was sort of a rule by consensus, and sometimes chaos. But nevertheless, these were extremely bright people who wanted to make things happen. Nobody was wealthy or from a privileged background. They all had their net worth on the line at all times. In that kind of environment you can see why everyone was sufficiently motivated to get the job done.

JESSICA BIBLIOWICZ (daughter of Sandy Weill and chairman of National Financial Partners):

There wasn't a lot of separation between the business and our family. It affected all of our moods in certain ways. This was the way Wall Street seemed to work. When I look back at it, I can remember how the business was doing by our lifestyle at the time. There were periods when we'd go out to dinner more often, and then there were periods when we ate a lot of pizza. When things were looking up, houses and apartments were bought, there was money to spend, stuff like that. You could kind of sense that things were okay. My father always was pretty tight so there was never excess, but you could see that there was more available.

Then, when times got tough, the tension was very high.

MARSHALL COGAN:

Our first real challenge as a new firm came when Tubby Burnham, who was the head of Burnham and Company, told us he no longer wanted to clear our trades for us.

SANDY WEILL:

When we started in the sixties we cleared through Burnham. Tubby Burnham is one of my heroes. I worked at his firm before we started [Carter, Berlind and Weill], and I watched the excitement and love of somebody building a business. But in the latter half of the sixties we were growing faster than they were, so they asked us to take our business out of their shop.

ROBERT LINTON (former Burnham and Company partner and former Drexel Burnham Lambert chairman):

I was the one who told them. That year we did $25 million of business. That's all of Burnham and Company. CBWL did $10 million that year. They were growing as fast or faster than we were growing. And they were interfering with our capacity to grow. We were swamped. I sat down with them and said, "Guys, we've had an executive-committee meeting and we're going to have to ask you to clear elsewhere or on your own because you're getting too big for us to handle."

I remember Sandy said to me, "Are you crazy? We're your most profitable account."

I said, "Yes, you are our most profitable account. But we have a lot of plans to grow and we can't accommodate your growth and our growth." That was it in a nutshell.

I. W. (TUBBY) BURNHAM (former chairman of Burnham and Company):

Sandy was the hardest-working guy we ever had. I wanted to make Sandy a partner but one of our partners opposed him because he looked down on Sandy's eastern European origins. Otherwise, he would have ended up eventually running the firm.

MARSHALL COGAN:

So Tubby asked us to leave. Why did he ask us to leave? He didn't want to do business with Marshall Cogan. He gave a dinner one night for CBWL. Arthur Carter had left by then and he believed highly in Arthur Carter. He didn't like me, didn't trust me. Of course, he's the guy who backed [former junk bond king Michael] Milken, just to give you a frame of reference. But the size of my institutional business was overwhelming Burnham. How could this young kid, twenty-six or twenty-seven years old, be doing this? He, Tubby, had been in the business for twenty-five years. What was going on here?

What made it all worse was I would not show deference to him at this dinner. He was an establishment Our Crowd Jew and he did not look kindly on me, even though I had gone to Boston Latin, Harvard, and Harvard Business. Personally, I resented that Tubby Burnham refused to show respect to Cogan, Berlind, Weill and Levitt, because our business was getting so substantial. So there was a blowup and it was only a matter of time before we were done.

ARTHUR LEVITT:

The day after the dinner Tubby and [Burnham president] Bob Linton called me into the office to discuss a very aggressive trade that Marshall Cogan had made. They said, "We're worried about your business. We don't think we can clear for you anymore." They felt that we were too aggressive and we might get them into trouble.

At that point I ran around and tried to get people to clear for us. The last thing we wanted to do was clear for ourselves. I went to see John Loeb at Loeb Rhoades and he turned us down. I went to Bache and they turned us down. I went to Lehman Brothers and they turned us down. Then Frank Zarb walked in off the street and said, "If you guys can get me a million dollars I'll build you the best clearing firm on Wall Street."

SANDY WEILL:

So we hired Frank Zarb, who was then number two in the back office at Goodbody and Company, a firm that eventually was merged into Merrill Lynch. Suddenly the back office became a key part of our company.

ARTHUR LEVITT:

Looking back, I can't tell you how many times we met at different homes during the tight business of that period and talked about dissolving the firm. But we were able to work out financing with ADP, which took a lease on our furniture and loaned us the million dollars. We gave it to Zarb and he built us quite a competent clearing operation.

FRANK ZARB:

We were living through the conversion of the securities industry. It was happening right before our eyes. When I started on Wall Street it was a bunch of partnerships of rich guys selling stocks to other rich guys. None of these partners wanted to invest their capital in their businesses. The partners wanted the capital for themselves. Now they were going to have to put money back into their businesses to build their back offices if they were going to survive. Needless to say, a lot of firms didn't survive. But for whatever reason, CBWL had that survival instinct.

MARSHALL COGAN:

Getting kicked out of Burnham turned out to be the best thing that could have happened to us. I will tell you that Berlind, Weill, and Levitt were in shock when it happened. But it forced a decision. We had to set up our own back office. We had to automate it, make it state-of-the-art. There would have been no Shearson Lehman, no Salomon Smith Barney, no Citigroup, if that hadn't happened.

CHAPTER 9

THE PAPER CRUNCH

By September 1970 conditions on Wall Street had reached a tipping point. The venerable old-line brokerage house Hayden Stone was about to go under, and the New York Stock Exchange leadership feared that a failure of such a significant firm would be catastrophic to the markets. So a rescue was arranged, with the onetime upstarts at Corned Beef With Lettuce taking over the troubled white-shoe firm. But a holdout contingent of Hayden Stone lenders wasn't convinced that it was such a great idea and refused to sign off. The clock was ticking and the market was on the brink of disaster. Something had to be done.

WICK SIMMONS (former partner at Hayden Stone and great-grandson of Hayden Stone cofounder Galen Stone):

The problem at Hayden Stone was we couldn't process our business. We were losing money on a profit-and-loss basis, and at the same time watching our capital decline for market and withdrawal reasons. To be a member of the New York Stock Exchange you needed to have a percentage of your net capital against your liabilities, and Hayden Stone's net capital fell beneath that. We had to throw ourselves on the mercy of the New York Stock Exchange. At that point in time the New York Stock Exchange went out looking for someone who would put in that capital and/or rescue Hayden Stone.

ROGER BERLIND (former partner at Cogan, Berlind, Weill and Levitt):

From a big-picture perspective, the danger in the failure of Hayden Stone was not only that their customers would be in deep trouble, and they had a lot of customers, but also what would happen to the outstanding accounts they had with every other brokerage house on Wall Street. Some of those firms would not have been in a position to simply write off the amounts owed to them because of a Hayden Stone default. So they would have gone under, too. It could have been a disaster, an immediate domino effect, and everybody realized that. It would have put a lot of companies out of business and shaken public confidence in the business beyond belief. It couldn't be allowed to happen. As a consequence everybody, the stock exchange and so on, was interested in getting this taken care of.

MARSHALL COGAN (former partner at Cogan, Berlind, Weill and Levitt):

Everyone on Wall Street saw what was going on with Hayden Stone. They were the second- or third-largest firm around at the time and they were going under. People didn't realize it then, but the stakes were high. Wall Street would have shut down if this hadn't gone through. The failure would have been in the billions. The headlines would have been "Calamity on Wall Street!"

Quite frankly, I was the partner at Cogan, Berlind, Weill and Levitt who conceived the Hayden Stone deal. Hayden Stone was a Boston firm, I was from Boston, and I understood their problems. I conceived this acquisition out of fear because I saw the institutional business of Cogan, Berlind, Weill and Levitt drying up. So we had to change the mix and do it rapidly. The fact that we had set up our own back office made us state-of-the-art. We could handle ten times the amount of business we were generating. So I said, "We ought to buy Hayden Stone." It was an establishment Wall Street firm and they were moving to a $700 million fail-to-deliver on the Street. So the timing was right for both firms.

FRANK ZARB (former executive vice president at Cogan, Berlind, Weill and Levitt):

It was the end of the sixties and start of the seventies, and the market was really starting to head south into a long correction. It was clear that we needed to find more volume to pump through this shiny new machine. Otherwise, why had we built the thing in the first place? There were two options: we could rent the back office out by clearing for other firms, which we looked into, or we could pursue acquisitions. I guess it's pretty obvious which path we chose.

WICK SIMMONS:

We were looking around for someone, out doing dog and pony shows, and we ran into Cogan, Berlind, Weill and Levitt. Our auditor, a fellow named Frank Borelli at Haskens and Sells, happened to be their auditor as well, and he lined up the initial appointment we had with them. That was after we had gone to Shearson, and Loeb Rhoades, and any number of companies, trying to find someone who would put their capital under Hayden Stone. What eventually happened was, we divided up Hayden Stone. A select group of branches, the better branches, were sold (and that's a euphemism) to Cogan, Berlind, Weill and Levitt, along with some financing from the exchange's emergency fund. The other branches were sold to Walston and Company. And that's how Hayden Stone disappeared in September of 1970.

SANDY WEILL (former partner at Cogan, Berlind, Weill and Levitt):

I'm sure it didn't feel right for them to be taken over by a bunch of New York City Jews.

WICK SIMMONS:

The CBWL guys were completely different from Hayden Stone. Their business was fast. It was new money. Ethnically, it was very different. It was Jewish, through and through, while Hayden Stone was very Catholic — not myself, but the firm. They were smarter than we were, but they had no tradition. They were members of no lunch clubs, members of no syndicates, and very much on the outside looking in at the securities business, whereas Hayden Stone had been on the inside, even though in many ways its people were less capable than those of Cogan, Berlind, Weill and Levitt.

SANDY WEILL:

We really made our pitch not so much to the Hayden Stone people as to some lenders from Oklahoma who had put their securities into a proud old investment-banking firm and in a few months found out that they were in a bottomless pit and might even lose all their money.

ROGER BERLIND:

There were 105 subordinated lenders to Hayden Stone, many of whom had put up their money in the last few months. Don Stroben, the firm's chairman, had gone and solicited investments to keep the company going. When we were structuring the deal to buy Hayden Stone we agreed it had to be all or none; there couldn't be different deals for different subordinated lenders. So the terms that we proposed were going to be taken by everybody or nobody, in which case there would be no deal. And by this point no deal would have been a disaster for Hayden Stone and the industry.

The last three days before the deal was going to close there were various subordinated lenders who were holding out and had to be satisfied in various different ways. One was in London, another was shooting birds up in Canada. People were flying all over the world to get signatures on the deal. The final holdout was a fellow named Jack Golsen in Oklahoma City.

MARSHALL COGAN:

Jack Golsen, who was from Boston, Massachusetts, but lived in Oklahoma, refused to sign. He felt he was getting screwed. He wanted his money back. All the other stockholders agreed, but he refused. The deal demanded that 100 percent of the controlling shareholders of Hayden Stone sign. So the key to the transaction was getting his signature.

JACK GOLSEN (former Oklahoma investor in Hayden Stone):

The CBWL deal was a cover-up. The New York Stock Exchange was in on it. They knew the real condition of Hayden Stone, and they hadn't disclosed it to us when we agreed to lend the money. They went along with Hayden Stone.

MARSHALL COGAN:

The deadline for the deal was Friday, September 11, at 10:00 a.m., when the New York Stock Exchange was going to ring its opening bell and Hayden Stone would go out of business. On Thursday night, Roger and I got on a private jet at Teterboro Airport in a driving rainstorm and flew down to Oklahoma to try to get Jack to sign. Sandy stayed back in New York. He was at the Plaza Hotel working on the last details for the deal.

I'd never been on a private plane before and I couldn't sleep at all on the flight. We landed somewhere in Oklahoma at about four thirty in the morning. I remember I said, "Look, I need a cup of coffee before we do anything because I'm just bleary-eyed here." I mean I was twenty-seven, twenty-eight years old and I didn't know what the hell was going on.

ROGER BERLIND:

We got Golsen out of bed and met in his office at like six in the morning to harangue him for hours. We told him the world was going to end. But he was just furious because he had been the last one in. He put in a big chunk of money and thought he had been misled. He also didn't think this deal was going to work. He thought he was going to get screwed twice and he wasn't going to stand for it.

JACK GOLSEN:

They came in and started [talking tough with me].

I said, "Just a minute. You're pouring salt on the wound. I'm the guy who's got the bitch, not you. You come in here and treat me like that? As far as I'm concerned you can leave right now."

Well, they backed off and changed their tune after that. Then they started to give me all sorts of reasons why I needed to do this.

MARSHALL COGAN:

Now Jack Golsen was a very smart man who happened to be Jewish and who also happened to feel that he had been deceived by the Hayden Stone establishment in Boston into putting his money in. This guy would rather have seen the firm collapse as a matter of principle. It was not money. Jack Golsen was not about money. He thought the white Anglo-Saxon Boston establishment had lied to him when he was putting his money in and now he wanted to stick it to them.

It was a very complicated issue. From about five in the morning until about quarter to ten I sat with Jack, at times with Roger, and then with Jack alone for hours. I got nowhere. By quarter of ten we'd had Felix Rohatyn talking to him on the phone, Bunny Lasker [chairman of the New York Stock Exchange] called him, H. R. Haldeman [President Richard Nixon's chief of staff] was on the phone. [Former Bear Stearns chairman] Ace Greenberg called Golsen because he was from Oklahoma. Huge pressure was being put on Jack. The president of the United States was putting pressure on.

JACK GOLSEN:

I got pressure from the guys at CBWL. I got pressure from the guys at Hayden Stone. I got pressure from Bunny Lasker, who was chairman of the exchange. They got President Nixon on the phone, but I refused to take the call. This was in the middle of the night, around three in the morning. They said, "We've got President Nixon here, he'd like to talk to you."

And I said, "I'm not going to talk to him." They were all in disbelief. I said, "If the president asks me to do something for the good of the country, how am I going to refuse? If I don't talk to him, I don't have to refuse him."

ROGER BERLIND:

Jack was getting a lot of pressure from Oklahoma interests. A guy named Bill Swisher, who was from Oklahoma, flew in from Canada, where he was shooting ducks, to talk to Jack Golsen. Bill Swisher was plugged into Oklahoma society and Jack Golsen was not. So Bill pulled Jack aside and said something about the social reality of his survivability in Oklahoma City if he didn't go along.

MARSHALL COGAN:

Fifteen minutes before the deadline I was on the phone with our attorney in New York, Ken Bialkin of Willkie Farr and Gallagher. I said, "Ken, I've tried everything. There's no deal. The collapse of Hayden Stone is going to happen." Now I also should make it clear that Cogan, Berlind, Weill and Levitt was in trouble too if the deal didn't go through. We needed their order flow desperately.

The net result of that was I *had* to have this deal. Jack Golsen came from Chelsea, Massachusetts. Chelsea is a part of Boston where the Jews from Russia emigrated. The reason I knew that was my grandparents lived there and every Sunday I would go with my mother and father to see my father's parents. So I knew the street that Jack Golsen was brought up on. I knew what Chelsea felt like and understood him.

I asked everybody to step out of the room except Jack and me. We went into the back room of his office and I said, "Now listen to me, Jack. You will be responsible for killing more Jews than Eichmann if you don't go along with this deal. You will do drastic harm to the legacy of Jews on Wall Street. I beseech you in the name of Judeo-Christian principles. Put aside your anger and think of a greater issue."

What I was saying was that Jack Golsen was a Jew and all of the partners at Cogan, Berlind, Weill and Levitt also were Jews. If he did not go forward on this transaction the Jews would be blamed for setting off a panic on Wall Street because one Jew would not go along with some other Jews. I was afraid of a wave of anti-Semitism like I'd never seen before. I was terrified of that more than anything else.

He shook my hand and said, "I appreciate what you said. Just, down the road, please help me out." I said I would do that on behalf of the company.

JACK GOLSEN:

Marshall made a big, big speech, and I have to say that had a major effect on me. Because you know how the Jewish people never want to be responsible for anything bad happening in this country. This country's been good to us, and I kind of felt that. That alone probably would have been enough for me once I believed that this was going to be a disaster.

ROGER BERLIND:

At five minutes to ten Jack Golsen capitulated and signed the deal. I had an open line to Sandy back in New York and said, "We got him." CBWL–Hayden Stone was born. The news was transferred to the floor of the exchange, and when the man on the balcony said, "Henceforth all trades in Hayden Stone will be designated CBWL–Hayden Stone," an enormous roar went up from the floor. The crisis was averted and few people knew how close the whole system came to collapsing. We were the heroes, at least for the day.

WICK SIMMONS:

There was a change in order we were going through. The old order had collapsed. And now the new order was coming in, looking at the wreckage, and trying to pick at the pieces and see what it could make work.

Wall Street wasn't out of the woods yet. Shortly after Hayden Stone was rescued the brokerage house Goodbody and Company fell into similar difficulties. This time the exchange turned to Merrill Lynch and its leader, Don Regan, to rescue the failing firm. Still, the pressures continued. Through the early 1970s, countless Wall Street partnerships went out of business or were bought at fire-sale prices before they collapsed. For the firms that did the acquiring, like CBWL and Merrill Lynch, there were real risks involved in bulking up their operations at this time because Wall Street was mired in a dismal bear market and nobody was sure that it was ever going to turn around. But these firms also knew that if there was a recovery, they would be sitting in the catbird seat.

CHAPTER 10

KISMET FUNDS

After the go-go years of the 1960s ended so abruptly, Wall Street entered a prolonged bear market that lasted throughout the 1970s and into the early 1980s. With interest rates climbing and the economy in a general state of morass, investors weren't exactly seeking out the hot mutual managers the way they were back in the heyday of the gunslingers like Jerry Tsai. For the mutual fund industry to thrive it was going to have to get creative. Desperate times call for desperate measures, and the 1970s were desperate times for mutual funds. So it's hardly surprising that two of the most significant innovations in the history of the fund industry — two products that today are the cornerstones of countless investment and savings portfolios — came during this period: the money-market mutual fund and the index fund.

JOE NOCERA (financial journalist and author):

Money-market funds are completely taken for granted today, but they were extremely important to Wall Street's development. To me, the money-market fund was the instrument that ultimately brought the middle class into the market. What happened was, economic conditions collided with government regulation in a way that made economic life in the country untenable for the middle class. The economic condition was inflation, which people in this country hadn't experienced on this scale in their lifetimes. The government regulations were the rules that covered banks and limited the interest rates they could pay their customers.

The government regulation of interest rates had existed for a long time; it was not new. Starting in the Depression, banks were limited in the amount of interest they could pay on a savings account. The idea was that people felt banks had gotten into trouble during the 1920s by paying too much in interest while competing for deposits. So the Federal Reserve established a rule — called Regulation Q, or Reg Q — that capped the interest rates banks could offer in savings accounts.

BRUCE BENT (chairman and cofounder of the Reserve Fund):

Regulation Q was designed to protect the banks from themselves.

JOE NOCERA:

From the 1950s through the 1960s, the interest rates paid by banks under Regulation Q rose from 3 percent to around 5 percent. Banks still were not allowed to pay interest on checking accounts. People had Christmas Clubs that didn't pay [market] interest rates. But as long as there was no inflation there weren't many complaints about Reg Q. People were completely content to earn 3 percent or 5 percent in a savings account if there was no inflation because at least they were making money on their money. The country really wasn't thinking in terms of the stock market and double-digit returns. People thought of their money in the bank purely as their savings; they wanted to save it and make a little interest on it.

Then inflation came along, accompanied by a gigantic rise in interest rates. Suddenly mortgages were 12 percent or 13 percent, inflation was climbing past 10 percent. Yet the money you had in the bank was still stuck at around 5 percent under Regulation Q. Something had to give. People who never had to think about interest rates or what was happening to their money in the bank suddenly realized that they were being screwed.

They were actually losing money by keeping their money in a bank because it wasn't keeping up with inflation.

So what were you supposed to do in this situation? Well, you could buy Treasury bills, bonds that gave you a market rate of interest, which was about 8 percent in 1970. And a lot of people did that at first. Believe it or not, in January 1970 people lined up outside Federal Reserve bank buildings around the country when the Fed was holding its T-bill auctions. They were waiting for a chance to buy a $1,000 T-bill. But the Fed governors started to worry about what having all these unseasoned investors holding government paper would do to the banking system. They also were concerned about their skyrocketing costs from processing the increased number of transactions. So what did the Fed do? It raised the minimum price of a T-bill from $1,000 to $10,000, effectively shutting out the middle class from this opportunity. And that's where money-market funds came in.

ROBERT POZEN (chairman of MFS Investment Management, former president of Fidelity Management and Research, and author of *The Mutual Fund Business*):

The fund industry really got pushed into money-market mutual funds because the seventies was such a lousy decade for stocks. Between 1968 and 1982, the stock market was flat. You'd had these great years in the sixties and then it just died. It was very hard to sell stock funds in the seventies. And there was a ceiling on how much banks could pay in interest on deposits. So when interest rates started to go to 10 percent, and the ceiling that banks could pay was 4 percent, it wasn't hard to see the compelling argument for the money fund. I don't think the mutual fund industry would've just decided to go compete with banks for assets. It was simply a response to the economic conditions of the time.

PETER LYNCH (former manager of Fidelity Magellan Fund):

The money-market fund liberated millions of former passbook savers from the captivity of banks once and for all. There ought to be a monument to Bruce Bent and Harry Brown, who dreamed up the money-market account and led the great exodus from the Scroogian thrifts [or savings and loan associations]. They started it all with the Reserve Fund in 1971.

BRUCE BENT:

Harry and I worked together at Teachers Insurance and Annuity Association. We both arrived together in September of 1963. He was the head of the department and I was the bottom of the department. I stayed there for a while, and then I went to work in the corporate finance department at Stone and Webster Securities. Brown stayed there for a while too, but he eventually left, or they wanted him to leave. He was not suited for the politics of that place. He was very outspoken.

So Harry called me and said that he thought we should start a firm together. That sounded like a good idea to me, and that's what we did. In March of 1968 we formed an investment bank. We named the firm Brown and Bent, and we had some success early on. We were doing corporate finance, mergers and acquisitions, things like that. But we came out at a bad time because the investment-banking business was drying up, not growing. Interest rates went through the roof. So we knew we had to do something different. The idea was, what could we do that would enable us to avoid going back to work for someone else?

That's when we noticed a huge aberration in the market. Under Regulation Q the banks were paying 5¼ percent and Treasury bills were trading at around 8 percent. We figured there had to be a way to get in the middle there and make some money. So we started looking at all the banking laws in the country, looking for a small old bank with a charter that wasn't subject to Regulation Q. Our idea was, if we could buy that charter we could take deposits, invest them in Treasury bills, and pay a market rate of interest. But for various reasons we weren't able to come up with a suitable bank charter. Then, in August 1969, while I was relaxing at my desk on the thirty-third floor of the J. C. Penney Building, I was hit by the masterstroke. I sat straight up, looked at Brown, and said, "Why not a mutual fund?"

He didn't think it was a great idea right away. He said, "I don't know anything about mutual funds." And I said, "I don't either, but I think this would work." I quickly sketched out my idea of a mutual fund that would invest in safe instruments like Treasury bills. It was so simple we had to pursue it. And that, my friend, is the birth of the money-market mutual fund. From there, all we had to do was a little research on mutual fund rules and how to put together a prospectus. But the main idea was already laid out in front of us. We decided to call our new creation the Reserve Fund.

JOE NOCERA:

Brown and Bent weren't the only ones who noticed this aberration in the marketplace. Across the country, a broker in Merrill Lynch's San Francisco office named James Benham was coming to the same conclusion that small investors were getting screwed by their banks. Without ever communicating with Brown or Bent he devised a fund that was almost identical in principle to the Reserve Fund, although Benham waited a year to file his idea for the Capital Preservation Fund with the Securities and Exchange Commission.

JAMES BENHAM (founder of the Capital Preservation Fund):

The average balance in a passbook savings account at the time was about $3,700. So it was obvious that they were shutting out the little guy on purpose. Meanwhile, I was a broker at Merrill. At that time, many people as part of a trade would, say, sell a couple hundred shares and have a few thousand dollars left over. So they'd buy T-bills and park the money in there. Well, now they had to have at least $10,000, so it left out a large segment of the population that could enjoy the rates that were there for people of more substantial means.

JOE NOCERA:

The money-market funds that Brown and Bent and Benham devised were designed to give people a market rate of interest without having to invest $10,000 in a T-bill. Under Brown and Bent's idea, called the Reserve Fund, a manager would invest a pool of money in a variety of low-risk instruments that earned unregulated market interest rates, like CDs, T-bills, and short-term corporate debt. Benham's Capital Preservation Fund was even simpler than the Reserve Fund; it bought only short-term Treasuries. But both were backhanded ways for the middle class to beat inflation. And the most alluring feature of these money-market funds was, they turned out to be so safe that they behaved like regular savings accounts, even though they paid a market rate of interest. So people didn't have to bend their minds or feel as if they were taking a tremendous risk to put their money into a money-market mutual fund. For much of the middle class it was just a natural leap.

So why didn't the Fed just outlaw money-market funds the same way they outlawed the $1,000 T-bill? Well, the truth is the funds were so blatantly designed to skirt federal regulations that they probably wouldn't have gotten off the ground if they hadn't come in below the government's radar screen. Benham purposely filled his prospectus for the Capital Preservation Fund with dozens of other investment possibilities to mislead regulators about what he planned to buy. If the Fed and the SEC had realized what he was doing the fund never would have been approved, or at least it would have been subjected to a $10,000 minimum because he was doing the exact same thing as the T-bill auctions. But by the time everybody woke up to what these funds really were, it was too late. The Fed would never say this exactly, but they couldn't kill something that was this popular.

BRUCE BENT:

We filed our prospectus for the Reserve Fund with the SEC in 1970, and they approved it in October 1971.

And then . . . well, nothing happened. We figured the world would beat a path to our door but we couldn't have been more wrong. When we first came up with the idea for the fund we actually saw it as more of an institutional tool, a way for corporate finance officers to earn a market rate of return on the spare funds their companies had sitting in savings accounts. That's where most companies kept their discretionary capital in those days, in a bank account earning practically no interest. Can you believe it? So we figured this would be perfect for them. We thought CFOs would fall all over themselves to get to us because now they could earn a market interest rate. But it didn't happen. In most cases we couldn't get in to see the CFOs, and when we did they wouldn't listen to us. We'd give our little spiel and the guy would say, "Yeah, that's nice. But we have a long-standing relationship with Chemical or Chase or some other bank, so we're not interested."

Then we turned to the brokerage industry. At that time most brokerage houses kept their customers' spare cash in what they called "free credit balances," which didn't pay interest. We thought our fund would be a tremendous service to the brokerage industry because their customers could earn interest if their free credit balances were placed in a money-market fund. That's how they do it today. But back then? Well, the securities firms didn't want to hear from us because they were too busy using their customers' free credit balances as trading capital for the firms' accounts. That's right — Wall Street didn't want to tell its customers that they could make money on their balances because it was too busy making money for itself. So I guess we shouldn't have been surprised when the brokers were about as excited to see us as the CFOs had been.

By 1973, things didn't look good for us. We were in trouble. I remember we were so poor that all we could afford to eat for lunch were hot dogs from this guy who had a cart on our corner. I used to joke that we should invest in the hot-dog guy because he seemed to have a business that was thriving. The truth is, we were actually thinking about selling a significant piece of our business just to keep ourselves afloat. And that's when we got our miracle, in the form of a story in the *New York Times*. I can't remember the exact date, but in early 1973 the *Times* ran a long article in its Sunday business section about this new cash-management vehicle that was a good way to earn interest on your surplus assets. The story was all about money-market funds.

The morning after that article ran our phone was ringing off the hook. By the end of February 1973 we had about $2 million in assets; by the end of the year we were up to $100 million. And we never had to sell that piece of the company.

JAMES BENHAM:

One interesting aspect of the success of money-market funds is that the banks really helped us to educate the public about these things. The banks could smell the competition from the money-market funds, particularly after Fidelity introduced the FDIT, which enabled you to write a check against your money-market mutual fund. At that point, the fund really started to look like a bank product, and it scared the banks. They were going to have to compete. So what they did was, they created these things called "money market" accounts. Basically, they paid money-market interest rates based on Monday's T-bill auction and put it in a CD. They paid you the T-bill rate on a CD they issued. But the key for us was, they called it a money-market account. From that point on, the term "money market" was legitimized. It became a household word. The business just grew and grew from there.

HENRY KAUFMAN (economist and former director of research at Salomon Brothers):

It should be noted that the success of money-market funds is one of those accidents of history where timing was at least as important as innovation. It was the period of sustained high inflation and interest rates beginning in the early 1970s that established an environment conducive to the creation of the money-market fund. If interest rates had returned to historic levels, there's a good chance that these investment vehicles might have slipped away without much notice. But when you look at the economic conditions of the 1970s, they were almost assured to succeed.

The other great innovation in the fund industry that came to life in the 1970s was the index fund. It too has its roots in the aftermath of the go-go years. Jack Bogle had been chairman of Wellington Management in the 1960s, when he merged with an investment company from Boston that specialized in go-go investing. But as the market turned sour in the 1970s, a dispute developed between the group of directors from Boston and the original Wellington directors in Pennsylvania. Eventually the Boston group won out, ousting Bogle from the chairmanship in 1974. But Bogle didn't go quietly, offering to buy out Wellington's mutual funds business rather than step down. Bogle put up a convincing fight, and as a result of his refusal to quit the business the index fund was born.

JACK BOGLE (founder of Vanguard Group, president of Bogle Markets Research Center, and former chairman of Wellington Management):

After they fired me I wanted to buy out Wellington Management Company, which was the part of the business that operated Wellington's funds business. We could've done it for about $10 million, and I think there was some interest in the idea. But it became highly politicized and in the end the directors didn't have the guts to do it. Instead, they went with another one of my ideas.

What they did was hire me as chairman of the funds, and allow me to hire an administrative staff. Then they did a sort of Solomonic "cut the baby in half" thing. They created a separate company, called Vanguard, out of Wellington. Wellington remained our investment manager and distributor because by charter, we, Vanguard, were not allowed to engage in investment management or distribution. Basically, Vanguard could only administer mutual funds. And it was out of this arrangement that I came up with the idea for the index fund.

The germ of the idea for index funds was in my thesis at Princeton, which was about mutual funds. In 1951, in that ancient thesis, I wrote, "Mutual funds can make no claims of superiority over the market averages." I didn't do an exhaustive statistical test, just looked at a dozen or so funds, but it was quite clear that beating the market wasn't something this industry was about to do. And then I saw the struggle we had at Wellington. I was on the investment committee and was part of the investment process. I realized how hard it was to beat the market, beat your competitors. It's a hard business. When I did the merger in 1966 I threw all that to the wind and believed that there were durably good managers for a lifetime. That was wrong. So at least I can claim that I learned something from experience.

GUS SAUTER (chief investment officer of Vanguard):

The concept of indexing really came about from the idea that active management, in aggregate, is going to underperform the market. That isn't to say that some managers might do better than the market, but on average they won't. So with that in mind, investors should try to get market performance and keep their costs to a minimum. The idea was you could significantly reduce the risk of an actively managed fund by simply investing in an index fund, settling for the market rate of return, and being satisfied that you're going to outperform 75 percent or so of the active managers, while also realizing that there will be active managers who outperform you. But really what you want to do is mitigate the risk of getting a subpar performance from an active manager.

JOHN NEFF (manager of the Windsor Fund for Wellington Management):

When you look at it, if you don't know who to invest with, putting your money in a low-cost index fund and looking for market performance isn't such a bad idea.

JACK BOGLE:

The very first thing I did once we got organized was statistical work comparing the results of the average fund out of the old Wiesenberger books, those manuals of investment companies that were so priceless, with the S&P 500 index. I went over page after page after page, added them all up and divided by the number of funds — this was very complex math we're talking about here — and figured out the average performance of an equity fund over the past twenty-five years. Then I compared it with Standard and Poor's S&P 500 index, and the S&P 500 won by about 1.5 percent per year. That was my entrée.

I wanted to get into investment management, but wasn't allowed to. And I wanted to get into distribution, but wasn't allowed to. So my idea was to get into investment management by creating a fund that didn't have any investment management — an index fund. The fund would hold the stocks that were in the S&P 500. Without an active manager I was not technically violating the charter, which said only that I was not allowed to engage in investment management. The directors gave me a hard time about it, but eventually they succumbed. We rolled out the Vanguard 500 on August 31, 1976. There wasn't a lot of fanfare, but at least we were on our way.

Like the money-market mutual funds before them, index funds were not a smashing success right out of the gate. Indeed, when Bogle first launched the Vanguard 500 fund in 1976 he couldn't even raise enough money to buy all 500 stocks. The stock market was in a prolonged slump and interest rates were at all-time highs, so there were few people looking to buy equity mutual funds. And with Vanguard's low-cost plan, there was little money for advertising and marketing. But as the seventies bear market gave way to the eighties bull market, Bogle's arguments for low-cost index funds would catch on with investors, and the popularity of index funds in general, and Vanguard's index funds in particular, would grow to levels that even Bogle never could have predicted. Eventually, the Vanguard 500 would become the biggest mutual fund in the world.

CHAPTER II

MAYDAY

One of the great ironies of Wall Street is that although it is the ultimate symbol of American free-market capitalism, from the moment of its inception it behaved like a cartel by fixing the rates traders could charge customers to do business on the New York Stock Exchange. For nearly two centuries the system worked fine — that is, until Mayday.

ROBERT BALDWIN (former Morgan Stanley chairman):

I came up with the term "Mayday" to describe what would happen when the New York Stock Exchange got rid of fixed commissions. I was undersecretary of the navy, and Mayday was the distress call that went out when ships were in trouble. "Mayday! Mayday!"

ROY SMITH (finance professor at New York University and former partner at Goldman Sachs):

Commissions had been fixed ever since the Buttonwood Agreement was signed, and it was partly done to keep people from undercutting each other. They wanted to have an orderly market where people could come, do business, and it would be done properly. What they found was that if everybody had the same commissions, all the business would flow through the exchange, and the volume of all that flow would enable it to become a more effective institution. That's why the fixed commissions were accepted widely. It was the same in every market in Europe and everywhere else. You couldn't have orderliness unless you took control of commissions.

CHARLES SCHWAB (founder of Charles Schwab and Company):

Price-fixing actually was very prevalent in our history as a country. And they managed to keep fixed commissions on the exchange for nearly two hundred years.

JOE NOCERA (financial journalist and author):

Of course, the cost of the commissions had gone up over the years — by 1970 they averaged about forty cents a share — but they always were fixed. And although the membership of the New York Stock Exchange had expanded to more than fourteen hundred by the early 1970s, it still was a highly restricted place that granted incalculable benefits to its members. Stock-exchange members still gave each other preferential treatment and all stocks listed on the exchange could only be bought and sold through a member firm. But as the business of Wall Street expanded it was obvious that a logical arrangement from two hundred years ago no longer made any sense. And nobody was screaming that louder than Don Regan at Merrill Lynch.

DONALD REGAN (former Merrill Lynch chairman):

I'd use this example all the time back then: We were operating like a cartel. We were practicing capitalists, bragging about our free society and free trade and all that, but we wanted to fix commissions. I used to say it was like Carrie Nation being caught tippling in the basement.

DAVID KOMANSKY (former Merrill Lynch chairman):

The leader of the biggest brokerage firm on Wall Street, Don Regan, was the champion of negotiated commissions on Wall Street. Can you believe it? Most people, myself included, felt he'd lost his mind. I mean, having fixed commissions was a terrific business model. Why would we want to mess with it? If you sold 100 shares of something for $50 [in commissions] you could just multiply by 10 if you sold 1,000 shares, or by 100 if you sold 10,000 shares. There was no discounting, no negotiating. Fixed prices meant fixed prices for the entire Street; we couldn't give you a discount even if we wanted to. It was the greatest thing in the world.

DANIEL TULLY (former Merrill Lynch chairman):

Well, we all agreed with Don, if you know what I mean. He had a way of looking at you and letting you know that your opinion was heard but not necessarily listened to. You didn't want to mess with Don when he was on one of his crusades.

LARRY RAND (financial historian and cofounder of financial public relations firm Kekst and Company):

The whole business of Wall Street was set up around fixed commissions. You had scads of these firms called research boutiques that did nothing but provide in-depth research on companies and stocks. H. C. Wainwright, Clark and Dodge, Mitchell Hutchins, these guys all sold ideas and got commissions based on those ideas. And for the most part they're all out of business now. The research firms got paid from things called soft dollars, which wouldn't have even existed without fixed commissions. Soft dollars were charges built into the commissions for services such as research, securities clearing, and stuff like that. As a customer, you had these soft dollars covered in your cost structure.

Then you had the give-up. Give-ups worked like this: Say I'm a mutual fund manager and you're a Wall Street firm, and I'm going to give you an order for a million shares of AT&T. Well, I don't think that my commission rate should be as high as that of the little old lady who's buying 50 shares of AT&T. Since you want my business, you agree to give me back, or "give up," a percentage of the commission on my order. It's a rebate, an extremely thinly veiled way of negotiating the commission rate with a few select customers without directly changing the rate. And as a major customer I also could direct you to pay a portion of your commission to the research boutique or broker who gave me the investment idea. That was another type of give-up.

So if you take a look at the real cost structure it was almost like the way the airlines operate today. The retail customer, paying full price, pays a lot more for his seat than the wholesale customer, Liberty Travel for example, that buys blocks at a discount. On Wall Street, the institutions could buy on a discounted basis; they could force down the price per transaction. In very real terms, the cost per transaction for the little retail investor buying a few hundred shares here and there was substantially higher than the cost per transaction for the institutional guy. On Wall Street, the squeeze was on the little guy.

DONALD REGAN:

Most of the people on Wall Street didn't appreciate my position on Mayday. My ancestry often was questioned — I thought I knew who my mother and father were. There were lots of things said behind my back, but nobody would dare say anything to my face. Down deep in their hearts they knew I was right, but I was breaking up their ball game. Nobody likes to have his ball game interrupted. The nicest thing they said about me was I was a bully. They also said we wanted to get all the business, even though I would have settled for 98 percent.

ROY SMITH:

Merrill was prepared to be a renegade at all times. Merrill was always on the other side of whatever the issue was that the rest of the Street seemed to agree on. Merrill didn't make it easy for anyone else. They had the idea that they were going to be the big winners because they were the volume players.

PETER LOW (member of the New York Stock Exchange since 1963 and former floor broker):

You were used to charging a certain amount for your services and now it could conceivably go to zero. We didn't know what to make of that.

DONALD WEEDEN (chairman of institutional trading firm Weeden and Company):

At the SEC hearings on commission rates well before Mayday, in 1968, we were asked if we thought fixed commissions were necessary for the vitality of the industry. We said that there was no reason for it. The industry will survive, the brokers will survive, and New York will survive. There aren't fixed commissions in the bond market or for preferred stocks, so why should there be for the New York Stock Exchange?

As the institutional business became larger and the total volume went up, the fixed commission enabled the brokers to have an unusual profit margin because the cost of processing 1,000 shares certainly wasn't 10 times the cost of processing 100 shares. So the institutions looked at this and decided that they would buy and sell stock in what we called the third market, which was off-exchange trading in listed stocks, so they could avoid going through the New York Stock Exchange. Or they would go to their broker and say that his commission was too large and that he should split the commission with other brokers for providing other services. So you began to have an undercutting of the fixed commissions through give-ups. And it was all because you had this monopoly pricing structure that was providing monopoly returns.

It was because of this that Bob Haack gave his famous and controversial speech at the New York Economic Club, saying that we have to do something about this. That was in '71 and that was the beginning of the end of the fixed commission structure.

ROBERT HAACK (former New York Stock Exchange president):

Toward the end of my tenure at the exchange, we began grappling with the issue of negotiated commission rates. In November 1970, I delivered a speech expressing my personal view that negotiated rates deserved a tryout. My basic thinking, which originally favored fixed commissions, was altered by the fact that the fixed commission schedule, in my judgment, was the root of many of our problems. First of all, there was no fixed commission schedule; it was fixed nominally. But you remember, this was the day of the give-up, the rebate. The commission dollar was being used for a lot of things other than compensating the executing firm. The firm that was giving away 40 or 50 or 60 percent of the commission was in effect negotiating a commission right there, because it was keeping only 40 or 50 percent. So the fixed-commission schedule was a myth.

CHARLES SCHWAB:

The little guy, the individual investor, has always had to pay the top price. He never got any kickbacks.

DONALD REGAN:

In October 1970 Bob Haack came to talk to me. This was his swan song; he was planning to leave the exchange soon and in November he was going to give what he figured would be his final speech to the Economic Club at the Waldorf. It was a big deal to him. So he said, "Don, I'm going to give this speech and want you to promise not to tell anyone what I'm about to tell you. I'm going to propose that the exchange go to competitive commissions."

I can't say I was surprised. I said, "You've finally seen the light of day, huh?" And he said, "Yes, and I know that you also have a speech to give in November and I don't want you to front-run me on this. I want this to be my announcement." Reluctantly, I said okay, and waited until two weeks after Haack's speech to give my first real talk on the topic. So Haack was able to get his headlines, which is what he wanted. But at that point I called in a bunch of my people and told them, "Here's how we're going to play it. Haack is going to gear up, so let's go for it."

ROBERT HAACK:

I was not for abolishing the thing overnight. The wording of that speech suggested that the exchange examine, analyze, and experiment with negotiated commission rates on large orders.

Still, all hell broke loose. My friend [former New York Stock Exchange chairman] Bunny Lasker was aghast. [Former PaineWebber chairman] Jim Davant was shocked. [Former Kidder Peabody chairman] Ralph DeNunzio was surprised. My good friend [former Morgan Stanley chairman] Bob Baldwin was mortified. On the other hand, there were a number of people who supported it. Don Regan supported it. [Former Salomon Brothers senior partner] Billy Salomon, some of the people at White Weld. So there was no 90 percent majority on either side. The Street was reasonably split.

JOE NOCERA:

By the time Haack gave his speech, the Justice Department had been after the exchange to reform for more than two years. Basically, Haack spouted the conventional wisdom of the folks who wanted change. But that doesn't mean people were happy about it.

MICHAEL LABRANCHE (chairman of LaBranche and Company):

There were people walking around down here on the floor of the exchange saying, "This is the end of our business."

ROBERT HAACK:

I said in the introduction to the speech that it was purely my point of view and I was not reflecting the position of the board of governors. There were some people who said I had no right to express a personal point of view. Well, I think that's hogwash. When they hired me to be president of the exchange, I don't think they, in the process, bought my silence for five years, my freedom of speech.

DONALD REGAN:

To me, Haack's speech meant that people were going to start to cut rates whether the exchange's leadership liked it or not. We'd already found this competition in block trading, where people were getting down to really cheap prices. It would eventually go to about a nickel a share because of the demand for the business. But the little guy wasn't trading in blocks and you couldn't compete for his business because commissions were fixed.

I could see that sooner or later somebody was going to figure out a way to get around this business and start charging less for the individual investor.

CHARLES SCHWAB:

Well, the SEC mandated a trial period for negotiated rates on small orders, $2,000 and below, and very large orders, $300,000 and above, in April of 1974. That's the wonderful New York Stock Exchange — "Try this for a while." There was a pretty big gap there, wouldn't you say?

So by all accounts it was a very successful trial. And of course from there they mandated across-the-board negotiation on all transactions in May of 1975.

DONALD MARRON (former PaineWebber chairman):

Some people thought Mayday would be the end of the business, but there were others who thought it would be a great nonevent. You know, they thought that commissions were high because they deserved to be high. That thinking turned out to be wrong; things changed dramatically.

PETER LOW:

Mayday caused dislocation and change, but the volume on the New York Stock Exchange exploded from there.

DONALD WEEDEN:

I was a founding investor in National Semiconductor in 1959 and came onto the board in 1962. So I've always watched what was happening in the semiconductor industry. There, there was a rule of thumb that prices of our chips would fall about 30 percent every year. You would ask, how can you survive? Well, it drove the industry to reduce costs. With prices falling and costs coming down, there was such a volume increase because of the attractiveness of these new chips in replacing the old ways of providing electronic services that the increases in volume more than made up for the falling price of each chip.

It occurred to me that this process could be applicable to our industry. I always felt that as the cost of going in and out of the market went down, the institutions and individual investors would increase their activity. And that's exactly what happened. It was kind of a mathematical reduction in commissions and a geometrical increase in volume. In the end it was to the betterment of the market.

DONALD MARRON:

Commissions came down right away and hundreds of firms that couldn't keep up went out of business within a few years. I remember the rates went down much faster than I thought they would. I thought that we had a system in place that would change, but that it would adjust gradually. Instead, the deep discounting came on much faster than I'd thought. All of a sudden you started hearing about guys like Charles Schwab, who ran this tiny, upstart discount-brokerage shop and didn't even show up on the radar screen before Mayday.

DONALD REGAN:

The pilings came undone much faster than I thought. I figured that over a period of five to seven years the discounts on commissions would hit rock bottom. But forces of competition ruled, and within two or three years they were down about as low as you could go.

CHARLES SCHWAB:

On May 1, 1975, which was the first official day of across-the-board deregulation of commissions, the *Wall Street Journal* had an article about this occurring and that Merrill Lynch's response was to increase commission rates by 10 percent. Of course, I was ecstatic about that. They had such market power and such wonderful arrogance that I thought they'd cut rates and try to put us out of business. But right there I thought, "This is the birth of a wonderful business." It was all about to unfold right before our eyes. Although I was a tiny company I could see that.

Why didn't they cut their rates? That's easy. It's called m-o-n-e-y. Why would they want to cut their existing revenues in half? It's the old story of the entrenched power against the new entrant. This was an economic decision on the part of Merrill Lynch.

So why did Merrill Lynch raise rates instead of lowering them when Mayday arrived? Although Regan never would admit it, it's pretty clear that his push for negotiated rates wasn't about his populist instinct after all. It was about Merrill's desire to be able to negotiate rates with the big institutions — the mutual funds and pension funds — that were controlling more and more of the trading on Wall Street.

But on another level Charles Schwab was right — there's no way Regan could've cut rates from an economic standpoint. At that point, Merrill Lynch was the dominant brokerage firm on Wall Street. Its 1974 revenues of $800 million were four times those of its next-largest competitor. It had an army of thousands of brokers, and ambitions to branch out into investment banking and trading. And the whole thing was based on how much commission income Merrill Lynch was generating. To slice commissions by 50 percent, which is what Charles Schwab was doing, would've been suicide for Merrill Lynch.

So Don Regan raised commission rates on Mayday, and in the process passed the baton to Charles Schwab as Main Street's new voice on Wall Street. As Joe Nocera put it in his book A Piece of the Action: *"At that moment it was Charles Schwab, not Donald Regan, who was poised to champion the causes Charlie Merrill had championed all his life. It was Schwab who picked up Merrill's old slogan about 'bringing Wall Street to Main Street,' and carried it into the modern age. Don Regan had known Charlie Merrill personally, had sipped brandy with the old man in Southampton, and had risen to run his old firm, something he did with tremendous vigor and no small amount of success. But he was not, in the end, Merrill's natural heir. Chuck Schwab was."*

CHAPTER 12

MAGELLAN FINDS ITS NAVIGATOR

Jerry Tsai left Fidelity in 1965, but under Ned Johnson's guidance, the firm continued to grow. And by adapting to the innovation of the money-market mutual fund in the 1970s, Fidelity in many ways actually was doing better than it ever had despite Wall Street being mired in a deep bear market. But one thing was missing from Fidelity's arsenal — the star fund manager. And that's where Peter Lynch came in.

Lynch was a research analyst at Fidelity, whose ties to the firm went back to his days as a teenager, when he caddied for Fidelity's president at a local country club. But by the mid-1970s Lynch was starting to get itchy for something more than just research. He wanted to run his own portfolio. Finally, Ned Johnson handed Lynch his dream, a tiny fund with some of the Johnson family money in it called Magellan. From here, Lynch charted a course that would lead Fidelity and the rest of the mutual fund industry into brave new waters.

PETER LYNCH (former manager of Fidelity Magellan Fund):

I was born in 1944 in Boston. When I was seven my father got cancer; he died when I was ten. He was pretty sick for about three years and my mother had to go out to work when I was fairly young. It's funny, my mother wound up being one of those people who bought Fidelity Capital Fund, Jerry Tsai's fund, very early on. Someone came around to the house selling it and she bought into it. Back then all these schoolteachers were selling mutual funds part-time, and she's one of those people who started putting a hundred bucks a month or something like that into one of them. I think she started with Capital Fund and then switched to Puritan Fund. I don't know if she knew who Jerry Tsai was, but the guy who was selling it did because I remember he told her about this Chinese fellow who was really smart.

Anyway, after my dad died I had to go to work, too. So in 1955, at age eleven, I started caddying at a nearby country club. Caddying as a kid was a great way to learn about the stock market. In the 1950s you had this great bull market, pretty close to the one we saw in the eighties, just a great decade. I caddied for all sorts of people, the president of Gillette, lots of doctors and lawyers, and D. George Sullivan, president of Fidelity. These were really successful guys. And they just seemed to talk about stocks all the time, constantly recommending stocks to each other. I'd try to remember the names of the stocks and then keep track of them in the paper. Invariably, after a month or so they'd be higher.

Obviously, we didn't have much money when I was growing up, certainly not enough money for me to go away to college. So I went to Boston College and lived at home. I remember tuition was $1,000 and I had this Francis Ouimet Scholarship for needy caddies. The scholarship was named after a famous caddie who won the U.S. Open in 1913. It paid $300 a year, which meant I had to make up the difference. So I continued caddying. By now I was a good caddie, making more than enough money on the golf course to pay for school. And that's how I started looking at the market myself.

When I was a sophomore in college I scraped together enough money to buy 100 shares of Flying Tiger Airlines. I'd done some work on the airfreight industry and thought it was going to be a great growth story. Actually, it was all I'd talk about for a while there — airfreight, airfreight, airfreight. Flying Tiger was an $8 stock when I bought it and it went to $80. So I made money, but it turned out I was totally lucky because it had nothing to do with airfreight. What happened was the Vietnam War was going on and Flying Tiger wound up getting a contract to haul troops to Vietnam. So the stock went up for the wrong reason, just a lucky stock. Anyway, I remember selling it in 1965 and paying for a good chunk of my graduate school at Wharton in Philadelphia. I had to go away to go to Wharton, which wasn't an easy decision. In the end I figured it was such a strong program that it was worth the gamble. I won a Shell Fellowship for my graduate work and Wharton gave me some additional money as well, but I still had to pay. I worked two jobs at Wharton, as a busboy and a waiter.

In 1966 my caddying experience came in very handy in an unexpected way — it landed me a job at Fidelity. Before my first year at Wharton I interviewed for an internship at Fidelity that would take place the following summer. I'll never forget those interviews — I met everybody, Mr. Johnson, Ned Johnson, Jerry Tsai. At Fidelity they take hiring very seriously, even for interns. There were something like seventy-five applicants for three spots, not great odds. But I had caddied for the president of the company, Mr. Sullivan, for nine years, so I got one of those spots. I remember when the three of us interns reported for work in the summer of 1966 they set us up in Jerry Tsai's old office, because he'd left in late 1965 to go start the Manhattan Fund. It's kind of eerie when I think about it now.

That summer I covered the paper industry, the chemical industry, and the publishing industry. The airlines were on strike for some reason, so I had to go visit companies in Ohio and Pennsylvania by bus. I saw Champion Paper and International Textbook. There were four or five companies that I had to catch a bus and go visit. I absolutely loved it, getting paid to research stocks. I knew this was what I wanted to do. That was it for me — I never took another job interview.

From 1967 to 1969 I was an army lieutenant, eleven months in El

Paso, Texas, and thirteen months in Korea. Luckily, I never had to see Vietnam. So, there I was, making money with no bills to pay. And I was living in Texas or Korea, so I didn't have anywhere to spend it. That's when I figured I could invest a little bit. It was hard because you couldn't make that many telephone calls. I needed Carolyn, my wife — we were married in 1968 — to make all the calls to my broker for me. Every time I wanted to do something I'd have to call home to Carolyn and hope she was there. It was a fortune to call and you'd have to drive a hundred miles to where there was a telephone you could use. This was before the Internet and 800 numbers and all that. I owned five or six oddball stocks; I remember Ranger Oil was one. Every week Carolyn would call my broker and find out what the prices were. Then I'd figure out what to do. I have to laugh about this because earlier today I noticed in the paper that somebody was doing a buyout of Ranger Oil. That brings back memories. It's thirty-three years later and it's probably the same price I paid for it.

Anyway, I made it through the army in one piece and when I got back to Boston in 1969 Fidelity offered me a job. I took it right away — that wasn't what most people I knew were doing. I had these friends who went out to San Francisco on interviews, but not because they were interested in the companies. They just wanted the free trips to California. If somebody was going to fly them out to someplace nice, wine and dine them, tell them how wonderful they were, they were there. Everybody was going on these trips. But I didn't want to do it. I had no interest. I knew I loved the stock market. I knew I loved Fidelity. There was no question where I was going to go.

I was hired as a research analyst to start. I assumed I'd run a fund at some point, but at first I just needed to learn. When you start here it's as if you know nothing. I came in, they gave me textiles, metals, mining, and chemicals, and I didn't know anything about them. I had to go see a company called American Metal Climax, AMAX, and I basically had no idea what I was talking about. Their major product was molybdenum and I thought it was pronounced moly-bee-dum. They got a kick out of that. I mean, I had no clue what it was, some chemical element. But you had to learn this stuff. When you go to Dow Chemical you have to learn about chlorine and caustic soda and bromine and magnesium, and where they get it all from. It's incredibly complicated, makes technology stocks look easy. But you just try to learn that and then figure out what makes companies get better or worse. Then from there you try to see whether the stock's cheap or expensive.

My first year at Fidelity I wasn't making much and the next year I got a $1,000 raise, so I still wasn't making much. After two years here, I was offered four times what I was making to go to New York for a Wall Street job. I would be an analyst in the same industry I was covering, exactly what I was doing here, but it was in New York for Loeb Rhoades. I was blown away. Obviously, I went and talked to them, but when I looked at it, it was just a lateral move for more money. I wouldn't be doing anything different. I decided to stay at Fidelity because I felt that eventually I'd be able to make my own decisions for my own fund, which is what I really wanted to do. It was the best move I never made.

Magellan Fund was sort of a closed in-house fund that had very few shareholders. Some of the Johnson family's money was in it — which was interesting (talk about pressure) — along with a few employees' and outside shareholders'. Ned originally ran the fund when it was formed in 1963. He wasn't running it anymore, but it was still closed to the public. I think Magellan had been a $6 million fund, but in 1976 they merged it with Essex Fund to make a $20 million fund. Then, a year later, I took it over — and I was ready to roll.

CHAPTER 13

THE THUNDERING HERD

By the mid-1970s, Merrill Lynch had reached a dominant position in the brokerage business. But now Don Regan wanted to broaden the firm's scope. He envisioned Merrill Lynch as a specialized bank and securities broker that catered to the financial needs of wealthy individuals. The trouble was, Glass-Steagall banking rules passed during the Great Depression in the 1930s, which separated commercial banks from the investment banks on Wall Street, prevented Merrill Lynch from overtly operating like Chase Manhattan or Citibank by offering its customers checking and savings accounts and other similar products. No matter what the firm did, its clients still needed to have a bank account.

And that's where the Cash Management Account, or CMA, came in. Unveiled in 1977, the CMA was a bank account wrapped in a brokerage account. Through a creative maneuver, Merrill Lynch found a way to offer its customers something that seemed to be a bank account but didn't violate the basic rules as outlined under Glass-Steagall. With Merrill's Cash Management Account, customers could put their money in a variety of securities and mutual funds, and the dividends and interest payments automatically would be swept into a money-market mutual fund earning interest rates much higher than what banks legally could pay under Regulation Q, which held savings accounts at about 5 percent at that time. For managing the CMA, Merrill Lynch would take a fee based on a percentage of the assets held in the account. In time, the CMA would change the way individuals interacted with Wall Street, and help Merrill Lynch grow to a size unimaginable in Charlie Merrill's wildest dreams.

DONALD REGAN (former Merrill Lynch chairman):

I wanted to get into banking, and CMA was the way to do it. I could see that we couldn't be — I hate this term — "stock jockeys" anymore. You couldn't just buy and sell securities. That was not the way to go.

WINTHROP SMITH JR. (former head of international operations for Merrill Lynch and son of former Merrill Lynch chairman Winthrop Smith Sr.):

For many years people referred to us as "the thundering herd," but meant it as a pejorative term. It was coined by the competition to refer to us as this huge, unsophisticated mass of cattle — an army of brokers selling stocks to the middle class. It certainly wasn't meant as a compliment. Of course, over time we turned it around and co-opted the phrase for our own use.

ROGER BIRK (former Merrill Lynch chairman and president under Don Regan):

The whole CMA thing really grew out of our need for fees. The fact was, brokerage commissions were going to start falling. Don was way ahead of his time on that. We had big studies on Mayday, Merrill Lynch and Goldman Sachs, and I think that we figured they would be down something like 35 percent in the first year. But instead they were down 65 percent in the first year.

WINTHROP SMITH JR.:

Don didn't have the idea for CMA. The idea came from a group headed by Tom Chrystie that went out to Stanford University to do some research. Chrystie was our CFO and had started our whole investment-banking business. Out at Stanford they came up with three concepts for Merrill Lynch: CMA, financial planning, and real estate. CMA was the most intriguing of the group.

The idea behind the CMA was to consolidate client relationships by creating an account that allowed them to keep all their assets at Merrill Lynch. It would provide easy access by offering checking and a Visa card. In those days Merrill Lynch couldn't offer a checking account because of Glass-Steagall, so we created a vehicle that gave people something that looked like a check, smelled like a check, but wasn't a check. It was a draft issued by Bank One that did the same thing. And we had a Visa debit card that acted like a credit card but it automatically took the money out of your account. That was a dramatic change.

JOHN L. (LAUNNY) STEFFENS (former Merrill Lynch brokerage-operations chief):

We felt there was going to be a convergence of services so it made no sense to have a structure where the client went to one place to do banking, another place to buy securities, and a third place for insurance. Having a legal structure that mandated this made no sense, but that's what Glass-Steagall did. So having a program in place that could put some of these things together was an important development. At the time, the banks were restricted in the amount of interest they could pay under Regulation Q. That was to our advantage because we could pay a real money-market rate of return.

The driving force in financial services today is the reality that there's only twenty-four hours in a day. There isn't a person around who doesn't want to figure out how to simplify his life and spend as much time as he can on the things that he enjoys. That's where CMA comes in. It makes managing your finances much easier. It's convenient and it's time-saving. To some people that's extremely important.

DONALD REGAN:

I thought, "Oh boy, here's how I get into banking." It was like Willie Sutton all over again. You know, why do you rob banks? Because that's where the money is. I wanted us to be a bank because that's where the money was. And here was my way to do it. You have to understand that at that time banks basically had a monopoly. Everybody had their money in a bank. The banks knew this and they were really — I won't say cheating, but — taking advantage of their customers. Take checking accounts: they were charging for checking accounts. They were charging you to put your money in their bank. It was ridiculous. Savings accounts paid 2 percent or 3 percent and then they were turning around and loaning it out at 12 percent and 14 percent. It was fish in a barrel.

God, there was just oodles of money and they had a monopoly on it, protected by the government. If anything happened to a bank did it go out of business? No. The Federal Reserve ran right in and propped it up, aided by the treasury of the United States. That's why when I was secretary of the treasury I wanted to let Continental of Illinois fail. Paul Volcker, who was head of the Fed at the time, wouldn't allow it. I said, "Too bad. We should let the bastards fail." Why not? They're competitors, they're bankers. Banks should have a right to fail. Of course, you certainly should make sure all the customers get their money — they shouldn't suffer. But a bank should be allowed to fail, and the bank officers and stockholders should be the ones to suffer. It's just like any other industry.

DANIEL TULLY (former Merrill Lynch chairman and director of sales and marketing under Donald Regan):

What do the people with money really want? They wanted convenience, a fair return on their money, the ability to make investments, the ability to buy and sell stocks, and so on. But the banks controlled all the dough and the banks were paying maybe 5 percent on deposits while issuing loans at more than 10 percent. You could drive a truck through those spreads.

DAVID KOMANSKY (former Merrill Lynch chairman):

This wasn't greeted with great joy and glee by the banking establishment. We essentially had to go state by state to get the product approved. In most cases we were forced into litigation because the commercial banks fought us tooth and nail. It took a tremendous amount of time. I've been told that as a firm we invested over $100 million on the CMA from its inception until the account structure broke even. In those days $100 million was a hell of a lot of money.

ROGER BIRK:

I think people really thought the banks were going to get us. We had a truth squad to combat them. In most states the bankers' associations were trying to get the state legislatures to outlaw it. So we had this flying squad that would zip around the country, go to Oklahoma one day, Minnesota the next. They'd basically work and lobby. We had to go state by state, fighting our customers, the banks. The clincher was in Utah. They had this big debate in the legislature and it was going to be really close. We literally were counting the people on our side. Finally, a little tiny schoolteacher got up and said, "I hope you don't outlaw this CMA because if I didn't have this money-market fund I couldn't live." It was all over after that. From then on it was more or less downhill. But no other firm was willing to do this with us. I think they thought it would all just blow over and that would be that.

WINTHROP SMITH JR.:

The Merrill Lynch brokers didn't like it one bit. They were saying, "Now I'm going to have to deal with checking-account problems? I'm not going to earn a commission on the money-market fund attached to the account?" The brokers also were getting a lot of flack from the financial institutions in their hometowns. Every local banker went into the nearby Merrill Lynch branch and threatened to stop doing business with us. Legislators didn't like it at all. If you had taken a vote there would not have been one broker or manager and probably no more than a couple of executives who would have voted to go through with CMA. In fact, the first year we didn't open many CMA accounts. At our annual dinner Tom Chrystie was given the Golden Turd award for the worst new-product idea of the decade. But Don Regan said, we're going to do it. So we stuck with it.

ARTHUR ZEIKEL (former Merrill Lynch mutual-funds chief):

Without Regan CMA wouldn't have happened. I don't think anyone else would have had the domineering sense to stand against the crowd and listen to the executive committee argue against it. "This thing is losing money; it's going to bury us." The history of the firm demonstrates this. Regan went into a meeting where they told him, "Don, we're going to get killed on this one." And Regan said, "There's only one way we'll get rid of CMA — over my dead body." You have to think of this mind-set that says, "Get it done." Regan had a real domineering presence. To a certain extent some executives, not all, were totally intimidated by him. There was almost a reluctance to go into his office simply because of him. I never found him to be that way. I thought he was like a beautiful Hollywood star sitting home on Saturday night because everybody was afraid to call for a date. My attitude was, "Go in and talk to him."

ROGER BIRK:

I don't want to say this wrong, but some people don't like conflict. Now I won't say that Don Regan likes conflict, but he's pretty close to welcoming it. And that's because he does well in conflict. He'll debate you until it's over. Annual meetings, most people hate them, but Don was prepared for them. I remember one time Don had a bout with Ménière's disease [a violent balance disorder] right before a meeting, and he basically had to crawl out of the bathroom. So I said I'd do it for him. But he wouldn't hear of it. He got up there, hung on to the podium, and got through it.

[Shareholder activist] Evelyn Y. Davis was at every meeting we had; that never bothered Don. "You're going to take me on, take me on. Let's go." I'm not saying this negatively, that's the way he was. Don was in the camp where the thinking was, "You want to attack me, fine. Bring it on." Marine Corps colonel, Harvard, quick, smart, good-looking guy, he knew he could handle himself. And he was ideal for us because he didn't give a damn about the rest of Wall Street. He was not part of the club, okay?

DONALD REGAN:

We decided to press ahead with it and selected some test cities. I appointed a committee under Ross Kenzie — John Fitzgerald was on it with quite a few others. I said, "Okay, you're a shadow committee. Observe this for a year and then come back and tell me what you think. Are we doing the right thing or not?"

So a year later they came in and we hacked it around in the conference room at Liberty Plaza. The majority of the committee was negative on it. The guys who had done work on it, like Paul Stein and a few others, said it had real possibilities. But the others said it was going to be a heartbreaker to get it through banking regulations in forty-nine other states. And there was that argument of, is this going to distract us from what we do best? The consensus was to drop it and concentrate on Europe or Asia or investment banking or trading or whatever else.

Now, the whole time I was more or less silent, though I'm never completely silent. I asked a few questions and tried to think the whole thing through. My instinct kept telling me, "No. They're wrong. This is it, don't lose it." Finally, after a long conversation I said, "You guys want to take a vote among yourselves or are you unanimous?" They murmured that the majority was against it. So I said, "Okay. I can see you're all against it. I'm for it, so we're going to do it." That's the rule. I had the scepter; I was the king. Throw me out if you will, and you can have your way. But as long as I'm here we're going to do it my way. And we did it.

DAVID KOMANSKY:

It took a long time, much longer than you would expect, for our sales force to embrace the concept. People were concerned that if something went wrong they would lose their customers. Basically, they felt that this was what a bank should do and now they might lose all their referrals from the local bank.

It took a while for people to understand what the account would mean. It probably took five years before it was widely accepted in the sales force. By that time I was managing the Manhasset, New York, office, and I remember how difficult it was to get my guys to accept it. We would run all kinds of sales-incentive programs and recognition programs around the CMA, anything to motivate them to really get behind the program. Once they exposed it to the clients they loved it. From the day I opened a CMA

I've never set foot in a bank. My wife has a checking account at a local commercial bank that she uses to pay bills, but that's it. I think there are millions of stories like this. But the challenge was getting these guys to tell their clients about it.

DANIEL TULLY:

Three or four years after we developed CMA it's amazing how many financial consultants said it was their idea. You want to talk about success having many fathers; you'll find five to ten people who take credit for CMA. But there's only one who deserves it, Don Regan — and maybe a few of us.

WILLIAM SCHREYER (former Merrill Lynch chairman):

I think the thing that may have surprised everyone was that people thought the CMA would replace what people did at the bank. But we found that most people used the CMA for their "serious" money, money they were saving — their kids' college fund and things like that. They did not want to use it for frivolous spending.

ROGER BIRK:

What's amazing is that nobody duplicated it for three years. To this day I don't understand it. So our guys just fanned out with it. Citibank finally had to develop a product similar to it, and they took out full-page ads in the *New York Times* and the *Wall Street Journal* forever, but they only got about two hundred accounts out of it. So it was a great product, but you still had to take people by the hand and say, "Here's how it works." It was the most tremendous sales tool, door-opener we'd ever had. And once the customers had it, they didn't leave. All their records, all their tax-planning documents, were with us, so they just stayed. It was wonderful.

WILLIAM SCHREYER:

Part of the strategy that followed CMA was this idea that we were not out there selling a stock or a bond to the customer. We were gathering assets, to use today's terminology. If you gathered all these assets and built up the size of the CMAs, the business would come naturally, whether it's an annuity product or a stock or a bond or anything else. It turned out that when customers found out how beautiful the monthly statement was and the service they were getting with this account they were more inclined to consolidate all their assets into it. In the old days people who invested in the stock market would have two or three different brokers handling their money just so they could get two or three more ideas. We were trying to take the customer from a mentality of simply trading stocks to managing assets, which is a more sensible way to handle your important money if you think about it.

Although it caught on slowly, as inflation and interest rates climbed in the late 1970s and early 1980s, the demand from investors for the CMA would build to a crescendo. More and more people were seeking the 15-percent returns in money-market funds, and the CMA seemed like a logical way to have that and a brokerage account at the same time. In 1979, Merrill Lynch brokers were adding three thousand new CMA accounts a week, and by the early 1980s that number would grow to six thousand. Indeed, the merger of Shearson and American Express in 1982 was in part driven by Shearson chairman Sandy Weill's desire to create a product to compete with the CMA. Today, it's something we take for granted. But if you think about it — if you have a brokerage account, it probably looks a lot like the CMA.

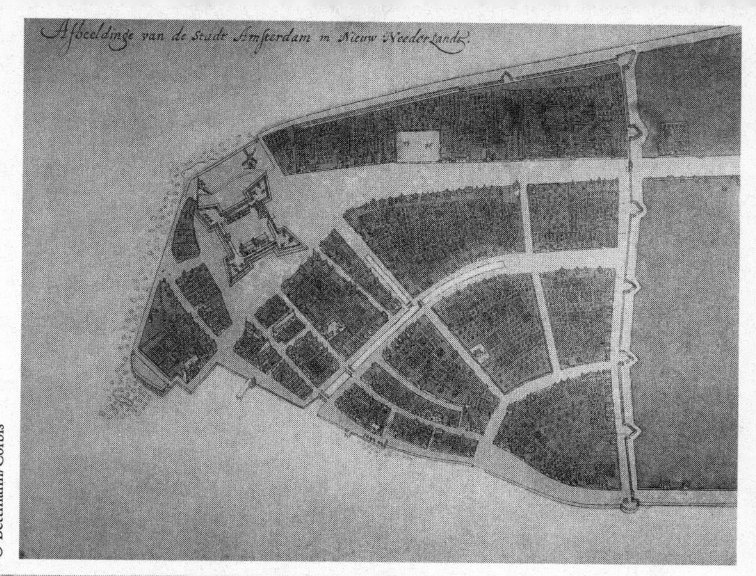

© Bettmann/Corbis

This map of New York in 1660, when the city still was under Dutch control, shows how Wall Street was flanked by a twelve-foot-high barrier designed to repel attacks from Indians and the British. But over time traders of stocks and bonds began to congregate alongside the barricade to conduct their affairs.

© Bettmann/Corbis

Traders in 1889 scurry about the old New York Stock Exchange trading floor at 10 Broad Street, just south of Wall Street. In 1903, the exchange moved down the block to a much larger space at 18 Broad Street. That trading floor still is in use today.

© Bettmann/Corbis

Panicked traders gather on Broad Street outside the New York Stock Exchange on October 24, 1929, the day of the great stock market crash. It would take Wall Street decades to recover from the sell-off. Note all the men wearing hats, as was the custom until the 1960s.

Photograph from the Merrill Lynch Archives

Charlie Merrill (left) and Win Smith (right) in 1950 plotting the future of Merrill Lynch on the terrace of Merrill's Sutton Place apartment. As Charlie Merrill's health failed he retreated from running the business full-time, leaving those responsibilities to Smith, his Mr. Inside. But Merrill's ideas and philosophies continued to permeate the firm, even long after he died in 1956.

(Opposite) Merrill Lynch advertised aggressively in search of customers, a practice considered "gauche" in most Wall Street circles. Still, this ad, which ran in 1948, was controversial even within Merrill Lynch. People said no one would read a 6,000-word treatise without any pictures. But they were wrong — it was an instant sensation, generated enormous amounts of new business for the firm, and is considered among the most influential advertisements in Wall Street history.

What everybody ought to know . . .

About This Stock And Bond Business

Some plain talk about a simple business that often sounds complicated.

WHY WE ARE PUBLISHING THIS INFORMATION

A little while ago we were talking with the editor of a big national magazine, a well-informed man. He said that he had never done business with a broker because he was afraid he wouldn't understand the "lingo they talk."

Since we are brokers, you can imagine that was something of a shock . . . made us think.

The financial business *does* use a lot of specialized words, but there really isn't anything complicated or mysterious about what those words *mean*. Because we've used them so long and so frequently, we've just assumed that everybody understood them.

That has been our mistake. And a big mistake. For if people don't understand what stocks and bonds are, they aren't likely to invest their money in them.

"So what?" you ask. Well, here's "what".

If people do not invest their funds in securities, American business and American government will not have the capital they need for growth — for new products, new plants, new jobs. That capital can come from just one place: People. Not just a few people with great fortunes — there aren't many of them any more—but from millions of people.

Or look at it from the social point of view. People who don't understand investments are easy prey for a wide variety of "get-rich-quick" artists.

Or look at it from the purely personal point of view. A lot of people might like to invest their surplus savings where they could earn a fair return on them. But if they are unfamiliar with securities, they aren't likely to invest their money in them.

For all these reasons, it is important that people should know as much as they can about this stock and bond business.

But where do you start?

Well, it would seem that a good place to start would be with the "lingo" that our friend the editor complained about. And we might as well go back to the most common words in the business. You may find a lot of this explanation pretty elementary. But the next fellow may not be wholly clear about the exact difference between a stock and a bond. So we'll start right there, in the belief that you'll be obliging enough to skip what you already know.

MERRILL LYNCH,
PIERCE, FENNER & BEANE

What Are Stocks?

The stock of a company represents the ownership of that company. If you own a share of stock in a company — let's call it the Typical Manufacturing Company — you own a piece of that company — a part of its plant, its production, a part of everything in that company. If the Typical Company has 1,000 shares of stock and you own 10 shares, you own one hundredth of the company, or 1% of it.

Some companies have only a few shares of stock and a few owners, while others — the big corporations like U. S. Steel and General Motors — have millions of shares of stock and hundreds of thousands of stockholders or owners.

Why Should Anybody Buy Stocks?

For the same reason that he might go into any other business for himself. To make money.

If you own 1% of the Typical Company, you own 1% of whatever it earns. Normally, some of those earnings or profits will be paid out to you and the other stockholders as dividends — so much on each share. The rest of the earnings will be put back into the business to do more work, make more earnings, more dividends.

How Big Are Dividends?

That depends on the company and how much it earns. Some companies pay out a substantial portion of their earnings as dividends. Other companies, particularly those that are expanding, may plow a greater proportion of earnings back into the business. Some companies pay no dividends. Of all the companies whose stocks are bought and sold on the New York Stock Exchange, about 90% are paying dividends. (That was the record last year.) The average dividend paid by these companies is a little better than 5% of what the stocks are selling at. Thus, if you bought one share of stock in each you could figure on making 5% on your money in a year. Some pay more. Some pay less.

Most companies try to pay dividends regularly. (The Pennsylvania Railroad has paid a dividend every year for more than a century.)

A company's board of directors decides what dividends will be paid and when. These directors are your representatives. You and the other stockholders elect them, each for a definite term. Ordinarily, you get one vote for every share of stock you own. The directors are the real heads of a company. The president and other officers are responsible to the directors for their management of the company.

What Do Stocks Cost?

The price of a stock, like the price of food or clothing, depends on how much other buyers are willing to pay for it, how cheaply those who own it are willing to sell. When a company first offers or "floats" its stock so that it can raise the money it needs to begin business, a specific price is set on that stock. But once the stock is traded in the market, its price is ***not fixed or pegged by anybody or any agency.*** It is determined by free and open bidding — by supply and demand.

That's why stock prices rise and fall constantly — sometimes rapidly. Some people who buy Typical Company stock do so not because they want to get the dividends that are paid on it but because they think the price of Typical stock will rise and that they will be able to sell it later at a profit. This is risky business for anyone who cannot afford to lose money, because the price of Typical stock may drop. Nobody ever knows for sure what's going to happen to the price of any stock.

What Are Preferred Stocks?

In addition to its common stock, some companies also have preferred stock, usually offered at $100 a share. This stock generally bears a set dividend rate, say of $4. Holders of preferred stock get those dividends before common stockholders get anything — that's one reason why it is called "preferred"—but if the company has a good year, preferred stockholders don't, as a rule, get anything more than the specified $4 dividend per share.

The stock is also called "preferred" because if the company is liquidated, holders of such stock get a first claim on whatever assets may be left after creditors' claims are satisfied. (Assets are property, such as plants or goods, that can be converted into money.)

Although preferred stocks differ widely in the *exact* terms of the preferred treatment which they provide owners, they always offer *some* preferences. Hence, the prices of preferred stock usually do not fluctuate as much as the prices of common stock over a given period.

Although preferred stockholders, like common stockholders, are part owners of the company, they often have no voice in management, no vote in electing directors.

What Are Bonds?

Bonds are a kind of promissory note. People who buy a company's bonds lend their money to that company, and the company agrees to pay them back at a set date, known as the maturity date. For the use of the money, the company generally agrees to pay a set rate of interest of, say, 3% per year. Bonds are usually backed by a mortgage on the company's property or by the general credit of the company.

Unlike stockholders, bondholders are *not* part owners of the company. They are *creditors* of the company.

Of course, as creditors their claims must be satisfied if the company goes broke, before stockholders — the owners — can divide so much as a dime's worth of the company's assets — if any.

Because bonds have this prior claim, they are regarded as the safest kind of security. That's why they appeal to conservative investors—widows, retired people, anyone who is willing to take a smaller return on his money, provided it's a surer one.

In times of economic uncertainty, bonds are always comparatively more attractive than stocks. Their prices do not fluctuate as much as stock prices, because they bear a fixed rate of interest and the element of risk is not as immediate a factor in the price.

Of course, the price of any bond is apt to be depressed, especially if there is any suspicion that the company is having a hard time.

In addition to corporate bonds, there are state, city, and government bonds. On state and city bonds, the revenue from taxes is frequently pledged as security for repayment. Back of U. S. Government bonds — the highest-grade investment there is — lies the integrity of the nation. Just that and nothing more, because nothing else is needed and nothing could add greater security. The integrity of the country is the standard of investment values.

State and city bonds are attractive to many investors, because the federal government does not tax the income from these bonds, as it does the income from company stocks and bonds or most U. S. Government bonds.

Bonds are usually issued in $1,000 units (sometimes $500), but as a matter of tradition they are usually quoted as though the price were a percentage of the face value. Thus, if a corporate bond is said to sell at 98½, it actually sells at $985.

Government bonds are quoted in 1/32nds. Thus a quote of 100.16 means 100 16/32 or in actual dollars, $1,005.

What Are Common Stocks Worth?

That depends on what people are willing to pay for them. And what they are willing to pay for a particular stock is largely determined by one factor — earnings. That includes what the company *has* earned (its past record), what it *is* earning (its present state of health), and what it *might* earn (its prospects for the future).

So you see it's not just a matter of figures. It's a matter of facts . . . knowledge . . . judgment. How aggressive is the company? How good is its management? How popular are its products? What part of earnings will have to be paid out as preferred stock dividends or bond interest? After all, these must be paid first, and what is available for common stockholders depends on how much is left.

Then you have to look outside the company and consider the whole industry in which it operates. Is its future bright? (The buggy industry once offered many good investments.) And what about competitors? Are they in better shape than your company? Might they take the market away from Typical Manufacturing?

Finally, you have to consider general business factors. For instance, will rising costs of labor and raw materials pinch your company?

These are just some of the questions to which the intelligent investor wants answers so that he can form a reliable opinion of what his stock is likely to be worth — *tomorrow.*

Investment values constantly change. That's why this firm has always urged stockholders to "Investigate — then Invest", and to keep on investigating afterwards.

Why Do Stock Prices Change?

At any given time, you may not agree with the price at which a particular stock is selling. You may think it is too high or too low.

There is a simple reason for that: What a stock is "worth" is a matter of personal opinion. But what it actually sells at is the sum total of a lot of individual judgments about it. The *price* of a security is nothing more than the collective expression of all the opinions of all the people who are buying or selling it.

If a number of people conclude at about the same time that a particular stock is overpriced, they may decide to sell it, and the price will probably fall. Or they may think it is selling at bargain prices and decide to buy it. Their combined orders may cause the price to rise.

That's why stock prices sometimes fluctuate sharply. Instead of changing by an eighth or a quarter of a point — which means an eighth or a quarter of a dollar — the price may change by several dollars, either up or down, in a short time.

Whenever there is a sharp price movement in either direction, it may pick up momentum and continue for a little while. That's because such a price movement is likely to attract other buyers or sellers.

For instance, if the price of Typical Manufacturing were suddenly to advance from $25 to $27 a share, others might notice the advance and quickly conclude that it was a good buy. So they might decide to buy it too, and that would lift the price still higher, perhaps to $28 or $29. At that point, some of those who originally bought Typical stock at, say, $25 might decide to take their profit of $3 or $4 a share and sell out. Then the price might start down again.

What Are Bull and Bear Markets?

Sometimes a great many people will decide more or less at the same time, perhaps just on the basis of the general business outlook, that it is a good idea to buy stocks—all kinds of stocks. Such general buying action raises the average price of all stocks. If the price rise is big enough and lasts long enough, we have what is called a bull market.

A bear market is just the opposite. The average price of all stocks drops because of widespread selling. To be bullish or bearish simply means to believe that stocks are going up or down.

Incidentally, it is a simple business to keep track of whether the market as a whole is moving up or down, because almost every major newspaper in the country publishes daily the average price of some group of key stocks and reports whether that average is moving up or down. The Dow Jones Averages are the best known of these indexes.

When Should You Buy or Sell Stocks?

Deciding when to buy or sell is often just as important as deciding what to buy or sell. This matter of timing is particularly important to the speculator.

But first, what is a speculator? And what useful purpose does he serve?

A speculator is a man who buys securities, expecting the price to rise so that he will make a profit on his purchase, usually in a short period of time. Or he may sell securities expecting the price to drop. The important point is that he doesn't buy securities as investments — for the sake of the dividends that they pay.

The speculator performs a valuable service in the stock market because he is willing to take risks — and risk, the risk of a sudden price change, is an inevitable part of any free market, whether it be a market for securities or foodstuffs or any other commodity.

Suppose you own stock in Typical Manufacturing, and suppose you want to sell that stock because you think the earnings outlook is bad. You might not be able to sell at anything like a fair price if it were not for a speculator and his willingness to assume the risk that you want to dispose of.

But no one should speculate unless he can afford to take risks. We've said that repeatedly in public advertisements and in counseling our customers. Nevertheless we are realistic enough to recognize the fact that there's enough desire for gain in even the most conservative investor so that he naturally wants to buy as low as he can and sell as high as he can. He doesn't want to lose an unnecessary dollar by an ill-timed purchase or sale. That's why we are always urging stockholders to make close and continuous study of the markets, for it is only through such study that one can reduce the risks in deciding *when* to buy or sell.

That point is especially important with respect to the *sale* of stock. If you own a stock which has risen to such a high price that you wouldn't consider buying it, it is only good sense that you at least consider selling it.

Too many people make the mistake of buying stocks, then putting them away and forgetting about them. That's bad business. If you want to invest successfully, you've got to pay attention to your securities and be always alert to new investment opportunities. What may have been a good buy last year or even last month may not be a good buy next year or next month.

Like everything else in this world, "securities are perishable."

How Are Stocks Traded?

There are thousands of different stocks and bonds — they are both called securities—but the ones that are bought and sold most frequently are those that are traded on the floor of the New York Stock Exchange. The securities of more than 1,100 major companies are "listed" on that Exchange, which means that they have been accepted for trading there.

All buying and selling on the Exchange is done between the hours of 10 A.M. and 3 P.M., New York time, Monday through Friday, and 10 A.M. to noon on Saturdays except in the summer.

What is the New York Stock Exchange? Physically, it is a large area, about two-thirds the size of a football field, in the Stock Exchange building at the corner of Wall and Broad Streets in New York City. Functionally, it is an organization consisting of 1,375 members who have bought memberships (commonly called "seats") on the Exchange.

Many of these members represent brokerage firms whose primary business is carrying out the orders of other people, the public generally, for the purchase or sale of securities. They are paid commissions for executing these orders for their customers. To provide service for investors throughout the country, these firms maintain many branch offices. All told, there are 609 member firms of the Stock Exchange that operate 936 branch offices in 370 cities. *This* firm alone has 98 offices in 96 cities.

What Is the Stock Exchange?

The Exchange is a voluntary association, as it has been since it was established 157 years ago, and it functions as an open auction market.

Before the Exchange agrees to list the securities of any company, it must be assured that the company is a substantial concern, that its securities are legally issued, that those securities are widely owned, and that the company agrees to issue regularly adequate public statements of its financial health.

Only member brokers can execute orders to buy or sell listed securities on the Exchange. If you give an order to someone who is not part of a New York Stock Exchange broker's organization, he turns that order over to a member broker. In such circumstance, you may be charged a small commission or service fee over and above the commission to the member broker.

What About Unlisted Stocks?

The New York Stock Exchange or "Big Board" is the biggest formal market for stocks and bonds, but there are thousands of security issues which aren't traded on that Exchange. Many are traded on the 24 other exchanges, such as the New York Curb Exchange, the Chicago Stock Exchange, or the Los Angeles Stock Exchange.

Still other stocks and bonds aren't listed on any exchange. These securities are called unlisted or off board securities; they are traded in what is popularly called the over-the-counter market. Government and municipal bonds are mainly traded in that market. So are the stocks of most banks and insurance companies, as well as the securities of many big corporations such as Time, Inc., Texas Eastern Transmission Corp., and the Weyerhaeuser Timber Co. By and large, however, unlisted securities are those of small companies that are apt to be better known locally than nationally.

They are bought and sold not only by many brokers who are members of the New York Stock Exchange but also by thousands of local security dealers.

Suppose a man in New York owns some stock in an Ohio machinery company and he wants to sell it. He doesn't know what it's worth because there is no regular market for that stock, and its price may not be published in the newspaper, as New York Stock Exchange prices are in many papers.

He goes to his broker, and the broker may ask for a price quotation by phone or wire from other brokers or security dealers who trade entirely in unlisted securities. He may find that the best bid for the stock is $23, while the lowest that anybody else is willing to sell it for is $25. If the stock is traded very frequently, the difference between bid and offer prices may be less. If it is almost unknown, the broker may have a hard time finding a market at any price. In this transaction, the broker acts as an agent and is paid a commission. However, in many over-the-counter transactions, the broker or dealer will buy the security himself, or he will sell such a security out of the supply of such stocks that he owns. In such trades, the dealer acts as a principal instead of as an agent, and the customer and the dealer agree on what is a fair ***net price,*** which includes a return to the dealer in place of a commission. In the end, the dealer may gain or lose on such transactions.

Merrill Lynch handles over-the-counter transactions either as a principal or an agent *as the customer chooses.* If a transaction is handled on a *commission* basis, it is the policy of this firm to charge commission rates that are even lower than those that now prevail on New York Stock Exchange transactions. If we handle such transactions on a *net* basis, we believe our price will be as low (if you're buying) or as high (if you're selling) as any you are likely to find. Further, we will trade only those stocks on a *net price* basis whose quality has been approved by our Research Division.

Who May Buy Stocks and Bonds?

Anybody — or perhaps we should say any honest and responsible citizen. For their own protection, brokers have to be sure about the responsibility of their customers because they accept oral orders to buy or sell. You'll find it a relatively simple matter to establish your reliability with a broker and to open an account.

Many potential investors haven't bought stocks and bonds simply because they don't know how to go about it. Some may have hesitated simply because they don't know a broker. They may even have thought of him as a somewhat unapproachable individual. He isn't. You can walk into any brokerage office in America without leave.

Finally, a lot of people probably have the idea that brokers only do business with people who invest thousands or tens of thousands of dollars at a time. Well, in our 98 offices we're proud to do business with people who talk in hundreds of dollars as well as people who deal in four and five figures. Last year, we found that 41% of our customers had incomes of less than $5,000 a year. At the other end of the scale were some who counted their income in hundreds of thousands. So you see, regardless of how big a customer you are, you'll always be welcome in any Merrill Lynch office.

But not everybody should buy stocks and bonds. We have consistently said that nobody should invest in the stock market unless he has savings sufficient to meet an emergency. And he should have insurance to protect his family. Then if he has surplus funds, he can probably invest them in stocks or bonds to his advantage.

You can tell your broker just as little or as much as you want to about your money problems, but whatever you tell him will be held in strict confidence.

Frankly, we hope you will want to tell us enough so that we can help you work out an investment program that will best fit your needs.

Does that mean that we will tell you how to invest your money? This is a point we want to make absolutely clear, for it involves a fundamental Merrill Lynch principle. Certainly, we'll try to help you if you want us to — if you *ask* for our advice and counsel. But we will not give you *unasked* advice; we will not foist our opinions or our recommendations upon you. What you buy or sell is your own business. We don't want to be accused of trying to make up your mind for you.

This firm spends about a million dollars a year in preparing and distributing to investors factual information about securities.

We'll give you all the facts and figures we have on any stock or bond you are interested in. There'll be no charge for them. We *want* you to have them — before you buy and *after* you buy. If you ask us, we'll even tell you how we think those facts and figures add up in terms of your own investment needs.

But in the end, the *decision is yours.* That's what we mean when we say

"Investigate . . . then Invest."

How to Buy and Sell Securities

How Do You Do Business with a Broker?

Here is what actually happens when a customer — let's call him Kenneth Smith — comes into our office, at 70 Pine Street to place an order for a hundred shares of Typical Manufacturing Company.

Mr. Smith goes directly to the desk of the man who regularly handles his business. (We'll call him John Ross.) Ross is registered with the New York Stock Exchange, which means that he is qualified as a man of good character and has passed an examination on the operation of the securities business. He is an employee of ours, with the title in our firm of "account executive." He's a man who thoroughly knows his business.

Smith might ask Ross for information about Typical Manufacturing from our Securities Research Division, and discuss the findings with him. But in this instance Smith has already checked on the company and knows that he wants to buy 100 shares of common stock. So he gets right down to business.

"What's Typical selling at now?" he asks.

If Typical Manufacturing were one of the major companies, Smith wouldn't have to ask, for he could look at the big electric quotation board which automatically shows the price at which the last previous sale was made. It also shows the high and low prices for the day and the closing price on the preceding day. The quote board in our 70 Pine Street office provides that information on 209 leading stocks, but Typical isn't among them.

"Sorry, I don't know the quote", says Ross, "but I'll let you know in a minute". Ross knows he can get that quote by a quick phone call, and the account executives in any of our 96 out-of-town offices can give equally good service by using the leased teletype wires that connect direct to our New York headquarters.

While Smith waits, he looks at the Trans Lux screen on which the ticker tape is projected to see if any sales of Typical are being reported right then. When a stock is sold on the Exchange floor, that transaction is reported on the tape. The price is shown and the number of shares involved in the sale. Because there are so many transactions, it is necessary to use a kind of shorthand, and the various stocks are referred to by initials or combinations of letters, such as C for Chrysler Corporation, CP for Canadian Pacific, and CGW for Chicago Great Western.

"Typical is quoted at 25 bid, 25¼ asked", says Ross in a minute or so. By that he means that $25 a share is the highest price that anyone is then willing to pay for it and that $25.25 is the lowest at which anyone is willing to sell it.

"Shall I place your order at the market?" he asks. A *market order* is one for immediate execution at the best price that prevails when the order reaches the floor of the Exchange, regardless of how the price may have changed — up or down a fraction of a point, sometimes more — in the interval between the time the order is placed and the time it can be filled.

Smith agrees. His order is immediately phoned over to one of our booths on the floor of the Exchange. There one of our floor brokers goes to the trading post at which Typical is bought or sold. There are 18 such posts on the floor of the Exchange, and at each of them a certain number of stocks are regularly traded.

At the trading post, our broker asks what the market is. Other brokers with orders to buy or sell Typical Manufacturing make their bids or offers in an audible voice. Secret transactions are not permitted on the Exchange floor.

Our broker immediately fills Smith's order at the lowest price at which the stock is offered, and Ross is advised by phone that the order has been filled.

The whole operation may have taken only two or three minutes. Smith may still be in the office. If he is, Ross will tell him that the purchase has been completed. If he is gone, Ross will telephone him.

As a matter of fact, most of our customers are apt to place their orders and handle all their business on the phone. Others do it wholly by mail. *It isn't necessary for a customer to come into the office at all to place an order.*

A customer can, if he wants, set the price that he is willing to pay. This is called a *limit order.* Smith might tell us, for instance, to buy Typical only if it could be bought at 24½. Further, he might say that any such order is good for a day, a week, a month, or indefinitely. Then if Typical is offered at 24½ within the time that Smith has set, his order to buy is executed, unless there are other similar orders on file that have precedence. Of course, the price of Typical might move right on up to 26 or 27. In such case, Smith would have lost his chance to buy at 25 or thereabouts. That's why any decision to buy that turns exclusively on the probable gain of a fraction of a point is apt not to be a good decision for most investors.

Limit orders can also be used in reverse — in selling stock. Thus, if Smith *owned* Typical, he might tell us to sell his stock for him, if we could, at 26.

How Big Does an Order Have to Be?

One hundred shares — a "round lot" — is the usual unit of trading on the New York Stock Exchange. But that doesn't mean that a customer can only buy or sell a hundred shares at a time. Many people want to buy only 5 or 10 or 25 shares at a time. These are called odd lots.

Suppose Smith wanted to buy only 10 shares of Typical. When we get that order we would fill it through an odd-lot dealer whose business it is to buy or sell in less than 100-share units. Such odd-lot dealers do business only with other brokers on the Stock Exchange floor, not with the public.

For rendering their service they charge one-eighth of a point or 12½c for every share of stock that they buy or sell to fill odd-lot orders for the customers of other brokers.

Apart from that extra eighth, odd-lot dealers don't charge any more for the stock that they sell than the price prevailing in the general market. On a 10-share order for Typical, Smith would pay that price which prevailed on the *next round-lot sale* after our broker gives Smith's order to the odd-lot dealer. Suppose the next sale was at 25. Smith would pay 25 per share, plus ⅛ for the odd-lot dealer, or 25⅛. If Smith were selling the stock, he would sell at 25, less ⅛ for the odd-lot dealer, or 24⅞.

What Does It Cost to Buy or Sell Stocks?

All transactions on the Stock Exchange are handled by member firms at reasonable commissions. The rates vary with the size of the order, being a little less proportionally on big orders than on small ones. At the present time, however, commissions on stock transactions average only 0.85 of 1%. On bonds the average commission is even less.

New York State and the federal government also levy transfer taxes on security sales or transfers, but these involve only a few pennies a share.

When Smith gets our bill the next day, it will state exactly what he bought, what price was paid, what commission is due, what postage or a tax, if any, is incurred, and what total amount is due. We do not make any charge for special services, such as research or information or carrying an inactive account or safe-keeping of securities, etc.

After Smith pays his bill — probably by check — he can obtain his stock certificate which shows that so many shares of Typical Manufacturing Co. have been registered in his name and that he is entitled to all rights, privileges, and dividends due stockholders in that company. But Smith, like an increasing number of our customers, may find it more convenient to leave the certificate in safe-keeping with us. That way he has protection against losing the certificate, and it is right here whenever the time comes that he wants to sell the stock. He will thus be relieved of the responsibility of personally delivering it at such time.

"WHAT'S THIS? . . . WHAT'S THAT?"

This isn't the *complete* story of how to buy stocks and bonds, of course. That would take volumes.

All we have tried to do here is set down answers to some of the most common questions that are asked us. And we have excluded a lot of things many people are curious about but that bear little relation to a program of prudent investment for *most* people.

For instance, there's "short selling", which simply means reversing the normal procedure — selling a stock first in the belief that it is overpriced, then buying it back at what you hope is a lower price.

Or maybe you'd like to know about buying "on margin", which means buying partly on credit.

In the main, these procedures are not important to the investor. But we'll be glad to tell you anything more you want to know.

Other market terms such as "rights", "ex-dividend", "stock splits", "debentures", "noncumulative preferred", "stop orders", and dozens of others we've had to omit simply for lack of space, but an understanding of them isn't likely to be important to most investors, except in occasional cases.

Again, for lack of space, we have not defined a whole host of financial terms that you are likely to encounter when you begin investigating various companies.

These terms are defined in a booklet, "How to Invest", which we have just published. A basic guidebook for all security owners, this new publication develops in greater detail the story of how this stock and bond business works. It reviews the basic principles of sound investing, such as the analysis of market trends, the diversification of holdings, and the management of a portfolio. We will be glad to send you a copy.

Copies of this advertisement in pamphlet form are available on request. No charge, no obligation. Just write or phone . . .

MERRILL LYNCH, PIERCE, FENNER & BEANE

Underwriters and Distributors of Investment Securities
Brokers in Securities and Commodities

10 Post Office Square
BOSTON 9

Telephone: HUbbard 2-5700

The former headquarters of Lehman Brothers at One William Street. The building, which also was the original home of the former Our Crowd firm J. & W. Seligman & Company, was built in eighteenth-century French style, but Bobbie Lehman had it remodeled to look like an Italian palazzo.

Milstein Division of U.S. History, Local History and Genealogy, The New York Public Library, Astor, Lenox and Tilden Foundations

Bobbie Lehman (right) sitting with Lehman Brothers partner John M. Hancock (left) in 1945. Although he wasn't considered a serious investment banker by his peers, Bobbie ran his firm "like a virtuoso piano player," collecting a wide array of competitive personalities and "playing them one against the other."

Time Life Pictures/Getty Images

© Bettmann/Corbis

Until 1943 women had never been allowed on the floor of the New York Stock Exchange. But during World War II women were called upon to do jobs traditionally held by men. Eighteen-year-old Helen Hanzelin was the first woman to work on the floor of the New York Stock Exchange.

© Bettmann/Corbis

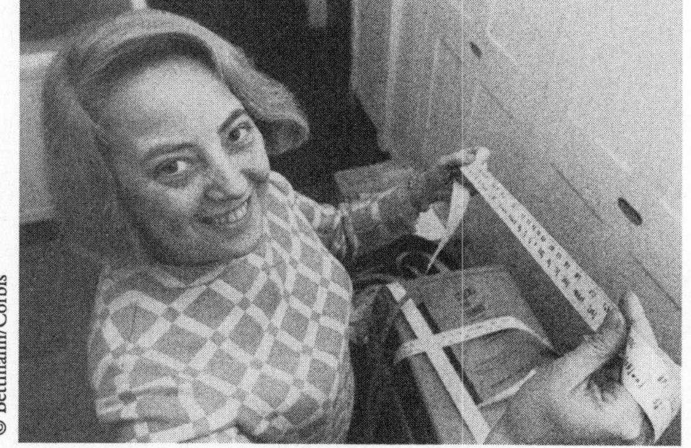

© Bettmann/Corbis

But women still were relegated to relatively menial jobs on Wall Street. Here a group of pages and quote girls gather at a trading post at the end of the workday in January 1944.

The New York Stock Exchange didn't get its first female member until it finally allowed Muriel "Mickie" Siebert to join in 1967.

© Omaha World-Herald

You couldn't get Warren Buffett to stop talking about stocks in the 1960s. When this picture was taken in 1966, the "Oracle of Omaha" still was running his partnership and still was bullish on the market. But by 1970 he was thinking differently. Just as the market was turning, he closed his partnership and kept one stock, Berkshire Hathaway, to be his investment vehicle.

A portrait of Jerry Tsai from 1966. As a Chinese man in a lily-white Wall Street world, Tsai stood out at the time. But it was his staggering returns as a mutual fund manager at Fidelity and the subsequent incredible popularity of his Manhattan Fund that made him a hero of the go-go 1960s — that is, until his flameout in 1968.

AP/Wide World Photos

Edward Hausner/The New York Times

Arthur Carter, Roger Berlind, and Sandy Weill (left to right), the brash, young founding partners of the brokerage house Carter, Berlind & Weill, pictured in 1968. Carter soon would push for changes in the firm, leading to his ouster and the emergence of two other partners: Arthur Levitt and Marshall Cogan.

Merrill Lynch Chairman Don Regan (left) and President Ned Ball (right) read the ticker tape as Merrill Lynch's stock symbol, MER, is listed for the first time in July 1971. Regan had wanted Merrill Lynch to be the first Wall Street firm to go public, but Donaldson, Lufkin & Jenrette beat him to the punch. "Those bastards stole my thunder!"

Photograph from the Merrill Lynch Archives

© Bettmann/Corbis

As trading increased, so did the amount of paper generated by Wall Street. Eventually the New York Stock Exchange was forced to shorten its trading hours and shut down for certain days just to keep up with all the extra paperwork.

By the late 1960s Wall Street's paperwork backlog had become a full-blown crisis. Stacks of stock certificates weren't getting delivered to the proper clients, and failed trades were becoming increasingly common. As a result, many of the old-line brokerage partnerships that refused to put money into computerized record-keeping systems were forced out of business.

Time Life Pictures/Getty Images

PART TWO

CHAPTER 14

HIGH-TECH MARKET

Throughout Wall Street's history the dominant, bellwether market has been the New York Stock Exchange. With its classic trading floor and august facade, the stock exchange is the image most people conjure when they hear the words "Wall Street." But in 1971 a new competitor to the New York Stock Exchange called the Nasdaq Stock Market was launched, and it was completely different from anything that had ever come before. Nasdaq was an electronic stock exchange. It had no trading floors or posts, just a bunch of brokers called market makers out in cyberspace repeatedly updating stock quotes on a computer screen. Nasdaq was very small at first. And it only traded over-the-counter stocks, the dregs of the equity markets, companies that couldn't meet the listing requirements of any stock exchange. So there was little reason for the New York Stock Exchange to take this upstart all that seriously.

GORDON MACKLIN (first president of the Nasdaq Stock Market and former chairman of Hambrecht and Quist):

When I started in the business there was no automated trading. The way quotes in over-the-counter stocks were disseminated in those days was each brokerage firm would write down the quotes of the companies they were trading, and somebody would come by, pick up the sheet of quotes and run it through a mimeograph machine, and then distribute it back out overnight to the brokers. So to the extent that the mimeograph machine can be considered automation, that was the rudimentary start of automated trading. But it worked. Every morning when you came to work there would be what we called the Pink Sheets. The problem was the Pink Sheets were gathered at different times, printed at different times, so the quotes were often old by the time you got them.

BERNIE MADOFF (founder and chairman of Bernard L. Madoff Investment Securities):

I started out in 1960 as a market-making firm, but that was before Nasdaq. So we'd make markets in the Pink Sheets. The Pink Sheets, which don't exist today in this form, was a set of sheets about the size of a legal pad that were actually printed on pink paper. It came out daily, published by the National Quotation Bureau. As a market maker, you would call the Pink Sheets every day and tell them what your quotes were in the stock, a bid and an ask. Then they'd list each stock with a group of market makers — there could be five or there could be twenty — and their quotes and their phone numbers. So people would call you up and say, "I want to buy this stock." By calling around to several market makers they'd try to get the best bid and ask, and they'd trade that way. It's not dissimilar from the way Nasdaq operates today.

GORDON MACKLIN:

Basically, the over-the-counter market was a joke. Just imagine trying to get best prices with that system. It was a joke. Nonetheless, it provided liquidity. What we really wanted to do was find a way to put this information on a real-time basis and make it available to everybody. It used to be that if my firm in Cleveland wanted to make a trade in a certain stock we would look at the Pink Sheets, find the stock, find the three brokers with the possible best prices, call up each one and try to make a trade. Usually if we did a trade like that it would be somebody from Cleveland trading with somebody from New York.

The National Association of Securities Dealers, NASD, was formed in 1938 under an act of Congress called the Maloney Act. At that time all the stock exchanges had their own regulatory systems, but nobody was watching trading that was going on off the exchanges in stocks that didn't meet the listing requirements of the New York Stock Exchange and the other stock exchanges around the country. So the assignment of the NASD was to regulate nonexchange-traded activity in the over-the-counter, or what we call the OTC, market.

NASD was a voluntary organization in that it was manned by volunteers from the industry at Merrill Lynch, McDonald and Company, or what have you. It was based in Washington largely because Congress wanted it to be located near the SEC. And, much like the Federal Reserve, the NASD divided the country into thirteen districts. I was living in Cleveland working for McDonald and Company at the time, and Cleveland was the power center of the Ohio and Kentucky area. So I was elected to a three-year term on the District Nine committee. The second year I was District Nine vice chairman, and the third year I was elected chairman. After that I went onto the NASD board for three years.

BERNIE MADOFF:

We were one of the firms that first asked the question, why couldn't you just automate the trading in the OTC market through the use of computers? By the 1960s the technology already was there for us to do it. You could develop a screen and be able to put up your quotation online, and it would be an automatically updating quotation as opposed to a quote that was just updated daily.

But there was a great deal of resistance from the industry to what we were proposing. The market makers didn't like it because it let everybody see what their quotes were. You had to show your hand, and they didn't want to do that. If somebody just called you up from the Pink Sheets, you could say the price was stale and give different quotes to different people. The system we were proposing would give prices a level of transparency. It was quite controversial. But we felt, as a small market-making firm, that this would level the playing field for us. So we pushed that concept, and I was not particularly popular with my competitors.

GORDON MACKLIN:

The whole history of the Nasdaq market is filled with fights. I was constantly butting heads with people as we tried to move this thing along. But I didn't care because I was convinced that this was the best thing for the market.

It was very expensive for investors to trade on the OTC market with the system we had, and it was impossible to keep track of price changes and actual transactions. The quotes in the Pink Sheets were old as soon as you got them, so you really couldn't tell exactly what the price was until you started calling around. And because of these inefficiencies, few people paid much attention to the smaller OTC stocks and it was difficult for them to build up price momentum. A lot of people started referring to the over-the-counter market as the "under-the-counter" market.

But that changed starting in 1963. The SEC published a special study on the conditions in the markets and made some recommendations for what should be done with the over-the-counter market. The key statement was: "There is on the horizon the likelihood of a computer system that would assemble all interdealer quotations and instantaneously determine and communicate best quotations for particular securities at any time. If such a system were established, the further possibility of using it in connection with executions and to compile actual price and volume data for over-the-counter transactions would exist."

Right there, you have the first description of what became the Nasdaq Stock Market.

ALFRED R. BERKELEY III (former president and vice chairman of Nasdaq):

You can't appreciate what Nasdaq did unless you understand Gordon Macklin and his philosophies. He was a man before his time and in many ways a visionary. He loved representing the little guy. He just hated the fake pseudoscientific elitism of the traditional markets and their exclusionary methods. He was all about inclusion. This was a profoundly radical idea in the formation of any stock exchange.

BERNIE MADOFF:

We were involved in the design of the Nasdaq technology. It wasn't genius, believe me. A lot of people give us credit for being these brilliant technologists, but the technology really was very basic. It was a matter of creativity, of taking the technology that already existed and applying it to Wall Street. And that had never been done before.

GORDON MACKLIN:

Bunker-Ramo agreed to build and operate a system for us under a five-year agreement. The system performed well, and they built a data center in Trumbull, Connecticut. The central processors were linked to a trader's desktop terminal with thousands of miles of telephone lines.

BERNIE MADOFF:

Bunker-Ramo built the system that we used to display the quotes, and there were five pilot firms that got involved in the development of an automated trading screen: us, Merrill, Allen and Company, Goldman Sachs, and Oppenheimer. We were in that mix, even at our size, because we were technologically oriented and we were pushing it. We were into automated trading and computer-type trading, so we were pushing that envelope. At that time the over-the-counter market was not controlled by the big wirehouses, like Merrill Lynch; it was controlled by people like us and some firms that no longer exist because they merged or went out of business. In those days, the Merrills didn't make markets in over-the-counter stocks. They relied upon going to wholesale dealers like me and other firms to get the business. So Merrill and the others looked at this as a great opportunity to compete with these wholesalers. And we, as a small wholesaler, looked at it as a way to get an equal footing.

MICHAEL BARONE (head of Nasdaq trading at William Blair and Company in Chicago):

Once it was possible for market makers to display their quotes and for other people to see them and interact with them, you had a market. It was rudimentary compared to what it's evolved into. But the basis of a market is seeing prices, and being able to buy and sell based on those prices. That's what the Bunker-Ramo machines allowed us to do.

BERNIE MADOFF:

We did a trial of that and it was successful. So the NASD said that if you want to be a market maker you have to display your quotes in this system. It was simply a matter of getting used to the technology and there we were.

GORDON MACKLIN:

After an appropriate warm-up period, the system came online on February 8, 1971.

BERNIE MADOFF:

Nasdaq was revolutionary because it was completely automated, whereas the floor of the New York Stock Exchange was a manual system. You could use technology to get an order to the floor, but once it hit the floor it still was a manual process with people running all over the floor to complete the order. Even though the exchange always says it has automation, picture it like a big funnel, where all the orders flow through a huge opening but when it gets down to the neck it's really tight.

The New York Stock Exchange is an auction-based specialist system; Nasdaq is a competing-dealer system. They're two completely different things. The dealer system has many different firms competing with each other to offer the best price and provide liquidity. It's used in currencies, commodities, government bonds — most things are done in a dealer environment, some of it manually, though today almost all dealer markets are automated. The way the auction system works is, you have one assigned broker on the floor of the exchange, known as a specialist, who is assigned to make a market in that stock. So if I'm the specialist in IBM, you have to come to me if you want to buy or sell IBM. The specialist is there basically as a traffic cop to match orders; he only steps in and provides liquidity when there isn't anyone on the other side of a trade.

MICHAEL BARONE:

In terms of the way we trade, Nasdaq essentially is the New York Stock Exchange except you have a bunch of competing specialists. That's the biggest difference; on Nasdaq you can have ten specialists or more bidding for your business. On the surface it looks as if there's a big difference, because Nasdaq's electronic and New York has a trading floor. But in terms of what you do it's really very similar.

ALFRED R. BERKELEY III:

Nasdaq was revolutionary because it provided transparency in pricing. That's at the heart of what the market wants to do. The difference between Nasdaq and the New York Stock Exchange is the Nasdaq market feeds on information. If someone posts a quote it's there for everyone to see. At the stock exchange you have specialists and the specialists' order book is opaque. How the federal government has allowed that opacity to exist in the market is beyond me.

BOB MCCOOEY (chief executive officer of New York Stock Exchange floor brokerage firm and trading house Griswold Company):

Something that I always try to keep in mind is that you always can buy a stock, but you can't always sell a stock. An example I use is the art market. Say pieces of art by a certain artist are hot and you buy one as an investment. Well, if you're willing to pay any price — $10 million, $20 million — you can just about guarantee that you can find someone who will sell it to you. But then say your situation changes and suddenly you have to sell the piece you bought. You don't know that somebody will be willing to pay $10 million for that painting. You don't know if there will be someone willing to buy the painting at all. Now at the New York Stock Exchange, there is someone who has to buy the stock from you, the specialist, because it's his job to add liquidity to the market. Obviously, the question is, at what price? But on the Nasdaq, if there are no market makers willing to bid, you're out of luck.

KENNETH PASTERNAK (founder and former chief executive officer of Knight/Trimark):

When you look at it historically, you have to look at Nasdaq really as the third exchange, with the first being New York and the second being the American Stock Exchange.

GORDON MACKLIN:

I think the people in New York just snickered at us at first. A lot of their companies did more volume in a day than the entire Nasdaq market. So there was a bit of arrogance on their part. The Amex [American Stock Exchange] was probably more affected by this. They used to be the second-biggest exchange in the country. Nasdaq came out in April 1971. In 1972, New York did about 5 billion shares of volume, Amex did 1.1 billion shares, and Nasdaq did 2.2 billion. And there it was out in print for everyone to see. The fact was that Nasdaq was by far the second biggest market. They couldn't deal with that. The first thing they did was to yell at the scorekeeper. They went to the SEC and complained that we reported our trades differently, but the SEC had already approved it. What they didn't want to face is that we had a better product.

MICHAEL BARONE:

Nasdaq was a market strictly for emerging companies, companies that couldn't come within even one-tenth of the NYSE's listing requirements. You had smaller retailers, franchisers, some fledgling tech stocks, some smaller telecom companies. In the early days, liquidity definitely was a problem in Nasdaq stocks. We had to commit a lot more capital just trying to keep some liquidity in the markets.

GORDON MACKLIN:

What we had was the miracle, but what we found out was, if we wanted to be a major player we had to make it more credible. One of the things we did was pass a rule that everyone who put up a quote on the system had to stand by that quote. And we had a series of upgrades to the regulatory operation to catch up to the exchange.

ALFRED R. BERKELEY III:

Gordon's philosophy was that disclosure was the key to the success of the market. Originally, there were no listing standards on Nasdaq. They would trade everything that was SEC registered — it was the OTC market. This allowed a respectable place to emerge where entrepreneurs could raise capital in a way they never could on traditional exchanges.

GORDON MACKLIN:

There is a not-so-coincidental tie between the growth of the high-tech industries and the popularity of Nasdaq. Part of the rationale is that on these old established exchanges you had to have earnings and assets in greater quantity than was really relevant to making the stocks more attractive. So these developing companies had us as the only option if they wanted to have a publicly traded stock. That helped us, without question. We had the market to ourselves for a long time.

DONALD WEEDEN (chairman of institutional trading firm Weeden and Company):

Nasdaq initially was set up in order to take care of the existing over-the-counter market, which in 1971 wasn't made up of very exciting companies. These were ones that didn't meet the listing requirements of the various exchanges, so many of them were riskier companies at more of a developmental stage.

But at about that time you had something else going on out in Silicon Valley and on other parts of the West Coast. A lot of new companies were being developed, none of which was making any money, but they were all exploring new areas of technology, and you could see the potential for real growth. They needed a lot of capital to do this work, so they went public, looking for investors who were excited about the future of computers and technology. Naturally, these companies ended up on Nasdaq since it was the only place at the time that would trade their securities. To this day, these companies remember that. Microsoft remembers that it didn't have a secondary market unless it went to Nasdaq. And so they have remained loyal.

ALFRED R. BERKELEY III:

Gordon made one decision that enabled so much of the advancement in the United States to happen, and he was criticized for it at the time. And that was to allow companies to become public without profits. It was a critical decision in the history of markets. Most people in his position would have said, "You can't list companies that don't have profits because they're speculative." But Gordon said, "It's not the market's job to decide what anyone invests in. It's your job to decide what you want to invest in."

LARRY SONSINI (chairman and chief executive officer of the law firm Wilson Sonsini Goodrich and Rosati and one of the leading legal advisers in Silicon Valley):

The phenomenon of taking early-stage enterprises public was primarily something that the New York Stock Exchange did not focus on. The requirements for listing on the stock exchange required more maturity from a company. So for these companies the only market that was available was the over-the-counter market, which with the growth of technology became Nasdaq. Through the evolution of Nasdaq it got identified with the technology industry.

GORDON MACKLIN:

We had a CEO in the Nasdaq market named Bill McGowan, the driving force behind MCI. I think God put Bill McGowan on earth to make life more pleasant, at least for me. He was so smart, instinctively smart, that it was as if he could see around corners. And he had more nerve than anyone I've ever met. He was raised in a freight yard and graduated from Harvard Business School. He was the perfect combination of a neighborhood tough guy and an absolutely brilliant executive. Big smiling Irishman — God, he was lovable.

Anyway, Bill would go around just ridiculing the idea of people selling stocks by going into a room and standing face-to-face yelling at each other. He couldn't understand why you'd want to do that when you could just as easily put it all together in a centralized electronic system. He'd say, "The

New York Stock Exchange? That's the way they sell fruits and vegetables in foreign countries." You see, there's no reason for everyone to be in the same room at the same time. Just feed your data in, and you could be on the West Coast, I could be on the East Coast, and we'd have the same instant communication as if we were in the same room yelling at each other.

MICHAEL BARONE:

Look at what companies like Microsoft were able to do because of Nasdaq. When Microsoft became public it wasn't a particularly big deal. But they came back to the market again and again for capital, and Nasdaq kept providing it for them. Today these are such solid companies — Microsoft, Intel, and all the others — and it all began on Nasdaq. The biggest reason for this was, the New York Stock Exchange listing requirements were much higher than anything these companies could bring to the table.

GORDON MACKLIN:

I had heard from a prominent venture-capital person that he had two companies he was deeply involved in and he put them both on Nasdaq because he felt the Nasdaq market was more liquid. More market makers to him meant more liquidity than just one market maker, like at the New York Stock Exchange. And then he brought down Gordon Moore of Intel and the chief financial officer of Apple. And Moore in particular saw right away how the Nasdaq market made sense.

ALFRED R. BERKELEY III:

Basically, you had a bunch of westerners, primarily Microsoft and Intel and Cisco and Qualcomm, and an easterner called MCI, who had a real rebel at the helm. And they said, "I don't buy your shtick, New York. I think what you're doing is a scam. I'd rather have this transparent, competitive market than a monopolist trade my stock."

What the New York Stock Exchange does is sell prestige. They say, "Be part of the Old Boys' club. Be part of the old establishment." This appeals to easterners; I'm an easterner and I can say this. A lot of people in the East care about where you went to school, and they're willing to claw their way up these old-line companies, and the last thing they want to have happen is to have to start over.

Well, on the West Coast these guys basically are serial entrepreneurs. They say, "Hey, if I screw this company up I'll start another one." And they don't buy the prestige according to what your daddy did. They're into meritocracy. That's the mistake New York made with these companies on the West Coast. The reason why so many companies have stayed loyal to Nasdaq over the years is New York tried to sell them something that they actually had an emotional disgust over. They think tradition and status have nothing to do with who your family is or what school you went to. They think it should be a by-product of a real measure of merit, like really good trades. And that's the most important thing a stock market can do, provide really good trades, right?

So when you look at it that way, nobody should be surprised at Nasdaq's success — though I think you might get a different reaction if you talked about it with the boys over at the stock exchange.

CHAPTER 15

HAVE YOUR CAKE AND EAT IT, TOO

The history of Wall Street is littered with attempts to find the keys to the kingdom, to unlock the magical vault that will make you rich beyond your wildest dreams. In the 1970s and 1980s, the vault was leveraged buyouts, and the keys belonged to the pioneering LBO firm Kohlberg Kravis Roberts and Company and its founding partners, Jerome Kohlberg, Henry Kravis, and George Roberts. In its simplest form, a leveraged buyout is using borrowed money to buy a company. The reason it was such a profitable enterprise in the 1970s is that the values of many companies were depressed from the grueling bear market that started in 1966. So if you were a savvy shopper you could snag some real bargains by putting up a little cash and borrowing the rest from banks, insurance companies, wealthy investors, and anyone else looking to get a better return on his capital than he would in the stock market. Do it well enough times, and you could become very rich.

By the end of the 1980s, KKR, as it came to be known, was one of the most powerful forces in corporate America, and its partners — who had neither the white-shoe nor Our Crowd ties that had dominated Wall Street in previous decades — were among the richest kids on the block. Sure, other companies did buyouts, firms like Forstmann Little and Company and Clayton and Dubilier, but none were as bold or as brash as KKR, the unquestioned kings of the jungle. Here's a statistic to give you an idea of what we're talking about: in 1989 the accounting firm Deloitte and Touche ranked its top clients. KKR was first. General Motors was second.

JEROME KOHLBERG (cofounder and former partner of Kohlberg Kravis Roberts and Company):

We'll put it this way: I am given credit for inventing the leveraged buyout, the LBO. But in fairness, people had used bank debt and other kinds of debt to buy companies before. They were originally called bootstrap deals, which referred to the fact that you were starting from scratch and buying the company with mirrors. You put in as little of your own money as possible. Guys like Charlie Allen and Herb Allen [of Allen and Company] had a nice private firm, and they did it a couple of times. Bear Stearns also did one or two.

The term "leveraged buyout" wasn't coined by me. I think it was the journalists who did that. But it had a less harsh connotation than bootstraps. Even so, this wasn't a highly regarded business. Gentlemen didn't do buyouts. When I started doing buyouts at Bear Stearns in the 1960s, the fact that you would borrow money to buy a company bothered people. Back then, buying anything with over 50 percent debt was ungentlemanly. Good, sound Wall Street people just didn't do that. But it was possible, and it was being done by a few guys.

GEORGE ROBERTS (cofounder and partner of Kohlberg Kravis Roberts and Company):

People have been borrowing to buy and sell companies since the Phoenicians invented money. The concept has always been there. I think our firm has pioneered the financing techniques that have been used to do it. To the extent that there's been creativity in this business — that's where it's come from. That's continuing to evolve. But I don't think that you can say one person invented the blueprint to do it because there never has been a blueprint. You're dealing with people and you're dealing with financial markets. This isn't a piece of machinery or equipment you're making. The concepts and kernels of knowledge were there, and we were able to craft and help develop markets to finance and do the transactions being done.

JEROME KOHLBERG:

Now this was the 1960s and I was at Bear Stearns. Bear Stearns was a trading firm, pure and simple. Cy Lewis was the head then, and Alan [Ace] Greenberg was his lieutenant and guardian. Cy was a trader. He loved to trade, and he was pretty good at it. He lost a lot of money, but he also made a lot of money. Alan, on the other hand, mostly made money. He knew you take your losses and ride your profits. That sort of attitude permeated the place — anything that you held longer than overnight was considered long-term.

I'd always watched Charlie Allen and wanted to be a merchant banker. Most people didn't know what a merchant banker was. But to me, it was somebody who put himself on the line, somebody who put his own money up and stood or fell along with everyone else who put up money. That's what the merchant bankers used to do in the old days. It was their money, J. P. Morgan and everybody else. Although J. P. also used other people's money quite successfully — the old "OPM."

Stern Metals was our first deal at Bear Stearns. I had known the family, the Stern family. They lived in Westchester and their plant was in Mount Vernon. I knew the sons slightly. Anyway, the old man, H. J. Stern, came to me because I guess he'd heard of me and knew that I worked on Wall Street. He was seventy-three at the time and wanted to plan his estate, which was all tied up in the business. He'd inherited it from his father, but he really didn't have confidence in his sons. He basically had a choice of either going public or selling out. So I suggested that he could retain part of the company, but that we would buy the rest of it. That way he could have his money for tax purposes and still run the company, which he did for a time. I put a group together and we proceeded to buy it. Bear Stearns put in a little money and the rest of it I raised myself. It wasn't that much, but a few institutions went in. I think Mass Mutual was one. It was a decent company and the price was right. H.J. continued to be chairman and gradually there was a transition to his sons. Then there was a transition away from his sons, and then we sold it.

GEORGE ROBERTS:

In 1965, when I arrived at Bear Stearns, Jerry was doing buyouts. There was a deal being done for Stern Metals Corporation, and I worked on that a little bit. Jerry and a guy named Walter Rockman and Steve Hirsch were the primary people working on it and it took about nine to ten months to get done. This was during the period of time when you had Stern Metals, you had Thompson Wire, Midland Glass — these were the transactions being done. I sort of connected with what was happening. I guess I was lucky to find something thirty-five years ago that I've wanted to do all my life.

JERRY KOHLBERG:

Cy Lewis was a great friend of Ray Kravis, Henry's father and George's uncle. I guess George wanted to work on Wall Street doing the kind of thing I did. I think I was head of investment banking then, so it was underwritings and all that. Cy called me in and said, "Will you give this kid a job?" Well, when your boss tells you to give the kid a job, you give the kid a job. So that's how it happened. He proceeded to be a real hard worker with a very good head.

GEORGE ROBERTS:

I would say that my dad and my uncle, Henry's dad, played a large role in my love of business. It was really Henry's father who got me a job one summer at Bear Stearns. Henry and I were roommates while he worked at Goldman Sachs and I worked at Bear Stearns. Our families were close and our fathers would talk about business from time to time. My ears would perk up whenever that happened, and once it was quiet I'd ask a lot of questions about what was going on. Just coming up in that family environment had more influence on me than anything else.

HENRY KRAVIS (cofounder and partner of Kohlberg Kravis Roberts and Company):

I'd never been to Wall Street until the summer after my freshman year in college when I worked at Goldman Sachs. I'd never even been down to Wall Street. That was my first exposure, but I caught on very quickly. I worked for three summers at Goldman, starting out as a runner that first summer. I did that for about half the summer, and then I went to the research department. Then, the next year, I was in the research department the whole time, working with some of the research analysts. Then I went into corporate finance for my last year.

GEORGE ROBERTS:

I'd attribute my success at Bear Stearns to the New York City subways. The first day I went to work — Henry and I were roommates, and he knew his way around New York, but I didn't. So we got on the subway and I'd never seen such a mass of humanity. There were all sorts of people getting on and off the subway, especially at Fourteenth Street as you went down to Wall Street. I quickly learned that if you went an hour earlier and left an hour later it wasn't as crowded. So I just started going to the office at seven thirty in the morning and leaving at six thirty or seven at night. I was working in the research department and Jerry was running the corporate finance department at the time. I think he probably figured, boy, there's a very ambitious young guy here. But I was really going in early and staying late just to avoid the rush on the subway.

We developed a friendship from that first summer, and the next summer I went to work for him in the corporate finance department.

JEROME KOHLBERG:

We were doing much smaller buyouts then — $25 million, $30 million, $50 million at the most. We also were spending a lot of time researching companies and a lot of time educating the institutional investors. And don't forget, we also had to do some underwriting and merger business to pay the overhead. If not, that would get the partners at Bear

Stearns down on us for not producing. So we had to do all these things. But we managed to continue to do it.

Deals were hard to find. The business was so new that a lot of people would throw up their hands and say, "You can't do this. It's not done." So we'd have to show them how we did it over here and over there. It took a lot of time to get things done. But it was changing. And if you could convince someone to do it, there were a lot of good opportunities. The values in the 1960s were much lower. Stocks were selling at much lower price-earnings ratios. If you could show people who owned these businesses how they could have their cake and eat it, too, they were more likely to come along. That was the pitch — you can have your cake and eat it, too. You were talking to the owner of the company, or even a chief executive who wasn't the owner of the company, and saying, "Your alternative here is to sell out and be part of a big company. Our way, you can make some money and still have all the satisfaction of building your company." That was our pitch, and I think it turned out to be honest.

I think the thing I brought to the buyout business more than anything else was the idea that management had to be an integral part of what we were doing. They had to have ownership in the business, something at stake. We made them buy stock and also gave them some options, so that they were on the same side of the table as we were. This took the place of high salaries and all that. They were going to make money, but they were going to make more money "on the come" than right away. Instead of emphasizing the perks and all the other things that corporate America enjoyed, we emphasized performance. You know, sink or swim. I think that was the real innovative part of the buyout — the involvement of management as partners with us.

HENRY KRAVIS:

In those days you went straight to business school after getting your undergraduate degree — you didn't take the time off to work the way you do now. I went to work for a short period of time for a venture-capital firm. Bear Stearns had offered me a job and Goldman Sachs had offered me a job, and I thought to myself that I'd really rather go to a smaller firm than be in a larger, more structured place. So I went to work for a firm called Faherty and Swartwood. But they turned out to be not as focused on venture capital as I thought they were going to be, and more into trading equities. I left there after about eight months or so.

I remember I talked to George and he told me that he was going to leave New York and go back to California. He had this idea. He said, "You could take my position here in New York and the three of us could work together this way." The thing is, Bear Stearns had offered me a job eight months earlier, and I'd turned them down. Now here I was asking for reinstatement. So I had to go back to Jerry Kohlberg, sort of with my tail between my legs. Jerry just said, "Fine, but you darn well better come here to work this time." No problem. I'll be there.

And that's how the partnership began. George went back to California in August to work in corporate finance, and I started in New York in August.

GEORGE ROBERTS:

It was July 2, 1970, and I got caught in a blackout in a Manhattan subway car for two hours. They finally evacuated people from the train and that's how we got aboveground. Then I had to walk home about thirty-five blocks because, of course, you couldn't get a cab at the time. I walked in the door completely soaking wet, and I said to my wife, "That's it. We're either going back to California with Bear Stearns, or I'm going to get another job out there."

After the Fourth of July, I went in and talked to Jerry. Basically, I said, "Look, I'm not going to make my life here in New York. Either Bear Stearns needs to start a corporate finance department on the West Coast or I'm going to start looking for a job." He was supportive of that and I returned to the West Coast.

JEROME KOHLBERG:

Over time, we must've done fifteen companies with Bear Stearns. We were constantly learning the whole time. I was thinking about this the other day — we actually had to get "key man" insurance for the top executive of any firm we were buying. The idea was, if this guy got hit by a truck it would be critical to the whole operation. As it turned out, that concept was better for an insurance salesman than a merchant banker. But we were learning. We were learning how to structure, how to hire. And we were educating the people at the insurance companies and banks, the lawyers, everyone and anyone we could think of who would invest in our deals.

HENRY KRAVIS:

We were a profit center for Bear Stearns but I don't know if we were ever popular there or not. It was basically the three of us who were doing these deals. Nobody else was all that interested in what we were doing; nobody really seemed to care much. Some of the partners would put up a little bit of the equity that we needed, but their attitude was, "The business is fine, but we're more interested in the fees that you get for closing one of these transactions. Maybe the equity will be worth something down the road, maybe not." Their focus was on finding out how much fee income we'd be able to generate from one of these things. That's all the firm cared about.

Clearly, it was a different thrust. We really have always taken a long-term view toward investing. At the time, Cy Lewis and Ace Greenberg and others who were running the firm had come from a trading background. They were extremely good at it, but long-term to them was overnight. That's why they didn't pay a lot of attention to us. They were busy doing what they were doing, and that's what the firm was built on. They gave us a lot of room to go and do what we were doing, as long as we were generating the fees.

JEROME KOHLBERG:

I'd been thinking about leaving Bear Stearns and going out on my own for a number of years. I'd talked to a good guy at Standard and Poor's and a few other people about doing buyouts as a business on my own. All the advice I got from close friends, and lawyer friends particularly, was don't do it. They said you needed a big daddy, a name, to open the door. Well, we had developed a very nice relationship with a number of institutions that had invested in us, the Pru and Mass Mutual and First National Bank of Chicago, and others, and I got a lot of encouragement from those people over drinks. I knew that I wanted to leave Bear Stearns no matter what. My philosophy differed from Cy Lewis's. I admired what he and Alan had done, but trading wasn't what I liked. I liked the idea of surviving on what you did, on what you were building with your own money. I didn't want to just collect a fee or a commission. So that started to grow on me. And I still had visions of this merchant banker in England that I admired. So I decided to leave.

I talked to George about it, and George definitely wanted to come. He was out there in California and his wife's family had money — he wasn't going to starve. So I decided we'd do it. But Henry was very hesitant. I'd decided to do it and George agreed, so we were going to do it, and it wasn't until then that Henry said he'd like to come along.

GEORGE ROBERTS:

I think the three of us had developed a camaraderie and chemistry. We all liked working with one another and respected one another. More important, this is really what we wanted to do. I didn't want to be out on the West Coast competing against Morgan Stanley and Goldman Sachs to get bond business from Pacific Gas and Electric. We didn't have a competitive advantage there. This business is really how I wanted to spend my time and effort. Plus, I wanted to work in an environment where I liked all the people I was working with, so a smaller firm seemed to make sense. In a way, I wanted to work for myself.

HENRY KRAVIS:

I've always been entrepreneurial in my outlook. Quite frankly, there were some people I was working with at Bear Stearns that I just didn't have a lot of respect for. I didn't want to be told that I had to do this or that. I just didn't believe in the project or the people, and I really wanted to work with George. So I figured if we could do this, starting out on our own, then we'd find out if we were really any good. If we could make it on our own it would be because of us. And if we couldn't make it work, then maybe our success was because of Bear Stearns having that umbrella over us. I wanted to find that out.

JEROME KOHLBERG:

I put up most of the money for the partnership, I think it was $100,000, and Henry and George each put up $10,000. We agreed that we'd all start as partners because they were taking a risk, too. The name of the firm was going to be Kohlberg Roberts Kravis, but we had Gershon Kekst as a public relations adviser, and he said KRK didn't sound very good, but KKR had a ring to it. It rolls off the tongue and is much more . . . what's the term . . . mellifluous. George was very good about it. He took the third position, and we became Kohlberg Kravis Roberts — KKR.

So we started. We got people to finance the overhead for us. A few people gave us $50,000 a year, and they had the first crack at the deals. I remember Henry's father was one, and my cousin and a couple of friends were the others. And that's how we started. Right about then, my old partner Cy Lewis tried to get the head of the First National Bank of Chicago not to do business with us. They were a very important client for us. We'd done business with them before, and they'd already agreed to do business with us in our new firm. But two people at the bank, Bob Judson, who was head of lending in the East, and a guy by the name of Stan Golder, who was in their equity division, both said no, they were going to back Jerry Kohlberg and continue to do business with us. They told their own boss, no. Cy was pretty angry, but he became reconciled.

HENRY KRAVIS:

When we made the decision that we were going to go on and set up our own firm — that was when Bear Stearns became unhappy. We gave them every opportunity to be a part of it. We actually went to them and said we'd like to do it within Bear Stearns, but they said no. Their attitude was, you can work here and do what we want you to do, or you can go off on your own. That made it pretty simple for us.

We had total capital of $120,000, that was what we used to get the firm started. We had two offices. George was in San Francisco, and Jerry and I were in New York. I remember when we first left Bear Stearns, we didn't have cell phones at the time so my office became a street corner and a phone booth until we could finally find a real office. We went in to deposit our $120,000 in what was then Chemical Bank, and they weren't sure that they could take it. I couldn't believe it. Here we were with $120,000 and they said, "We'll call you back." We had to wait a day or two to open up the account. That's how we got started.

We started on May 1, 1976, and we finished out that year by getting ourselves organized. In the next full year we bought three companies. The first transaction we got involved with was out in California — A.J. Industries. Then we bought L. B. Foster and we bought U.S. Natural Resources. So that kicked us off. We were constantly calling on companies. We tried to explain to the investment bankers what we were doing and they didn't have a clue what we were talking about. I remember speaking to some Goldman Sachs people, showing them what we were doing, and they said, "You can't do that. It just doesn't work." So we just went about it on our own.

I can remember George and I would be driving along on our way to visit some company and we'd see a nice-looking plant so we'd write the name down. We didn't have any idea what they did, but we'd come back and look it up on Dun and Bradstreet and get a report on the company. You know, dissemination of information in those days was not what it is today. We'd find out what the business was all about and we'd write them a letter or call them, and sometimes it would lead to something.

JEROME KOHLBERG:

Houdaille Industries, which I think we did in 1978, was the first company on the New York Stock Exchange to go through one of these deals. They were represented by Goldman Sachs. And the president of the company was a lawyer who lived up in Buffalo, where the company had been headquartered, and he was having some qualms about being on both sides of the fence, the seller and buyer, so he elected to retire. A whole new top team came to the fore. They just loved the idea of what we were doing. They persuaded the lawyer to do it. And in fairness he couldn't have been more wonderful. They were forthright and straight with us the whole time. We knew where the problems were, but this was a well-managed company. He cooperated and congratulated us on it at the end. He was a very decent man with integrity.

But the Houdaille deal opened up Wall Street's eyes to what we were doing, particularly at Goldman Sachs. They have very quick vision, and they saw the money to be made, the fees to be made. And I know they started to think about doing this, and formed a department not too long afterward.

HENRY KRAVIS:

Houdaille showed that you could do a large deal. In those days a $355 million transaction was large. Nothing like that had ever been done before — it was the first large public-to-private transaction. We didn't do it as a tender offer. We did it as a merger of Houdaille into "Newco." So we had to do a filing with the SEC and put out a proxy statement, which meant that shareholders had to vote on the deal. Now, to give you a sense of how new this was, the SEC actually asked us to explain what we were doing. I mean, they didn't have a clue. We kept trying to explain it to them and describe it to them, but they just couldn't get it. Finally, they said, "Nobody's going to understand what you're doing. They're not going to understand how these guys that nobody's ever heard of are going to come up with $350 million and buy a Fortune 500 company. Would you please diagram it?"

If you go back and look at the 1979 proxy statement for Houdaille, there is a diagram in there that became a famous business-school case because it laid out who was merging with whom and what was going where. It also showed where the capital was going. We had so many layers of capital because the markets weren't deep or broad, so the deal became very complicated. So we had to diagram the whole thing in this very thick proxy statement before we could do the deal.

JEROME KOHLBERG:

Of course, what we were really doing, in my view, and I've thought about this a lot, was taking earnings or value that should've gone to the shareholders and bringing it unto ourselves. Corporate America was still working on salaries and perks. The chief executive chose his own board. They had airplanes and hunting lodges and everything else. They should've cut these things out and given it to the shareholders in the form of a higher stock price. I can think of two companies where the chief executives were under potential attack, they knew they were vulnerable, and they told us that we could save $300 million a year. You multiply that by seven or eight, and the multiples were higher than that, that's a lot of dough. We bought the companies and stepped in and made those changes. And that redounded to our benefit, and then to the public's benefit to a certain extent. But it really should've gone to the old shareholders in the first place. Corporate America, executive America, was responsible for a lot of this. That's the way I look at it. You have to ask the question, why didn't they do it themselves?

As the 1970s gave way to the 1980s, KKR continued to find opportunities in the market. Then, in 1984, the firm received a massive boost when it teamed up with Drexel Burnham Lambert and its junk-bond dynamo, Michael Milken, in the purchase of Cole National Corporation. The combination of Drexel's cheap capital and KKR's shrewd eye for value was devastating. The deals became larger in scope and the profits went off the charts.

Around the same time, Jerome Kohlberg required a series of serious medical procedures that eventually caused all the partners to rethink his role in the firm. In 1987, after months of haggling, he finally stepped away to form his own buyout firm, Kohlberg and Company. Like most personal and professional breakups, this one had its share of acrimony, and to this day hard feelings remain on both sides. But even Kohlberg acknowledges, "We viewed things differently. It was time." That left Kravis and Roberts as the firm's leaders. From here, the two cousins would chart KKR's future.

CHAPTER 16

A LICENSE TO PRINT MONEY

By the mid-1980s, as the financial markets rebounded, America found itself in the midst of a full-scale mergers-and-acquisitions, or M&A, revolution. And the currency of this revolution was junk bonds. Simply put, junk bonds are the bonds of companies that are not deemed to be "investment grade" by debt-rating agencies like Standard and Poor's and Moody's Investors Service. To account for this added risk, junk bonds carry a higher interest rate, or coupon, than regular corporate bonds. In essence, the market has deemed these bonds to be "junk" compared with standard investment-grade bonds.

Historically, junk bonds originated as investment-grade bonds that had fallen into junk status as the company underlying the debt got into trouble. So obviously, junk bonds — or high-yield bonds, as their issuers like to call them — have been around for as long as there have been companies that have issued debt and then hit hard times. What was new in the 1970s and 1980s was the development of a liquid market for new junk bonds to be issued by companies, and traded as an asset class by investors. This market was created and managed by Michael Milken at the upstart Wall Street investment bank Drexel

Burnham Lambert. Milken's central thesis was, sure, these bonds were risky on their own, but if you held a portfolio full of them the rewards from the ones that worked out would more than make up for the defaults on the ones that didn't. So ultimately, investors could earn a far higher rate of return, without taking on significantly more risk, by holding a basket of junk bonds than by simply owning safe U.S. Treasury bonds.

Knowing the history of the financial markets, it isn't surprising that this revolutionary idea came out of a relatively obscure corner of Wall Street. Drexel Burnham Lambert hardly was a household name in the 1970s. The company had been formed through the merger of Drexel, an old-line Philadelphia investment bank that had bottomed out like so many other Wall Street partnerships, and Burnham and Company, an ambitious brokerage firm. The name Lambert referred to Compagnie Bruxelles Lambert, a Belgian outfit that had invested $20 million in one of Drexel's merger partners in the mid-1970s. But the Belgians never exerted any control over the company, and their participation in the business was largely in name only. So, for the purposes of this story, the key names are Drexel and Burnham — and, of course, Milken.

ROBERT LINTON (former Drexel Burnham chairman):

To understand how Drexel Burnham came together you actually have to go back to Firestone — you know, the tire company. Firestone had, in addition to its traditional business, a bank in Switzerland. And their management in the 1960s wanted to get into the U.S. investment-banking business. They invested in what was then Drexel Harriman Ripley, and the firm became Drexel Firestone. Drexel was the Philadelphia partner of the J. P. Morgan bank. They were the powerhouse in traditional investment banking until the 1930s, when the Glass-Steagall laws were passed that separated commercial banking from investment banking. So they had as good a pedigree as you could have in investment banking.

Anyway, in about 1972, Firestone realized they had made a mistake and wanted out of the Drexel holding, which wasn't working well for them. A man named Archie Albright, Drexel's president, brought the deal to us at Burnham and Company. The primary reason Drexel Firestone suited us was we wanted to become a major underwriter. We were a very active submajor in the syndicates at that time, but the chances of our becoming a major were pretty distant. Drexel historically was a major. That was the motivating force behind the deal.

Burnham and Company had been started in 1935 by I. W. Burnham II — or Tubby, as the Street called him — and four other men, each of whom had been partners in lesser firms on Wall Street. So we were newcomers relative to what Drexel had been. The main business of Drexel was underwriting corporate America, particularly the major-sized companies, many of which J. P. Morgan and his people had created. So these were absolutely different cultures.

I. W. (TUBBY) BURNHAM (founder of Burnham and Company and former chairman of Drexel Burnham):

If I'd called it Burnham, Drexel, we'd still be a submajor. I remember I told my mother about it, and she said, "How can you? The firm has been Burnham since 1935." I said, "Mother, I want this. It will be worth millions to us."

ROBERT LINTON:

Now, sitting in the back room at Drexel was Michael Milken, whom we didn't even know about early on. He had a very unfavorable deal at Drexel. His department had to bear all the losses, there wasn't much overhead, and they didn't allocate much capital to him. So he was getting ready to leave Drexel. When we made the acquisition, he sat down and talked with our principal people, who rather quickly recognized his potential and made him a completely different kind of deal. His deal never changed in the entire time he was there. He got a $200,000 salary, never more, never less, and 35 percent of the profits of his department, if there were any. So when you ask how he could have made $550 million in 1987, it was very simple. That year his department made $1.5 billion in profits, and the more he made, the more we made. Some people criticized us for that. But what do you do, take your best salesman and biggest earner and cut him back? The answer's no.

MICHAEL MILKEN (former head of Drexel Burnham Lambert's high-yield bond department):

By 1973 there were more than two hundred firms making a market in what was later called junk bonds. They all might not have been making markets for $10 million at a time, but they were making markets. Loews had a lot of junk debt — issued when they acquired Lorillard. Loews had a $400 million junk issue — in today's dollars that would be way over $1 billion. I didn't invent all that. It was there when I was just getting started.

FRED JOSEPH (former Drexel Burnham Lambert chief executive):

I met Milken probably six months after I joined the firm. I'd heard from a couple of people outside the firm that there was this fellow trading low-grade corporate bonds who was absolutely brilliant and I ought to meet him. I'd also heard this from some people inside the firm. So I made it my business to get to know him.

PETER ACKERMAN (former Drexel Burnham Lambert executive vice president and deputy to Michael Milken in the high-yield bond department):

The high-yield bond department at Drexel had three parts: we bought and sold on the street, we bought and sold for our clients, and we researched all the credits [debt securities]. Milken's innovation, which I think will dub him the hero he was in finance, is that he said, "I'm going to create a real market in this stuff." At that time it was a market that was opened and closed like the IPO market. But Milken said, "I'm going to make a market every day. You may not like the price that I bid or ask, but I'll make a two-way market every day." To make a two-way market successful you have to grow it so you don't end up buying every single high-yield bond. So he did a lot of evangelical work on high-yield bonds, in terms of the risk-adjusted return. And he used the same portfolio-management theory that's now completely validated in the marketplace. Milken wasn't the first guy to deal with the high-yield bond. He was the first one to create a consistent market-making activity.

FRED JOSEPH:

The high-yield market was made up of former investment-grade issues that had fallen on hard times. People took to calling them fallen angels. There were a lot of these REIT [real estate investment trust] bonds that Milken became the dominant force on, in terms of research knowledge, trading knowledge, and the ability to place the bonds. He and his staff knew more about the Penn Central bonds than anyone else on Wall Street at the time. So they had a really nice niche. They had a lot of knowledge about lots of securities that people were not terribly interested in, and built up a constituency of investors who did very well. In 1974, we were in a recession, interest rates had spiked up, and people were demoralized. And with those conditions, there were lots of investments that he found for people at twenty cents on the dollar that were at eighty cents on the dollar a year later. His name spread from there.

MICHAEL MILKEN:

The turning point was 1974, when interest rates spiked, the stock market fell 45 percent, and large financial institutions, faced with their own problems, stopped lending to all but the highest-rated borrowers. Thousands of below-investment-grade debt instruments — including those of municipal governments and utilities — were then tagged as "junk" because their issuers were supposedly on the verge of bankruptcy. When the issuers survived, investors in those high-yield instruments received a stunning 100 percent return in the next two years.

ROBERT LINTON:

In 1977, Michael moved the entire high-yield department to California. Michael was from California, and both his children were not 100 percent healthy. He felt they'd do much better out there. Also, his father got very sick around that time, and he wanted to spend more time with his parents. And, as surprising as this may seem, he thought he could put in more hours if he was on California time. His people could really get a jump on the market and then wind down in the afternoon. It suited him to go out there for those reasons. That happened just at the time that I became CEO, and we did have some reservations about management and control. But he convinced us that his department would thrive there and communications were such that it would work. So we went along with it, not without a little trepidation.

PETER ACKERMAN:

It was a very exciting atmosphere in the Beverly Hills office. We were in a field that most people on Wall Street were content to neglect, and that's always good. High-yield bonds were considered junk, and therefore we were considered purveyors of junk. But in the office, it was an environment where research into credit allowed you to really offer value, as an investor yourself and to your clients. It was an exciting, growing time.

Working with Mike was both taxing and delightful. There were two things that I most admired about him. One, he was an incredibly quick study, just incredibly bright. And two, he never asked anyone to put out any more than he put out himself. He was always there first and always left last. Now, let me give you an idea of exactly what that means. Showing up first means leaving your home at 4:15 in the morning and getting into the office at 4:35. And leaving last means walking out the door at around 7:00 at night. I used to have a competition with him. When he'd slip sometimes and show up at 4:45, I'd say, "Ah, gotcha!" But the next day he was there at 4:30. He always won.

MICHAEL MILKEN:

By 1977, dozens of Wall Street firms were issuing high-yield securities for a broad range of below-investment-grade companies. Although considered "high risk," these securities turned out to carry less portfolio risk than higher-rated instruments because yield premiums more than compensated for defaults. Lenders of small and medium-sized firms with good prospects, who had been dependent on relationships with individual banks and insurance companies, could now turn to a market-based system with thousands of institutional buyers, including mutual funds, which would eventually grow larger than the banks.

ROBERT LINTON:

We were not alone in the junk-bond business. Lehman Brothers and Bear Stearns had sort of dabbled in it. And we did not even do the first junk-bond underwriting. Lehman Brothers did the first few in the 1970s for companies like Zapata and LTV. But there wasn't much out there, and Michael really thought we could do some business in this field.

FRED JOSEPH:

I remember Mike pointed out a Lehman deal to me. I said, "We have lots of clients who could use that capital. Could you sell the bonds?" And he said of course he could. We didn't really know that he could do it, but we knew that he thought he could. The first one we did was for Texas International Petroleum, and of course he sold all the bonds.

ROBERT LINTON:

He began developing more and more contacts and ideas. I'll pick one out of a hat — Steve Wynn. Steve had this run-down casino in Las Vegas called the Golden Nugget, and he had an idea to open one in Atlantic City, which had just legalized gambling. If I remember, his gross balance sheet was around $18 million. Steve also was from Philadelphia, also from Wharton, like Michael, and he was very bright and aggressive. They hit it off. So Michael came to us and said, "I want to raise $150 million for Steve Wynn to build a casino." We looked at the numbers and thought he was out of his mind. But he convinced us not only that this was a deal that made a lot of sense, but that he could place the securities himself and we wouldn't have to worry about it. He developed that deal off the drawing board. And, of course, the rest is history.

PETER ACKERMAN:

In the benign sense, the liquid high-yield bond market gave financing to companies of the future, companies like MCI, Turner, Metromedia, and health-care companies, telecom companies, and cable companies, which couldn't get financing otherwise. We could finance them based on their cash flow, whereas at banks they wanted to know what their assets were. These companies were generating cash flow, but they didn't have the collateral to get loans from banks.

The high-yield bond was a quasi instrument between equity and debt. It was debt in the sense that it had a maturity and coupon, and if you failed to pay you were going into bankruptcy. But it was like equity for the company because as debentures they were subordinated, so you could put more debt on top of it. But more important, the indentures were not constricting on management the way past indentures were in the private-placement subordinated-debt market. It was a much more pliable instrument, much more management-friendly.

Our job was to create a bouquet of these things so that as an investor you didn't mind giving all that latitude to management in a variety of situations because you had an excellent portfolio of these names. It was the portfolio-creation element of the high-yield market that really was so valuable. In other words, if we had five hundred clients and we put each name into everybody's portfolio, that's diversification. You have a great portfolio of these instruments. It was like insurance — they'd get a better risk-adjusted return than in government bonds. The managements would benefit because they didn't have to finance as if they were the last man standing. So the standards you could use for the financiers to be intrusive to management were much lower. It allowed good management to come to the fore and control more assets.

JAMES GRANT (author and publisher of *Grant's Interest Rate Observer*):
You have to understand that junk bonds are nothing new. Debt securities of the revolutionary American government were speculative-grade instruments, or junk bonds. Before there was a constitution, the revolutionary government was raising money in Holland in speculative circumstances. So the idea that Milken invented this thing is not at all historically accurate. The nineteenth century was full of examples of railroads financing themselves with debt securities. I guess people didn't view owning the railroads as speculative grade, but enough of them folded that the idea could not have been far from the minds of the creditors.

What was perhaps new in the seventies and the eighties was how speculative a speculative-grade security could be. The bond market was full of junk bonds in the thirties, forties, and fifties, but typically these were instruments that had begun their careers as investment grade and then through adverse circumstances turned into speculative-grade securities. What was new in the seventies with Milken was this widespread issuance of speculative-grade securities right out of the gate. Now you had stuff that was underwritten as junk in connection with a change in corporate control.

FRED JOSEPH:

The really controversial move was when we decided to use our financing capability to help us build our M&A activity.

JOSEPH FLOM (M&A lawyer and partner at Skadden, Arps, Slate, Meagher and Flom):

In every era, the single dominant factor of whether there's takeover activity is the existence of liquidity in the market. Liquidity doesn't mean just cash. Obviously, cash is a kind of liquidity, but it can be bonds, stock, or high-yield bonds, which really are a cross between equity and debt. To the extent that junk bonds created liquidity in the 1980s, they also increased the action in takeovers tremendously.

DANIEL HERTZBERG (deputy managing editor of the *Wall Street Journal* and former M&A reporter):

Junk bonds made financing easy. You had these people called raiders, who we really don't have right now. They were guys who had limited amounts of money, but who would just go after companies. You also had the leftover conglomerates and other companies that just weren't really well run. What was going on in the eighties was a major restructuring of a lot of big American companies, and in many ways the results of that can be very painful, particularly for the people who get laid off.

T. BOONE PICKENS (former chairman of Mesa Petroleum):

I was always amused by the term "raider." It was hard to see how we could be considered that. The financial press was just so uninformed. I'd invested a lot of money and was now the largest shareholder in a company. But I'm a raider? Explain to me what that's all about. We were the only ones with money in the deal. Management certainly didn't have money in the deal. So immediately after you take a position you get sued by the company. Now I'm being sued with my own money. You're the largest shareholder, and they're suing you. Whose money's that? And you've got nothing to say about it.

MARTY LIPTON (M&A attorney and partner at Wachtell, Lipton, Rosen and Katz):

The market really went down through 1973 and 1974 and didn't come back until the middle of 1982. We essentially had a flat market for eight or nine years. You had inflating asset values and you had cheap debt. Junk bonds essentially were very cheap for the risk that was involved. So you had all the makings for takeovers. It was almost like shooting fish in a barrel if you could use cheap currency in the form of junk bonds and take over assets that had a depressed valuation in the stock market, yet the assets were showing appreciation. It was a natural for financially structured deals.

T. BOONE PICKENS:

At the end of the 1970s I was conscious that oil- and gas-finding costs were going way up. We were spending a lot of money, but having a lot of difficulty finding oil and gas. And we were good oil finders, too. We started out with zero reserves in 1956, and when I left the company in 1996 we'd produced 3 trillion cubic feet of gas and 150 million barrels of oil. So we knew what we were doing. Which is why we also knew what we were doing when we could see that our finding costs were too high. In the late seventies I thought, gosh, there's got to be a better way of doing this. My thinking was, you're entrusted with so much capital and what you've got to do with that capital is deploy it in the areas where you can get the highest rate of return possible. When I looked around I figured, hell, I'm better off trying to buy another company than I am going looking for oil and gas because I'll have to pay too much for what I find. It wasn't a hard conclusion to come to, but it was a hard decision to make — that instead of finding oil and gas you were going to buy companies with the idea of changing management or making something happen.

PAUL STEIGER (managing editor of the *Wall Street Journal*):

There was an enormous shift in the recognition of the relative competitiveness of U.S. companies. It became clear to smart people in the investment-banking business and elsewhere, as well as to the smarter corporate leaders, that an enormous restructuring of American industry was required. The dramatic shift of energy prices and competition from abroad, particularly from Japan, made it clear that American companies were the high-cost producers. There was an infrastructure of middle management, of capital assets, that was simply unnecessary, and that made it impossible for American industry to compete in an environment in which it no longer was insulated from foreign competition. So there was a tremendous need for restructuring of American industry.

PETER ACKERMAN:

On the corporate acquisitions side, the high-yield bond gave people who would have been shut out of the market for corporate acquisitions a huge stick. They could do leveraged acquisitions, and unfriendly leveraged acquisitions, particularly with companies that were conglomerates. The conglomerates turned out to be a very bad idea in finance. You slapped together many companies that didn't have a reason for existing together. So you'd have all these companies under the same umbrella, and then management would put on an oversight infrastructure that became more and more distant from the operations themselves. It was just an extra layer of management. Not surprisingly, the rates of return in these companies would go way down because there was this enormous bureaucracy. That's why a lot of them were selling at huge discounts.

JAMES GRANT:

There was a great deal of truth in that. Many of these companies were profit-making bureaucracies — rigid, not meaningfully answerable to the stockholders, and inclined to reinvest free cash flow on acquisitions, perquisites for executives, and just about anything else other than paying special dividends for stockholders. The entire shareholder-rights movement was way off in the future. The junk-bond movement sped its coming.

At its best, it caused managements to anticipate the demands of shareholders and thereby to protect themselves against unwanted raiders. At its worst, it caused solid-operating businesses to become overburdened with debt and driven into bankruptcy when the business cycle turned against the company. Something I've learned is that every good idea on Wall Street is driven into the ground like a tomato stake. The idea of shareholder power — of corporate executives being answerable to people other than a handpicked board of directors — is relatively new. These are all great ideas that were taken to excess, and the junk-bond market was instrumental in bringing about those excesses.

FRED JOSEPH:

Once we began to finance the leveraged buyouts and the unfriendlies, high-yield bonds leveled the playing field between the large companies and the small companies. It really caused a reaction among the Fortune 1000, which began to hear the footsteps and dramatically revamped their operations to enhance shareholder value. We did very few acquisitions of New York Stock Exchange–listed companies. But the majority of the Fortune 500 restructured in a way that was good for shareholders because of the footsteps they heard.

BOBBY STILLWELL (longtime legal consultant to T. Boone Pickens):

We had a hard time hiring investment bankers at first. The big bulge bracket firms didn't want to touch us because they may have felt pressure from their Fortune 500 clients to not do business with us or anybody else in the takeover business.

DANIEL HERTZBERG:

There was a lot of controversy because the corporate establishment was not happy about hostile takeovers. The Business Roundtable was not happy at all. There was a lot of opposition to it. But the people in the market weren't unhappy. They saw a company get a hostile offer and the stock price go up. In some cases a raider trying a hostile takeover would drive a firm into the friendly hands of an LBO firm, in what was called a white-knight deal.

So there were lots of people who, in a sense, actually had a vested interest in Drexel's success, just as there were lots of people who were competitors and would have rather had the junk-bond market to themselves. But the M&A business really is a community. People who are on opposite sides of one deal may be on the same side in the next. They all know each other and they all create business for each other. You do a hostile takeover, the target goes out and hires investment bankers and lawyers and everything else. It generates business.

PETER ACKERMAN:

The Gulf Oil deal, which was in 1984, was the seminal deal of the 1980s for us. It's often been suggested that in 1979 we had a vision, and that by 1987 we had infested the entire American economy with these raiders that we selected [ourselves]. It was just the reverse. These people came to us with a vision of how to transform a company, but they had no access to capital. So we worked deal by deal by deal. Each deal taught us new things, new techniques. It taught us where the market was and how to access it.

Now, the Gulf deal was important because, for one, it was huge. Nobody had ever attempted a $1 billion deal, and we were doing a $3 billion unfriendly deal. And two, it showed how skewed management's motives became in terms of trying to control assets to get paid versus doing what was right for shareholders. Boone might've been an obscure figure to them, but the fact was the stock went from $40 to $80, and $6.5 billion in 1984 dollars was created among the shareholders and pension funds. Corporate-governance ideas changed radically at that moment. You might not believe it, but at that time it was the practice of insurance companies and pension funds never to vote against management. Never. That all changed. Obviously, we're in a different environment today.

FRED JOSEPH:

There was a speech I used to give about how things change over time. In the 1940s and 1950s, families owned these companies. There was a family that controlled Ford and Bethlehem Steel and these other major companies, and cared how they did. By the 1970s, that ownership had transferred to the anonymous institutions, the pension funds and mutual funds, that didn't like to exercise their rights as shareholders. Most didn't even visit the companies they were investing in. The managements were accountable to no owners. And while the noise from us far exceeded the actual activity, the fact that shareholders could develop a way to have a say led to board actions.

PETER ACKERMAN:

What was really going on was, the managements of these companies were getting paid based on the size of their asset base, not on the performance of their companies. So if you were management, all you had to do was make the company bigger and you got paid more. But that says nothing about how the company actually was doing. That's why when T. Boone Pickens went after Gulf Oil there was such a fight. The fight wasn't over what was good for shareholders. The fight was about how to protect what was going on in Pittsburgh.

BOBBY STILLWELL:

At the beginning the institutional world was largely against you. So if you saw that Fidelity or Chase Bank owned 30 percent or 40 percent of a company, you knew that you had a tough road ahead.

T. BOONE PICKENS:

One thing about the institutions: in the beginning they were against you, but they kind of quietly sat on the sidelines and patted their foot and clapped lightly because you'd increased the value of their holding. They kind of liked that. But they damn sure didn't want to be connected to you. Then, as time passed, it became more and more evident to them that you were creating value, and a lot of it. Just go back to the Gulf deal. When we first started buying the stock it was at $33. We bought stock clear up to around $50. So let's say the average price we paid for Gulf was $40. When Chevron eventually bought it as Gulf's "white knight," the company sold for $80. At $40 the company's worth $6.5 billion, at $80 it's worth $13 billion. So everybody can see what was created there. This was a company with the highest finding costs of any major. They had not replaced their oil and gas reserves, and instead were depleting them. It was a dismal situation, and all of a sudden the value went up by $6.5 billion. That got a lot of attention. After that, if they even thought you were looking at someone, the rumors became rampant. Everybody was interested.

ROBERT LINTON:

The stock market was undervaluing a lot of these great traditional companies because they weren't maximizing the earnings on their assets. So some of these raiders, if you want to call them that, or entrepreneurs, which is a nicer word, saw the opportunity that if they could get the financing they could go in and shake the tree. Sometimes in the end it was really the threat that mattered.

MICHAEL MILKEN:

The Disney deal was originally brought to us by Roy Disney, who felt his family franchise was being dissipated by the people who were running the company. Later, Saul Steinberg approached Drexel and asked us to represent him in an offer for Disney. The end result was that Disney got new management, and the value of its stock increased tenfold.

SAUL STEINBERG (former chairman of Reliance Insurance):

Disney was a great company but had a horrible management. Walt Disney had died and they forced Roy Disney out of the company. Walt Disney's son-in-law [Ron Miller] was running the business, and every afternoon he'd play cards with his friends and drink. Anyway, the company just went downhill. Wall Street got completely disenchanted with the company and sold off the stock. I mean, it was selling for less than book value, less than ten times earnings. Then you had an oil crisis and people said no one's going to go to their parks anymore. But it was still the best entertainment property around. I was still young with six children and they all wanted to go to Disney World, Disneyland, all of their parks. I said to myself, "These guys on Wall Street who are selling all this stock must not have young children." The idea that the gas crisis was going to cause people to stop going to Disney's amusement parks was ridiculous. Who cares if it costs two dollars more to drive or ten dollars more to fly — if your kids want to go to Disneyland, that's where you're going to go. We saw that.

So we went to buy the stock, and we worked out a whole plan of how to manage it. We were going to have Barry Diller run Disney. We thought he was the most creative guy in the whole entertainment area. It turned out that they fired the son-in-law and hired Barry Diller's protégés, Michael Eisner and Jeffrey Katzenberg.

BOBBY STILLWELL:

We weren't stupid. We knew that the possibility was there that a company we were interested in acquiring could make a deal with somebody else to avoid us. Typically, acquiring the company would have been our favored outcome because that's where we could've made the most money. But we had an insurance policy that as a backup we could make money on our stock position if they made another deal. We looked at that as insurance.

T. BOONE PICKENS:

There was no downside risk in what we were doing, with one exception — if we had no outcome. So something had to happen. There had to be a change. If they were able to stymie us and just sit there, we would've been in trouble.

BOBBY STILLWELL:

We also knew that in a world populated with investment bankers and lawyers, the possibility that nothing would happen was virtually zero. Bankers and lawyers were going to make something happen. No transaction just wasn't going to be acceptable to them.

DANIEL HERTZBERG:

So, on the one hand you had raiders who had figured out how to finance off the assets of the company by saying, "If we get the company we'll sell you junk bonds." You don't need any money. And then you have the KKRs of the world, the financial engineers. They were doing it from a friendly perspective, though not always quite as friendly as it looked. They were coming in and saying, "We'll protect you from the raiders."

Of course, there was this wonderful symbiotic relationship between the respectable LBO crowd and the raiders. The raiders made people nervous and often literally drove them into the arms of the KKRs and the Forstmann Littles. Then, since the KKRs and Forstmanns had figured out that the equity was undervalued, they would offer managers a piece of the action. They could get managers to do it because they told them, "We'll make you rich." And they did.

MARTY LIPTON:

The LBO crowd were not raiders. They were doing negotiated deals, deals that the management of the company wanted to do. They were the white knights that came in to rescue the target company. The LBO was a friendly deal. Raiders were doing hostile deals. The LBOs in this period were not creating the kind of leverage and the kind of dislocation that the raiders were. When you got into 1988 to 1989, the leverage in the LBOs had gotten out of hand and they began to overuse junk bonds.

HENRY KRAVIS (cofounder of Kohlberg Kravis Roberts and Company):

From our standpoint junk bonds and Drexel Burnham made our lives a lot easier. I'll give you an example. When we were starting out and dealing with the large insurance companies we'd have meeting after meeting with an insurance company's investment group to explain the business. They'd want to come out to the company we were buying and spend quite a bit of time trying to understand it. The deal would go through a series of review processes before it finally got to a board of directors. And we didn't know if the board had approved the investment until we finally got that call giving us the go-ahead. In fact, there were several situations where we made proposals to, say, Prudential, as an example, and the staff recommended the deal, but we got a call saying they were sorry but the board had turned us down.

Now jump forward to 1984, which is when we first worked with Drexel on a company called Cole National. The markets were somewhat tight at that time but we decided to give it a try anyway. So we went out to see Mike Milken. He'd been talking to us for a while about this crazy idea for the high-yield market. So I went out there with the CEO of Cole National, Jeff Cole, and we spent about two hours giving a presentation to Mike Milken, Peter Ackerman, and two of the savings and loan people, Tom Spiegel and Fred Carr. Then there was some poor guy from a home-insurance company who was just walking through the office and they grabbed him and dragged him into the meeting, too. This guy had no idea why he was sitting there. So for two hours we laid out our plans for Cole National and at the end of the meeting Mike said, "Okay, it's done. Here are the terms and you've got your money." That was it. We thought that was pretty good. It certainly was a far cry from what we had to go through before. Nobody was going out and kicking the tires. It was a dramatic change for us. We never looked back from there.

Having access to capital enabled us to get control of companies, on a friendly basis, that were much larger than anything we'd done before. We could show, on a much larger scale, how we were able to restructure corporate America and create more value for shareholders. But you needed to have that capital to buy these larger companies. Otherwise, we'd have been "stopped out" at maybe $1 billion. Don't forget, even with the banks, there were only a handful of banks that were involved in the buyout business in the early eighties. You had First Chicago, Continental Illinois, Security Pacific, Chemical Bank — a lot of these names have disappeared — Manufacturer's Hanover, and a little bit of Chase. That was it. Even Citibank didn't do much then because they'd only do it as a secured loan, a loan secured by the assets. We said that we didn't do that. Our loans were all unsecured, cash flow–based loans. You also had a few insurance companies that would invest in this, and that was Prudential, Allstate, the Equitable, Mass Mutual, Teachers, and a few others. Basically you had very few financial institutions providing capital and it was constraining. Companies were all constrained if they wanted to buy anything of size unless they had a big balance sheet of their own.

Let me put it in perspective. In 1979, when we were buying Houdaille Industries, the total purchase price was $355 million. To raise that, we had to go around and figure out how much money was available in each category. Here's how much we can probably get from the banks, here's how much we could get from the insurance companies, here's how much senior subordinated debt, how much junior subordinated. So we first had to figure out what the size of the market was, then we could come up with our capital structure. Today, it's the exact opposite. You set your capital structure and then you have a million places to go raise money. The change came from the combination of Drexel's ability to raise large amounts of money from institutions that we never would've even talked to and what KKR was able to do with a company once we bought it, in terms of restructuring and creating new value opportunities.

BOBBY STILLWELL:

For a company like us, our size, the only money we had access to was bank money, or basically margin money plus our own Mesa capital. So we could put together $400 million or $500 million to put into a deal, plus the margin value of any stock that we acquired. But that was the only financing source that we had access to. Milken created a whole new web of financing through these contacts that he had. He had raised money for several hundred of these kinds of companies through junk-bond financings, and those companies, in turn, were candidates through his networking to invest in transactions like ours.

JAMES GRANT:

Separate and distinct from the validity of Milken's argument was the institutional setup. Drexel and Milken had a daisy chain — I like to use the metaphor that they persuaded customers to take in each other's wash. Fred Carr [former chairman of First Executive] would issue bonds and Tom Spiegel [former head of Columbia Savings and Loan] would buy them. The issuers would issue more than they needed, knowing that with the extra funds they would purchase somebody else's bonds. Drexel created an extended family of willing buyers, and it was this daisy-chain arrangement that determined the inner circle of the family.

If you wanted the cash that Milken was sitting on in the junk-bond market, you would have to participate. You couldn't just get financed, go away and run a great American enterprise. You had to thank them — and the thanks they wanted wasn't an appreciative letter to Mike. No, you were expected to participate. You were expected to buy other people's junk bonds, whether you really wanted them or not.

PAUL TIERNEY (former partner at Coniston Partners):

Part of my reluctance in using Drexel's capability, which is what you're talking about when you start talking about doing junk bonds in the 1980s, was I didn't want to be beholden to Drexel and Michael Milken. I'm not trying to be critical of what they did or any of the people there. But there was a feeling of independence that we wanted to maintain. I was leery of getting involved with them.

PETER ACKERMAN:

The Drexel community was mutual funds, insurance companies, pension funds, S&Ls, big, huge institutional buyers. I would say 99 percent of the buyers were institutions. That's who our customers were. It's amazing how that's been misperceived over time. These were true professionals who understood perfectly what they were buying and why they were buying it. They had research departments that could analyze these securities, very smart people who were quite capable of judging value.

FRED JOSEPH:

By the mideighties, Drexel had really emerged. We were a dominant player on Wall Street, not just in junk bonds, but also in many other businesses. We were someone you had to deal with. We were the most profitable securities firm in the world and the most profitable private company in the world in 1985.

ROBERT LINTON:

We went from being sort of a secondary factor in the Wall Street world to being a firm that everybody had to pay attention to. Love us or hate us, we were there with a big stick in our hands.

PETER ACKERMAN:

It's a funny thing. I think that we made a lot of mistakes. When I say we, I don't mean Mike Milken. I mean the firm from a cultural point of view. I think the firm was arrogant toward its competitors. But in a way that was understandable because our competitors would compete with us by asking potential clients, "Why do you want to be associated with those guys?" That was how they tried to win business from us, so really, what were we going to say? And our competitors didn't want to work as hard as we did or become as knowledgeable as we did. But having said that, we gloated too much and were rough with them on underwriting allocations. Maybe in hindsight we should've done a better job with that.

So we didn't make too many friends on the Street — in fact, we made enemies. But let me stress that all this has become focused on Mike, and this wasn't Mike's doing. I don't think anybody was trying consciously to be arrogant. We just felt that we were making it happen, and if they wanted to compete with us, compete on merit. In the process of doing that it was very easy to slide into saying, "We're better than you are." Of course, that can be taken to mean, "You're incompetent." And people get embarrassed when you say that.

By the middle of the 1980s, fledgling high-yield bond departments were springing up at numerous major firms, including Merrill Lynch, Salomon Brothers, and Goldman Sachs. Still, the anger that Drexel engendered in its competitors was very real. In the years ahead, the firm would pay dearly for poking the establishment with no allies in its corner.

CHAPTER 17

TRADING UP

Despite the growth of the securities business in the mid-twentieth century, Wall Street and Main Street still largely remained miles apart from one another. But in 1981, they took a few steps closer with the acquisition of Shearson Loeb Rhoades by American Express. Shearson, at that point, was the second-largest brokerage house in the country after Merrill Lynch, and American Express was, well, American Express — one of the most prestigious and recognizable brands in the world. While the combination did not defy the Depression-era Glass-Steagall regulations that separated commercial banks from investment banks, it did send an undeniable message that those rules eventually would be heading to the boneyard.

For Sandy Weill, Shearson's chairman and CEO, the sale to American Express was supposed to be a crowning achievement. Less than a decade earlier, Weill had taken charge of CBWL–Hayden Stone when his partners picked him to be their leader over Marshall Cogan. In time, Cogan and CBWL's other key partners — Arthur Levitt and Roger Berlind — drifted away to pursue careers elsewhere, leaving Weill in complete control.

Through the 1970s, Weill led his firm on five successful acquisitions of once-prestigious failing partnerships and created a brokerage powerhouse. In 1974, he bought Shearson Hammill and changed CBWL–Hayden Stone's name to Shearson Hayden Stone. In 1979, he bought Loeb Rhoades and changed the firm's name to Shearson Loeb Rhoades. And by 1980, he was ready for something new.

SANDY WEILL (former Shearson chief executive officer and cochairman):

By 1980, internationalization and securitization were beginning to make it clear that companies had to have access to a lot of capital and that technology was really going to be key. So I was wondering, how do you get both? And I was not averse to doing something with another company where personally I might have an opportunity to try something different. I had been running Shearson for eight or nine years, and we had the best numbers in the industry.

JUDITH RAMSEY EHRLICH (coauthor of *The New Crowd*):

One day in late August of 1980, Weill was having breakfast at the New York Stock Exchange luncheon club. His companion was Sandy Lewis, the son of Cy Lewis, Weill's first boss at Bear Stearns. Lewis proposed a striking idea to Weill: sell Shearson to American Express. As he described it, the combination of Weill's diversified brokerage house and American Express, with its global charge-card and traveler's-check services, international banking division, and Fireman's Fund insurance company, would create a financial empire rivaling any in the world. It would be a superbroker.

SANDY WEILL:

Sandy Lewis was very friendly with [American Express chairman Jim] Robinson and he approached me, and I said, "Geez, I don't see how that's possible. I don't think that Jim is ready to retire, and if he's not, I don't see how we can do anything. But I'll meet with him." And we met and we talked about the future, and we decided to see if together we could create a product competitive with Merrill's Cash Management Account, using the American Express card. We courted each other a little.

JEFF LANE (former Shearson executive under Sandy Weill):

The CMA had come out a few years earlier and it was a really attractive product. I decided that one way of one-upping Merrill Lynch would be if we could offer an American Express Gold Card with the account instead of a Visa card. I told Sandy that we ought to give American Express a call and see if they would allow us to use the American Express Gold Card for our FMA account, Financial Management Account, which is what we called it. That may or may not have started the discussions.

PETER COHEN (former Shearson executive and right-hand aide to Sandy Weill):

In March of '81, Prudential bought Bache, and Sandy sort of heard the elephants coming. He said, "What happens if somebody buys E. F. Hutton or Dean Witter? Where does that leave us?" Whether it's instinct or fear that drives Sandy, it's a good combination. Plus, his ego was at work here. He wanted to leverage into the next big thing in his life.

JUDITH RAMSEY EHRLICH:

Sandy Weill and his wife, Joan, learned of the Prudential Bache deal the morning it was announced, in March of 1981. They read about it in a newspaper article in the *South China Post* while they were staying at the Mandarin Hotel in Hong Kong. They were with former president Gerald Ford, now a Shearson director, visiting the local Shearson office.

For some years, Bache had not been a serious competitor for Shearson. But now, Bache would be owned by one of the world's biggest financial institutions, which had more than $60 billion in assets. Sandy was convinced that other firms would sell out to large corporate entities so they could remain competitive in the new world of financial superpowers. From his point of view, the balance of power on Wall Street had shifted, and a merger with American Express became even more attractive.

WICK SIMMONS (former Shearson executive):

I didn't see a need for us to do a thing. I can only speak for myself, and others obviously did. But I thought we were on such a roll that we didn't need to take this step. I mean, we had come so far after being this nothing in September of 1970, when Hayden Stone got together with CBWL. Here we were, ten years later, on a roll. We were the most efficient operator in the brokerage business, bar none. That's what made us attractive to American Express. But I thought we could've just kept on going. I have every reason to believe that to this day.

JESSICA BIBLIOWICZ (chairman of National Financial Partners and Sandy Weill's daughter):

It was the same story you'd hear today. It was scale. It was consolidation. It was being the biggest player, cross-selling, having all these accounts in a financial supermarket. It was the most exciting story you ever heard. And it was American Express. I mean, my father's firm was a bunch of guys with their sleeves rolled up. This was *the* American Express. There was no greater name in the country at the time. Maybe Pan Am was a broader name, but not by much.

PETER COHEN:

It started in March. He met Jimmy Robinson. I was away on a trip to Israel and when I came back I met secretly with Robinson because by now I was clearly the number-two guy in the firm. It really was a very close call as to whether that deal was going to get done. We had a management group of about nine or ten guys in the firm, which by now was pretty sizable. I think we had about twelve thousand people at that point. And the management group was not necessarily in favor of this idea. They wanted to go it alone. Wick Simmons felt that way. Duke Chapman thought he was a loser in the whole thing, so he didn't want to do it. Buzzy Faulkner, who's been deceased a long time now, was very much on the fence. A lot of the other guys also weren't sure what they wanted to do. So it was a real iffy thing.

DUKE CHAPMAN (former Shearson cochairman):

I thought it was a good idea that Sandy was talking to American Express. It seemed to me that was the way the industry was going. Amex couldn't have been a higher-profile company to become a part of.

JESSICA BIBLIOWICZ:

I remember that deal perfectly. I came home from college for Passover — I think I had friends with me — and I was thinking that I would be the center of attention, the focus of the family. Well, I quickly learned that was not to be the case. You could tell that this was *the big one.* I don't know that I completely understood what was really happening, that my father was selling his firm and all that meant, but it definitely had a different tone from all the other deals. Before, it was a very positive thing, they were the ones doing the acquiring and they were all very confident in the decision. This was just totally different from all the other deal activity I saw. They were the ones being bought.

The talks were around the clock. As always, there was tension, but it was different this time. When you sell your company there are some people who are more excited about it than others. This was much more delicate than anything I'd seen, and the energy was much more below the surface. But there was one guy in there who figured out that he could change everything, and he liked to do that, so he was very excited about it. And that was my father. He loved to break the rules. Absolutely.

SANDY WEILL:

We worked out a deal over Easter weekend. We did the financial part of it in two minutes. Who did what to whom personally took a lot more time.

PETER COHEN:

I could see that on balance this was good for the people who worked for the company and the shareholders. Our employees owned about a third of the company's stock so it would be good in two ways for them. Then, I had a little trouble with the way the deal was being structured.

Originally, we would be given three seats on the American Express board, one for Sandy, one for me, and one for Ken Bialkin, our lawyer at Willkie Farr and Gallagher, who's now at Skadden Arps.

It was Good Friday, 1981, and we met with American Express. George Sheinberg, who was a member of our management group, and I basically carved out the financial terms of the deal with the American Express people while Sandy and Jim dealt with things like boards and committees. Sandy went into that meeting saying, "Look, it's three board seats for us or we're not going to do this. It's me, you, and Bialkin or nothing." We wanted our lawyer on the board as sort of an outside guy.

So Sandy and Jim came out of their meeting and we finally agreed on all of our terms. We decided that on Easter Sunday night we'd all meet at Skadden Arps, which were American Express's lawyers, so we could give American Express a letter of intent to take to their board on Monday morning. Sandy had to convene us, the Shearson management group, on Saturday to draw up this letter. Of course, that weekend not only was Good Friday and Easter, it also was Passover, just real crazy timing. But we agreed to get all the guys up to Sandy's house in Greenwich, Connecticut, on Saturday morning to review the terms we accepted on Friday.

We then left the meeting and caught a cab uptown. We dropped Sandy off, and as he was getting out of the taxi he leaned in and said to me, "By the way, Jim changed his mind in terms of the board seats. We'll only get two. So it's going to be me and Bialkin." He was like throwing me away. George Sheinberg was sitting there right next to me — I couldn't believe what I was hearing. As he turned from the cab he said, "There's been a change. That's all. I'll talk to you later." Then he walked away. He couldn't face me.

I went berserk. I mean, I was absolutely nuts about this. He called me later that night and asked me to come to his house early the next morning so he could talk to me before the other guys showed up. He basically wanted to convince me not to queer the deal with the other guys.

When I got there the next day I said, "I'm not going to talk anybody out of this, but I'm not doing it for you. I'm doing it because it's the right thing for the firm and the people who have worked for us for the last ten years. That's why I'm going to do it." That made him happy. Then I said, "But I'm giving you and Jim Robinson no commitment beyond year-end that I'm going to be here. I really feel like the rug's been pulled out from underneath me."

Jim called me that Saturday night and I told him exactly how I felt, too. On Sunday, we went up to Skadden Arps to take a look at the letter of intent. At that point they informed Sandy and me that we would have to sign five-year noncompete agreements. I said, "I can understand why Sandy should sign one, but I don't know why I should. I'm not getting any special consideration." And I wasn't committing to staying beyond year-end.

Monday we went into work, and American Express's board was supposed to meet first thing, agree to the letter of intent, and then let us know that we had a deal. But the entire day went by, and we heard nothing. All we knew was that they were in a board meeting that was lasting the whole day. Meanwhile, Sheinberg and I were telling Sandy, "First of all, there have to be problems if it's taking this long. And second, don't do this deal if you think you're going to push Jim Robinson out of a job, because it's not going to happen."

JEFF LANE:

I never heard Sandy say he wanted to be CEO of American Express. Early on, I think what he wanted was to be chief operating officer. Besides, there was not a chance that Sandy was going to become their chief executive. Number one, they were happy with Jim. And number two, Sandy was of the wrong religion. I may be incorrect, but I think that was a factor also at that time.

JUDITH RAMSEY EHRLICH:

There was not a single Jew in the upper management of American Express back then. Jews would not be easily accepted in that environment, not at the very top.

WICK SIMMONS:

Of course, Sandy thought that he was going to become chairman of American Express. I mean, it was never going to happen, but of course he thought it was. The guy had built a terrific business here that had been acquired for a huge sum of money compared to what we were worth just a few years before. But there was no way at that time that a Jewish guy was going to run American Express. It would never happen.

PETER COHEN:

Sandy absolutely wanted to be chairman of American Express. And Sandy absolutely thought he could become chairman of American Express. He figured that somehow he'd maneuver his way in there and do it. But we said, "It's never going to happen, Sandy."

Of course he always denied it. "That's not what I aspire to . . . you don't know . . . blah, blah, blah."

We just kept saying to him, "If you really want to run American Express you stay with Shearson after the merger and build it into an undeniable force within the American Express family. If you make Shearson the company, you can do whatever you want to do."

Anyway, that day just kept dragging on and on and on. The anxiety was unbelievable. Sandy was pacing, chewing his nails, twirling his hair, and drinking. Everything was going on. Then Jim called and said he wanted to talk to Sandy. So Jim came over, and Sandy had his wife, Joan, who's sort of his sidekick, there. He always has her around. Joan's a great salesman for Sandy because she'll bullshit the hell out of anyone better than most of these slick guys on Wall Street. She's lost a lot of friends over the years because of all the mergers. Joan always tries to patch things up — "That's just Sandy. It's not me." But this is what happens anytime you mix friendship and business the way they do.

So Sandy and Jim met for about an hour, and we were all hanging around waiting to hear what's going on. When he came out of the meeting, he gave me this look, this sneer, as if I'd undermined him. Then he said, "You're on the board after all, Peter."

I was stunned. That was it. He just walked away. Jim came over and said, "The board decided and feels very strongly that we should have you join the American Express board. We want to try to make you a big part of the future of this company." Whether it was the five-year lockup, or that they felt they could control me more than Sandy, I don't know. Maybe I fit into their plans because if things didn't work with Sandy at least somebody would be around who knew the business. Whatever the reason, I got the board seat.

But from that day on my relationship with Sandy was never the same, even though I didn't do anything other than point out that the original deal was not what was promised to me. I mean, I wasn't going to disrupt the deal, but I wasn't promising to stay under those conditions either. I was never a guy who put a money gun to anyone's head.

SANDY WEILL:

It's no secret that Peter and I don't have a real close relationship — God knows why.

JEFF LANE:

I didn't think that Sandy's involvement with us would end with the American Express deal. I thought he'd continue to be involved with Shearson. As it turned out, he and George Sheinberg went to American Express, and Peter became the CEO [of Shearson/American Express]. Then Peter and Sandy had this enormous falling out, and that was that.

PETER COHEN:

We closed this deal in September and by November he was gone, over to American Express. He still wanted to control Shearson but didn't want to be there day in, day out. So he said, "You run it." He was starting his push over at American Express, and his first move was to leave our office and move over to the corporate headquarters.

JUDITH RAMSEY EHRLICH:

Sandy wanted to move to the corporate office to be at the center of power. And he watched some of his colleagues move over. Soon after the merger was completed George Sheinberg of Shearson was named treasurer of American Express. Duke Chapman became vice president of its international banking arm. And Robert Reilly moved over as senior vice president in charge of planning. By early 1982, Weill was ensconced in a corner office on the fortieth floor of the American Express Tower. He was diagonally across from Jim Robinson's suite.

PETER COHEN:

When he left Shearson to go over to American Express, it was over for Sandy at the company. If he'd stayed at Shearson he still would have been king of the mountain. When he left I said, "You're making a mistake leaving. Believe me, from a personal standpoint it's not in my best interests to tell you this, but you shouldn't leave."

SANDY WEILL:

I'm one of the world's great rationalizers, and I feel things have a way of working out for the best. Everyone told me, including Joan, that I should keep my power base at Shearson to force my way into a stronger position at American Express. My decision was not to do that. If I had wanted to run Shearson still, I wouldn't have sold the company. I wanted Shearson to grow in the American Express environment. If I had to do it all over again, I would have done the same thing.

WICK SIMMONS:

Sandy sold us to American Express and never found his footing there. I'm not sure they were ever going to give him a footing, but for whatever reason he never found it at American Express.

What American Express ultimately refused to do was turn over the names of their American Express card members to Shearson. The whole reason for this deal originally was, with the sales force that we'd built up in conjunction with this relatively high-net-worth group of American Express cardholders, there were tremendous synergies. But there was no way that Lou Gerstner [the head of American Express travel-related services at the time] was going to turn over the names of his card members to us.

Well, if you weren't going to do that, why the hell should we be together in the first place? So it turned out to be a huge mistake in conception.

JEFF LANE:

It didn't work, but it didn't work for a lot of different reasons. My concept was that we'd use the American Express Gold Card as our vehicle, and American Express would introduce their wealthy clients to us, and we would to a limited extent introduce our clients to American Express. But they had no intention and no interest in introducing anybody to our company. They were always concerned that our brokers would do things they shouldn't do, and two bad things would happen: one, there'd be a lawsuit; and two, they'd lose their client. So there were no introductions of American Express customers. But that was the hope.

Sandy was inappropriately used at American Express. Jim thought he was a threat rather than an ally, which was unfortunate. I'm of the view, for what it's worth, that if Jim had embraced Sandy and made him chief operating officer, there's a chance that all of us would still be at American Express. They could've been really great partners. Sandy at that time was the "king of the inside." Of course, as it turned out, he's really king of the inside *and* king of the outside. But at the time, Jim clearly was in charge of the outside stuff at American Express, and Sandy would've been wonderful in the inside role. I'm not sure that anything terrible would've happened.

SANDY WEILL:

I wasn't even number two going into Amex. I was number three [after American Express president Al Way].

JUDITH RAMSEY EHRLICH:

Despite the status and perks that went with being president of American Express, Weill soon found that he had little leverage or power. He wanted to make policy and management decisions that would shape the future of the company. But he had few responsibilities in the day-to-day management of the firm. Instead, he handled superficial chores, odd problems, and corporate projects as they arose. He supervised the building of the new American Express Tower in the World Financial Center. He lunched with promising young company executives. And he helped build the corporate image with the media and press. In fact, Robinson felt he was getting too much attention from the press. Nonetheless, Weill was locked into a tight little box and there didn't seem to be any way to get out.

In 1983, Robinson gave Weill the assignment of rescuing American Express's Fireman's Fund, based in San Francisco. To many of his friends at Shearson, it appeared that Weill was moving away from the power base at American Express and that Robinson was responsible. From December of 1983 through March of 1984, Weill, though still president of American Express, was spending three-quarters of his time in California as the new chairman of the Fireman's Fund. Sometimes he'd fly home for weekends, and occasionally Joan would join him there. And, in what some call "the December debacle," he fired 1,150 of the 14,000 Fireman's Fund employees, including virtually all the senior executives. While Weill was out there making his mark with Fireman's Fund, Robinson saw to it that another link with Shearson was severed. Robinson directed that the brokerage house report to him and not to Weill.

JAMIE DIMON (president of JP Morgan Chase and former assistant to Sandy Weill):

When they had all those problems with Fireman's Fund, Sandy became CEO of that. Then they started talking about spinning it off, and Sandy said, "I have a better idea. I'll buy it."

But Sandy also knew that once he started that conversation, if it didn't work he'd probably have to leave. There really was no turning back from there. So he put together a group of people, and we set about trying to buy Fireman's Fund. But once it broke, he knew he was in a compromised position because there were two teams working on this now, two negotiations. It just wasn't going to work anymore.

I remember the second it broke he wanted to do his exit agreement right there. We were at the office until two, three in the morning. Marty Lipton [Weill's attorney] came down and helped draw it up. The whole thing was only a couple of pages long, typed. It was announced the next day, and he was gone. It was never bad blood, though there were some difficulties between a few of the departments. But Jim and Sandy kind of stayed friendly. And they're friends today.

SANDY WEILL:

The biggest lesson of these twenty years is that I'm happier running my own show. This doesn't mean I shouldn't have gone to American Express; the experience was valuable. For one thing, I learned that my skills are transferable. But I forgot how much I enjoy being the top person. I also believe that eventually you have to move on and leave room, leaving a good team behind.

Sandy Weill resigned from American Express in June 1985. He took an office in the Seagram Building on the East Side of Manhattan with his assistant, Jamie Dimon, and started looking for another company to run. In the coming years, the ambitions of both Weill and Dimon would play out on an even grander stage. Meanwhile, with Weill out of the way, his former protégé, Peter Cohen, emerged as Shearson's new CEO, free to pursue his own ideas to further expand the firm's reach. And it wouldn't take long for an interesting opportunity to catch his eye.

CHAPTER 18

CULTURE CLASH

With the arrival of Mayday, which allowed traders to negotiate commissions with their clients, and the emergence of the computer as a quantitative tool, trading stocks and bonds had become a much more profitable business on Wall Street by the 1970s and early 1980s. But for many of the old-line Wall Street partnerships, the trouble was, you had to spend money to make money because trading also had become extremely capital intensive. Traditionally, their business was one of relationships, where a few partners put in as little money as possible and earned enormous fees for advising and financing companies. Now, Wall Street had to grow or die. Not surprisingly, many of the old-line partnerships disappeared. But Lehman Brothers survived.

Bobbie Lehman, who collected people as well as he collected art, had put together a powerful group of personalities underneath him. Unlike the other Our Crowd investment banks, Lehman Brothers was able to keep its blue-chip underwriting and advisory business and successfully build a mighty trading operation that rivaled anyone on Wall Street. Indeed, by the early 1980s, the trading business was arguably more important to Lehman Brothers than in-

vestment banking. This did not go unnoticed by the firm's head of trading, Lew Glucksman.

Of course, the rising importance of trading also brought its own set of complications. There was a clash of cultures at Lehman Brothers between the sophisticated, Ivy League–educated investment bankers and the traders, whom many Lehman partners considered inferior. Over time, these tensions would result in an all-out war within the firm and a palace coup against chairman Pete Peterson. And in the end, the loser would turn out to be Lehman Brothers.

PETE PETERSON (former Lehman Brothers chairman):

You almost have to be a social psychologist to understand the relationship between bankers and traders on Wall Street. Clearly, the bankers tend to see themselves as the preferred, first-tier group because they're the ones that have not only technical sophistication in corporate finance but also the social sophistication. They deal in the top of the corporate world, whereas traders are seen as being down in the trenches doing the heavy lifting. Not to engage in a lot of psychobabble, but I'm sure if you did a psychological profile you'd find that traders are much more short-term oriented and less patient. But there's also probably a class thing going on there between the investment bankers and traders. At that time the traders tended to not have MBAs; some of them didn't have college degrees. There was a cultural difference in the way bankers and traders looked, dressed, interacted, and so on. You could do a whole book on that subject alone.

WARREN HELLMAN (former Lehman Brothers partner):

On Wall Street in general, the division between the investment banks and sales and trading firms was evaporating. There was always a difference between Lehman Brothers, Morgan Stanley, First Boston, and Goldman Sachs, and Merrill Lynch, Salomon Brothers, and the rest. But those guys, the Merrills and Salomons, started to do a better job of winning investment-banking business based on their ability to distribute to their clients. It was only so long that we could say, "We'll just hire Merrill Lynch to be in our syndicate." Eventually, Merrill Lynch was going to say to the company, "We'll do it ourselves."

ANDY SAGE (former Lehman Brothers partner):

We were not a trading firm classically. In the 1950s I don't think we did any trading business, but as we moved into the 1960s it started to become more important. Bobbie Lehman may or may not have been aware that there even were traders. Certainly they weren't anything he went home and lost a lot of sleep over because no one had lost him a significant amount of money. Bobbie had a one-track mind — he wanted us to get IBM and every other damn piece of business we could. He wanted the prestige of doing the big business and would do just about anything to get it.

WARREN HELLMAN:

Bobbie Lehman was pretty much disdainful of traders, or what we called salesmen. We'd never had a salesman as a partner. The first guy from sales and trading to become a partner was Marvin Levy. When the partners wanted to bring him up, Bobbie was just aghast. He said, "But those guys smoke cigars." The sales department was on the second floor. I don't think Bobbie visited the sales department more than once a year.

But Bobbie also was very admiring of Goldman Sachs, which had a dominant commercial-paper business. And Lew Glucksman brought the commercial-paper capability to Lehman Brothers. Lew was at A. G. Becker, and he came to us and said, "I can bring a bunch of guys and start a commercial-paper business for you." That's how he got to Lehman.

ANDY SAGE:

Commercial paper is very short-term debt, fairly low-risk stuff. The business was successful, but not extraordinarily so. It didn't come close to dominating the investment-banking business. But it was there and it helped. Our motive wasn't necessarily to do well at commercial paper. It was to find another avenue to get underwriting clients. That was the plan. All of a sudden you're working with the treasurer of the company on some short-term financing, and you could introduce him to some of your investment bankers who might have some larger ideas. That was the motive, but I don't know that it ever paid off the way we'd hoped.

LEW GLUCKSMAN (former Lehman Brothers chairman and chief executive):

From my kind of background, Lehman epitomized a level of success in banking that was not generally available. They were the pillars. You looked upon Lehman as the furthest you could go.

BOB RUBIN (former Lehman Brothers partner):

The trading business at Lehman Brothers started to become more important within the firm because it was proportionately more profitable than it had ever been. In the 1960s, trading was nowhere near a dominant part of the earnings. But that was the source of Lew's strength. Over time, the businesses that Lew was responsible for started contributing to a larger share of the firm's overall earnings.

SAUL COHEN (former Lehman Brothers in-house counsel):

Lew Glucksman is a very bright guy, very capable. But until about 1983, Lew was a total slob. His shirt was always unbuttoned. I'll tell you a story. I was at a meeting in the office of a guy named Paul Cohen, who was a senior-level administrative person in Lehman's commercial-paper department. Anyway, Lew walks by, sees us in the room, and decides to take a look in at what's going on. The meeting stops and Paul says, "Lew, your pants are ripped." Now, when most people's pants are ripped they've got a seam open. But this looked as if someone had taken a hacksaw to them from the cuffs to his waist. Lew looks at me — I'll never forget this — and says, "God knows I have the intelligence, but the image is sadly lacking." I remember it word for word.

STEPHEN SCHWARZMAN (former Lehman Brothers partner):

Those of us who worked with Lew realized that sometimes he just behaved in a strange way, whether it was yanking telephones out of the wall and throwing them, or opening his shirt by ripping all the buttons off, or screaming at people in what appeared to be an uncontrolled rage.

PETER SOLOMON (former Lehman Brothers partner):

Starting in the late sixties there was a regrettable confluence of events that changed the firm. First, Bobbie died, and there was no real successor.

ANDY SAGE:

When Bobbie died nobody was going to be able to replace him. Before he died he made various people heads of the firm. General Clay was the head guy for a while. Paul Mazur was the managing partner for a while. But it didn't make any difference. Bobbie could've made everybody else in the firm a sultan and himself a runner, but everybody would still know it was his firm. So when Bobbie died I was the managing partner and the first president, but I wasn't Bobbie Lehman. Toward the end of '72 I said I wanted to do something else.

ROBERT BERNHARD (former Lehman Brothers partner):

Somehow or another Fred Ehrman was chosen to be senior partner. About as ill suited a man to be senior partner at any firm that I've ever met. Bitter? He was nasty, a really nasty individual. His close friends were Gus Levy and Cy Lewis, and he thought that their talents rubbed off on him. They didn't.

ANDY SAGE:

Freddy really was a good guy. But he was crude and rude. He was not universally loved — they called him "Friendly Freddy." Freddy kind of was shy in a way, so if somebody would get in the elevator and say, "Good morning, Mr. Ehrman," he'd be as likely as not to answer. That doesn't go over well. If a junior partner said something in a meeting that Fred didn't think was right, he would say, "That's the stupidest thing I've ever heard." That's not the way to make friends. But he was smart and a really good technician, best technician I knew in the business. He could do preferred stock, convertibles — he could price them, he could do them, he was a real pro.

Nobody in the place could match Fred as far as knowing the investment-banking business. But he did not get on well with people. I knew it was going to be a problem, and frankly, I didn't want any part of it.

WARREN HELLMAN:

By 1973, Fred, who was my uncle, was the chairman, the firm was hemorrhaging, there was no internal communication, and we were losing something like $3 million a month. We were very, very close to the line. The fixed-income division, Lew's division, had taken some positions. I don't entirely blame Lew for this, because the firm was so secretive that I'm sure he didn't know how small the firm's net capital actually was. Anyway, they had taken a huge long position in governments, I believe, assuming a drop in interest rates. Instead, interest rates went up, and there was a drop in the face value of the positions. But to be fair to Lew, nobody communicated to him our financial condition.

It's the old story — had Lew been able to hold his positions long enough we would've come out great. But we were not in a position that we could do that.

BOB RUBIN:

I'd worked with Lew from the beginning. Lew was in the interest-rate business, whether it was commercial paper, or CDs, or bonds. When you're in the fixed-income business your success depends on being a good trader or investor, and it also depends on interest rates. Any fool can make money in the fixed-income business if interest rates are going up.

So I was brought in, I think at first to fire Lew. But what they did was make me chairman of the commercial-paper division and told me to supervise him. The one incident that always sticks in my mind is that I started getting a weekly report from Lew. So I called his secretary and asked who got this report. Well, everybody who was complaining that Lew had done these terrible things that nobody knew about had been getting this report. Did they read it? Who knows. But there was nothing hidden about the weekly changes in inventory and what was happening to interest rates. It was all there.

STEPHEN SCHWARZMAN:

Pete [Peterson] was brought in right before that as vice chairman and sort of a well-known personage. At that time Lehman collected people of that type. There was a fellow by the name of George Ball who'd been deputy secretary of state, the only deputy who actually attended cabinet meetings, serving in some cases as the de facto secretary of state. There were people like Paul Davies, who'd been chairman of FMC Corporation. Lehman had a tradition of bringing in high-profile non-investment bankers, and Pete was brought in along that vein. This dates back to Bobbie Lehman. But within about six weeks of Pete's being here, we had that problem in the trading area.

SAUL COHEN:

Pete Peterson was a standout in American business. He'd been president of Bell and Howell in his thirties. He was a member of Nixon's cabinet as secretary of commerce, and he was fired from Nixon's cabinet because, as he said to me one day, "I wouldn't click my heels for Haldeman." That was probably the best thing that ever happened to him, getting away from the Nixon White House before the disaster hit.

PETE PETERSON:

So I was brought in as vice chairman at Lehman. Three weeks later the controller comes in and says that we've just lost $15 million or $20 million in fixed-income positions. I said, "What?" I mean, we only had about $17 million or $18 million of equity at the time. This was kind of devastating because it consumed a lot of capital, and the firm became very uneasy about the leadership. There was a fellow by the name of Fred Ehrman who was chairman. I'd only been there about six weeks when George Ball and a few others came to see me and said, "You've got to run this place." I'm saying to myself, wait a minute, I've only been here a few weeks, I don't even know how I feel about the business, and I really came in to do the investment side of things. By then I'd put all my money in the place, though I didn't have all that much money. But part of the requirement of being in a partnership is you have to put your capital in, so my capital was in the partnership.

I'll never forget the meeting in which they told me they wanted me to take over. I said, "You know, I've always believed in orderly transitions." Clients don't like it when there's upheaval in your organization. So I said that I'd take the job on the condition that I'd go in and see Fred with George and Warren Hellman, his nephew. Fred had had two or three heart attacks and had become extremely unpopular. Frankly, he was getting blamed for the whole trauma when he hadn't put up all the losses. But you know what happens, people want to make a change. I wanted to have the transition take place at year-end. I'd still be vice chairman, the only difference would be how I'd function. I said, "The guy's been here his entire life, and he's had this health problem. Let's give him a dignified send-off."

They were really reluctant to do that. "No, no, no, throw the son of a bitch out." But I said, "If you want me to do this, this is the way it's going to be done. I'm not going to be part of a bloody coup."

So we went in there, and I explained to Fred what was going on. Warren was kind of terrified of his uncle and was staring down at his socks. He always wore these white silk socks that were too short and falling down all over the place. He wouldn't look his uncle in the eye, just kept looking at those socks. But I looked him in the eye. His answer was, "No way. Fuck you!" I said, "Fred, why wouldn't you want to do it this way? You're sixty-eight years old, you've got this health situation." But he kept saying, "Fuck you." And that was my introduction to the Lehman culture.

WARREN HELLMAN:

It's funny, I think we wanted Pete for one reason, but when he got there it turned out he had tremendous talents in another area. We wanted him as a guy with a great Rolodex who could attract great investment-banking business. Oddly enough, he turned out to be a hell of a manager.

PETE PETERSON:

The first thing you had to do was get your costs down. Next you had to get out of the bleeders. We were in the real estate business and it wasn't working. We got out of that. I thought asset management was going to become an increasingly interesting business, and a bread-and-butter business that transcends the cycles of Wall Street. It has a steadying effect on your cash flow, which is very difficult to do in that business.

I was presumably educated at the University of Chicago, and Adam Smith was my patron saint, so I believed in comparative advantage. When looking at our business I realized that I didn't know anything about the trading and capital-markets side of the business. I guess you could say I was at a comparative disadvantage there. So I decided to make Lew president, because by then we were beginning to perform very well and the fixed-income business was becoming increasingly important.

BOB RUBIN:

Trading really started to become important to the firm in the late 1970s. When fixed commissions went out it changed the whole equity-trading business. Before, what the hell, you didn't have to do anything. A guy wants to buy stock, you sell it to him and collect your commission. You didn't have to put up your own capital or anything. It was a gravy train for people who were in the equity-trading business, which was never very big for us, actually. But that changed the whole trading business, the need for capital in the equity business, and so on.

PETER SOLOMON:

Glucksman was a guy who could and would intimidate people. He would intimidate people about their jobs. He was intimidating, acted intimidating. But he was doing well. He ran a pretty good operation. He was making money; he was the moneymaker. Trading was becoming more important. Pete came up to my office one day and said, "I think Glucksman should be president."

I said, "I don't have a problem with that. He's working hard, doing a good job." So there are two sides to this coin, and both of them are real.

SAUL COHEN:

The firm was very aggressive, but highly dedicated to doing things properly. These were very ethical people. I can give you a specific example.

I remember a trader coming to Lew Glucksman and saying, "We screwed up a trade and the guys on the other side think we should make good on it. It's a $3 million loss."

So Lew said, "It's our trade — we'll eat it." That was a $3 million loss, and that was a lot in those days. I don't know if that exists on the Street anymore, but that's the way the place ran. Your word was your bond.

PETE PETERSON:

So I made Lew president, and he did a damn good job. As time went on, Lew and I developed what I thought was a good working relationship. I'd gotten a lot of our corporate clients and they were impressed with our fixed-income capability. It was not an area I knew much about, and I really believe in the importance of being complementary in an organizational relationship. That's how I viewed our relationship.

LEWIS GLUCKSMAN:

If I could avoid being with Peterson, I'd avoid being with Peterson. I couldn't stand the monologues.

PETER SOLOMON:

Glucksman was a guy who could never take yes for an answer. He always wanted more.

BOB RUBIN:

What happened was, in 1982 and 1983, the bankers owned two-thirds of the firm, but the earnings were 60 or 70 percent non-investment banking. So they owned two-thirds of the firm, they got the bulk of the incentive compensation, and they were not contributing as much. This contributed to disagreements between bankers and non-investment bankers. Lew was leading the charge for the non-investment bankers. And Pete, who was supposed to be the CEO and leading the charge for nobody, was leading the charge for the bankers. It was a problem.

PETE PETERSON:

So one day Lew and I were having breakfast — when Lew was president and I was CEO we'd have breakfast once or twice a week — and [Goldman Sachs co-senior partner] John Whitehead had wanted to come over, so he paid a visit and brought [Goldman Sachs co-senior partner] John Weinberg along with him. And I noticed that they were getting along very well. I think Lew was fifty-eight at the time, and I was fifty-eight. Anyway, I remember I was talking to my wife one night after that and I said, "You know, I've been at this for ten years and I've gotten a lot of credit. I deserved some of it, but certainly not the lion's share. The business is doing well. Lew and I are the same age, and we seem to be getting along well . . ."

I think this was the middle of May 1983, and I called him in one day and said, "I've been thinking. We've been getting along well. The firm's getting a lot bigger and you deserve more credit. Why don't I make you co-CEO?"

All I can tell you is what he told me, which is that he was thrilled. We put out an annual report with the two of us. We sent letters to all our clients. I said that I'd draft the letter but I wanted him to sign it with me. I told him that I wanted him to get to know the corporate clients that I know, and we'd be in this thing together. And it all seemed fine.

BOB RUBIN:

In my recollection, that is absolutely untrue. Pete was interested in protecting Pete. I have memos from Pete in 1980 and '81 where he's sort of asking me to consider whether it's okay for him to invest money with one of his friends from outside the firm because he was concerned about his long-term financial situation. But at the same time he also was saying that he was going to devote all his time to the firm. Pete was interested in himself. Maybe he can say it was his idea because that was the only way he could think of to stem the tide of either him being sent on his way, like Fred, or having Lew leave. If Lew left, what would he do about this business that he knew nothing about and was contributing 60 or 70 percent of the earnings? In his mind it may have been his idea, but it was not one he embraced, and it was not one that was successful. I think the co-chief executive arrangement lasted only a few months.

PETE PETERSON:

It was in June of that year [1983] that Lew was nice enough to have a party on my tenth anniversary with the firm. I've always been a modern-art nut — Rothkos, Diebenkorns, Mirós — I've got a lot, and I love it. Lew knew that I'd seen a Henry Moore, and much to my amazement he presented it to me at the party and said some really nice things. He wrote me a note that I probably should have saved about how good the relationship was, how much he'd enjoyed it, how much he'd been learning, and so forth. I was happy to give him a lot of credit.

But it was only a month later when this famous meeting was held. I'd gotten another piece of business from the CEO of Continental. We'd had this great meeting and I was telling him about it. And then he starts this monologue that has been variously reported and exaggerated, I'm sure. He was talking about wanting to be the captain of the ship, and then he started talking about how he needed to run the firm by himself.

I remember my reaction was one of real surprise. We'd made all these changes and all these announcements. If you've never run one of these firms for ten years, let me tell you, it's one tough job, particularly with the Lehman culture. There's greed; there's envy.

BOB RUBIN:

If there were two people that you could think of as being opposites in personality, demeanor, personal goals, and anything else you want to describe, you couldn't find two more disparate people than Lew Glucksman and Pete Peterson. Any cooperation between them was forced by circumstances. Peterson loved to acquire people, and he did at Lehman Brothers. He was able to get people to be "his" people, whether they were in the firm or not in the firm. And I think it's fair to say that Glucksman was disdainful of wanting to, or being able to, do that kind of thing.

PETE PETERSON:

So when Lew and I had that famous meeting, and he told me that he wanted to take over, I was very surprised, particularly since I was offering him a transition. I didn't want to fight. I said, "Why didn't you tell me about it?"

But he was going on and on about how he wanted more, and this guy was getting too much, and why was this guy getting this? He thought he could do a better job running the company. I actually was very proud of the organization we'd put together. I'd made arrangements where Lew got as much money as I did, or he'd get more. I voluntarily reduced my stake in the firm. Steve [Schwarzman] can tell you this — I had 8 percent of the firm but I reduced it to 3 percent so I could give the young guys like Steve Schwarzman and Steve Fenster 2 percent. We'd flattened out the organization.

So I said, "If you'd just told me about it." I mean, I was getting tired. The whole thing had become so draining to me.

LEW GLUCKSMAN:

My principal concern was that the best thing that could happen would be an orderly and a quiet transition to benefit the business. I wanted to do it quickly. The key in any financial deal is to keep the momentum going.

On July 26, 1983, Pete Peterson stepped down as chairman of Lehman Brothers, with a severance package that ultimately would be worth about $18 million. Lew Glucksman, a trader, installed himself as chairman and chief executive. For many of the investment bankers, the response was open rebellion. Within nine months Lehman Brothers would be gone.

PETER SOLOMON:

I didn't realize Glucksman was going to move against Peterson. I was out doing enormous amounts of business, having an incredibly wonderful run in the 1982 to '83 period. I wasn't paying any attention to the politics of the firm. I was shocked by the confrontation.

STEPHEN SCHWARZMAN:

Having Pete forced to resign in such a threatening manner by Lew had almost a Shakespearean quality to it. The trading side was doing well, but somehow the wrong person wound up in the wrong position, and you could sense that something very bad was going to happen as a result. I think that was the feeling that most of the people in the banking area had. It wasn't as simpleminded as the fact that their economics were going to change, because with strong-performing individuals that wasn't really a concern. The main concern was that the firm was in the hands of somebody who could do damage to it because the position of CEO in this business is complicated. The people who work in the business have to rely on the judgment, fairness, and consistency of vision and leadership of the CEO. And I think people were concerned that because of Lew's sometimes-erratic personality, it was the wrong decision for the business. And that turned out to be the case.

BOB RUBIN:

The same thing happened in 1983 that also happened in 1973. Interest rates went through the roof, and the fixed-income business — commercial paper, bonds, everything — was losing money. The investment bank made about $20 million and the non-investment bank, particularly the fixed-income business, lost about $20 million. People went bananas. The partners, owners, went bananas. That's what stimulated the move to sell the business.

PETER SOLOMON:

It wasn't a capital problem. It was an inability of Glucksman to run the firm. We refused — I refused. I, in retrospect, maybe could've handled this better.

STEPHEN SCHWARZMAN:

There were so many different things going on at the firm at the time that it's hard to re-create the instability that existed by simply explaining it.

Many of the partners, certainly on the banking side, wanted the firm to be sold because of the potential losses. I think many people were scared that they were going to lose their capital. There was a divergence of views on this because some people thought we could ride these positions home, while other people thought that if we let it ride any more we could end up with nothing. In any case, there were significant partners who wanted the firm sold simply as a resolution to the breakdown in confidence with Glucksman.

LEW GLUCKSMAN:

The trading partners were generating 60 percent of the profits and never had received as much as 40 percent of the compensation. In the end, the bankers, who controlled 65 percent of the partners' shares, had the option of selling the business, and that's what they did.

PETER COHEN (former Shearson/American Express chairman):

I always had my antennae up for what was happening with Glucksman and Peterson. About a year before we actually bought them we were solicited by Peter Solomon and some of the other senior guys there. We had this secret meeting across the river at an Italian restaurant in Queens. We didn't want to run into anyone we knew. Peter Solomon, to his credit, said, "These guys are going to bury this firm. We're a good fit with you guys because you have holes where we have strength and vice versa."

But I told him, "Look, I'm not about to step in and try to resolve this Peterson-Glucksman mess you have on your hands. If there's a time when it's appropriate for us to engage in a deal after you've straightened this stuff out, we'd be interested."

We were waiting for something to happen. Then, Glucksman shot Peterson and war broke out. One day, Steve Schwarzman shows up at my house — he was my neighbor at the beach — and says, "You've got to buy Lehman." They were all worried about the place imploding, which he was right to worry about, because if we hadn't done it, Lehman would have disappeared.

STEPHEN SCHWARZMAN:

Peter was my next-door neighbor out in East Hampton. I was very active in the merger business, so I was a logical person to be involved in that. I wasn't sure if anybody wanted me to do anything about it, but I went to Shel Gordon, who was appointed by Lew to run the whole corporate finance side of the business and was very loyal to him. Shel said, "I think that's the right thing to do."

I checked with him two or three names, and I assumed that Shel was speaking, not just for himself, but also for the senior people who worked for Lew and realized that the firm was falling apart. I didn't assume that he was speaking for Lew, of course. Lew didn't want anything to happen to the firm, but a lot of people around him did.

PETER COHEN:

He promised me that Glucksman would step aside if we came in and that they could deliver a deal any way we wanted it. Eventually I just said, "I don't know, let me think about it." Then he left. Of course, the first thing I did as soon as he walked out the door was pick up the phone and call Jim [Robinson, American Express chairman]. Jim knew about the meeting I'd had in Queens the year before, and I said, "I think our time has come."

STEPHEN SCHWARZMAN:

Really what they were concerned about was whether Lehman had received such a body blow that there would be nobody left standing by the time the deal closed. As long as there was no problem of that type, he was very enthusiastic about it.

PETER COHEN:

I got the go-ahead from Jim and from Sandy [Weill, American Express president], who wasn't even a part of Shearson anymore, but I wanted him to feel good about it. As a matter of fact, the first person I had lunch with in the Lehman partners' dining room after we bought them was Sandy. I said, "Let's the two of us go over there and enjoy a little bit of this."

BOB RUBIN:

I wasn't happy about the deal, but I also wasn't Bobbie Lehman. It's a partnership. If you have fifteen people on the board of directors, and I'm making that number up, and then you have three or four people voting against it, you can be a hard-ass for only so long. When you're in the minority, you're in the minority. I think there were four of us who did the whole deal, and we did what we had to do. But happy, I was not.

PETER SOLOMON:

We sold the firm for bupkes. The firm would have been worth billions, and we got $350 million. It was a pathetic sale. But it was a liquidation of a political problem. The politics had gotten so terrible, the divisiveness. It was unbearable.

STEPHEN SCHWARZMAN:

I think panic sales by definition aren't good. But the problem at Lehman wasn't just about Lew Glucksman, because that's too simple. The problem really was the next layer of partners and the fact that they could not, as a group, find a way to work together and replace Lew when it became clear that he needed to be replaced. What should've happened is that group of senior partners should've worked together to bring in some outside capital and rebuild the firm. They would've done very, very well. So to blame the failure of Lehman on simply Lew Glucksman and his leadership, or the greed of other people, is a bit simplistic. One needs to look at why the remaining senior partners couldn't work together to find a suitable management structure and replacement. Looking through the mist of time, that is the failure.

PETER SOLOMON:

The whole thing was totally driven by personalities. It was a lack of governance, a lack of leadership and a compass of how people should work together. Ultimately, this was the fault of Robert Lehman. I'll use the analogy of beekeeping. When the queen begins to die the worker bees sense that the queen is failing. They create a whole new set of queen cells.

One queen usually emerges, and she kills all the other queen cells. She establishes herself as the queen, order is resumed, and life goes on in the beehive. But sometimes the queen dies quickly, before there are enough queen cells. Then, what you have is a lot of queens who can't lay new eggs. They run around and eventually the hive dies off. That's what happened at Lehman Brothers.

LEW GLUCKSMAN:

My biggest mistake was to make them all so rich. I'm serious.

CHAPTER 19

DAWN OF A BULL MARKET

The greatest bull market in the history of Wall Street began in the summer of 1982 and ran essentially unabated — other than a few hiccups, most notably in 1987 — through the end of the twentieth century. The rally started as a long-awaited rebound from a dismal period that began in the late 1960s and ran through the early 1980s. By the time 1982 rolled around, the last thing anyone expected was for Wall Street to heat up. And yet, that's what happened.

There were several factors underpinning this explosion, but the primary trigger was the 1979 decision by the Federal Reserve, headed by then chairman Paul Volcker, to break the crippling inflation that was strangling the U.S. economy. There also were some fundamental changes taking place in the financial markets. First, mutual funds started to grow in popularity, largely spurred by high-profile fund managers like Fidelity's Peter Lynch. With his distinctive silver hair and knack for explaining investing in simple terms, Lynch in the 1980s became one of Wall Street's true celebrities. Of course, it didn't hurt that he also was about the best investment manager on the planet at that time. And Presi-

dent Ronald Reagan pushed through Congress a radical tax-reform package that slashed taxes for the upper and middle classes, and, through a host of tax incentives, brought about the creation of new savings plans that completely changed the way Americans put away money for retirement. It used to be that the bulk of a U.S. worker's retirement savings was in a pension plan that provided a set payment based on a percentage of the worker's salary. But with the new 401(k) plan, so named for the section of the tax code that provided the loophole that essentially created it, and the individual retirement account, or IRA, workers instead could invest their own money, and money contributed by their employers, in a host of financial instruments, and receive favorable tax treatment as long as the money stayed in the plans for a certain amount of time. Finally, Wall Street had a captive audience.

Perhaps not surprisingly, this newfound prosperity eventually led to excess. By the time we reached the mid-1980s, some wondered whether the stock market's momentum had gone beyond reason. But with new innovations like computerized program trading and so-called portfolio insurance, Wall Street refused to heed the warnings, and the good times continued to roll. So, when the calendar hit 1987, it clearly was time for a sanity check.

HARRY POULAKAKOS (former owner of Harry's of Hanover Square bar and restaurant):

I started Harry's at Hanover Square in 1972. Wall Street was much smaller then. The actual business of Wall Street was confined to about six, seven blocks down here. The market was bad then, the early 1970s were very bad and things were pretty quiet. And I think everybody was looking for a little excitement, and at least my place was exciting.

But then the eighties came, and Wall Street started creating its own excitement.

ARTHUR ZEIKEL (former head of mutual funds at Merrill Lynch):

You had a number of things going on in the late seventies and early eighties. Expectations were very low. The market was selling flat on its heels. The prevailing consensus was that America had seen its best days, that the corporate sector was in disarray, the sun was setting, and we needed to develop quality control like the Germans and Japanese. They were seen as the wave of the future. That was the conventional wisdom.

Now, what happened? First, the American corporate sector began to regenerate itself. Second, the political atmosphere in this country changed and the more liberal agenda, and its excesses, came under attack from two directions: Margaret Thatcher and Ronald Reagan. With them in power, the idea of free markets became politically acceptable. At the same time, American technology started to work. And the concept of the IRA and 401(k), that individuals ought to be in control of their future financial affairs, started to take hold.

So all of a sudden you had freer markets, a growing economy, and these things called IRAs and 401(k)s where you were supposed to invest your money for the future. Mutual funds became the ideal vehicle to fit that client need. They offered convenience, investing expertise, record keeping — they just solved a whole host of problems. And, as all this was happening, the market started to behave in a way that nobody expected.

PAUL STEIGER (managing editor of the *Wall Street Journal*):

In the seventies you had all kinds of economic turmoil, the rise of inflation, the two gasoline crises, the horrific experiment with credit controls that Jimmy Carter undertook briefly, and at the end of the period the two-humped recession of 1980 to '82, which was probably the most serious recession in the postwar environment.

So you had all this turmoil, but people don't realize that you also had the equivalent of a stock-market crash in that period. At the start of the seventies, the market dropped from a peak of around 1,000 down into the 700s. That was a 25 percent decline or more in a pretty short period. And, furthermore, it was happening in an environment of quite high inflation. So, if you adjusted the market for inflation in the seventies, you had a very serious decline in stock prices. By the time we hit the early eighties stock prices were very depressed.

At the same time you had Paul Volcker's Fed determined to get inflation under control. In the past, under Nixon and Ford and Carter and their respective Congresses, anytime the Fed tried to get really tough on inflation you would get jawboning from the political side that forced them to relent. Throughout the seventies, you had these series of cycles in which each inflation peak was higher than the last, and each inflation trough was higher than the last. There was a sense of despair about the ability to ever bring inflation under control — sort of the notion that political realities wouldn't allow it, you couldn't sustain the level of unemployment that would be required to do this. Then along came Volcker. Jimmy Carter, who appointed him first, was sufficiently desperate, so Volcker could essentially do what he wanted in that brief crossover period.

KENNETH GUENTHER (former chief executive officer of Independent Community Bankers of America and former assistant to the Federal Reserve Board under chairman Paul Volcker):

Volcker came in as Fed chairman in August 1979. He inherited a sluggish economy with high inflation, and determined that something drastic had to be done. The economy was just dragging along. You had stagflation, which was no growth and inflation. So there was a need for some shock therapy. He came back from Brussels on October 6, 1979, and decided to get the monetary aggregates [a group of key monetary statistics] under control, the assumption being that this would have a direct and immediate impact on inflation. And to do this he started moving up interest rates very aggressively. The federal funds rate was moved to 15, 16 percent, and all the other interest rates followed.

HENRY KAUFMAN (former Salomon Brothers economist):

This was a very difficult time for the United States, the late seventies and early eighties, just exceedingly difficult. When Paul Volcker became chairman of the Federal Reserve in August of 1979, the United States was tottering economically and financially. I was deeply concerned about the extraordinarily high rate of inflation in the United States, which culminated in the first quarter of 1980, when consumer prices rose at an annual rate of 15 percent, something that's difficult to fathom today. This was at a time when we didn't have full control over monetary policy, and fiscal policy became distorted in the United States. The country itself was drifting very badly.

PETER LYNCH (former manager of Fidelity Magellan Fund):

In the 1970s and early 1980s, the key thing was inflation. Inflation was going up, and people didn't know where it was going to stop. Stocks didn't seem to protect you from inflation. That theory wasn't working.

JAMES GRANT (publisher of *Grant's Interest Rate Observer*):

These inflationary periods tended to be few and far between throughout much of our history, most often associated with wars. So the response in the Second World War was to suppress unwanted price rises through controls. Those controls lingered in some form or another into the Cold War era. The textbook response to price inflation is, of course, to constrict monetary growth and run a budget surplus. Those policies actually were not followed much in the seventies. Monetary growth in general was quite easy, and it wasn't until the Volcker program of October 6, 1979, that there was a real clamp put on monetary growth.

The rise in interest rates was the by-product of the policy. The thrust of it was to control the growth of the money supply as defined. There were many definitions, and everybody on Wall Street hung over the Dow Jones Newswire every Thursday afternoon, waiting for the Fed to inform everybody what the money supply was doing. It was the one thing everyone had to know for a couple of years.

As you know, rising rates are the reciprocal of falling prices. What it meant for the holders of fixed-income securities was unimagined marked-to-market losses and equally unimagined opportunities for reinvesting interest income at rising interest rates. That resulted in terrific volatility and complete disorientation, which is something not to be underestimated. All the known markers of behavior of interest rates turned out to be wrong or meaningless. It was known that 6 percent was a very high rate for a government security. But that was followed by 7 percent, then 8 percent, then 9 percent, and everyone who thought that 9 percent was high enough was discredited when it went to 10 percent. Finally, at 15 percent people stopped caring. They knew it was going to 20 percent.

PETER LYNCH:

I remember all these people were always predicting gloom and doom. There was this thing called *The Bank Credit Analyst* and it would say the "M3B" is growing too fast or the "M26" is growing too fast. They had all these terms to prove that today is Tuesday. I thought it was a bunch of crap.

The reality is that when you're in 1981 to '82 and it's a horrible recession you have to know that auto sales are at a seven-year low, cars are getting very old, and there are inspections in forty-nine states, so eventually they're going to have to replace their cars. You have to know where you are in the economy. If you're in a strong economy and auto sales are strong you have to say, someday they're not going to be so strong. But if you're in a weak economy and cars are getting old you have to say, someday in the future this is going to get better. That's why I bought Chrysler. I said, "Someday in the future, I don't know when, there's going to be a great auto demand." They were at breakeven in the middle of a bad recession, so you didn't have to be brilliant to see that they could still cut costs and if we had a good economy they'd make a lot of money. That's the only economics I ever cared about. What's going on right now? Trying to tell me what's going to happen in the future is like weather forecasting in New England, not Arizona.

HENRY KAUFMAN:

It took time for Volcker's approach to breed results. It worked by slowing down the economy, lowering expectations, indicating to participants in the market that inflation would not bail them out with continually rising prices. It required a recession. It is not easy to overcome huge excesses.

KENNETH GUENTHER:

What it did was drive the economy into a short, but deep and profound, recession. It broke the back of the savings and loan industry, leading to the failure of literally thousands of savings and loans. The S&Ls were sitting there with fixed-rate mortgages in their portfolios and interest rates were going through the roof. So there was a mismatch in what they were receiving in interest payments on the old fixed-rate loans and what they had to pay out for new money from the Fed. The business became cost prohibitive. So the S&Ls were driven into the corner and made desperate. So of course they reached for anything that would bring more money in. It drove them to junk bonds. It drove people to some desperate acts and in some cases criminal acts.

Of course, the flip side of that sharp rise in interest rates is that it did break the back of inflation. It worked. Then the Reagan tax cuts came down the pike, fueling a very sharp economic recovery. And with that you moved into the start of the bull market.

ROBERT FARRELL (former chief market strategist for Merrill Lynch):

One of the things I remember making a big point of at the time was that the old Nifty Fifty stocks had gone through their major bear market and they weren't going down anymore when the market went down. If you plotted their price versus earnings, their earnings were going on a steady growth trend all through the seventies, but the price had gone from being way above that trend to way below and stabilizing. There was at least the indication that a new cycle was likely to develop.

JAMES GRANT:

In '82, Merrill Lynch launched a new campaign called "Dawn of a Bull Market." They took out full-page newspaper ads trumpeting this. I had some fun with that in my column at *Barron's* because it was like, how could these guys be right? But they were. It was a great call by Merrill.

PAUL STEIGER:

A critical moment was August of 1982, which is the point when I would date the start of the most recent economic good times and what I consider to be essentially an unbroken bull market. Even though there was a crash in '87, the crash was so sudden that you couldn't even see it in the annual data. The Dow was up slightly in '87.

But in the summer of '82, Mexico defaulted on its loans and Volcker was sufficiently frightened of a debacle in the banks, a meltdown in the banks. And I think he also felt they had squeezed enough of the inflation out of the system. I never asked him this, but my sense is he saw for the first time that the trough in inflation was lower than the last trough. There was a sense that they had made serious inroads on inflation for the first time. Second, the concerns about recession were there. I think we were coming out of a recession by then, but you got some comments from some quotable analysts expressing concerns about another Great Depression in this kind of environment.

So Volcker, in August of '82, took the pressure off and began to loosen money. And the markets responded. Money became much more available very quickly. There was a surge of economic activity, so you had both financial and real surging in that environment.

MICHAEL LABRANCHE (chairman of New York Stock Exchange specialist firm LaBranche and Company):

It didn't really start to get good until August of 1982. I feel as if the market turned around in one day. Interest rates had been going down, the prime rate went from about 21½ percent to 12 percent. Then, Henry Kaufman at Salomon and Albert Wojnilower at First Boston came out and said that interest rates had peaked. They actually were behind the curve because rates had peaked much earlier. But they were the respected economists, so we got this huge rally.

I really felt that was the beginning of the bull market, right then. I swear you could feel it. It happened right in the middle of the afternoon, and it just felt like, here we go! Before, it was really quiet. It was getting better and volumes were up, but it was still pretty quiet. After that, it just really took off and became a big business.

HENRY KAUFMAN:

I can only tell you that the response was a surprise to me, but I never know how markets will respond. Sometimes I've made projections where the market responded, sometimes I've expressed views and the market didn't respond. So I never sit there and say, "What will the market reaction be?"

JAMES GRANT:

So Henry capitulated, or saw the light, or changed his mind, however you want to put it, on August 12, 1982. It was a very big day because "the Pope" blessed the bull market. And it didn't look back much from there.

PETER LYNCH:

The shift to defined-contribution [savings] plans created a huge market. If you think about it, there was a period of time when people would work for a company and not worry about the stock market. When they retired they got 50 or 60 percent of their last year's salary, and it went to their spouse if they died. They didn't have to care about stocks and bonds. They knew they had a good pension coming, they believed in Social Security, and they had some savings. But they really thought their pension was their deal. I remember I had friends who would talk about their pension plans, how good their pension was. I thought that was dumb. But they didn't care about the stock market. Then things changed.

All of a sudden, a lot of firms don't offer pensions, and if they do it's in early retirement when you get a lump sum and they say, "Okay, this is your money. You take care of it." That led to people buying funds directly. Or, they went through a 401(k) or 403(b) for public workers and schoolteachers. It takes a certain kind of person to go to your bank, and take money out of your bank account, and invest it in the stock market. We got some of those people in Magellan. That's a person who's willing to take a risk. But the broad-based people in their twenties and thirties who are now taking money out of their paycheck every week and investing it, that's a totally different audience. Those people didn't exist in the 1960s, 1950s, or 1940s. I mean, people don't even look at it anymore. The money's already taken out into a retirement account and they live on the rest.

GUS SAUTER (chief investment officer of Vanguard):

In the early 1980s the 401(k) plan was created, and millions of people started using them to save for retirement. Mutual funds were a natural investment for 401(k) plans. Their prices were recorded in the newspaper and their performance was tracked in the newspaper. This really brought a whole new type of investor into the marketplace. Many of the people who saved money in 401(k) plans had never bought a stock in their lives. Suddenly, here they were tracking mutual funds.

ROBERT FARRELL:

In the 1980s, you had a major low, where people really had just come through a period of about eight years when mutual funds were mostly being redeemed. People didn't own equities. They owned bonds because the high interest rates attracted them. They had their CDs and their money-market funds, and they were getting paid a lot for not being in stocks. So what you really started with was a new ownership cycle where most people were out, and the eighties were about bringing them back in.

ARTHUR ZEIKEL:

I think one difference between Peter Lynch and anyone else who came before him — Jerry Tsai or Howard Stein [of Dreyfus] — was he had much more widespread publicity because the media had grown by the time he came along and more people were starting to pay attention because the market was really moving. It was just a function of the whole game getting bigger.

ROBERT POZEN (former president of Fidelity Management and Research):

When you talk to Peter about any stock or industry he just bubbles over with information. I think he was inspirational to a whole group of younger analysts and people who became managers. They worked with him because they embraced his enthusiasm and learned his approach to stock picking, which was very much bottom-up, company by company. Peter combines great technical analysis with an exceptional feel — you know, the artistic side of the business. I've always viewed portfolio management as part science and part art, and Peter was very good at both.

PETER LYNCH:

People started saying hello to me in airports or when I was on the checkout line at the supermarket or at movie theaters. By the end of my time running the fund [in 1990] one out of every hundred Americans was in Magellan. That was probably true the last five years I ran it. These were small folks, not some guy living on an estate. They'd tell me great stories about how they put $5,000 in and now they're using it to pay for cars and homes. That was rewarding, it made me feel good about what I was doing.

ROBERT FARRELL:

Through the mideighties things heated up, and we really climbed this "wall of worry" until about '86 or '87.

JOHN PHELAN (former New York Stock Exchange chairman):

About 1985, early 1986, we had some teams of people who went out to the major member firms to see what they were doing systemswise and so forth. They picked up that several of these major member firms were beginning to use computer technology to do program trading, and some of the institutions were beginning to nibble at something called portfolio insurance.

TIM METZ (former reporter for the *Wall Street Journal* and author of *Black Monday*):

Portfolio insurance was an idea that was turned out by the major Wall Street houses — often through mathematicians, who were consultants or people they brought on staff — that made it possible for the S&P 500 future to act as a proxy for exposure to all equities in terms of a stock portfolio. So if the market was going up, a portfolio manager would look smarter if he owned more stock, and if the market was going down, he'd look smarter if he owned less. The S&P 500 future became an economical way to do this. You were hedging your position with financial futures.

The S&P 500 future wasn't born until 1982, and by the time portfolio insurance got going it really was about 1986. So the concept of hedging with financial futures was new to most money managers. Often they had restrictive covenants on what they could invest in, which was particularly true of the pension managers. The futures markets often were one of the things they couldn't invest in. But in the commodities markets this was an easy call. So portfolio insurance tapped equity institutional investors and made them hip to commodity-style investing for the first time.

LEO MELAMED (former head of the Chicago Mercantile Exchange and the creator of financial futures contracts):

The reason there were agricultural futures [in Chicago] is, this is where the product came and went from the grower to the user. So futures were a natural way for the grower to offset some risk and the buyer to earn a profit. It was the right and natural place for it to be. And it wasn't necessarily about finance. No one figured that financial instruments also would work their way into the schematic. This was an agricultural thing. And if I hadn't come along, perhaps it wouldn't have happened.

JOHN PHELAN:

Chicago was always pushing the derivatives [financial futures are a type of derivative], but their product was very different from ours. Their product was highly, highly leveraged, and ours was not. So this whole business of portfolio insurance and program trading was adding a magnitude of leverage that hadn't been seen in the modern marketplace.

JAMES CRAMER (CNBC talk-show host, journalist, and former hedge-fund manager):

Look, you can't insure everything. Some things can't be insured. "If a fire engulfs your street I guarantee your house won't burn." Well, you can't guarantee that because if the fire burns down your neighbor's house, guess who's next? It's a bad bet.

JOHN PHELAN:

There was an outfit in California called Leland O'Brien Rubenstein Associates, and they were the gurus on portfolio insurance. So, sometime in the summer of '86, I had one of their three major partners in for a luncheon to go over this whole business of portfolio insurance. After he went through his whole thing, I said, "If everybody's doing the same thing, what is going to prevent this from going down to nothing?" And he said that in theory this was correct, but in fact, as securities went lower that would attract more buying, and it would even out.

Well, it seemed to me that this was a formula for disaster, and I developed at that time the term "meltdown" to describe what might happen because we'd just had Chernobyl and they talked about an atomic meltdown. Well, this seemed to me to be a potential securities meltdown, which might not happen all at once, but which slowly but surely within a couple of days would drive the indices down. I began to talk more about this in my public pronouncements at the board and so forth, and by the end of 1986, people who were involved in this thing got very upset with me whenever I mentioned it.

LEO MELAMED:

In the early months of '87 as a trader I believed that the stock market had gone awry. Don't forget we were trading stock-index futures, and it was the biggest success we'd had. So we were very tuned in. And I was a trader first and foremost. So my little band of traders and I believed that the market had gone far beyond its value levels.

JAMES CRAMER:

In many ways it was an unbelievable bull market from the spring of 1987 into the summer before the crash. For me, there was no reason to think about anything else. The run from the April 17 low to the August 25 high was extraordinary, with the exception of Gap stores, which was the only stock that really wasn't participating. I mean, you had Merck doubling in the first three months of the year and then doubling again. This was Merck — a big established company, not some fly-by-night operation. And there were many other stories out there like it.

JOHN PHELAN:

By the fall of '87, it seemed that there was at least a speculative bubble building, not just in the real estate markets, but in our markets as well. Part of it was genuine investor demand, and part of it was based on these new products based on derivatives that had entered the market and had so much leverage. So we continued our concern and continued to prepare in case something happened.

By most objective measures, what history has come to call the bull market of the 1980s ran for five years, from August 1982 to August 1987. In that time, the Dow Jones Industrial Average rose 250 percent, from a low of 777 on August 11, 1982, to a peak of 2,722 on August 25, 1987. And while the market started to decline somewhat as summer gave way to fall, few people noticed — they were too busy trying to figure out where the next surge was going to bubble up on Wall Street. Indeed, in the weeks leading up to October 1987, some market experts were predicting that the Dow soon could be heading up to 3,600, which was considered an astronomical figure at the time. Investor enthusiasm for stocks had reached a fever pitch. Clearly something had to give.

CHAPTER 20

BLACK MONDAY

PETER LOW (member of the New York Stock Exchange since 1963 and former floor broker):

If you work on Wall Street long enough you'll experience your share of panics. For example, I became a member of the stock exchange on April 18, 1963, and on November 22 Kennedy was shot. So I was still new to the business when it happened. I remember it was a quiet Friday afternoon about 1:20, and I was standing with a fellow by the name of Harry Neufeld, who was a specialist in Polaroid. A broker walked by named Jimmy Phillips (his father was a good friend of my grandfather's) and he said, "Fellas, the president's been shot." I'll never forget that. And then, all of a sudden, utter pandemonium broke loose. I'd never seen anything like it in my life. U.S. Steel was selling for three different prices because there was so much confusion in that one trading crowd. You couldn't have an orderly market. It was just too chaotic.

Now obviously that's an extreme example because it's not too often that something dramatic happens like the president being assassinated. In fact, I never experienced that level of pandemonium again — well, that is, until October 1987.

JOHN KENNETH GALBRAITH (author and Harvard University economist):

In the 1980s there was a speculative bull market, no doubt about it, and one that was recognized. I would venture to say that I was one who not only recognized it at the time, but also warned against it. The investing public as it is called, or the speculative public as it should be called, has a short-run intelligence of its own. That is something that you must always keep in mind when looking at periods of financial euphoria. The problem here is not poor economics — it's poor history.

PAUL STEIGER (managing editor of the *Wall Street Journal*):

You can talk to a hundred people on Wall Street today, ninety-eight of them will tell you that they saw the 1987 crash coming and that they had taken all their money out of the market.

Of course, that's ridiculous. At the time you had people saying, "This is a sure sign of a top." But then you also had other people saying, "No, here's why it can go higher." That's why we have markets. People disagree, and at any given point in a market movement you've got some people who think that it's overdone and other people who think that it has more to go. Then in retrospect everybody can see why it was inevitable for it to turn, how there were all kinds of signs of animal spirits and voodoo like that. It's the nature of markets and '87 was no different.

MICHAEL LABRANCHE (chairman of New York Stock Exchange specialist firm LaBranche and Company):

Of course, there's a reason why some people were starting to get nervous. The market was up a lot in 1985 and 1986. You'd had these really good years, and by August of 1987 the Dow was up about 35 percent for the year, from about 2,000 to 2,700. In those days 35 percent was unheard-of. Just a few years earlier it seemed the market hadn't gone up 10 percent in a while. Suddenly, it was up 35 percent on a lot of speculation. And all this was happening in the face of rising interest rates.

DANIEL HERTZBERG (deputy managing editor of the *Wall Street Journal*):

In retrospect it all seems clear. The long bond was at 10 percent and the dollar was falling. I mean, that's a bad fundamental situation for equities. You want to know what caused the crash? That caused it. The market was overvalued again and interest rates ran up, but the market hadn't reacted yet.

JOSEPH GRANO (UBS PaineWebber chairman and former Merrill Lynch executive):

Wall Street just got fat and happy between 1982 and 1986 going into the 1987 crash. We were making the same mistakes we always made during good times. You saw brand-new buildings going up with the mahogany and the marble. It became very euphoric, and then — *boom!* I have this adage: if you're worried about the market, look what's going on with brokerage-firm real estate. You'll get more scared with every new marble foyer.

ELAINE GARZARELLI (former Lehman Brothers market strategist):

I turned bearish in late September, and then a week before the crash I went on CNN and said there was going to be a collapse like '29. The valuations were bad, and my indicators had turned down to a level of around 7 percent. They varied from zero to 100 percent, and anything below 30 percent was negative. They'd gone to as low a level as they had when I back-tested them to '29, so they were very bad. And the indicators are such things as money factors, economic factors, valuations, and sentiment — all those things had turned negative, except for free reserves.

MICHAEL LABRANCHE:

During the week before the 1987 crash the market was down for three straight days. On Wednesday it was down 95 points, then 57 points on

Thursday, and 108 points on Friday. It really created a lot of pressure because people had bloated inventories. Nobody had ever seen the market down 100 points — ever. It had never been down 100 points in one day before that.

PETER LYNCH (former manager of Fidelity Magellan Fund):

Up until 1987, I don't think my wife and I had taken a single vacation in the entire decade of the 1980s. Now it was the middle of October 1987 and we were finally going to Ireland for two weeks. We left on Thursday night, October 16. Wednesday and Thursday were severe down days in the market, and we left after work Thursday. We got in sometime on Friday morning and spent the day driving around County Cork, saw the Blarney Castle, kissed the Blarney stone. By the time we hit three in the afternoon we had done a lot of stuff.

Three in the afternoon in Ireland is ten in the morning in Boston and New York. So I called in to the office to see what was going on. I heard that the market looked as if it was getting ready to head south on Friday. So I called again later and asked, "What's the market doing?" I think it was down like 115 at that point. That was really bad, worse than I could ever remember. I said to Carolyn, "If the market goes down again on Monday we're going home. But while we're here let's enjoy Ireland."

Over the weekend I talked to my office a few times about which stocks to sell, which to buy. Other than that, Carolyn and I basically played golf and did some sightseeing along the Ring of Kerry. I tried to forget about work. But it wasn't easy.

LEO MELAMED (former head of the Chicago Mercantile Exchange):

The week before the crash I was very bearish and had a terrific week trading in the stock-index market. I actually had been bearish for some time and was quite concerned about where things were headed. Now as any good trader knows, after a week like that you get out, take your profits, and go home. Unfortunately, I had such a good week trading that that's what I did. I had nary a position coming in on Black Monday. The biggest down day in history and I wasn't even in the market. But you can't look back when you've had a good week. You know, "You'll never go broke taking profits." It actually turned out to be a blessing. In the aftermath of accusations and investigations, of analyses and reviews, it would not have served my interests to read stories about how the leader of the Merc was short the market [betting on a big decline] and made a lot of money on Black Monday.

JOSEPH GRANO:

The weekend before the crash I was at a resort in Vermont giving a seminar on real estate. This doctor from Philadelphia came up to me and started explaining how he had hundreds of options positions all over the place and how he was highly leveraged. I looked at him and said, "You're out of your mind. This market is very tenuous and if I were you I'd deleverage myself now."

Unfortunately, he chose to stay in Vermont for three more days — he got totally wiped out.

HENRY KAUFMAN:

On Sunday, October 18, I appeared on *Meet the Press*. Not surprisingly, the journalists pressed me to prognosticate about what the market might do the next day. I tried my best to sidestep such questions by pointing out that there was no analytical way to specifically forecast an extraordinary event such as a crash happening tomorrow. The large setback on Friday already had investors on edge and I had no intention of adding to the turmoil with my remarks. So I sounded more vague and reassuring about the situation than I really felt.

Treasury Secretary James Baker, who was questioned by the panel after me, did not mimic my tactic. When asked about some of the signs that seemed to indicate a deterioration in international monetary and foreign-exchange matters he said, "We will not sit back and squeeze growth worldwide on the expectation that the United States somehow will follow by raising its interest rates." That remark surprised me and after the program I went up to him and said, "Jim, that was quite a candid statement. The market may not take it the way you may have meant it."

I'll never forget his firm reply. "Henry, some things need to be said."

MICHAEL LABRANCHE:

I remember clearly that I was sitting home on the Sunday morning before the crash, and Jim Baker, who was then treasury secretary, was talking on *Meet the Press*. They asked if he was concerned about the stock market sell-off and he said twice, "No, because remember stocks are already selling off from high levels." Now, I don't think he meant to do this, but he sent the message that he didn't mind if stock prices went down. That's what the perception was. He probably meant to be reassuring, saying the stock market's fine and we just had a sell-off. But I'm sitting there thinking, "Oh, this is not good at all. The market's going to be down another hundred points tomorrow."

LEO MELAMED:

That weekend the *New York Times* and every major periodical, whether it was *Barron's, Chicago Tribune, Los Angeles Times,* all compared what was happening to the 1929 crash. Media analysts on financial markets over the weekend on television all were speaking of comparisons to what happened in 1929. This is October again. Could we go through another Depression? Those comparisons had a great impact on the psychology of investors. If you couple that with the momentum of the week before and the real concerns about the valuation of the dollar versus where interest rates were headed, what you had was a mixture of fear, greed, and concern that was combustible.

PAUL STEIGER:

There was a sense of things coming unglued. There was a level of tension in the air that was palpable. We had people working all weekend long just picking up fear and loathing, no question. So when it did hit, the only surprise was how low it went. I mean 500 points — that was awesome.

LEO MELAMED:

Early Monday morning, on my drive in to work, John Phelan [chairman of the New York Stock Exchange] called me in the car. I'd spoken to John before but this definitely was the first time he'd had to reach me on the car phone. So this wasn't a social call. He wanted to alert me that the projection for the Dow opening in London was at least 200 points down. That was a number we had never heard before. He said, "It's going to be bad. Keep in touch."

JOHN PHELAN (former New York Stock Exchange chairman):

I called a meeting on Monday morning in my office with the heads of any of the New York firms that could get in at eight. We had a meeting — I think there were twelve to fifteen of them — and I just said, "Listen, there's no guarantee, but it looks like we're going to be in for a rocky time here for the next couple of days. I want all of you to understand and prepare for it. And I want all of you to understand that no matter what comes, the exchange is going to stay open and trade." Our method for overcoming problems was to shut down individual stocks, not the whole exchange.

WILLIAM SCHREYER (former Merrill Lynch chairman):

I spent some time Monday morning talking to the White House, mainly Howard Baker, President Reagan's chief of staff. Howard was one of the people who I asked to serve on our international advisory board. We got to know each other that way. When the crash happened Howard called a few times. He wanted to know what our position was and how we were handling it. We told him what we were doing — that we were staying positive and counseling our offices to talk to their customers, be professional and helpful, that kind of thing.

Basically, the White House wanted to know what was going on from our point of view. I remember Howard was desperately trying to chase down Alan Greenspan, who had just taken over as chairman of the Fed. We were all very concerned about the liquidity in the market and Howard was going to find out what they were going to do about it.

MICHAEL LABRANCHE:

On Monday, October 19, the market started down, things were very nervous out there. Everybody was holding a lot of stock from Friday, all the dealers [dealers, or specialists, are traders on the floor of the New York Stock Exchange that manage the trading in specific stocks.] I remember I had some AT&T to sell. The last sale was 30⅛. I opened it at 28¼ and bought on the opening. Then another institution came in with 250,000 to sell. I bought a lot of that. I thought the market would rally because, you know, we took AT&T down from 33 to 28. But it just got worse and worse. The selling just poured in. Most of it was computerized, coming in through the DOT [electronic trading] system. The programs just sold all day. They never stopped — well, except maybe from ten thirty to eleven in the morning.

So finally, AT&T was trading at 26½, and I was holding about 450,000 shares. Now I know that doesn't sound like a lot by today's standards. But believe me, in those days, to me that was *a lot.* At that time 10,000 shares was considered a big position. And here I am with 450,000 AT&T at 26½. I went up to a senior partner who was running a big stock that was just getting pounded. He was surrounded by a crowd of people, and I went up to him and said, "I'm long 450,000 AT&T and it looks like it's going lower. I'm just telling you."

I remember he left the crowd for a second and said, "I've got my own problems." Then he turned and was gone. I didn't talk to him for the rest of the day. At that point I realized everybody was trying to figure out what to do.

DONALD MARRON (former PaineWebber chairman):

The mood had changed — the psyche of fear kicked in. People were thinking, "There hasn't been a crash in a long time and after the last one the country went into a depression. And if that happens it's all over."

I remember being down on our trading floor, and looking in the eyes and faces of the people trading. They were really scared, petrified. Clearly, it was something they'd never seen before. As it always is in this business, the guys on the front lines were young. So they really didn't have a long history and they were scared. Stocks would shut down. You couldn't get people on the phone. Think about this — you're trying to do business but you can't get anyone on the phone and they won't call you back. Prices are going crazy. Clients are screaming at you. People who you always dealt with in a nice calm way all of a sudden are abusing you and coming after you because there are all these problems. You'd be scared, too.

MICHAEL BARONE (head of Nasdaq trading at William Blair and Company in Chicago):

The phones were ringing and no one was answering them. Basically, no one at the New York firms was picking up the phones.

GORDON MACKLIN (first president of the Nasdaq Stock Market):

What happened was, you're on a Nasdaq trading desk and a big customer calls and has 5,000 he wants to sell, and there was an assumption that all the quotes on the exchange were good — and they weren't. So people just didn't pick up their phones. It was a disaster. I don't think too many people were affected, but some were. And we probably shouldn't be surprised because you can't expect people to just stand out there and commit economic suicide. But it's not as if the [New York Stock] exchange's quotes were good and ours weren't. Their quotes weren't good at all either.

DONALD MARRON:

And there was this specter of "This is what we were worried about. It's '29 all over again. Game over." That was the big difference, game over. You weren't just worried about stock prices. You were worried about the impact of the crash on the country, the world, the economy, morale, people, everything.

WILLIAM SCHREYER:

For most of the crash I was in [Merrill Lynch president] Dan Tully's conference room. We had offices at opposite ends of the hall, but I put the stock-quote machine in Tully's conference room. That machine always distracted me. As a leader I was focused on Merrill's long-term strategy, not the short-term stock price. Of course, when something like this happens strategy goes out the window. So we were in Tully's conference room for the crash. As the day unfolded we brought in all our research guys to keep us abreast of what was happening while we kept one eye on that quote machine.

As I remember it was one of those beautiful fall days in New York City, sunny and comfortable. After a while I got fed up and looked out the window and thought, "This isn't the right day for something like this to happen."

DANIEL TULLY (former Merrill Lynch chairman and president under chairman William Schreyer):

We had all the executives come in and talk to us — Bill and I — to keep us posted on what was happening. When the market was going down I was thinking about what we could do for our clients and how we could navigate our way through this. Others were getting up, going over to the quote machine and checking their own portfolios over and over and over. My concern was that this person couldn't react as rationally as I needed him to because he was so deeply involved in the markets on a personal level. Employees at Merrill Lynch are no different from anyone else. We're a microcosm of the world, with our share of stiffs and winners. We just don't know who the stiffs are until situations like this.

WILLIAM SCHREYER:

You won't believe this, but right in the middle of the crash I hosted a Penn State luncheon here at Merrill. I was chairing a fund-raising campaign for the school, we were trying to raise $250 million, and all the leaders of the campaign were in our dining room for a meeting at around noon. [Penn State football coach] Joe Paterno was there and he still talks about it. I remember one of them said, "Gee, Bill, this seems like a bad time. Do you want to cancel?"

"Nah," I said. "We've done all we can do. Let's eat."

PETER LYNCH:

On Monday, Black Monday, Carolyn and I were still in Ireland. We played golf in the morning and then we stopped in this pretty little town called Dingle, which is out on a peninsula, and checked into a hotel there. We had the ocean and mountains behind us, just a beautiful spot.

And that's where I spent the crash. Luckily, because of the time difference we finished our round of golf before the opening bell on Wall Street. I spent the rest of the afternoon calling in to get the updates. At the end of the day Magellan shareholders had lost 18 percent of their assets, $2 billion. On Tuesday morning we left for Boston.

ROGER SERVISON (former head of marketing at Fidelity Investments):

It was pandemonium in the Boston office. The important thing was, particularly for the phone reps, we kept saying you've got to sound calm, you've got to talk to people, but you can't linger on the phone. Because, you know, we were getting killed with all the phone calls. So we said, be polite, tell them that things are fine, but try and get off the phone within three minutes so you can get onto another call. We just can't linger with people.

We got several hundred thousand calls that day, and I think an average day back then was seventy or eighty thousand. I mean, this was huge. Every possible person we could find was on the phone. There were times when the New England Telephone switch into this part of town was jammed and people were just getting automatic busy signals.

MICHAEL LABRANCHE:

The market sell-off didn't really accelerate until three in the afternoon. If I'm not mistaken the market was down around 300 at around three, and it went from down 300 to 500 in an hour. There were rumors that they had put up barricades at Fidelity, where people were trying to get in. I mean, when you see the market's down 300 you're wondering what's going on.

It seemed surreal. It went from down 300 to down 500 without any resistance. It just picked up steam. People were running by and throwing orders at me. When it finally ended we looked up and saw the market was down 508 points. We couldn't believe it.

JOHN PHELAN:

Nobody had ever seen anything like it. It wasn't just the points; it was the percentages. Within three days the market was down more than 35 percent. Markets had gone down that much before, but over a period of time, never in such a time frame.

LEO MELAMED:

It was a shocking experience. I had never seen anything like it before. There were absolutely no bids for the S&P 500 futures contract. The prices that emerged from the S&P 500 futures pits that afternoon were really only from a smattering of orders. Then there was this enormous vacuum before there were any other prices. Then there was another vacuum before there were more prices. It was unprecedented.

The market was in pure shock. I had never seen that before. There were no limits so it was just this abyss heading down. I tell you, I have few memories of my life where I would describe myself as petrified. This is one of them.

JOHN L. (LAUNNY) STEFFENS (former head of brokerage operations at Merrill Lynch):

During the crash Merrill Lynch was sponsoring a golf tournament in Tucson, Arizona. We had maybe fifty of our best clients out there, and I was there with them. On Monday I played golf with Payne Stewart and a fellow who probably was Merrill's biggest individual account at the time. Now, Tucson is two hours behind New York. So we teed off and the market was down about 100 points or more. When we got to the ninth hole it was past two in the afternoon and my wife was standing there. By that time the market was closed back in New York. I said to her, "How'd we do?"

She said, "You don't want to know." And I said, "You can tell me. I can take it."

But instead of telling me, she went over and whispered something in Payne Stewart's ear. Then Payne turned to me and said, "You really don't want to know."

Our group ended up finishing the nine remaining holes, but around the fifteenth hole, the client who was with me said, "Launny, I think I'd better go home." I understood. After the round was over I gathered all our clients together — remember, these were our *major* accounts — and told them what I thought they ought to do. Nothing. I said, "Tuesday's probably going to be a fairly important day and clearly it would be foolish to buy or sell right now. But if Tuesday works out to be a day where we don't go down and it stabilizes a bit, it might be a good time to do some buying of some good companies."

MICHAEL LABRANCHE:

That afternoon we came up to the office to figure out our inventories. I remember working until seven thirty or so and then driving home to Long Island. When I got out of the car it was so silent with the crickets and everything, it seemed like a perfect juxtaposition to what I had experienced that day. It was just so quiet and serene, as if the people out here couldn't possibly have known what happened that day.

PAUL STEIGER:

That whole day I was focused on getting out the paper, the *Wall Street Journal.* The computers couldn't keep up with the flow of quotes. The quotes from the AP were late. It was really tough getting the paper out.

So at the end of the day we were just exhausted, and I had to go out to the airport. My then wife was an executive at a money-management firm, and she had gotten on a plane Monday morning to go out to L.A. to start a weeklong trip in California visiting clients. Around Pittsburgh she got on the phone in the plane with the office. They were telling her that the market was down 100, down 150, down 200. As she went across the country it got worse and worse. She just kept the phone open, and spent the time consoling clients and getting more concerned herself. By the time she landed in California she decided it made no sense to continue the California trip. So she got on another plane and came back to New York.

I went out to Kennedy Airport to pick her up at eleven thirty at night. Now while I was tired, I also was on a high. I mean, this was one of the greatest stories I'd ever been involved in covering, and I thought we'd done a really good job. So I was up and excited. But then I took one look at her face and I wasn't up anymore. She was just ashen, thinking about people whose money she was responsible for who now had 22 percent less than they had when the day started. It really brought home what had happened.

Then when we got back to our apartment I checked messages on the answering machine. We had a call from a very dear friend of mine, a college classmate who's now dead. He was in the movie business and he had this house in East Hampton, Long Island. His name is Roger Swaybill. Roger's claim to fame was that he wrote the script for the movie *Porky's,* even though he didn't get screen credit for it. Instead of getting a screen credit he got points. He got like a $2 million check at the end of it, and much of that $2 million was invested in this house in East Hampton. So there was this message on the machine that starts off with a brief apologetic note, something like, "I'm very sorry, you must be very busy, but can you just give me a call and tell me what this means for real estate prices in East Hampton?"

And you know, that was a very good question for a journalist to hear. It showed how people were desperate to know what this meant for them. The drama of the market is fine, but they want to know "What does this mean for my life?"

JERRY CORRIGAN (Goldman Sachs managing director and former Federal Reserve Bank of New York president):

As Monday unfolded it became very apparent that this was one of those "perfect storms," call it what you will. It's also true that it really wasn't until the end of the day that one could begin to focus on the order of magnitude of the issues that were on the table. So, one of the big questions as markets closed here in the United States was, how is this going to play out in the rest of the world?

JOHN PHELAN:

At six or seven that night, Corrigan called me and said, "What can I do for you?" And I said, "To begin with, you can provide liquidity to this market." In a position like that everything dries up, everybody pulls back. The financial crises in the eighties, and in the nineties as well, have been liquidity crises. The question is always, how will people react? So Corrigan and I talked about that, and his point was that they'd do whatever they could to help us. He said, "We will provide liquidity to all the markets."

LEO MELAMED:

I had a conversation with Alan Greenspan at around eleven on Monday night. By now it was obvious that the collapse in our S&P 500 futures pit in Chicago was accelerating the disaster everywhere else. His question was, "Will you open tomorrow morning?" But Greenspan and I both knew what we were really saying when we talked about whether we would open the market the next day. We actually were discussing whether the longs would be able to pay the shorts.

You see, if the world thought for a minute that some long at the Chicago Mercantile Exchange couldn't pay a short for an S&P 500 futures position, it would mean Morgan Stanley, Goldman Sachs, Salomon Brothers, whoever, couldn't make payment. Think about that for a second. It would set off a chain reaction of gridlock. Nobody would pay anybody if they suspected somebody wouldn't pay them. So the fear was gridlock.

JERRY CORRIGAN:

As we got into Monday night I was talking to a lot of people. Greenspan — who was brand-new as chairman, he'd come in August — during the afternoon hours was on a plane to Dallas to give a speech to the American Bankers Association Tuesday morning. When he got off the plane he found out that the market had closed down 508 points. This came as a little bit of an eye-opener to him.

That night, when I was talking to Phelan and everybody else, my primary focus was learning as much as I could as a matter of intelligence from people in the markets. But much more important, I was working with

Chairman Greenspan and others as to what we thought the appropriate response of the central bank should be. The immediate question on Monday night was how this was going to play out in other markets around the world. One of the great institutional accidents — and it's not entirely an accident — is that the international community of central bank governors is a very close-knit society. This is still true, but back then we used to meet literally in person, together, every month. We all knew each other. We all trusted each other. So in circumstances like this, the network and the old-fashioned telephone was a remarkably effective device. We were able to monitor what was happening around the world literally as the sun rose in different places. As that occurred, it became quite apparent that the events of Monday in the United States were having profoundly important effects elsewhere.

So over the course of Monday night one of the questions that came up was, should we as the Federal Reserve be prepared to issue a statement, and if so, what should that statement say and when should it be issued? That naturally was a lively topic of conversation. I don't think there was much difference of opinion on whether we were going to have to issue a statement — we were. The real question was, what should it say, and when should it be issued? There's a lot of folklore around this, and maybe it's a bit of an exaggeration, but the original cut of the draft statement was rather technocratic. I, in particular, felt that this was not the environment where you wanted a technocratic statement. You wanted something short, sweet, tight, and to the point, no nuances, no nothing. Fortunately, that's the way it ended up. Then, the next question was, when to issue it? We were all quickly of the mind that the optimal time to issue it would be before the markets opened in the United States Tuesday morning. As I recall, I think it was issued at eight thirty on Tuesday morning.

JOHN PHELAN:

The next morning Greenspan announced that they would provide liquidity, which was as good a statement as anybody could possibly make. And they did work with the banks to make sure they were lending, not only to the floor of the exchange, but upstairs as well.

MICHAEL LABRANCHE:

I remember I came into the office and everybody was watching TV. All of a sudden there was this report that the Fed said they were going to pump money into the system. If you read John Kenneth Galbraith's book *The Great Crash, 1929,* the big mistake he said the Fed made in 1929 was it drained the system instead of supporting it. Maybe Greenspan read that book, because the first thing he did was pump liquidity into the system, which was smart. Basically, he was saying that money was going to be available.

DANIEL TULLY:

Liquidity clearly was a problem — the lenders were really jumpy. In the middle of the crash one lender called me and said, "You need X number of dollars to cover your positions and we need it here in ten minutes — or else."

I'll never forget that. I said, "Hey, you son of a bitch, calm down. Relax. This is Merrill Lynch. You'll get your money. But you'd better not do what you said you were going to do. Or else? All these years we've done business together on certain terms of payment and now you want it in ten minutes?"

But the lenders panicked, see. I'm not going to mention who that was, but I never forgot it, I'll tell you that. It was god-awful how people, professionals, panicked.

JERRY CORRIGAN:

What you can never do, as a central banker, is tell people what to do. It doesn't work. And even if it did, you're superimposing your credit judgment, your risk judgment, on them. You have to do this in a way that they are the ones who make those decisions.

Now, I knew all these guys, and they knew me. So there's kind of an art form to this. You call them up, and you say, "How are things going? What do you think?" And then you finally get around to saying, "Look, let's make sure we've got the right perspective on this. You have to make your own business and credit decisions. That's up to you. But let me remind you of the consequences of what will happen if all of you make the wrong decisions. Let me remind you of the consequences of gridlock." You just kind of put it to them in those terms. These guys aren't dunces. They get the picture.

MICHAEL LABRANCHE:

At the opening on Tuesday morning all the orders were to buy, and a lot of stocks opened up on the enthusiasm from the Fed's liquidity statement. But the rally didn't hold at all. I mean, it opened up like 200 points in the first hour and the rally just didn't hold. A lot of stocks started trading late because of delayed openings, and they put pressure on the market, dragging it back down. When the market sold off badly, people were very upset.

So by midmorning we were testing the low levels of the day before. It actually became worse than the day before because at one point before noon IBM had one million shares for sale and no bids. They just shut it down. That was like the bellwether stock. There were a bunch of other stocks that stopped trading, too. I remember thinking, "That's not good. That's *really* not good." It was just quiet. Silent.

JOHN PHELAN:

I guess around eleven or so it was off 100 points, so I walked down to the floor, just to see how that was, and the volume had dried up and there was a stillness there. It was almost as if everybody was in a daze. We'd shut down at that time somewhere in excess of eighty stocks, and a lot of these stocks were big stocks, particularly the stocks that were in some of the indices.

I got the four floor directors together and said, "Remember, we're not going to close this place down. But we'll continue to shut down stocks."

They said, "Well, we have eighty or ninety down."

So I said, "Get them open. Indicate them, so everybody knows what the prices are. And keep rotating them." I walked off the floor, and something struck me. It was as if a hurricane had hit the place. And I had to figure out if it was the eye of the storm, or if the storm had passed.

JERRY CORRIGAN:

As you got into the late morning, the pressure on the market was just immense. I had all my trusted people in a room with me, and between us we probably had more than fifteen telephones. I was on the phone and off the phone in rapid-fire succession. I truly can't remember the sequence in which the conversations as to whether the market should be closed or not took place, but those conversations certainly took place. There were conversations between John Phelan and me. There were conversations between Washington — specifically, Howard Baker, who was President Reagan's chief of staff at the time — and me. And it is true that I took the position that closing the exchange was a bad idea. I remember somebody saying to me, "Why do you think it's such a bad idea to close the exchange?" And I distinctly remember saying, "If you close it, you're going to have to figure out how the hell to open the thing."

JOHN PHELAN:

The market was down 700 points in a day and a quarter. Stocks were getting down to the point where no matter what happened they were really inexpensive. As soon as everybody got their wind back and looked at it, I was sure that other buying would come in. Now, there were two good things that happened Tuesday morning to help it along. One was the Fed announcement about liquidity. Then later on, around noon or so, some of the major companies started to announce stock buyback programs. Those were two real signals that the storm was over.

LEO MELAMED:

The corporate buyback programs kicked in, and kicked in big. The SEC relaxed its rules and allowed companies to buy back shares of their stock immediately rather than wait to make a formal announcement. Suddenly, all the specialists were getting encouraged again. They had huge orders in their hands to buy the majors, the General Motors, the IBMs, the General Electrics. It turned out that this was the perfect opportunity for those corporations to buy back their own shares at beyond bargain-basement prices. It was such a natural thing to do. And it got most of those stocks up and trading again.

JERRY CORRIGAN:

Anybody who tells you that they know exactly why the market came back is full of prunes. They don't know. I can't tell you. If I had to single out one thing that I think contributed to it, it was the stock buybacks. Starting early on Tuesday morning, a fairly large number of blue-chip companies were buying back their own stock. I don't know if that was decisive either, but it didn't hurt. But those people who think they know the trigger are wrong.

JOHN PHELAN:

The other thing we did that was good that morning was with program trading. My operations people wanted to ban program trading. I decided not to do that, but we did take them [the program traders] off the trading system so they wouldn't clog it up. This way, the individual investors and small institutions could get their orders in.

And what happened was, somewhere around one or one thirty the market began to bottom out. Then it started to rally, and the rally looked like a good one. We got several more calls asking if we were going to shut down, and we said we're not, the market's turning around. From there, I thought things were going to be all right. The market was exhausted. The selling was over. There was just nobody else to sell.

DANIEL HERTZBERG:

It's funny, if you read the news accounts at the time, people really didn't know how close we came to a total shutdown on Tuesday. The market finished up in the afternoon. It actually finished up over 100 points on Tuesday, and another 187 points on Wednesday. By Wednesday afternoon more than a hundred major companies had announced plans to buy back their stock. So the market came back. But if people actually knew what was going on in between they would have been really frightened. It was very scary while it lasted.

JERRY CORRIGAN:

It took the better part of two weeks to really get things sorted out. You wouldn't know it by looking at the stock indices, but there were a host of hangover issues that had to be dealt with. One of them was in the United Kingdom but it was very important. Right in that time frame was the initial public offering of British Petroleum. This was the British government, Margaret Thatcher, with their first big privatization. Mrs. Thatcher being Mrs. Thatcher said, "We've got to go ahead with this no matter what." That was a great drama by itself, and there were many others.

DONALD MARRON:

It's ironic; in the rally that followed the crash it turned out that the institutions, with all their portfolio-insurance devices and the like, were selling and the individuals were buying. The original scenario was that the little guy would panic and that would be it. But in the end it turned out to be the little guy who survived and the institutions that had the problems. The other thing that was worrying people then, as now, is whether the mutual funds would be forced to sell stocks to cover redemptions. That apparently didn't happen either. Believe it or not, the individuals acted in a way that was smart and sophisticated.

If you think about it, it makes sense. Things were pretty good at the time, and the crash happened so quickly that there wasn't much you could have done to get out of the way. By the time it was done there was this wonderful sale. So individuals really weren't left with much choice. They woke up and said, "We had a crash. We're still here. The world is pretty good. The market's down and stocks are cheap."

JAMES CRAMER (CNBC talk-show host, journalist, and former hedge-fund manager):

I think the overall lesson from the crash is what I call "the Federated effect," as in Federated Department Stores. You know, there's gonna be a sale so you might as well wait for it before you buy.

LEO MELAMED:

Buying stocks when markets are falling, "buying the dip" as they say, can be dangerous business as a trader. You can't assume that it will go back up in time for you to capitalize on it. It may be true that the market always goes back up, but what if this time it takes twenty years? Big deal. I'll be dead by then, or at least a very old man. The trick is to get out ahead of the break and wait to see what happens.

WILLIAM SCHREYER:

Our message at Merrill Lynch through the entire crash — in our commercials, in our communications with our clients and employees — was to sit tight because fundamentally everything was okay. I mean, we didn't come out and say the market was going to rally tomorrow. All we said was, "This is a long-term thing. The economy is strong. The fundamentals are good. This is a time for cool and reasoned judgment. We continue to be bullish on America."

JOHN KENNETH GALBRAITH:

When markets crash, Wall Street's first reaction, and we'll definitely see this again, is to say that the fundamentals are solid. That word always appears — "fundamental." It was repeated in 1929 and 1930 and 1931. They will always argue that this is not a fundamental reflection of the economic situation, but something that has a life of its own. That's what Wall Street says.

I regard such statements as something between mysticism and black humor. Don't listen to anything these people say. Just be guided by history.

CHAPTER 21

KILLING THE GOLDEN GOOSE

Throughout the 1980s, financial entrepreneurs like the corporate raiders and leveraged-buyout practitioners dominated the M&A landscape, taking over companies many times larger than themselves and then selling them off or taking them public for tidy profits. These men were advised by a select group of investment bankers and lawyers who considered themselves Masters of the Universe and who collected exorbitant fees for their services. But eventually the underlying driver behind the frenzied era would be exposed in a single, mammoth fight — unbridled greed.

BRYAN BURROUGH (coauthor of *Barbarians at the Gate*):

RJR Nabisco basically was a company that never should have been. It was the combination of R. J. Reynolds Tobacco and Nabisco foods that had been formed in a merger in 1985. It probably seemed like a good idea at the time but the problem was, when you put those two companies together, their combined stock price was artificially reduced because of concerns about the tobacco business. This, of course, ignored the great potential value of the Nabisco franchise, or so the company felt. By the time we reached 1987, RJR Nabisco was swarming with investment bankers trying to find ways to fix this, looking at all sorts of alchemy to get them out of this mess.

F. ROSS JOHNSON (RJR Nabisco president and chief executive officer):

It was a little frustrating.

BRYAN BURROUGH:

Ross Johnson was the CEO of RJR Nabisco. He had been the CEO of Nabisco Brands. A man named Tylee Wilson was the CEO of R. J. Reynolds and Johnson edged him out to become head of the combined company. The LBO idea was Johnson's solution to fix the jam the company had put itself in with the merger.

HENRY KRAVIS (cofounder of Kohlberg Kravis Roberts and Company):

Don Kelly [chief executive of Beatrice, which was owned by KKR] said to me that he had an idea. What he wanted to do was have Beatrice be part of the buyout of RJR. So Don said, why don't we get Ross to come over? That's what we did. Don and Ross came over to my apartment and had dinner, and we talked about the idea. This was probably 1987. So Ross listened and from that he knew exactly how it worked, even though he walked away and said it wasn't something he wanted to do. And that was it.

GEORGE ROBERTS (cofounder of Kohlberg Kravis Roberts and Company):

RJR Nabisco actually was a company that we had looked at from afar for three or four years. It was a perfect example of corporate directors not doing their jobs. There was quite a bit of fat in the company, so much wasted spending of shareholders' money. It was pretty bad. With its stock price reduced it was a great candidate for us.

BRYAN BURROUGH:

I think, in essence, Ross felt, "Everybody will win in an LBO. Shareholders will get a price they never would get otherwise. My friends will get rich. I'll get rich. My investment bankers will get rich." You know, he figured there would be a chicken in every pot. The only people who would get screwed in all this were the bondholders. And nobody really cares about bondholders anyway — you can always buy them off for millions of dollars when all this is long said and done.

But the peculiar aspect to the RJR LBO was that instead of doing the deal with KKR, the most experienced team on the block and the undisputed kings of the business, Ross decided to go with somebody who'd never done a deal before. He went with Peter Cohen at Shearson Lehman Hutton.

J. TOMILSON HILL (head of M&A at Shearson Lehman Hutton):

It made sense that Ross Johnson chose us for this deal. Ross was a longtime client of Lehman Brothers, which at this point was part of Shearson Lehman Hutton, which was owned by American Express. Andy Sage, the former president of Lehman Brothers back in the seventies, was Ross's personal adviser. Andy advised Ross in the Standard Brands deal, was a board member of RJR Nabisco and a consultant to RJR Nabisco. RJR and Nabisco were both clients of Lehman Brothers. Ross also sat on the American Express board, and he and [American Express chairman] Jim Robinson were also very close.

PETER COHEN (Shearson Lehman Hutton chairman):

Jim Robinson called me up one day and said, "You're going to be getting a call from Ross. He wants to talk to you about hiring Shearson."

Johnson called me up shortly afterward and told me that he wanted us to do an analysis of how to create value at RJR Nabisco. He wanted us to help them figure out how to create the maximum amount of value for their shareholders. I knew right away what the end result was going to be — way before we even started the analysis. You had to take that company private, do an LBO. It had all this cash flow, so you could afford to pay a big price for it and service the debt. The stock was at about $50 at the time, which was pretty cheap. I didn't think you could steal the company, but you could pay a fair price for it.

BRYAN BURROUGH:

I think Johnson went with Peter Cohen and Shearson for two reasons. The stated reason was that Johnson's best friend on Wall Street had always been Jim Robinson, chairman of American Express. American Express owned Shearson, so that was the stated reason why Johnson picked Peter Cohen.

I always felt the unstated reason for the selection was that Ross clearly did not want to become a pawn of Henry Kravis. He wanted a "special kind of deal," where he would call all the shots. Clearly, going into business with a first-time LBO doer gave Ross tremendous leverage over Shearson. And Shearson essentially did give Ross everything he wanted, a "special deal" that ultimately blew up in everyone's face.

J. TOMILSON HILL:

Ross didn't want to get involved with KKR because Henry wanted to control everything. KKR has a very simple philosophy in their buyouts, which is, they control the company. Ross wanted much more of a partnership arrangement between his management team and his LBO sponsor.

PETER COHEN:

We did the analysis for Ross over the summer and the conclusion was: do a buyout. So we met with Andy Sage and Ross and told them that. We also gave them a range of prices that we thought would be financeable for a deal like this. Ross wanted to go to his board and propose to them that he propose a buyout. He didn't want to just go in and make a formal bid for the company. He was going to tell them that we'd done this work, reached this conclusion, and we'd like to come back to them with a proposal. He also wanted us, Shearson, to lead the deal and help raise the equity.

So on October 19, 1988, Johnson went to that board meeting and told them that he was thinking about doing an LBO. They said, "What kind of price are you talking about?" The stock was at about $55. And he said that he had been informed by his advisers at Shearson that based on the information we'd seen to date an offer of around $75 a share would be eminently financeable. Then he told them that how much more he could afford to pay would be a function of our doing more due diligence, more work on the deal. That's all he said.

Of course, what got reported the next day was he made a bid to buy the damn thing for $75 a share. But he never made a formal bid! There was never a formal proposal put to the board. He never did it. All he said was, "Based on what work has been done to date I am being advised that a $75 bid is eminently financeable."

But that started the whole process.

J. TOMILSON HILL:

There were a lot of mistakes that were made in this deal, but the fundamental mistake was that Ross misread his board and didn't understand that there was another dynamic at work here. I think there were some board members who wanted to get Ross, set him up in a curious way. He didn't know that. So they sent out a press release announcing what he'd done. That was not the game plan at all. The idea was to put this together as quietly as possible with the board's help so we could avoid the competition.

We were very aware of Henry Kravis. We talked about it a lot. We said, "Henry is probably going to be interested in this." We talked about what we wanted to do if he surfaced. The basic idea was, let's see if we can figure out a way to cut him in.

It turned out the press release was how KKR found out. And to Henry, it was as if somebody had walked into his home and said, "I want the following five things from your house — that painting, this sculpture," and so on. I mean, he took it as a direct challenge to his business franchise. He could not stand for this.

HENRY KRAVIS:

Let me tell you something, if I was worried about protecting a franchise and that's how we went about making offers, we wouldn't have a franchise. I heard the same things and read the same things, but the reality is that was never something that even entered my mind. We'd looked at this company on and off for two years and I thought $75 a share was cheap. It wasn't as if we didn't know what we were talking about. This wasn't a hard business to understand, and we were very familiar with it going back to my dinner with Ross. We kept worrying if we wanted to be in the tobacco business. Was that something we wanted to do? But when they announced at $75 a share, I said, "This is stupid. It's an absolute steal. That company's worth a hell of a lot more than $75 a share. It's a no-brainer."

PETER COHEN:

The night after Johnson's proposal to the board was made public, Friday night, I met with Henry.

Now I'd known Henry a long time socially — our kids were friendly — so this wasn't a big deal or anything. One of the ironies in all this is that my daughter and Henry's son Harrison, who died in 1991, were best friends. They went off to Brown together, the whole thing. She was with him in Colorado when he was killed. With all this acrimony between us it was a very awkward, sad time. He was a great kid. In fact, Henry's first wife, who's also deceased now, used to bring the kids to wherever we, and a few others, were going around Christmastime because we were always going away someplace as a group.

So I met with Henry that Friday night. It was a miserable, rainy night. We talked about doing the deal together — he was basically insisting that he had to be in the transaction. I said, "Look, this is not my call. It's Ross Johnson's call and I have to talk to him first. I will call you on Monday after I speak to Jim and Ross over the weekend."

Then I went home. I remember I got home at around eight thirty and I spoke to Jim. I think Ross was traveling so we got to him later over the weekend. Ross actually was not opposed to sitting down with Henry and seeing if we could do this thing together — none of us were opposed to that. Frankly, KKR had a lot of experience in doing this stuff. Henry had Drexel so it would take away one of the deal's natural competitors. Instead of having a fight on our hands we could do it cooperatively. Both Henry and I said during that Friday-night dinner that it would make a lot of sense if we could do it together.

I remember that weekend so vividly. It just rained the entire time. My son played football in a Saturday league and I went out to Randall's Island and stood there in the rain watching him play. Then we came home soaking wet and tired. I was home all Saturday night and never left the house on Sunday. I knew that on Monday I was going to call Henry and tell him that we wanted to sit down.

Meanwhile, Henry spent the weekend getting whipped up into a frenzy by Bruce Wasserstein, Jeff Beck, and all the other bankers on his team, who told him that we were having a board meeting on Tuesday and we were going to sign a contract with RJR. Understand that this idea was leaked by the board on Thursday, and he now was thinking that on Tuesday we were going to sign a contract to buy the company. He obviously figured we'd been working on it a long time and that we'd just been waiting to pounce.

So I left the house around seven thirty Monday morning to head downtown and go to work. While I was in the car I got a call from my wife, who said, "Henry just called the house. Here's his number. Call him back." When I got Henry on the phone the tension in his voice was palpable, right there on the surface. He said, "I know what you're up to and I know what you've been doing over the weekend. At eight o'clock we're announcing a tender offer for RJR."

I was stunned. I said, "What do you think we're up to?"

"Well, I know that you have board meetings tomorrow, American Express and Shearson, and you're going to sign a contract to buy the company."

I said, "Henry, these are our regularly scheduled monthly board meetings that have been on the calendar for a year now. Nothing's going to happen, there's no contract that's going to be signed. Your information couldn't be further from the truth — I was going to call you when I got in to tell you that we wanted to sit down. You're making a big mistake."

But he just said, "It's too late." That was it. And at eight o'clock they announced the tender offer for $90 a share.

HENRY KRAVIS:

They started the game by making the bid. Now, I've never spoken to them about it, but I'm sure Ross was sitting there thinking, "There's no way anyone else can come in. I've got the board and it's my company." Ross really did think of RJR as his company, and nobody was going to try to come in and take it over with him at the helm. But as soon as I saw the $75 come across the tape, I said that it's an absolute steal. All we had to do was refresh our numbers, which were not that far out of date, and take a look and see what we could pay. That's how we came up with the $90 offer.

PETER COHEN:

When we first started down the road to this deal we didn't know that Ross had actually had this meeting with Henry the year before where they discussed doing an LBO. That sort of came out when Henry started screaming, "I gave him the idea! I met with them and that's my idea!" Johnson never told us that; we heard it from Henry, loudly. I mean, he was berserk when he heard about it.

So we had to have a series of meetings with them, KKR, to see if we could work together on the deal. We even offered to step out at one point. We said to Ross, "If you think you want to do this deal with KKR or if you think you're better served with KKR, just tell us and we'll step aside. We're here to give you advice, but you're the client." At another point KKR offered us $100 million to step out of the deal. I called that a bribe — Henry didn't like that at all.

GEORGE ROBERTS:

From our point of view the main question was, who's going to do the financing for the transaction? Shearson and Solly [Salomon Brothers] wanted to do all the financing. Now this was a $5 billion high-yield financing, which they'd never done. We weren't prepared to let them drive the boat, quite frankly.

PETER COHEN:

We had our problems with Drexel, but not like Salomon. We had done some joint deals with Drexel and we'd had some bumpy spots along the way in dealing with them, but we didn't harbor the same level of animosity toward them as Salomon did. John Gutfreund, who was Salomon's chairman, just absolutely hated them. He thought they were crooks. He thought they were bad competitors, dishonest. I can't even begin to describe the things he would say about them. He would rant and rave about Drexel and Milken, how they're crooks, and on and on and on. He was fixated on it.

Now, this is a very important point, and for me this was perhaps the greatest mistake I've ever made as it's affected my life. Being the lead in this thing, what I could have done was go to Gutfreund and say, "John, we're going to do it with KKR and Drexel and either you're in or you're not. That's just the way it is." Instead, what I did was stand behind his desire not to have Drexel in the deal. That ended up in KKR and us blowing apart. Had I done that, the deal would have been done at a lower price, we would have made a lot of money, my life would have gone on, and I could have been a hero for pulling together this great deal. My life definitely would have been different.

I regret not doing that. I made the mistake of mixing up loyalty and whatever with the practical consequences of this transaction. Jim [Robinson] gave me the freedom on that one. He didn't tell me, you've got to do this or you've got to do that. He said, "It's your call." Not that I came to this alone. All the Shearson guys felt we ought to stick with the Solly guys rather than stick it to them.

HENRY KRAVIS:

Then we decided to go it alone. We tried very, very hard to do something with Ross and Shearson and Salomon. I'll never forget an all-night meeting we had with them where we just couldn't agree. To tell you how stupid it became, it got down to who was going to be on the left side of the tombstone and who was going to be on the right. That literally was part of the discussion. Salomon had this ridiculous fight with Drexel. John Gutfreund kept on saying, "We have to be on the left because we have to show that we're better than Drexel Burnham. We'll never be on the right to Drexel — ever."

We saw that and said, "We're putting up all this money and Drexel's going to be financing this. That's final." That was how you had to do it because otherwise they didn't have a clue how to finance it. So Salomon really ended any possibility that we could work together.

J. TOMILSON HILL:

Salomon only wanted to win because they saw this as their avenue into the high-yield area. That was John Gutfreund's and [Salomon president] Tommy Strauss's single focus, "This is our ticket into the high-yield business and to crush Drexel." Of course, that was totally unrelated. It had nothing to do with the deal.

JOHN GUTFRUEND (former Salomon Brothers chairman):

I thought we were competent. Our people had spent a considerable amount of time on the deal and I didn't think it was appropriate that we had to share it. We were perfectly capable of doing the job. Our firm had taken a beating over the past few years because we hadn't been as aggressive in junk bonds and this was how we wanted to move forward.

J. TOMILSON HILL:

I think everyone — all the bankers, lawyers, advisers — saw a cornucopia of potential fees, whether they were fees on advising, fees on financing, fees on refinancing. Literally, there were billions and billions in fees at stake here. Forget about the company and how you were going to run it and how you were going to pay off the debt! People were thinking about fees.

This was not Wall Street's finest hour.

PETER COHEN:

The board decided to convene a special committee and set up a process that would lead to a sealed-bid auction for the company on the Friday before Thanksgiving. They hired Skadden Arps and Dillon Read and Lazard to advise them on it. Anyone who was interested in the company would have to come up with a bid, show where the equity was coming from, the whole nine yards, by 5:00 p.m. that Friday.

Now, you remember how I said along the way leading up to the bid we had a few meetings with KKR to see if we could get together on a deal? Obviously, those talks collapsed, but at one of those meetings at some suite in the Plaza Hotel — I think we had two rooms there — we showed KKR our management-compensation model, the specific incentive deal the management would get if the deal went through. We didn't want to give them the term sheet, so we said, "We'll let you read it, but we want it back."

Jack Nusbaum, our lawyer from Willkie Farr, and Steve Goldstone, RJR's outside counsel, had the responsibility of working that through with Dick Beattie, Henry's lawyer from Simpson Thatcher. Dick said, "Let's discuss this term sheet." And with that he stepped out of the room and made copies of it. Then he came back, handed Jack the original, and Jack took him through everything that was in it.

[Eventually someone leaked a copy of the term sheet to] Jim Sterngold at the *New York Times* and told him, "Ross Johnson is going to make a billion dollars." That story ran on a Saturday.

When I saw the paper I went absolutely berserk. Number one, it was a clear violation of the understanding we had about how the information should be handled. Number two, it was a complete misrepresentation of the facts. I said to Jim Sterngold, "Not that anyone will ever know this, but you've been totally had." In order for Ross Johnson to make a billion dollars, or for the management group to make a billion dollars, the equity in this deal had to compound at some ridiculous rate. Seriously, the returns for the equity investors and bondholders would have been enormous — inconceivably humongous! But when the *New York Times* says a billion dollars . . . well, the board didn't want to hear any of it.

In the haste and emotions of what was going on, nobody on the board wanted to take the time to understand the assumptions underlying the figures in the *Times*. All they thought was, "Ross is trying to pull the wool over our eyes." They were afraid this great grab was going to take place, but nothing could have been further from the truth. The management group would have done okay. They would have made a few hundred million dollars under reasonable circumstances over five to seven years.

That story completely turned the board against Ross and actually made it impossible for them to want to give him the company.

J. TOMILSON HILL:

The fact of the matter is the story in the *New York Times* was accurate up to a point. We had an understanding with Ross that if the price went up his package invariably was going to go down. That's where we were going to find the money. If shareholders were going to get more he was going to get less. He was okay with that because he was a shareholder himself.

PETER COHEN:

But that wasn't even the worst of it as far as the bad press in this deal was concerned. We submitted our bid on the Friday before Thanksgiving. Then, on the day after Thanksgiving, Ross Johnson was interviewed by *Time* magazine down in Jupiter, Florida. Now, Linda Robinson was supposed to be his PR adviser. So I said to Linda, "Look, Ross is capable of being such a wild card, don't you think you should be there?" She said, "Oh, he can handle it." Sure he can. As it turned out, Ross destroyed himself and shot all of us in the process. The following Monday, December 5, *Time* magazine came out with Ross's picture on the cover underneath the words "A Game of Greed."

BRYAN BURROUGH:

So everybody came in with their bids on November 18 at 5:00 p.m. Ross Johnson won outright at $101 a share because Kravis and Roberts, for whatever reason, got cold feet and came in at $94. By all rights Johnson should have won right there, and he would have if not for something that happened later that night.

The board's representatives got a letter from First Boston, which was the only major investment bank on Wall Street that had no stake in this deal and of course badly wanted one. First Boston had a harebrained scheme to use some tax loopholes that expired in a matter of months to bid as high as $118. Well, of course nobody took them seriously, but the lawyers did show it to their tax attorney, saying, "We assume we can just throw this out." Unfortunately, the tax lawyer came back and said, "Well, we can't just throw it out. We need to at least look at this." So that Sunday, two days later, the board said that because they needed more time to look at the First Boston offer all the bids would be thrown out and there would be a second round of bidding.

PETER COHEN:

That first round of bidding was completely unfair. We submitted our bid at about $100 a share. Henry submitted his bid at $94. And then First Boston lobbed this crazy bid in. They were going to pay way more than $100 a share, but the whole thing was predicated on this esoteric tax issue that turned out to be bogus. Of course, we didn't know that yet. So if you looked at the pecking order it was these guys with the crazy tax thing in first, we were second, and KKR was third. When it turned out that the First Boston thing wasn't going to work, we got the company, right? Wrong. The board decided there would be yet another round of bidding.

BRYAN BURROUGH:

During the ensuing seven days First Boston fell out; its deal was as harebrained as it looked. Henry Kravis and George Roberts put out word that they were out of it. Henry spread the word that he was going skiing in Vail. In fact, he made a point of telling Linda Robinson he was going skiing because he knew she'd run back and tell her husband, Ross Johnson, and Peter Cohen. George went back to California. And all the other KKR people scattered. They put out word that they didn't know what they were going to do. Kravis's thinking was, if they weren't going to bid again they might as well walk away and not waste any more time on it. And if they were going to come back they might be able to capitalize on the element of surprise. Well, that's exactly what happened — it was "the head fake."

Basically Ross, Peter, Tom Hill, and their advisers assumed they had won. But Henry and George and the folks at KKR came back from their vacations and decided that they really did want this company. So the management group bumped their bid by a dollar, but Henry Kravis came back strong at $104 and just swamped the Johnson team, really put them on the defensive.

HENRY KRAVIS:

That was a strategic move. We had planned to go to Vail for Thanksgiving anyway. But I remember I was talking to Linda Robinson and I said, "I don't know what I'm going to do with this thing, Linda. I'm going skiing and getting out of here." What she didn't know, and nobody else knew, was that we'd already done all our work. There wasn't anything else to do and it was just a matter of fine-tuning it when we got back. We had a day to fine-tune it on Monday because we didn't have to submit it until Monday night or Tuesday. I think that when Linda asked what I was doing for Thanksgiving, she thought that if I was staying in New York I'd be working on the deal. But I told her the truth, that I was going to Vail, which I did. We've got telephones and fax machines in Vail, you know.

PETER COHEN:

That's a load of crap! Of course I knew he was going to bid. Henry goes to Vail every year around Thanksgiving. He takes his kids and it's the beginning of ski season. I've been in his living room and I know he's got a fax machine right next to the damn fireplace. Of course he was going to bid — Vail wasn't going to prevent him from doing anything. We knew exactly what was going to happen.

Now, Linda Robinson was saying that Henry was out of it. Or, perhaps she and Henry had decided to try to convince us that he wasn't going to bid.

LINDA ROBINSON (Ross Johnson's PR adviser and wife of American Express chairman Jim Robinson):

I thought Henry was trying to snow me. He was trying too hard.

PETER COHEN:

Anyway, in the second round KKR made its bid at $104 and we were at about $101. In the middle of the night, actually at around two in the morning, it became apparent to us that as of that moment KKR was the winner.

Ross Johnson almost didn't care one way or the other because he had this huge options position and he was going to make $50 million if he lost. He was a winner either way. Jim and some of the American Express board members probably preferred that we lose rather than suffer the scrutiny from this deal. It was apparent that there were going to be hearings in Washington over this whole business, the Dingell committee, so I think they became indifferent. And there were people on our team who believed that Linda Robinson, Jim's wife, had started working adversely to our interests. She was trying to feed information to Henry to make sure that KKR won. There was a strong feeling among several members of our group that this was going on.

But we had made our bid, we had done our work, and we thought that this could be done very well. We weren't about to back away at that point. So we left the offices of Willkie Farr at two in the morning, totally dejected. I got up around six thirty — I couldn't sleep much — and I called Jack Nusbaum, our lawyer at Willkie Farr.

I said to Jack, "You know, nobody's been playing by the rules that were established. It was supposed to be one bid, best bid. We had the best bid and should have won, but now they created this second round. Ross conceded, but that's Ross. Is there anything to prevent us from making another bid?"

Jack said, "Actually, no." He was rarin' to do it.

So I got hold of Gutfreund and said, "Look, the fact that Ross is out of this now doesn't matter. We can pull him back in if we need him to run the company. Why don't we think about making our own bid? There's been no announcement yet so we have to believe no contract's been signed."

Meanwhile, the board was trying to work out a bunch of things, they had this whole process going on, and they had Kravis waiting in the wings. His deal wasn't done yet. We got a group together and announced a bid for $108, which threw the place into a total tizzy. Kravis went nuts. He was like crazed. The board came back to both of us because they had a fiduciary obligation to explore this bid because we were now $4 a share over Kravis, which was about $200 million. They said to both of us, "Okay. Last bid, best bid." Kravis bid $109.

We went back to Ross and said, "Here's the management deal. We've completely cut the shit out of it. We're going to bid $112."

Ross took one look at it and said, "I agree." That never really came out. To keep an acceptable level of returns on the deal we had to take money out of somewhere, so we took it out of the management. And Ross was willing to go along with it.

So now it's $112 to $109, right? We're the winner. But we're not the winner because the board didn't want to give it to us. They kept coming up with conditions. Would we guarantee this? Would we guarantee that? Most of this was okay, until they said, "Will you guarantee that the debt you're going to use will trade at par [meaning one hundred cents on the dollar] eighteen months from now." The shareholders were going to receive debt in return for their shares and the board wanted to guarantee that they'd have a par-valued piece of paper.

That's when John Gutfreund said, "I won't guarantee that anything will trade at par. You can't do that." But KKR was willing to make that guarantee.

J. TOMILSON HILL:

The management bid, our bid, was not the higher bid. The bids were so different, and by the end of the whole process it was clear that the independent committee would do just about anything to prevent Ross from buying the company. They felt the only criticism they could face in retrospect was somehow selling the business to Ross. So they looked at the financing conditions, the willingness to be unconditional on the bridge loans, and things like that. There were ways for the independent committee to find holes in the RJR management bid. And that's what they did.

Now, if they put the KKR/Drexel bid under a microscope they might have found contingencies there, too. Although you have to give Drexel credit, they were operating under such a cloud at the time but they still really owned the high-yield market. The board probably said to themselves, "If there is a risk of not getting this financed, Drexel probably has a better chance of getting it done, even though they're under this cloud." See, there was always this issue of can this thing get done? Can it get financed?

HENRY KRAVIS:

It was a very difficult and nerve-racking process. You get so focused on your objective and it becomes all-consuming. We were getting calls at eleven at night. Can you come over and meet with Ross Johnson? Can you meet with the investment bankers? It was this constant on-again, off-again thing. There were seven of us who worked on the transaction and we'd sit around my office and talk about all the issues that are so important besides the numbers. What does it mean to the firm if it doesn't work? What does it mean to you and your family and the other people at KKR with the amount of time and effort it's going to take? We knew this was a transaction that was so visible we had to make it work. What did we really feel about the cigarette business? None of us smoked — how did that affect how we felt about the deal? What does this mean in Washington? How are they going to view us and the rest of the buyout world? These are the kinds of things that we were constantly talking about, and they became very troubling to all of us. This wasn't just, let's buy another company. We had to really think through all the issues that were confronting our making the acquisition. But in the end we did get the company.

PETER COHEN:

After we lost I spoke to Felix Rohatyn and Ira Harris from Lazard, who were advising the board on the deal. I said, "We just don't understand. We were the high bid."

"There were other considerations," was how they put it. You know, this and that, this and that.

Bull. It was very clear that the board had turned against Ross. They felt that he hadn't dealt with them in good faith. Now, I don't think that's the case, but I understand how, based on the way he handled it, they could only conclude that.

F. ROSS JOHNSON:

I think the board found themselves in something they never anticipated. They were really in the hands of the investment bankers. I think they had doubts reading what they had to read.

J. TOMILSON HILL:

In the end we really came to view losing as winning because of the price we would have to pay if we actually bought the company. There's no question that from a fiduciary standpoint — where we were looking at the American Express shareholders and investors in our private equity fund — we were better off not having bought RJR Nabisco. There's just no question about that. Look at how the investors in KKR's fund suffered as a result of it.

After KKR bought the company, RJR ran into trouble because of two things that nobody quite anticipated. These are things that would have hurt no matter who bought the company. The first was the decline in the growth of the tobacco business, because everyone was positing that this could grow for years. And second was litigation [from cigarettes]. Nobody really quantified that. So when the junk-bond market collapsed in the early 1990s after the demise of Drexel, RJR Nabisco almost went bankrupt. Those bonds were sold at very high rates and then the market just crashed on them.

BRYAN BURROUGH:

This had all become so unseemly, our stories every day chronicling the bad feeling and name-calling; all the cinematic aspects of it had created almost a main-event kind of atmosphere. Everybody was following this like the World Series. George Roberts and Jim Robinson were especially concerned about this, not that the public would become upset with it, but that Congress would somehow come in and regulate the golden goose. That's what scared everyone.

So symbolically, this was the deal that killed the golden goose. What that meant was, every CEO in America was scared. See, by this point every CEO had at least looked at doing an LBO. Now every CEO took those LBO plans, put them in his desk drawer, and locked it. Keep in mind Ross Johnson had been all but burned in effigy. He was *the* evil man, as constructed by the press. And everyone saw what you could do if you made a wrong step. As a result, nobody would do these deals anymore.

GEORGE ROBERTS:

Looking back, other than not buying the company in the first place, I wouldn't change a thing in the RJR deal. It's been a lousy investment for us. We'll basically get our money back plus a very small rate of return. We put over a decade of hard work into it and have gone through an awful lot of crises with it. So it's been a disappointment. If I had to do it all over again I certainly wouldn't do it.

CHAPTER 22

GREED IS BAD

The RJR Nabisco deal may have shown that the M&A craze had gotten a little out of hand, but the 1980s takeover era really came to an end at the hands of regulators pursuing the most far-reaching series of criminal investigations in the history of Wall Street. Starting with the arrest of Dennis Levine in 1986, the Securities and Exchange Commission and U.S. attorney's office in Manhattan began unraveling a web of corrupt investment bankers, traders, and lawyers with ties to some of the major Wall Street firms at the time. Prominent players — such as star M&A banker Martin Siegel, who had moved from Kidder Peabody to Drexel Burnham Lambert, and powerful Goldman Sachs trader Robert Freeman — ruined their careers by trading on inside information. But despite the fact that several key people were brought down in the scandal, many on Wall Street suspected that the real prizes for the financial police were Drexel Burnham Lambert and its junk-bond king, Michael Milken.

The critical moment for the government was when Ivan Boesky decided to cooperate in a plea agreement. Boesky, the reputed ideological model for the

Gordon Gekko character in Oliver Stone's film Wall Street, *was a merger arbitrager, which basically meant that he was a trader who bet on the outcomes of mergers. He had racked up impressive returns in the 1980s, and earned himself a fortune in the process. But in time it became clear that his seeming clairvoyance actually was the result of his ability to gather inside information. And everyone on Wall Street assumed that Boesky had the goods on Milken and Drexel.*

GARY LYNCH (Credit Suisse First Boston executive vice chairman and former director of enforcement at the Securities and Exchange Commission):

The year I'd say when things got really out of hand in terms of insider trading was 1981. There were two deals that year, Seagrams and St. Joe Minerals. There was massive trading through the Swiss banks, much larger than what we had seen before in other matters. But in all the matters at that time there were these huge run-ups before the announcements. So there was much more of a focus on insider-trading cases and many more people started working on those cases. They also became cases that people thought were interesting to work on. Everyone in the division wanted to do the insider-trading cases.

RUDY GIULIANI (former New York City mayor and former U.S. attorney for the Southern District of New York):

I remember we did a survey of the number of insider-trading cases that had been prosecuted by, and were pending in, the U.S. attorney's office. There'd be a prosecution, someone would plead guilty, and there was very little attention being given to it. We thought that there should be a little more attention paid to this because it could act as a deterrent to people who were involved in insider trading. We did a survey of a number of cases to see if there were a lot of cases, or just a few. And I remember seeing the chart that was compiled and being surprised at how widespread illicit insider trading was.

GARY LYNCH:

Frankly, for all the cases we were bringing, it didn't seem to be stopping. The run-ups were the same and it really appeared as if insider trading was occurring unabated. Then, in 1985, about the time that I became director of enforcement, there was an article that appeared in one of the newsweeklies about the "unwinnable war" against insider trading. It made my then boss John Shad furious, just furious, because it suggested that the SEC wasn't effective and perhaps should just give up the fight. Shad was a true believer that insider trading was bad and he didn't want to hear this at all. If anything, he wanted to redouble the efforts in the area.

At about this same time, completely fortuitously, the Dennis Levine investigation began. It was a gift really. Things might not have fallen together the way they did if that hadn't happened. There was an incredible series of cases that came out of that one case, Dennis Levine. We got Ivan Boesky, Martin Siegel, Michael Milken, out of Levine. And for a long time those cases had an enormous effect on abuses in the markets.

DANIEL HERTZBERG (deputy managing editor of the *Wall Street Journal* who covered the 1980s insider-trading investigations as a reporter):

Dennis Levine was the start, but if you're saying, did we know that Dennis was going to lead to Michael Milken? No. Dennis's was a big case — there had never been anything that big. But nobody knew that it was going to lead to where it ended up.

FRED JOSEPH (former Drexel Burnham Lambert chief executive):

I was shocked when Gary Lynch called me about Dennis Levine. Before I got the call I thought Dennis was a good young banker, maybe a little too aggressive. You had to control him. He had joined us, I think from Shearson Lehman Brothers, not too long before this happened. So we had no idea that he was running a major scam, primarily because it mostly happened before he got to Drexel.

My first question to Gary was, "Are you sure?" He said, "We're absolutely positive." So I said, "Well, I'm on your side. What do you want me to do?" He said they had everything well in hand, but that we should secure his office. It was a sad, shocking, dismaying day. You know, the fact is, and this is cold comfort, that nobody I ever hired out of school for corporate finance has ever been accused of any wrongdoing, and there have been hundreds of them. The two people in Drexel's corporate finance department who were accused of wrongdoing, Dennis and Marty Siegel, both started their bad behavior before they got to Drexel. Marty at least had the sense to stop once he got here. Dennis continued.

ROBERT LINTON (former Drexel Burnham chairman):

With both Dennis Levine and Martin Siegel, their insider-trading problems predate their arrival at our firm. One I knew very well — Siegel was with Kidder Peabody and really was considered one of the leaders in his profession. Why he wanted to go and basically trash his career I'll never understand. Levine I didn't know at all. But it certainly made for bad publicity for the firm because when they had their problems and went on trial, they were identified as having been with Drexel Burnham. What they'd done happened elsewhere, but that point usually got lost in the headlines.

GARY LYNCH:

Beyond the fact that it was a huge amount of money in comparison to any other case prior to that time, Dennis Levine was the first case against someone who was, well, I wouldn't say Dennis was a major player, but he was the kind of noted Wall Street banker who was invited to SEC roundtables. But at that point we didn't have any evidence of a wider conspiracy on Wall Street. There was concern that a wider conspiracy was going on, for sure. I used to get calls from people all the time — "If you look into so-and-so and so-and-so I know they have to be insider trading." But there was never any evidence, and some of the stuff was pretty ridiculous. Basically, you had a lot of accusations being hurled at major figures in the business without any factual basis.

But the Levine case suddenly was there, a major case. And he very quickly gave up the other bankers. We knew there were other people because we had other names on our list and all of these deals weren't Drexel deals. So there had to be other bankers involved. He gave those names pretty quickly, Ilan Reich and Robert Wilkis and a few others. He also gave up Ivan Boesky, but in a very murky way.

Unlike the other guys, where there was direct evidence linking them, the Ivan Boesky evidence was soft. There was no documentary evidence. No money ever changed hands. The meetings were at the Harvard Club. We were very doubtful that we were going to be able to make the case, actually. It's one thing to prove insider trading when you have someone who's not trading hundreds of millions of dollars' worth of stock a day, but if you have trading in enormous volumes, the way Boesky was doing, proving insider trading can be very difficult. All trading is in accordance with a pattern; there's always some reason for a trade. And we'd cut a deal with Dennis Levine, so his credibility was going to be called into question. It looked as if he was going to be one-on-one with Ivan Boesky — that was our case. But then Boesky just caved very quickly. I think something like twenty-seven subpoenas were sent to him and his various entities in one day, all with the message that Dennis Levine had turned him in.

DANIEL HERTZBERG:

Boesky was the most prominent arb, another one of these guys who wanted to be well-known. When he got hit, calls went out all around Wall Street because people knew this was big. He was extremely tied in, considered the biggest or among the biggest arbs. Therefore there was the assumption that if Boesky pleaded guilty he would be in the position to reveal things.

JOSEPH FLOM (M&A attorney and partner at Skadden, Arps, Slate, Meagher and Flom):

I knew enough not to deal with Ivan Boesky. Early on I decided that we didn't want to represent arbitragers. Who needs to take a chance with those guys? If they read my body English and figure out what's going on in a deal, I don't need that. A lot of the big firms started working with the arbitragers and I got some irate calls asking why I told my people not to talk to them. They said they weren't looking for inside information, that they just wanted to get something clarified. Bullshit.

MICHAEL MILKEN (former head of Drexel Burnham Lambert's high-yield bond department):

It was obviously a terrible mistake ever doing a single trade with him. But people forget that in the 1980s Boesky was celebrated by the media. Just about every investment house on Wall Street dealt with him, and those that didn't mostly wanted to. In 1986, Boesky was the commencement speaker at Berkeley's business-school graduation exercises. Everyone thought he was a great arbitrager and wanted his business. But he was only a tiny part of Drexel's business.

PETER ACKERMAN (former Drexel Burnham Lambert executive vice president and deputy to Michael Milken in the high-yield bond department):

I don't think we fully understood the impact we were making on the world. I know I didn't. I didn't realize how deeply people felt about us until afterward. And then you also had the fear that we engendered in corporate America. So in that environment, when Ivan Boesky said some bad things about Mike it was a huge opportunity for someone to take action. It was sort of like the perfect storm that evolved to a crescendo.

GARY LYNCH:

Boesky was trying to cut the best deal possible, which is what anyone would do in that circumstance. He gave us a number of people — including Martin Siegel and, of course, Michael Milken. We wanted to get a deal cut with Boesky relatively quickly, too, because the U.S. attorney's office wanted to wire him and send him to meet with Mr. Milken and maybe others. The only way that could be done effectively was if it happened before word got around that Ivan had some problem. I was really concerned about a leak. We did the whole deal — from the approach, to the meeting, to the documents — in probably about a three-week period.

RUDY GIULIANI:

Milken took the whole investigation to a level beyond any it had gotten to before. He was involved much more substantially in many more situations. The thing I am sure that must have struck the judge is how many different crimes the people involved were able to commit. They didn't confine themselves to one or two. They pretty much did a checklist of crimes. And also the sophistication of it; it wasn't as if they were blundering into criminal activity.

GARY LYNCH:

Drexel was very helpful with Dennis Levine. I dealt with Fred Joseph, giving him a heads-up. They were very helpful. But they were not helpful on Milken. I think everyone on the government side was a little naive in thinking that as the war moved from Boesky to Milken that Drexel would see the handwriting on the wall and adopt a cooperative approach as they did in the Levine case. But Milken was much, much, much more than Levine. Milken may not have been their entire franchise at that point because Drexel had gotten so big, but he certainly was a key part of their franchise, and they rallied around him initially.

FRED JOSEPH:

When it became clear that Boesky was pointing a finger at Milken I had a lot of reasons to think that Michael wouldn't be doing stuff like that. Some of the early things that they said Michael had done were demonstrably untrue. They said we'd positioned something, and I'd have them go check out records and it turned out we hadn't done it. So I ended up in the wrong place, which was convinced that Boesky had to give up the bigger fish, and that was Michael. I had numerous discussions with Michael over the years about this kind of thing. I'd say, "Michael, do you have the best job in the world?"

He'd say, "I think I do."

So I'd say, "You know, if you put one toe over the line they'll cut your foot off."

And he'd say, "Fred, do you think I'm stupid?"

Now, I'd never presume to think that Michael was stupid, but I'd always ask him if he'd made any promises to anyone that I should know about or his brother [Lowell Milken, legal counsel for Drexel Burnham's high-yield department] should know about. He'd look me in the eye and say, "I know people keep saying I'm promising favors to people, but I'm not. I know the securities laws. My business is way too good for me to risk it."

I don't know if he was setting me up, or what. I think his obsession was getting done what he said he'd get done, meeting his commitments. That led him into some excesses that got him in bad trouble. A lot of people have talked about his obsession to do every piece of business. But I don't think it was that. Michael was obsessed with the idea that if he said something was going to happen, it happened.

GARY LYNCH:

The major thing Boesky had on Milken was this transaction where Boesky was raising money on a private placement and there was a settling up in the ledger that was created to record monies that Boesky owed Milken on information that had worked out favorably versus losses that Boesky had taken in order to help Milken do something. That was the primary thrust of the whole Milken-Boesky connection. We thought for a long time that this ledger had been destroyed on both sides. Actually, I think it was destroyed at Drexel, but the Boesky sheet was located and it was just a devastating document. By the time the thing started unraveling and Drexel started to think about settling, two and a half years later, that document was the key. The practice could no longer be defended.

PETER ACKERMAN:

Mike was charged with "parking," and that's a serious crime. But at the same time, an infinite number of incidents of parking have been handled on a civil basis. Be clear, I'm not here saying that Drexel was screwed because its members behaved perfectly. My problem with what happened is, it's a question of proportion. And if prosecutors are prosecuting to create deterrence, they failed miserably, because nobody knows what Drexel really did wrong. You ask the average person what went wrong at Drexel and he'll say, "insider trading." Well, that's nonsense. These were technical violations. And they killed the firm. If you're supposed to mete out justice in proportion to the crime, where's the proportion?

FRED JOSEPH:

So we started talking to the SEC. There were very intense conversations on day one, and we refused to settle. On day two, they called us in and gave us a sanity check. They said, "Are you nuts?" We said, "No. Indict us." So they said, "What will change your mind?" And that's where we got into the real negotiations.

GARY LYNCH:

The negotiations started off contentious. We'd all get together at these big meetings where they'd bring in Fred Joseph, [Drexel mergers and acquisitions chief] Leon Black, and a couple of others, and all of their lawyers, and we'd sit there. Eventually somebody would say something that would piss somebody else off, and the meeting would dissolve. Maybe it wasn't a shouting match, but it wasn't constructive, shall we say. As the weeks went on and the group thinned, many of the major issues were taken care of in small meetings with Joseph and me. Occasionally it would be with Joseph and John Sturk, the associate director, Jerry Tannenbaum, one of their lawyers, and me. That's really how it got done.

FRED JOSEPH:

The negotiations went on for a long time. Finally, in the fall of '88 I think, the government said, "You're nuts. You're really not going to settle until we show you what he's done. This is unheard-of, but we're going to show you."

They showed me spreadsheets with the calculation of the $5.3 million payment to Boesky, some trading tickets with signatures on them, and other incriminating documents. They also had me listen to tapes where you could hear people trying to affect the price of the stock, which is by definition manipulation. All I can say is, it was troublesome. It was a powerful batch of information. By this time, I'd also learned about how [Milken had] stripped the warrants from certain transactions and put them in his children's accounts. With the accumulated information they showed me, and the new stuff I learned, it became clear that some things that shouldn't have been done were done. As you can imagine, it had an enormous impact on the way I was thinking.

GARY LYNCH:

Drexel and Joseph, in particular, were concerned throughout the settlement negotiations that getting rid of Milken would destroy the firm.

FRED JOSEPH:

Once you get into a war with the government you're going to lose. They've got the guns. They've got the jails. They've got the unlimited resources. They win. There's no amount of money or power that can stand up to the government. I never for one second thought we could. But Drexel had done an immense amount of good. There were eleven thousand people here. In the end they charged seven people with criminal wrongdoing, two of whom did it before they got here, and one of whom dumbly committed perjury for her boss. So really four people at Drexel out of eleven thousand had violated securities laws, and the government absolutely didn't care how much damage they did to us.

I argued with Giuliani that a $150 million fine gives them the biggest headline they could possibly get, and capital is the lifeblood of a securities firm. What about our government-securities business, and our commodities business, and our retail business, and all the other 10,996 people who were working? He could've cared less. I think that once a government gets a head of steam it's going to do anything it can to win.

ROBERT LINTON:

It was all about the blind political ambition of Rudy Giuliani. He wanted to use this to promote his political career, and he managed to do that successfully. The RICO [Racketeer Influenced and Corrupt Organizations Act] charge was the most interesting part of the whole case. What brought the firm down was Giuliani told us, "I'm going to bring a RICO charge against you on Monday." As I'm sure you know, the RICO law was meant for the Mafia, and after this happened the law was declared invalid in white-collar matters.

FRED JOSEPH:

Our choice was, if we didn't settle they were going to indict us. And if they did indict us it would be under RICO, which meant that they could demand an enormous bond because RICO crimes carry huge financial penalties. We'd set aside $1 billion to handle it. Then they were going to announce that there would be a superseding indictment with a superseding bond of an indeterminate amount, which meant that nobody in their right mind would lend us money. It meant with 100 percent certainty that we'd be bankrupt within a week unless every financial institution in the United States went absolutely nuts. We had $2 billion in capital and $30 billion in short-term secured borrowings, and some unsecured borrowings. Nobody was going to let that stand. We had to settle.

GARY LYNCH:

During the course of the negotiation it became pretty clear that they were going to have to get rid of Milken. All the evidence pointed to the reality that if they were going to continue to operate as a firm, they could not have him as part of the team.

FRED JOSEPH:

One of the conditions set by Giuliani and the SEC was that we'd have to terminate Milken. That wasn't the biggest issue, because by then we knew it was going to happen. He was negotiating with them, and because of what else we knew, we also knew he'd have to settle. The bigger issue was, would the firm plead guilty to six felony counts and pay a $650 million fine?

Eventually I called Michael and said, "We have to terminate your employment. If you want to resign you can. If you don't want to do that, you'll force us to fire you."

So he said, "I'd hoped to spend my whole life here."

And I said, "Well, me too."

That's when he told me that I should fire him. I said that I thought that was a mistake because there's some PR benefit to resigning. So he called me back about twenty minutes later and said that he'd changed his mind. He wanted to resign. I said, "I think that's a good idea, Michael." And it was done.

On December 21, 1988, Drexel Burnham Lambert settled with the Securities and Exchange Commission and U.S. attorney's office, pleading guilty to six complicated felony counts and agreeing to pay a $650 million fine. From there, the focus of the investigation turned to Michael Milken himself. On April 25, 1990, Milken pleaded guilty to six felonies, four of which related to his dealings with Ivan Boesky, and agreed to $600 million in fines. Then, on November 21, 1990, Michael Milken received his sentence from Judge Kimba Wood: ten years in prison.

RUDY GIULIANI:

When you look at it compared to other sentences, it is higher. But it should be. Because his involvement and the scope of his criminality was greater, before you even get to analyzing the lack of cooperation. Just based on an analysis of the scope of the criminal activity, it was the correct sentence.

ROBERT LINTON:

I was stunned when I heard Michael's sentence. In the end, I feel that his having spent a couple of years in the kind of institution he did was probably not far from where it should've ended up. But you have to understand that Michael never intended to do anything other than fight this to the very end — until his brother was implicated. His plea bargain was very much predicated on the fact that they would not bring any charges against his brother, Lowell. He felt completely responsible for whatever was going to happen to Lowell. He has said, and I believe him, that that's what led him to make his deal.

JUDE WANNISKI (chairman of Polyconomics and former associate editor of the *Wall Street Journal*):

Milken never did anything wrong. Nothing. He was so harassed by the government and the media that he came to believe he would be attacked for the rest of his life unless he came to terms with his adversaries. He refused to admit he did any of the almost one hundred felonious acts with which he was charged, but there were technical violations of the law. He chose a few of these, as for example, his failure to file a report with the SEC in timely fashion (which his secretary should have done). He believed, incorrectly as it turned out, that his plea bargaining would allow him to avoid prison. Boesky, of course, did in fact commit felonious acts, and was successful in getting his punishment reduced by feeding Rudy Giuliani a line on Milken.

GARY LYNCH:

So he got to see a lot from his vantage point. I always thought that was pretty cut-and-dried stuff. Take 13D violations [the SEC rule requiring investors to register if they own more than 5 percent of a single company's stock]. Explaining their significance to a man on the street is hard. But is it something that's bad and should be punishable? Absolutely. I never thought that was a gray area. Manipulation has always been a bad thing. Was this the kind of manipulation where you jack the market up ten points or down ten points? No, it was more sophisticated than that. But it was still manipulation. Did he violate the law at every turn and with every opportunity? Clearly no. He was involved in so much and so many transactions that I wouldn't even say illegality permeated his business. But was it a factor in some of his transactions? Yes.

SAUL COHEN (former SEC-approved in-house counsel for Drexel Burnham Lambert):

Now, I'll tell you a story about what was wrong with Drexel. About a week before Drexel filed for bankruptcy one of the compliance people came to see me. We had a hundred-person compliance department, and these guys were stars. They had brilliant systems for looking at everything that was happening in the firm, all the trading, on computers. Anyway, one of the compliance guys comes in with this printout from the computer (today this would all be electronic) and he shows me how a couple of traders in one of our branch offices had bought certain bonds for their own accounts. Okay. So he says, "Today, just after the close came an announcement that the company's redeeming the bonds at par. They paid about fifty-one cents on the dollar. I think they had inside information."

So I say, "Let's not jump to conclusions." Then I call a senior guy out there. He gets on the phone, and I say, "Hi, this is Saul Cohen here in New York. One of our compliance guys has come in with this stuff about these bonds and I've got some questions." There's a long, long pause and then I hear the following . . . I don't know if that got picked up on your tape, but it's the sound of a man slapping himself in the head from thousands of miles away.

He says, "How stupid can we be?"

And I say, "I don't know."

"What were we thinking about?"

"I don't know."

He says, "Is there anything that can be done?"

I say, "What would you like to do?"

"Could you break the trades?"

And I say, "Yeah."

He says, "Would you break the trades?"

"Yeah."

And he says, "Oh, bless you. Thank you. We'll never do anything like this again." Okay. That was it. We hung up.

Now, you'll notice we never discussed insider information. So I'll ask you a question: who did they buy the bonds from? The answer is, they bought them from *Drexel's* inventory. The bonds were sitting there in the inventory, and they didn't consider it trading on inside information because they were just buying them from the house. They were ripping off Drexel — who cares? They had been taught to rip off everybody, and they didn't differentiate. That's what was wrong with the place.

FRED JOSEPH:

I don't think the firm was dead as soon as Milken was gone. The public relations nightmare from the settlement definitely hurt, and we were weaker, no question. And we had cut back — by the time we went bankrupt we'd gone from eleven thousand employees to under six thousand. But we actually did fine for a while. We made money the following year, which was 1989. We did the RJR deal, which had a $250 million fee in it. In the end, it was a thousand small cuts that did us in. It was every state regulator giving us a hard time. It was the New York Stock Exchange jumping on us. It was the willingness to change our capital requirements. In aggregate, it was expensive, time-consuming, diverting, aggravating, and ultimately, once they took the capital away, there was no place to turn.

Drexel Burnham Lambert filed for bankruptcy on February 13, 1990, after defaulting on $100 million in loans. For all intents and purposes, Drexel was dead, although it still took several years to fully unwind the firm's positions. Michael Milken ultimately served two years out of his ten-year sentence in a federal prison and paid a total of $1.1 billion in fines and restitution. Milken emerged from jail having survived a bout with prostate cancer, and since then has spent most of his time on philanthropic efforts aimed at finding a cure for the disease. Meanwhile, Ivan Boesky served twenty-two months of his three-year prison sentence and paid a $100 million fine after pleading guilty to one count of conspiring to make false statements to the Securities and Exchange Commission.

Fred Joseph also was punished because of his failure to adequately supervise Milken. The New York Stock Exchange censured him, and the SEC barred him from having a supervisory role at a securities firm for three years and banned him for life from holding the title of chairman, chief executive, or president in the securities industry. And, in an ironic coda to the story, Rudy Giuliani, also a prostate-cancer survivor, in January 2001 wrote a letter to President Bill Clinton urging that Michael Milken be pardoned in recognition of all the beneficial work he's done for cancer research since his release from prison. The letter was ignored. Milken continues to wait for a presidential pardon.

But Milken wasn't the only major figure contemplating leaving Wall Street as the eighties closed. The year 1987 had not been a particularly good one for Peter Lynch. First he was stuck in Ireland during the stock-market crash. His Magellan Fund posted $2 billion in losses. And then, at the end of the year, the public learned that Lynch had failed to outperform the S&P 500 index for only the second time in his career. In response, Lynch threw himself into his work, and using his traditional stock-picking techniques of making big, bold bets on businesses he believed in, he succeeded in dramatic fashion. Magellan climbed nearly 23 percent in 1988 and a whopping 35 percent in 1989, outpacing sizable gains in the S&P 500 in both years. What makes this performance all the more remarkable is that by this time Magellan Fund held roughly $12.5 billion. In essence, he was successfully steering a yacht through roaring river rapids.

Still, none of this means he was happy. As the 1990s dawned, Lynch started to realize how much of his personal life he'd surrendered in pursuit of success. He'd more than made up for the losses Magellan posted during the 1987 crash and no longer had anything to prove to anyone, including himself. So, on March 28, 1990, Peter Lynch stunned Wall Street by announcing that he'd be retiring at the relatively youthful age of forty-six.

PETER LYNCH (former manager of Fidelity Magellan Fund):

Everybody talks about how frightening the 1987 crash was, but to me 1990 was a much scarier time. In 1987 you had big companies taking a hit, but the fundamentals were fine. It actually created opportunities. In 1990, banks were failing. The savings and loans were in trouble. Real estate prices were falling. In the 1980s we had a big run-up in real estate values, and now people's homes were falling in price. That's frightening to anyone. The financial system was in trouble. You had Chase Manhattan Bank, Citibank, Manufacturer's Hanover, big banks, and people were saying they were going up in flames. Bank of Boston was selling for three bucks a share. Banks are very important to the economy because they make loans, and when the banking system is in real trouble it's pretty scary.

Then, on top of that, you layer on the fact that we were in a recession. And just to make things a little worse, we now had five hundred thousand troops in Saudi Arabia about to fight Iraq, which was supposedly a mighty army, the fourth largest in the world. People were sitting on their sofas debating body bags; that's what all the talk shows were about. Taxes were going up, we were going to war, not a pleasant environment. It was really ugly, almost as bad as 1981 to '82. You have hyperinflation, spiraling property values, and people worried about Chase Manhattan and Citibank going under. If you line up all those things, it was the worst set of circumstances in my thirty-year career. All of which made it seem like a perfect time to walk away from Magellan.

I stopped running Magellan in May 1990, and I think the market was at 2,700. By July, it was up to 3,000. That's when Saddam Hussein walked into Kuwait with his army. The market went from 3,000 to 2,300. We had a 20, 25 percent correction. But guess what? We were able to have the war and it was over in a month. And the banks didn't go under. The market didn't anticipate a quick recovery, so 1991 was one of the best years in a long time to be in stocks because most people were looking for a rebound maybe in 1992 to '93. Of course, by then none of the good news mattered to me anymore, at least in terms of running a fund. That was already over for me. But the stock market really had nothing to do with that.

Look, I liked my job, but I love my kids. That's really all there was to it. I stopped running Magellan because I wanted to see them grow up. I know a lot of people say they're leaving their job because they want to spend more time with their families, but they really mean something else. Well, I meant it. And I haven't regretted it one bit.

Like a great professional athlete who stops playing before fans can see his skills diminish, Peter Lynch went out on top and kept the mythology that surrounded him intact. He never returned to running a mutual fund or started up his own fund family, as anyone in his position might have been tempted to do. And as other hot fund managers came and went in the years following his retirement, Lynch's star continued to shine. He has remained at Fidelity, but only in an advisory capacity. His books on investing are best sellers, and although he hasn't been active in the business for more than a decade, he continues to be the most effective advertising pitchman the mutual fund industry has ever seen.

PART THREE

CHAPTER 23

THE TECHNOLOGY AGE

The 1990s brought the technology age to Wall Street. Sure, the financial-services industry was computerized by the 1980s, but in the 1990s there was an explosion in technological developments that made trading, managing portfolios, and just about every other possible financial-services activity under the sun less expensive and more efficient. And then, with the development of the Internet and the World Wide Web, an entirely new industry was born — discount online brokerage. Suddenly, with the click of a button on a computer, individual investors could be managing their money, buying and selling stocks and mutual funds, and doing research on other investments. The appeal was irresistible, and as access to the Internet spread and the bull market continued to roll on, participation in the stock market by Main Street investors erupted. Clearly, if you had to point to a single force that was most responsible for the democratization of Wall Street in the late twentieth century, technology would have to be it.

ALFRED R. BERKELEY III (former Nasdaq president and vice chairman):

When you look at it in terms of decades, the biggest difference between Wall Street in the 1990s and Wall Street in the 1980s is technology. With each new computer terminal, each new program, each new software package, trading got faster and information became more readily available. When you think about Wall Street today you have to think about technology. But it wasn't that long ago that this wasn't the case.

KENNETH PASTERNAK (founder and former chief executive officer of Knight/Trimark):

I think technology democratized the stock market in three ways. There was informational democratization because people could get information about stocks and use technology tools that previously had been unavailable to the self-directed individual investor. You had execution democratization, where people could act on this information by trading electronically. And it reduced costs, which made it much more affordable for individuals to participate in the market actively and aggressively.

Firms were spending $1 million to $5 million a year on technology in the midnineties, and we were spending $50 million to $100 million five years later. If you had told CEOs that they would be spending $50 million a year on technology they would've looked at you as if you were on drugs.

JACK BOGLE (founder of Vanguard Group, president of Bogle Markets Research Center, and former chairman of Wellington Management):

In the late 1980s, I think it was 1988, I said to *Forbes* magazine, "We don't want to be the technology leader. We can't afford to be." I was a bit of a Luddite. But three years later, at a meeting of senior officers, thirty or forty of us, I put up that headline from *Forbes* and I wrote a new quote saying here's where we are today: "We are going to be the technology leader because we can't afford not to be."

HARRIS BRUMFIELD (chief executive officer of Trading Technologies International and former trader in the futures pits at the Chicago Board of Trade):

I got my start trading in the futures pits in Chicago, so I know what it's like to work on the trading floor. But when you put it on an electronic platform, the world becomes your pit. That's a massive difference. On the floor you're restricted to several hundred people who you can trade with. But when you take it out to the world, your opportunities are unlimited. There are a lot more people now who have a level playing field because of technology, and it has dramatically opened up our markets.

DAVID LANDES (chief executive officer of Bondsonline.com):

In terms of technology making a difference on Wall Street, there were some significant developments in analytics for traders, programs, software, and things like that. But the real leap was made with the development of the Web in the mid-1990s.

JERRY PUTNAM (chief executive officer of Archipelago Holdings):

The distribution possibilities of the Internet were enormous. In the old world you had to hook up people on a point-to-point basis. With the Internet you could hook up once, and suddenly the whole world's your customer.

WILLIAM HAMBRECHT (chairman of WR Hambrecht and Company and cofounder of Silicon Valley investment bank Hambrecht and Quist):

What the Web allows you to do is on a real-time basis communicate with literally millions of people all at once. No one has ever been able to do that in the marketplace. I think what it's really doing is — and I know this sounds corny — but it is democratizing the business process. For example, use the metaphor of the department store. For the first eighty or ninety years of the last century, department stores were the place you had to be if you wanted to sell your product to the consumer. You had to get shelf space there, because that's where they came to make their purchases.

Little specialty stores were hard to do. If you were really good at it, you could pull it off, particularly at the high end, where there are always those kinds of stores. But effectively, department stores were the places where people shopped. Then, along comes this thing where people can communicate exactly what they want directly with the supplier, and that transaction can be done even more cheaply. So the department store starts to go away. Now you have a proliferation of suppliers of specific consumer needs or goods, and the consumer can communicate directly with them. That's really what the Internet has done.

DAVID LANDES:

The big Wall Street firms were really reluctant to get involved in the Internet. They were nervous about security and whether data could be delivered accurately and timely. But the discount brokers weren't concerned about that and they're the ones that really capitalized on it.

FRANK PETRILLI (former chief executive officer of TD Waterhouse):

Even in the eighties it was clear that automation was the smart play. We didn't have the online trading or the Internet, but we had phones, and that was the first form of automation — touch-tone trading. Before the Internet 30 percent of our trading was touch-tone trading.

RODGER RINEY (founder and chief executive officer of Scottrade):

When you looked at the Internet and the discount-brokerage industry, it just seemed as if it couldn't miss. Your customer could go to a computer, log in, transmit an order, and have it executed without anything having to be touched by human hands. That to me was a very compelling strategy. To this day, I don't think there's a better use of the Internet than the brokerage business. It's a perfect match.

BLAKE DARCY (former chief executive officer of DLJDirect and CSFBDirect):

The discount-brokerage industry in the 1980s basically was Schwab, Quick and Reilly, and Fidelity, with Waterhouse in there to a lesser degree.

There were some smaller, mom-and-pop shops around as well. At the time it was very clear how discount firms were different from the full-service firms like Merrill Lynch. Discounting meant cheap transactions, placing a trade for a stock through an 800 number or branch office at a greatly reduced rate. And the full-service firm did all the research for you and told you what you should do with your money.

FRANK PETRILLI:

When I joined this firm in 1995, the discount-brokerage business had just 15 percent market share of all trades. And even that was misleading because we were charging a discounted commission, so in terms of revenues we actually were well below 10 percent of the brokerage industry's commission base. Discount brokerage was very small and really not much of a factor. Schwab was investing in technology and so was Fidelity, but that was about it. The full-commission guys weren't afraid of us at all. They were misguided. They did not understand what we understood, that the mass affluent population was going to be the fastest-growing segment of wealth, and their business models were flawed — seriously flawed — for dealing with it. It wasn't until the mass explosion of online trading that they realized they'd better do something to protect their flanks. And you know what? By then it was too late.

RODGER RINEY:

I think the 1980s bull market helped the discount-brokerage business tremendously because people started to get interested in the market and see their investments grow, and then they wanted to take control of their finances. Once people felt confident making decisions on their own the math was undeniable. It became, if I'm going to buy 1,000 IBM from my Merrill Lynch guy it's going to cost me $900 or more, but if I buy it from Charles Schwab or Scottrade (though we were then called Scottsdale Securities) I'm going to pay $50 to $150. The savings were mind-boggling, and it convinced many people who had the appropriate level of sophistication to make the switch. But it wasn't really until the online technology came along that the business really exploded.

BLAKE DARCY:

There had been attempts at doing online trading, but it really hadn't worked. We [DLJ Direct] had an exclusive on Prodigy [a private online service] before the Internet even came along, and I think that was simply because every other online effort had been such a money loser for everyone else that nobody wanted to take a chance. But what we saw was that while it would take a while to grow, this was clearly a superior way for investors to gather information, make the transaction, and monitor their investments over time. All of it's always at their fingertips. On top of that, from a brokerage-firm standpoint, all of that was less expensive to process from a back-office point of view, so you could lower the price, which brought in more customers. It ended up being a wonderful virtuous circle. But frankly we had to be patient, because when we launched with Prodigy they had a total of thirty thousand people. It wasn't a very big pool. Then we joined with America Online's service, which was growing at an extremely rapid pace, and it just picked up from there. So by the time the Internet came along and people started figuring that out we already knew what we were doing online.

RODGER RINEY:

We bought a computer that we put under a conference-room table. And we had one guy who kind of babysat it. We bought some software. And all of a sudden we were in the online trading business. It just blossomed very quickly from there. Once word got out about the $9 commissions, we couldn't hire enough people or buy enough computers to keep up with the demand and the changes in technology. It was like a freight train.

CHARLES SCHWAB (founder of Charles Schwab and Company):

Here's a way of looking at it: 80 percent of our new-business customers come to us through a local branch office — that's how they come in with their check. And yet, 80 or 85 percent of our transactions take place over the Internet. It's the ultimate clicks-and-mortar strategy.

FRANK PETRILLI:

A customer of mine who traded five to seven times a year went to thirty times a year as soon as he went to the Internet — the very same customer. And that's not all. All of a sudden his account balance went up two or three times because instead of that small chunk of money that he used to play with at our firm, he emptied his full-commission account and put the whole thing with us. Because it was so easy, and effective, and low cost, people felt comfortable migrating to a discount brokerage firm and, eventually, trading more.

BLAKE DARCY:

By the mid- to late nineties, with the onset of online trading, where anyone with a computer had access, discount brokerage became something that was available twenty-four hours a day, seven days a week. You get all the research, analysis, news, and information at your fingertips. You have a full range of products — stocks, bonds, mutual funds — at your disposal. And you can trade with a click. Suddenly, the difference between a discount brokerage and full service didn't seem all that great. The playing field had been leveled for everyone.

CHAPTER 24

DIGITAL BABYLON

There are many different ways to look at the development of the Internet and its impact on society. From Wall Street's perspective, the story of the Internet bubble of the 1990s starts with the initial public offering of Netscape Communications, a company in Silicon Valley, California, that was founded in 1994 and developed a popular Web browser. By 1995, Netscape still had no profits, but it had strong revenues and demand for its service clearly was growing. The company planned to sell five million shares to the public to raise capital, and originally its underwriters set a target price of $12 to $14. But as more people clamored to get in on the offering, they ratcheted up the price to $28. That put the company's market value at $1.4 billion, an astronomical figure for something that wasn't even making money.

On August 9, 1995, shares of Netscape hit the public market, and all hell broke loose. At first, the stock was halted for ninety minutes while traders tried to sort through the imbalance in the supply of Netscape stock and the demand for the shares. When Netscape finally opened for trading, its price was astounding — $71. The stock had more than doubled before it even began to trade. By *the end of the day, it had cooled off somewhat and was down to 58¼, still a very fancy price for such a highly speculative company. The revolution was under way.*

MICHAEL LEWIS (journalist and author of *The New New Thing*):

The Netscape IPO is where the financial Internet begins. It wasn't the first Silicon Valley IPO, but it was the one that really went nuts. Netscape is what introduced the Internet to investors. It also is what captured the attention of the Silicon Valley engineer. When the Netscape IPO happened in 1995, a lot of smart people said, "Whatever we do next is going to be Internet related because the market has this incredible appetite for it." The market at that point began to believe the story that the Internet was going to change the world — and that these Internet companies were going to be very valuable. It turned out that part of that was true. The Internet is going to change the world. The problem is, that doesn't necessarily mean these companies are going to be very valuable.

LISE BUYER (Google director of business optimization and former senior equity analyst in Frank Quattrone's technology group at Deutsche Morgan Grenfell and Credit Suisse First Boston):

Netscape changed the way people thought about technology stocks because it blasted through the roof and kept on going for quite some time. I think everybody knew that technology stocks were high risk, high reward, but somehow when you really see that reward, you kind of forget about the risk. The thing about Netscape was that the people who were paying attention to the technology were talking about this life-changing breakthrough. It was on the covers of newspapers and magazines. It was the PC era all over again, only much bigger.

WILLIAM HAMBRECHT (cofounder of Hambrecht and Quist):

What the Netscape offering did was attract a lot of capital. It allowed a lot of companies to get very high valuations, which also attracted the very large investment banks. We operated out here for a long time without the big banks. It was Robertson Stephens, and Montgomery Securities, and

Alex. Brown, and us. These were small investment banks that were able to grow and develop with the industry. Goldman and Morgan came in a little, primarily at the high end on the big ones. But suddenly, when $20 million deals turned into $200 million deals, they all came charging in. CSFB in particular, with [technology investment banker Frank] Quattrone, came in and scooped it up. It became a very attractive business for the big firms because the deals were so big.

LISE BUYER:

To be fair, Netscape went through the roof, but that was in August of 1995. Then Yahoo, Lycos, and Excite came in 1996, and they languished. In fact, Yahoo traded beneath its IPO price for months. Nobody wanted to own it. But what happened was a lot of people started using AOL, which had gone public years earlier, and it became an early way for people to communicate with each other over the Internet. The whole e-mail thing started catching on.

At the same time, folks like E-Trade and Ameritrade and Schwab were running online brokerage businesses, and they were putting all sorts of financial information online for the first time. So not only were people reading about the Netscapes of the world in the newspaper, they also were able to get a whole bunch of information about their own finances that they'd never had before. People had been terrified to do banking online in the early nineties, but now this seemed like a good idea.

These changes meant two things: one, people had more information about investing; and two, they had an easy way to trade stocks through these new online brokerages. What happened was, within two years of Netscape going public we saw a demographic shift in the kinds of people who were investing on Wall Street, as more people signed up for these online trading accounts. Suddenly, you could trade from your desk, and it was kind of fun.

JENNIFER WILLIAMS (New York Stock Exchange floor broker for Griswold Company):

I just remember the late 1990s as being ridiculously busy on the floor.

Any announcement about an interest-rate change caused an explosion. There was volume like nobody had ever seen before.

PETER LOW (member of the New York Stock Exchange since 1963 and former floor broker):

Something else we saw during the nineties was that the Fed chairman, Alan Greenspan, became a public hero in a way that I don't remember ever happening before. Ordinary people were listening to every word the man said because they wanted to know which direction interest rates were headed.

JOHN KENNETH GALBRAITH (Harvard University economist and author):

The Federal Reserve attracts attention because the rate of interest does have some importance with regard to borrowing. But mostly it attracts attention because it is within the simple range of public understanding. Everybody, without care and without thought, focuses on the lending rate of the Federal Reserve because it doesn't require knowledge of all the complexities affecting economic behavior. Therefore it's a simplification of economics, which is a very attractive escape from a very difficult subject. And this is a game where there can be master players, none more skilled than Alan Greenspan. He is extremely good at drawing attention to the Federal Reserve's lending rates. This is one of the brilliant theatrical exercises of all time.

PETER FISHER (former head of the Federal Reserve Bank of New York's markets group and former undersecretary of the treasury for domestic finance):

In the midnineties something very different happened in terms of our success in squeezing inflation out of the system. The soft landing for the economy that the Fed engineered in 1994 to '95 was really the only time in Federal Reserve history that that was accomplished. Interest rates rose from low recessionary levels without inflation accelerating and without throwing the economy into a recession — indeed, stabilizing the economy at high real rates of growth. Never done before, but the Fed pulled it off notwithstanding a lot of volatility in the market at the time. I think that historic event was really what laid the basis for the fascination over what Greenspan's going to say. It worked, and it really came from substance, not mechanics.

KEN GUENTHER (former chief executive officer of Independent Community Bankers of America and former assistant to the Federal Reserve Board under chairman Paul Volcker):

In 1996 Greenspan gave his famous Irrational Exuberance speech about the investment patterns in the Internet, and the phrase "irrational exuberance" is now an integral part of the vocabulary. But people don't seem to remember that he failed. He was trying to jawbone the market and it didn't work. The irrational exuberance went on for several more years before it went into its decline.

ROBERT E. RUBIN (former treasury secretary):

I'm not sure Alan was even intending to express a view about stock prices. But markets thought the "irrational exuberance" phrase was deliberate and the Dow declined the next day, from 6,437 to 6,382. Then the bull market resumed its run — for another 5,000 points. The only lasting effect of Alan's comment was to win him a probable future entry in Bartlett's Famous Quotations.

JERRY KENNEY (Merrill Lynch executive vice president of research and corporate strategy):

I've been on Wall Street for thirty-five years now, and in every cycle there's some level of euphoria. But there was nothing of the magnitude of the Internet. People got euphoric over copy machines, personal computers, and other forms of technology. When radio was becoming popular, RCA was the hot stock. It went public in the 1920s, and never hit that price again.

ROY SMITH (finance professor at New York University and former partner at Goldman Sachs):

Technology has always been able to capture people's fascination. The big boom in the twenties, which began in 1925 and ran to 1929, was a five-year period when people were focusing on radio, refrigeration, and electric power. Those are powerful economic signaling devices and all of a sudden people wanted to get in on them. The nineties was probably the period when people started to realize they were in the computer age. It was growing at a very rapid pace and you had all this fascination with Intel and Dell and companies like that. In that latter half of the decade it sort of morphed into a fascination with the Internet, which was driving everybody into excessive glee because it was doubling every twenty seconds, or something like that.

BLAKE DARCY (former chief executive officer of DLJDirect and CSFBDirect):

In America we're always looking for the next big idea. Now it's the next Microsoft that everyone wants to find, but there have been other companies in the past. The whole idea of the Internet was fascinating on a lot of levels. You could buy things online. You could do research online. You could talk to your family and friends online. The possibilities really stirred the imagination, particularly of the media, in a way that fueled this idea that here was the next big thing. You had all this talk about the new economy and so on. I used to go to all these online conferences in the nineties and it was the same group of people. But all of a sudden they were packed. Everyone thought online was such a great idea, that everything was going to happen immediately and the possibilities were limitless.

JERRY KENNEY:

So in every cycle there are these hot areas that have gone to overvaluation. But nothing was this massive and this destructive. This affected all industries and all companies. It undervalued companies that were not involved in the Internet and grossly overvalued those that were. It got to the point where telecom and tech were 45 percent of the U.S. market, and just about the same percentage of the foreign market. There'd been nothing of that scope.

RODGER RINEY (founder and chief executive officer of Scottrade):

The development of the Internet itself produced an almost insatiable appetite for hardware and software. It was pulling us along, and I'm sure many other industries felt the same way. We just couldn't buy stuff fast enough to keep up with the technology. We couldn't hire people fast enough to man these machines. It didn't matter what the price was, it didn't matter what you had to pay people. You had to do what you had to do to keep up with the band. At one point it looked as if this was going to take over commerce as we knew it. Department stores were scared, malls were terrified, and stores of all varieties didn't know what to do because it was so much cheaper to do things on the Internet that it looked as if everything was going to move online. As the logic of that started to take hold, and people convinced themselves that this would last forever, things just got bid up out of sight.

KENNETH PASTERNAK (founder and former chief executive officer of Knight/Trimark):

The epiphany in the nineties was that the Internet changed all the rules — that individual investors would rise from 10 percent of the market to 50 percent, many trading via computers.

LISE BUYER:

The professional investors sat back in '96 and '97 and said, "Okay, I see this frenzy going on, but there's nothing fundamental over here." The problem was, the stocks kept going. They kept going into '96, they kept going into '97. By 1997, this was a front-page story. You were reading stuff about it all the time. And the mutual fund companies and big institutional investors were getting pressure from their investors, who were saying, "I'm paying you to manage my money and you don't own this stuff? What's the matter with you?"

ROBERT POZEN (chairman of MFS Investment Management, former president of Fidelity Management and Research, and author of *The Mutual Fund Business*):

The mutual fund industry had roughly $1 trillion in total assets in 1990, and by 2000 it was roughly $7 trillion. There were a number of factors that drove this. The first is that the stock market over that period had great returns. Then you had the rise of the 401(k) plan and the rebirth of the IRA, which surely was important because they were tax-advantaged savings plans and mutual funds were such natural investments for them. I think in particular that 401(k) plans introduced people to the idea of mutual funds, and then they became comfortable investing in them on their own. And finally, the mutual fund industry was offering a broad array of products at a variety of pricing strategies, which attracts customers. You had about two thousand funds in 1990, and about eight thousand by the time you got to 2000. And those funds varied from low-cost, no-load index funds to highly specialized Japanese small-stock funds.

JACK BOGLE (founder of Vanguard Group, president of Bogle Markets Research Center, and former chairman of Wellington Management):

Never confuse genius with a bull market. The Investment Company Institute people say, "We must be doing something right. We're a $7 trillion industry." The mutual fund industry probably would be under $1 trillion without the great bull market. We ride the coattails of stock prices. The mutual fund industry is the most stock-market-sensitive industry ever created. You see it in the cash flows, booming at market highs and petering out at market lows. So it was the bull market that really created the mutual fund industry as it exists today.

ROY SMITH:

Remember, we had five years of the market growing at over 25 percent [a year]. That means you are committed to a momentum-investing kind of mode because you don't want to miss this. If you'd just invested in nontechnology stocks you'd be growing at 8 percent a year while the indices were growing at 25 percent and everybody would dump your fund. So that's what was happening. You were compelled to be in on all this. I think people realized that research was less helpful than the latest tip. Mutual funds built up such a strong interest in gathering assets and stoking what was there that they weren't too worried about which investments were going to go wrong. All they had to do was stay even with the indices.

SHERRON WATKINS (former vice president and accountant at Enron):

To me, the biggest problem in the 1990s was the mutual funds, pushing and pushing for a higher stock price, all very short-term. When I think about Enron's investor-relations department, they were consistently meeting with the large mutual funds, trying to sell them on buying Enron.

BLAKE DARCY:

I'd say it was a bit of a shock to me that, when we were going on our tour for the DLJDirect IPO, there was limousine after limousine lined up at the mutual fund companies and money managers because everyone was doing a road show trying to cash in on this phenomenon. But then you'd walk into the meeting and it seemed clear that the people who were talking to you had never even read the prospectus. It was quite disheartening.

Of course, I could sort of understand what was happening because they didn't care. They knew our stock was going to go up, and up big. So the question in their minds was only, how many shares can I get? I think in many instances they were afraid to ask too many tough questions because we might not give them as many shares as they wanted. It was kind of an unreal environment. You could tell that people were in it for anything that they could get. And sure enough we had the second-largest Internet IPO of its time, which is pretty hard to do.

JACK BOGLE:

The other thing that happened to mutual funds is they went from being a management business to a marketing business, a business of stewardship that turned into a business of salesmanship. The idea isn't to sell what you make; it's to make what you sell. The idea is to gather assets, to market better, not to manage better. So funds appeal to the baser instincts of the investing public. If telecommunications is hot, let's do a telecommunications fund. If technology is good, do a technology fund. These things come and go. They're born to die. Unfortunately, they take a lot of innocent people's money with them.

So we brought out Internet funds, we brought out telecommunications funds, we brought out technology funds, all at the high of the market, without any thought of whether any of this would be good for investors. They were good for the managers because they enabled you to gather a lot of assets, and if you gather a lot of assets you gather a lot of fees. We did $500 billion of aggressive growth in the two years up to the boom. We're talking really big money. But bringing out funds only a moron would buy is not illegal.

ROBERT POZEN:

Mutual fund managers, most notably Janus, rode that curve and gathered a lot of assets, and then rode it down. I was under a lot of pressure when I was the president of the management company at Fidelity to start an Internet fund, a dot-com fund. But I felt very strongly, and Ned [Johnson, Fidelity chairman] agreed with me, that this was not an investment category. It was a technology that could be used across industries, but not an industry unto itself. I think in retrospect that our decision not to start an Internet fund was a wise one. Companies that launched Internet funds, especially the ones that came out late in the game, really did their investors a disservice.

LISE BUYER:

Normally, all this would just bubble up and subside, but it went on for way too long. The only way to stay out of the market by 1998 was to be supremely arrogant and assume that you knew more than everybody else out there. Generally, these little moments of hype last, and then implode. But this one didn't implode — two and a half, three years later it was still going. At some point you have to say, "Is the whole world wrong, or am I?"

LARRY SONSINI (chairman and chief executive officer of the law firm Wilson Sonsini Goodrich and Rosati and one of the leading legal advisers in Silicon Valley):

In the late nineties you had a tremendous amount of venture capital being focused on the Internet. Billions of dollars in venture capital in a rather short period of time was being invested in everything and anything related to the Internet. We weren't sure what the Internet really was. Many people thought of it as a business model. Other people thought of it as a tool to a business model. In essence that's what it is. But during those days, in the nineties when the boom came, anything that had the word "Internet" in it was getting financed. And many of those entities that were being financed really didn't have sound business plans. They were being valued on the number of clicks on a Web site as opposed to sound fundamental business. But that was part of the euphoria.

Many, many of these companies don't make it. If you hit it, you hit a home run. And it all comes down to risk-reward. Yeah, you're taking a risk, but the reward can be massive. When you look at the goals for a technology venture-capital fund — you have ten deals; two of them hopefully will be home runs, two to four of them will be okay and maybe you'll get some money back, and at least four will go belly-up. You assume two wins, four losses, and the rest are up in the air.

MICHAEL BARONE (head of Nasdaq trading at William Blair and Company in Chicago):

The year that I first remember noticing that Nasdaq was really heating up was 1996. That was the largest IPO year Blair had ever had, just a huge year for IPOs. That was the year that I first remember seeing those really dramatic first-day price jumps in technology IPOs with some regularity. You started to see more and more professional traders getting involved. The tide was starting to rise, and if you didn't jump on real quick you were going to get washed away.

ALFRED R. BERKELEY III (former president and vice chairman of Nasdaq):

Nasdaq was the stage on which the hopes and aspirations of all these speculators were played out. We had a classic speculative bubble and judgment was suspended. You have to understand the game theory of the markets. There are always three games going on in the market at any one time: a game of chance, a game of skill, and a game of strategy. Games of chance are gambling; games of skill are speculating; and games of strategy are investing. The best way to understand this is to look at the definitions. Investors, like Warren Buffett, want to find the underlying value of a company. The time horizon is the same time horizon it takes to work out the company's strategic plan, usually years and decades. The speculator doesn't care about the underlying value of the company. He cares about the underlying demand of buyers and sellers in the stock. He's looking at the beauty-contest aspect — will people like the stock and bid it up or not. It's judging human nature. And the gambler is just a more speculative speculator, making a bet because he's got a hunch that he knows what's going on.

So when you look at what happened in the 1990s, there wasn't much investing going on, but there were a lot of people speculating and a lot of people outright gambling. And that's a perfect recipe for a bubble to develop.

CHAPTER 25

A RISKLESS TRANSACTION

The advent of computer technology on Wall Street in the 1990s primarily meant two things for traders: higher levels of profitability and greater levels of volatility, or risk. Computers enabled the securities industry to create all kinds of new products and trading strategies that had the net effect of dramatically increasing the amount of money flowing around the Street. For many people in the financial community, these revelations were a godsend, as complex, high-tech trading operations started raking in cash like never before. But at the same time, these complicated new products and strategies also were causing securities firms and investment partnerships called hedge funds to operate at levels of risk that hadn't been imagined before. In time, they would nearly trigger a financial calamity similar to the one we experienced in 1987.

At the center of the controversy were financial instruments called derivatives. Derivatives are so named because their values actually "derive" from other financial instruments. Take, for example, stock options. Options give the holder the right to buy or sell a certain stock for a certain price at a certain time in the future. So, say IBM is trading for $100, and for $1 you can buy an option *that gives you the right to buy IBM for $105 one year from today. If at that time IBM is selling for more than $106, you made money because you can pay $106 — the $1 cost of the option plus the agreed-upon price of $105 — for something worth more than that. But, if IBM is trading for less than $106, the contract is useless, and you're out the cost of the option, $1. So, the option is a contract that enables you to make money from your belief that IBM is on the way up without actually paying for the stock. The contract itself is just an agreement. It actually "derives" its value from IBM, the underlying stock.*

While they clearly are inherently risky instruments, derivatives themselves have very legitimate uses in helping companies manage their finances. The key difficulty in trading them, however, is figuring out how much they should cost. What's the proper price for the level of risk you're taking in that options contract? Using complex mathematical formulas, Nobel Prize–winning economists developed models that would calculate the price of a derivative. One such example is the Black-Scholes options pricing model, which was created in the 1970s, and for which Fischer Black, Myron Scholes, and Robert Merton won the Nobel Memorial Prize in Economic Sciences in 1998. These mathematical formulas helped savvy traders spot pricing anomalies where the financial markets had set the cost of risk in a certain security either too high or too low. As Wall Street soon found out, exploiting that difference, known as a spread, through arbitrage trading can be a highly profitable — and risky — business.

TOM STRAUSS (former Salomon Brothers president):

Salomon had a close-knit culture that really revolved around bond trading. That's what the firm was known for, and it's what we were particularly good at.

MICHAEL LEWIS (former Salomon Brothers bond salesman for John Meriwether's risk-arbitrage department and author of *Liar's Poker*):

What happened at Salomon Brothers in the 1980s was related to the bull market and a revolution in the financial markets. The computer was making the financial markets much more complicated. All sorts of new asset classes were being created, interest-rate options and futures, interest-rate swaps, mortgage bonds — complicated securities, more complicated than ever before. Pricing them accurately required a bit of sophistication. So what you had on the Salomon Brothers trading floor was the collision of two very different kinds of people. One guy was the old-fashioned trader, who had a high-school education, and the nerve to take risk, and a feel for the markets, kind of savvy. The other guy was a newfangled kind of trader, with a fancy education and an aptitude with a computer. And the flash point for this conflict at Salomon was John Meriwether's risk-arbitrage department.

TOM STRAUSS:

John's a very good trader, good risktaker, has good instincts for people, and is very much to himself. He's not the kind of guy who's going to stand up and do a lot of shouting.

MICHAEL LEWIS:

Meriwether figured out that there were huge sums of money to be made by analytically putting accurate prices on these new securities that were being invented, the options, futures, interest-rate swaps. He saw that a lot of these securities were being mispriced in the marketplace because the old-fashioned kind of traders simply couldn't understand them. So he realized that if he brought in people who could understand these securities and knew what the Black-Scholes options pricing model was, he could make virtually riskless profits. He built a trading department out of these guys, and very quickly they were running the place — very quickly there was a sense that the entire firm was in some way an extension of John Meriwether's trading desk.

ROGER LOWENSTEIN (journalist and author of *When Genius Failed*):

The guy who formed Long-Term Capital Management was John Meriwether, and he left Salomon Brothers after a celebrated scandal in 1991. A trader there had gone bad, and through a failure to sufficiently supervise and in retrospect punish this trader, a number of heads rolled. Meriwether was the top trader, and he was gone. And John Gutfreund, who ran the firm, was gone.

MICHAEL LEWIS:

Paul Mozer, who was charged with putting in bids to the Treasury market for the Treasury-bond auction, was accused, truthfully, of placing false bids so he could in a sense corner the market in a Treasury-bond auction. He was submitting false bids to manipulate the auction — basically, using customer accounts to buy bonds for Salomon so he could control the market. And when Gutfreund found out about it he didn't report it to the Fed, or anyone else.

Something I learned after the fact is that Gutfreund had the opportunity to tell Nick Brady, who was then the treasury secretary, about it in a meeting they had after it happened, and didn't. So Nick Brady felt lied to. There was a very real discussion at treasury over whether to put Salomon out of business. So, Warren Buffett then stepped in — he was the largest shareholder of Salomon Brothers — and became the mollifying agent. He came in and said, "I'll clean house and steer it through this time." Part of the deal was that Gutfreund lost his job and John Meriwether, who oversaw Paul Mozer, lost his job.

So when Meriwether leaves, all his boys are pissed off because they don't understand why he had to take the fall for something that he wasn't really involved with. The boys are all ready to up and leave too, because their loyalty isn't to Salomon — it's to Meriwether. And you can see why, because Meriwether had sheltered and protected them in the early days and made it possible for them to succeed. When Meriwether decides to create Long-Term Capital, they're more than ready to join him.

ROGER LOWENSTEIN:

Meriwether brought along Larry Hilibrand, Eric Rosenfeld, Victor Haghani, all ex-Salomon people. And they became the nucleus of this hedge fund that was going to deploy its bond-trading expertise just as it had at Salomon. They also brought in two celebrated financial scholars and future Nobel Prize winners, Myron Scholes and Robert Merton, who had in fact devised the formula for pricing a stock option. Then, just for good measure, they also brought in the former vice chairman of the Federal Reserve, David Mullins. It was quite an extraordinary bunch.

DANIEL TULLY (former Merrill Lynch chairman):

I'd never met John Meriwether until one day after he left Salomon he called and said he wanted to see me. I'd read about him, so I knew who he was, but we'd never been introduced. Quite honestly, I thought he was looking for a job. I remember we just sat and talked. He was a very likable person. I didn't want to do a formal interview or anything, so I just told him we could talk like friends about what he wanted to do with the rest of his life. Then he told me that he had this idea for a fund, and I said it sounded interesting. The way we left it was, if he was interested in getting back into the business we'd be interested in hiring him, and if he wanted to do a fund we'd be interested in participating. I also introduced him to [former Merrill Lynch chairman David] Komansky, who was running fixed-income at the time. When he eventually decided to raise the fund, we helped him do it.

ROGER LOWENSTEIN:

There are always people who want to feel that they're smarter and investing with the experts. And this was particularly true in the 1990s because as the market grew, more people became concerned that it was due for a fall. So they wanted to invest in a way that would protect them from that, but would still count them in on whatever good times still were to be had. Hedge funds, because of their ability to go long and short, and because of their systems, seemed like a way to do it — to have your cake and eat it, too.

ARTHUR CASHIN (director of New York Stock Exchange floor operations for UBS Financial Services):

The first hedge fund was started by a man named Alfred Jones back in 1952. Jones wanted not just to buy stocks he liked, but to be able to short [bet against] the ones he didn't like. Jones had another, more controversial idea. He thought his expertise was so valuable that clients should pay him a piece of profits that he made for them. Because of federal laws, that meant he couldn't start a regular fund, so he started a private partnership that could not advertise or openly solicit people. But he may have been as good as he thought, because within a decade, magazines were writing that his performance had outstripped regular mutual funds. Pretty soon, folks were clamoring to become clients, others clamored to be imitators. Hedge funds began to spring up everywhere. Some, like George Soros's Quantum Fund and Julian Robertson's Tiger Fund, were so profitable that they became legendary. And hedge funds didn't just trade stocks. They started to trade bond futures, currencies, commodities, even customized derivatives.

JAMES CRAMER (CNBC talk-show host, journalist, and former hedge-fund manager):

The word "hedge" came from the idea that these funds would be long in one position and short in another. You would have a paired trade, like Long-Term Capital. Ford's worth X and GM's worth Y — if you go long one and short the other you will eventually capture the disparity. In practice, none of these funds work this way. They're just a way to participate in the long side and the short side with the client, as opposed to getting just a percentage of the assets. That's the only definition of a hedge fund you need.

BILL SEIDMAN (former chairman of the Federal Deposit Insurance Corporation):

Most investment funds are heavily regulated and not really set up to do hedging or selling short or whatever. But the hedge funds were the swingers; they could do whatever they wanted because they had no capital standards or anything like that, and they could still keep it really quiet because they had no disclosure rules. Once people saw how much some of these guys — like George Soros and Julian Robertson — were making, they started to take notice. Pretty soon everybody wanted to invest in a hedge fund.

ROGER LOWENSTEIN:

The partners of Long-Term Capital knew there was going to be a huge demand for their fund because of their unbelievable reputations. So they got themselves an even better deal than most hedge funds had at the time. They charged a 2 percent management fee instead of 1 percent, and then 25 percent of the profits also went to them. And you had to keep your money in for three years, while most other funds were a lot more flexible about allowing investors to withdraw their capital. But it's funny how people respond to something like this. Nobody wants to buy an $18,000 Mercedes; they want to buy a $60,000 Mercedes. If you charge a lot of money, people have this reaction that it must be a really good thing. The idea of investing with titans and geniuses, Nobel Prize–level scholars, just dazzled people.

DAVID KOMANSKY (former Merrill Lynch chairman):

You have to realize that this was a brilliant group of people. John Meriwether, Myron Scholes, Robert Merton, Eric Rosenfeld, and all the other people who were involved were an amazing collection of geniuses, Nobel Prize winners with unimpeachable reputations. These were truly recognized experts in their field. At the time we started doing business with them I was running fixed-income. One of our guys brought Meriwether and Scholes to see me. They wanted us to raise the fund for them, which we did. They also wanted us to be what they called a "strategic investor." They had about a dozen "strategic investors" who put in $100 million apiece. We didn't do that. But we reinvested the fees we earned from raising their money back into the fund. I think it was $15 million or something like that.

WILLIAM MCDONOUGH (former Federal Reserve Bank of New York president):

The strategy of Long-Term Capital was to use complex mathematical formulas to identify temporary price discrepancies between different interest rates. For example, the firm might notice that the yield on corporate bonds relative to Treasury yields was higher than the range observed in recent years. If Long-Term Capital believed the former relationship would reassert itself, it would buy corporate bonds and sell short Treasury bonds. If the spread narrowed as expected, the firm would profit. If, however, the spread continued to widen, the firm would incur losses. This basic strategy, and many complex variations, was followed across many interest-rate products in the United States and many overseas markets as well.

ROGER LOWENSTEIN:

In real general terms, bonds trade at an interest rate and they sell for a price. The way it works is, the higher the price, the lower the interest rate, and vice versa. Bond traders relate the interest rates of one bond to another — so if General Electric yields a certain interest rate, Amazon presumably will yield a little more because it's a less reliable, less profitable company. In governments the same is true — Belgium yields X, and Nigeria, which is not a First-World economy, yields more than X.

Now, since bonds are all related to each other, experience has bred into the bond market a general sense of wisdom about what the difference, or what we call the spread, should be between one bond and another. So if you discover that Mexico yields one percentage point more than U.S. Treasuries, that's okay. But if you discover that Mexico is 14 percentage points more than the U.S., then you'd say that's not right. That spread is way too much, it's not properly accounting for the reality that this is Mexico, not Afghanistan. What Long-Term Capital did was come along and look for places where this spread was too high or too low. This is obviously in very general and simplified terms, because most of their trades involved four, eight, and sometimes even sixteen different interest rates.

WILLIAM MCDONOUGH:

Anticipating that some positions would move in their favor and some would move against them, the firm relied on diversification across a large number of product and geographical markets. Long-Term Capital proved quite successful at this strategy, generating returns in excess of 40 percent in 1995 and 1996, though somewhat less in 1997.

Perhaps their success went to their heads. Long-Term Capital took on larger and larger positions. They also leveraged their investments at higher levels, returning capital to their investors but not, apparently, reducing risks.

BILL SEIDMAN:

These aberrations usually weren't large, so what they were really doing was making many very small bets over and over again. And in order to make this strategy really profitable they had to borrow a lot of money, which they did. The problem with this was, if things didn't revert to normal as they'd expected, they were going to get creamed.

ROGER LOWENSTEIN:

If you did these trades once you'd make a little sliver, pennies on the dollar. It wasn't a lot because these spreads weren't usually off by a whole lot, and there were a lot of people out there doing what they were doing. But you could make a sliver, what Myron Scholes called "plucking nickels out of the air." With leverage, borrowing, you could own many more trades and invest in many more of these paired bets, because you not only had your capital, but had all this capital from other people. So if you could make that bet twice, or four times, or sixteen times, you'd suddenly have much, much more on the table. Instead of a nickel, you were making fifty cents or a dollar. That was the game.

The importance of leverage to Long-Term Capital was like the importance of syrup to Coca-Cola. It was the firm.

JAMES CRAMER:

Some guy would e-mail me and say, "I'm up 300 percent, and you're only up 30 percent." Well, he probably is fully leveraged, which means he's taking a lot more risk. You can say, so what, but my lesson is that in '87, the guys who were that levered couldn't stop it. So I'm willing to accept the fact that I won't make it the way he did, but I'm willing to give up some of my upside to protect my downside. That's as analytical as I'll get. I think that you can empirically prove that if you borrow a lot of money, you can juice your returns.

So what struck me was that Long-Term Capital really wasn't all that good at what it did. Despite all that leverage, their numbers were just okay. I was able to get their numbers without their leverage. So with a massive amount of risk they were only doing okay numbers.

Leverage allows you to magnify your returns greatly. It's fabulous if you get it right. If I had a fantastic call that semiconductors are going up I would conceivably borrow some money for a couple of days to juice the returns on that bet. That's a situation where I think I have such a good call that I want to put as much money on the table as I can. But these are people who are walking around and doing it all the time with every position. That's how they're making their money. These same people, if you put them in a casino in Atlantic City and said, "Here's $10,000, you have to bet all this money on every single hand," they'd say, "That's crazy. I'm not going to put all my money out there." Then how about this? "Here's $10,000 and a line of credit for $100,000. Put it all out there every time." They'd say, "That's crazy. I could lose everything." I know these people would have that level of sense at Trump's or Bally's Park Place, but they don't have that sense in the stock market.

PETER FISHER (former head of the Federal Reserve Bank of New York's markets group and former undersecretary of the treasury for domestic finance):

Looking at the economic conditions at the time, it's easy to see why there was an underappreciation of the importance of credit risk in the late nineties. You had equities going up and up and up, but a pretty firm monetary policy from the Fed and a flat yield curve. But over the course of 1998 we ended up losing a lot of liquidity in the credit markets. That didn't just switch on a dime on Labor Day. The monetary authorities of the United States and Japan had intervened in the exchange market the prior spring when the dollar-yen ratio was going up through 140 to 150. That was a very technically successful intervention, but it ended up inflicting a lot of losses on Japanese investors and hedge funds and other levered investors. Also over that summer, some firms withdrew from fixed-income arbitrage. They were nervous about the risks and pulled back, decreasing liquidity. And then the Russian default occurred. Suddenly, investment vehicles like hedge funds, whose premise had been that they could always turn a position in the market, found that they couldn't do it. And it was in that environment that LTCM found itself in the position of mounting losses and no way to get out of its positions.

WILLIAM MCDONOUGH:

While hubris may have set them up for a fall, it was the extraordinary events of August [1998] in the global markets that appear to have tripped them. On August 17, the Russian government announced an effective devaluation of the ruble and declared a debt moratorium, shocking investor confidence all over the world. Over subsequent days and weeks, equity and debt markets the world over became increasingly volatile, with U.S. equity markets falling and the spreads between U.S. Treasury securities and higher-yielding debt instruments widening sharply.

ROGER LOWENSTEIN:

Finance is very much a creature of trends and fashions, and in the mid- to late nineties there was a fashion for emerging markets, emerging being a publicists' term for not yet emerged. Russia was the darling of this fashion. Consultants were visiting insurance firms and other institutions telling them that they had to be in Russia. There was this idea that in only a matter of years Russia was going to look like a slightly less developed part of Switzerland, or something. It's pretty astonishing. A lot of the world was invested in Russia. Goldman was out floating Russian paper, and it was quickly unloaded.

JULIAN ROBERTSON (former head of Tiger Management, at one time the largest hedge fund in the world):

A lot of people were playing that bet — we had a Russia bet on. Russia was doing well, and most people thought that it wasn't in the interests of anybody in the world for the ruble to fall. Many of us were waiting for something that would intervene. It was a big shock when it hit.

TOM BROWN (founder of the hedge fund Second Curve Capital and former head of the financial-institutions group at Tiger Management):

The Russian bond default didn't just affect Long-Term Capital. Tiger lost $1 billion in a single day in September 1998.

BILL SEIDMAN:

They all figured that Russia would not be allowed to default and that the world would come to their rescue. But it didn't. Suddenly, a lot of people had these huge loans and instead of being ahead they were behind. In fact, they were behind so much that many of them were just about broke.

HERB ALLISON (TIAA-CREF chairman and former president of Merrill Lynch):

The collapse of the ruble and the problems in Russia precipitated a number of bankruptcies of hedge funds and others who were counterparties on hedged trades. You know, if you're going to be "hedged," you need somebody to take the other side of the trade. So when these little firms started going bankrupt, they turned out to have major exposures themselves. And that triggered exposures throughout Wall Street. Suddenly, what you thought was hedged no longer was.

JERRY CORRIGAN (Goldman Sachs managing director and former Federal Reserve Bank of New York president):

I would say that 1998 and 1987 were the two most challenging events in the financial markets over the past thirty, forty years. And in both cases what made them challenging were credit questions. Am I going to get paid? Somebody's supposed to deliver securities to me, somebody's supposed to deliver collateral to me, somebody's supposed to deliver cash to me, am I going to get valuables when I'm supposed to get them? The market is based on this kind of informed trust.

ROGER LOWENSTEIN:

When Russia went bust it shocked everybody. You know [former Citicorp chairman] Walter Wriston's old thinking, "Countries don't go bankrupt." Well, it turns out they do go bankrupt. The problem here wasn't only Russia, which was sort of the hydrogen bomb of emerging markets, and on its own would've meant a lot. But it also suggested that some of these other countries out there are probably pretty lousy, too. In fact, Brazil went in the tank shortly after. And then there was a reaction where people didn't want to have anything to do with risk. I don't want Russia. I don't want Brazil. I want the safest thing you've got.

JOHN CALAMOS (chairman and chief executive officer of Calamos Investments and an expert in convertible arbitrage):

LTCM's problems really came down to those professors believing that everything in the market could be measured as a statistical event. The statistical measure of the market is a convenience, a way of looking at it. But it isn't reality. It's just a representation of reality. Unfortunately, sometimes things that aren't supposed to happen do, and suddenly those statistical measures are wrong. If you're making a lot of money betting that markets will behave normally, you have to remember that markets don't always stick to what our definition of normal is.

MYRON SCHOLES (Nobel Prize–winning economist and former Long-Term Capital Management partner):

In August of 1998, after the Russian default, you know, all the [statistical] relations that tended to exist in the past seemed to disappear.

PETER FISHER:

The shocker here was that all the markets in which they operated started to correlate. And what was getting them correlated was a lack of liquidity. Once people start losing money in one market it reduces their risk appetite to make prices in another market. You get smaller and smaller market-making capacity spread across all the markets, and suddenly everything is correlated.

ROGER LOWENSTEIN:

In September there was sort of a momentum effect. There were plenty of people out there in Long-Term's straits — including, by the way, Salomon Brothers, which unloaded a Russian position precipitously, and quite astutely. People realized that all the people who owned Russia, all the people who owned the risky stuff, were dumping it. Two things happened. If you owned that stuff and were thinking about dumping it, you dumped it. Who wants to stand in front of a moving freight train? And second, even if you didn't own it, you sold it short because you could make money on the way down. You said, "Hey, these suckers are stuck with it and they're going to have to sell. I'll sell first." So there was a ganging-up effect. There was a lot of evidence that people knew Long-Term was sitting on a lot of this stuff and would have to sell. And Wall Street is not a place brimming with sympathy.

JOHN MERIWETHER (founder of Long-Term Capital Management and former Salomon Brothers vice chairman):

We didn't fully understand that a variety of people had become much more involved in these types of activities, and more important, their behavior in a time of panic. It led to a complete breakdown of the fundamental thesis of how we evaluated risk.

JULIAN ROBERTSON:

LTCM got into trouble because it was so successful for so long that a lot of the investment banks that LTCM had hired would follow them into their positions. In other words, if LTCM did something, they were so successful that their investment bankers did it, too. Then when LTCM got into trouble and tried to unwind these positions, these people saw that and ran for the exits, too. And when everybody tries to get out at once there's a problem. So in a lot of ways they were victims of their own success.

RICHARD R. LINDSEY (former director of market regulation at the Securities and Exchange Commission):

On September 2, 1998, LTCM announced that during the period from January through August 1998 it had lost $2.5 billion, or 52 percent of its $4.8 billion of equity, since the beginning of 1998. Of those losses, 84 percent, or $2.1 billion, occurred in August.

ROGER LOWENSTEIN:

Long-Term, throughout late August and early September 1998, called people for money. They called Warren Buffett. They called George Soros. They called Merrill, Goldman, Morgan — who do you call if you need a couple billion dollars? You don't call you or me. But for various reasons these deals didn't go through. Nobody is eager to invest in a falling stone because each day it was getting cheaper. They were losing hundreds of millions of dollars by the day. There didn't seem to be any chance of catching the bottom because each day there was a new one.

TOM BROWN:

I remember when the senior management of Long-Term Capital, Meriwether and the rest, came to see Julian. They were having some major problems and they needed capital. And this was one of the things that I really respected a lot about Julian. He basically said, "I didn't understand anything that they were doing. So I decided that I couldn't give them any money."

JULIAN ROBERTSON:

It was just too big a thing for us to have done. We were having our own problems at the time and it was outside our realm at that point.

ROGER LOWENSTEIN:

It's important to emphasize that Long-Term had started the year with $4 billion, which seemed like an impregnable amount of capital. By late September it had all but evaporated. Hundreds of millions, day after day, in a portfolio that they had figured would never lose more than $40 million in any one day, certainly not day after day.

ROBERT E. RUBIN (former treasury secretary):

LTCM was faced with massive losses that threatened to become much larger than the remaining capital the firm held. The immediate public-policy question this raised was what kind of harm a forced liquidation of LTCM's assets could do. In normal circumstances, governments shouldn't worry about the tribulations of any particular firm or corporation. But if a situation threatens the financial system, some kind of government action might be the best among bad choices. No one wanted to rescue LTCM's partners or investors. But there was a concern that liquidating such large positions could lead to a general unraveling of the markets. With the hedge fund's creditors — Chase, Citigroup, Goldman Sachs, Bear Stearns, Morgan Stanley, Merrill Lynch, and many others — all selling into the same decline, the entire financial system could freeze up, with a spillover into the real economy.

WILLIAM MCDONOUGH:

A team from the New York Fed, led by Peter Fisher, the head of our markets group, and joined by treasury assistant secretary Gary Gensler, met with the Long-Term Capital partners at their offices on Sunday, September 20. During this meeting, we learned the broad outlines of Long-Term Capital's major positions in credit and equity markets, the difficulties they were having in trying to reduce these positions in thin market conditions, their deteriorating funding positions, and an estimate of their largest counterparty exposures. The team also came to understand the impact that Long-Term Capital's positions were already having on markets around the world and that the size of these positions was much greater than market participants imagined.

PETER FISHER:

The individual creditors had exposures running in the range of several hundred million dollars each. But if you told me it was going to stop there I wouldn't have been worried. What you had to think about was the mechanics of how this was going to unfold. If Long-Term were to default, all of those assets that they were holding on leverage — borrowed money — would revert to the creditors. That's what repo financing is all about. So suddenly they would be stuck owning a lot of stuff that had been sinking in value. It was going to be a race to see who could liquidate first. That sets up the risk of continual selling and bringing other asset values down as well.

DAVID KOMANSKY:

It was on a Sunday afternoon, and I was at home reading a book on the deck, thoroughly enjoying the sun. My wife called out to me and said that Jon Corzine was on the phone. I knew this was serious. While Jon, as chairman of Goldman Sachs, was a good friend, it was highly unlikely that he would be calling to pass the time of day on a Sunday afternoon.

So I picked up the phone, and Jon said, "We've got a little problem.

Our bankers spent the weekend up in Greenwich at Long-Term Capital and it's a real mess. Looks like we're heading to a default."

Now, the next day was Rosh Hashanah, and I had to be in temple. So I told him Herb Allison, who was our president at the time, would get in touch with him. Herb and Jon spoke, and the next day they sent another team up to Greenwich.

PETER FISHER:

Monday morning, September 21, Asian and European markets were selling off dramatically — I think the Dow was down around 180 points at one point. And the talking heads were saying that this was because of the videotape of Bill Clinton's deposition in the Monica Lewinsky affair, which was going to be aired that day. Of course, some of us who understood just a glimmer of LTCM's volatility positions thought maybe it had something to do with people hedging their exposure to the risk that LTCM would not be there anymore. Once I saw the dramatic impact this was having on the equity markets, and that this was not about Bill Clinton, the risk of a downward spiral in stock prices seemed quite real.

HERB ALLISON:

It was imploding rapidly. We sent some people up to take a look at things, and they came back shell-shocked by their exposures. Our information was that Long-Term could go down the next day. They had to be able to repay their funding every day, but they were going to run out of money.

PETER FISHER:

There was a pivotal breakfast at the New York Fed where we had several of the major New York firms [Merrill Lynch, Goldman Sachs, and J. P. Morgan] together discussing what was the right way to fix this problem. One idea was a consortium to recapitalize the firm and try to stabilize it. There were other different ideas about how you could lift the positions out or try to restructure it or buy it.

HERB ALLISON:

J. P. Morgan's idea was that they would identify all the counterparties for Long-Term Capital's debt portfolio and all the counterparties for their equity portfolio. They wanted to work out a way to solve each problem independently. And Goldman's idea was to partner with an outside major investor — who they would not name — and they would buy out Long-Term Capital together.

So I listened to both of those and right away could see that the Morgan idea was impractical. It would take far too long and there was too much negotiating required for it to work. With Goldman, I said, "If you can find a buyer, great. I wish you luck with that." Goldman told us that they were confident they could line up this person within twenty-four hours. It turned out to be Warren Buffett — that's become public. I had a feeling that it was, but it didn't matter. I said, "That's fine, go ahead and try that. But there's got to be a better solution."

To me, the best idea was to take an approach that was deliberately crude. You were never going to find out the real exposures of all those banks. Ideally, what you'd like to do is say, "Bank X, you have a billion of exposure, so you should put up more than this other bank that only has a hundred million of exposure." But they were going to argue to death about what their losses were and what their exposures were, so you had to do something that would cause the same amount of dollar pain to every single institution. We figured there were about sixteen institutions and about $4 billion in losses that had to be covered. So we came up with about $250 million per institution, and they'd have to put it up within twenty-four hours.

PETER FISHER:

While the firms were arguing about that, I think my only substantive addition to the proceedings was to suggest that rather than sitting there arguing about which idea was best, why didn't we put together groups to work on all of them for a day. If they could agree to stand behind one of the ideas, then I would invite people in to have them propose the idea. And it was really through their work during the course of that day that the only idea left standing was the consortium of major creditors to recapitalize and stabilize LTCM.

HERB ALLISON:

The Fed wanted nothing to do with making any proposals or compelling anyone to take part in any program to solve this problem. They wanted to remain totally neutral.

DAVID KOMANSKY:

Our people worked the whole day, an army of bankers up at Long-Term Capital. By that night, it was obvious that the consortium idea was the only one that would work. On Wednesday morning we had to get everybody together to form the consortium, and word had gotten out of what was going on. As I called around to get people to participate, some of the leading lights on Wall Street were reluctant to get involved, and others flat-out refused to come to the meeting [at the offices of the New York Fed]. I did as much as I could to convince people to be there.

HERB ALLISON:

It turned out that Goldman had come up dry. So the only solution left was this very crude consortium. I made the proposal, and we got some comments around the room. It looked as if this wasn't going to fly. That was my take. We took a break, and Dave and I both felt that the chances of this thing working were slim to none. But we got together again and that's when we began that hard negotiating, which went to about midnight.

DAVID KOMANSKY:

Then, during the course of the negotiations, some people tried to back out. I did as much as anybody to hold the thing together.

ROGER LOWENSTEIN:

Bear Stearns was the clearing broker for Long-Term. If you think of the function of a clearing broker, money is washing in and out all the time. They're paying out debts, and collecting on them, but they have to make sure that they have a receivable to cover every billable, otherwise they're stuck. So Long-Term kept a capital account there, a cushion. Well, Bear at a certain point announced that if Long-Term got to a certain threshold they were going to stop the game because they weren't going to be stuck with Long-Term's bills. Nobody was happy about that.

There were fourteen banks at that meeting with the Fed, the key players on Wall Street. And when they went around the room asking who would contribute to the consortium, Bear Stearns said they would not. People were shocked. But Bear Stearns, well, they look out for Bear Stearns. Particularly because Bear was the clearing broker, the other bankers wondered, "Do they know something we don't know?" They called Jimmy [Cayne, Bear Stearns chairman] into a sort of "in camera" private session with several people, including Dave Komansky, who was chairman of Merrill Lynch.

HERB ALLISON:

This deal depended on getting everybody involved because if one or two dropped out then the others would have to pick up the load; and each time someone dropped out you'd have a bigger burden on the others. So we had to try to keep everyone in. There was a lot of rancor about that. People started yelling at Jimmy Cayne.

DAVID KOMANSKY:

Bear Stearns was doing the prime brokerage work and clearing for them. They also had a $500 million deposit from Long-Term. We weren't even their largest counterparty. I felt that the firms involved, all of whom were the leading firms on the Street, were in this thing together. I thought it was a noble cause, a critical thing to do. Now, I know Jimmy quite well, and I was very unhappy with the position he took.

ROGER LOWENSTEIN:

When Cayne came out of the meeting he said, "We're not contributing. But I'll tell you that I'm not doing this because I know any information that you don't. And if you contribute and recapitalize it, we'll continue to clear their trades."

HERB ALLISON:

But it wasn't just Bear. There were big rumors that Lehmen was going down. Lehman was under great pressure, and Dick Fuld said, "Look, I can't put up $250 million." We had a lot of negotiations with them, and they decided that they could put up $150 million. We thanked them very much for that effort because it was key to at least keep them in there.

Then, at various times, Morgan Stanley backed out. But Goldman hung in. Corzine was one of the braver people in those meetings. But Corzine's company was about to go public; they'd already announced that they were doing an IPO. They were staring at what I would estimate to be a loss of $1 billion to $1.5 billion. It killed their IPO. That's why they were so desperate to get Buffett to come in, because it would save their IPO. The partners were furious at Corzine for having gotten them into this situation, they blamed him for this. And I could see that there was a fracturing of the partnership at Goldman that you rarely saw. They were fighting with each other over this situation.

In the meantime, the markets were starting to freeze. There was no liquidity. The bond market throughout the world didn't trade for about eight weeks. You couldn't trade anything. And the stock market was starting to keel over. We were looking at Doomsday. I mean this was doom, potentially worse than 1929. So just by portraying the risk of what we were dealing with, gradually people got the message. Others tried to bow out, and the deal fell apart five or six times, but we kept Long-Term going for about seven days. Eventually they agreed to put in $300 million each.

DAVID KOMANSKY:

From there we reached the basics of the agreement. Then Herb Allison took over and really drove the details of the deal. I think that was Herb's finest hour. My role was to keep everybody on the reservation; Herb's role was to get the agreement done.

HERB ALLISON:

The main way we got there was by threatening these banks with the enormity of the problem that they were going to create, that they were going to be responsible for. They were going to have to explain to the public why they wouldn't put up the money.

ROGER LOWENSTEIN:

The solution was for each of the banks to chip in a few hundred million. A few of them got a discount, but the idea was to recapitalize the fund, to invest more money in Long-Term so that this box at Bear Stearns, where the money was, could be filled up again. Since the value of a Long-Term share was basically nil at that point, all the ownership in the new fund went to the new investors, the banks who recapitalized it. This is the same thing that would happen if a company on the stock exchange went down to $1 [a share] and then new investors came in. They could buy so much stock at that price that the old stock would become worthless.

ALAN GREENSPAN (chairman of the Federal Reserve Board):

On September 23, the private-sector parties arrived at an agreement providing a capital infusion of about $3.5 billion in return for substantially diluting existing shareholders' stake in LTCM. Control of the firm passed from the current management to a committee determined from the outside by the new investors. Those investors intended to shrink LTCM's portfolio so as to reduce risk of loss and return the remaining capital to the investors as soon as practicable.

BILL SEIDMAN:

Essentially, the lenders got together and decided they'd be better off saving the thing than putting it into bankruptcy and liquidating. It was so big it would've disrupted markets everywhere. So the banks stepped in and financed it and kept it alive. It's what old J. P. Morgan used to do back in the old days. I thought it was a pretty good example of how the private sector can step in and solve a problem in a way that mitigates their loss and doesn't cause a disruption.

ROGER LOWENSTEIN:

So the fund was recapitalized. And then, for another couple of weeks, it tanked all over again. Of the $3.65 billion the banks put in, they lost $750 million over the next couple of weeks. Finally, after Greenspan cut rates a couple of times, the markets calmed and the bond market finally stopped seizing up.

JERRY CORRIGAN:

People didn't see the "world is ending" headlines in 1998 because it didn't cause the stock market to crash. But in informed, sophisticated financial circles, there was a very real sense of panic in 1998. We probably weren't very far from the point where we could've had a big blowout in the stock market. There were things that happened in 1998 that didn't even happen in 1987. For example, the market for United States government securities, credit-risk-free securities, virtually went into gridlock in '98. This is a very technical thing, but if you go to any computer screen and look up the price of the so-called on-the-run ten-year Treasury note, the difference between the on-the-run and off-the-run notes was a 40-, 50-basis-point spread. Illiquidity in financial markets, but not the stock market, was the problem in 1998.

DAVID KOMANSKY:

I remember that infamous day when Jon Corzine and I went to the Fed to take a look at [LTCM's] book. This was the first time we got to see their positions across the industry, and it was disturbing. In my mind there was never any doubt that if this thing went under we ran the risk of a systemic failure.

JOHN KENNETH GALBRAITH (Harvard University economist and author):

We don't know what would have happened if Long-Term Capital Management had been allowed to go under. It had some very influential investors, and they have not been inclined to minimize the economic and social importance of the forces that saved their money. You follow me? If you get into the kind of trouble that Long-Term Capital Management did it's very good to have public expression coming from the New York Federal Reserve Bank and the big New York bankers.

PETER FISHER:

If you look at what happened over the fourth quarter of 1998, some of the firms that helped recapitalize Long-Term and stabilize it saw their share price cut in half. It's not that no one took any pain here. So with the benefit of hindsight I'm prepared to say it was a reasonable success to take this problem and tie it to the share price of the creditors who created it and make them responsible for cleaning it up.

ROGER LOWENSTEIN:

I think if they'd been allowed to fail there would've been disruptions, but the world would've gone on. Some of the banks would've lost money, and some would've cannily traded around it. But I think there would've been more urgency about reforming the derivatives world if Long-Term Capital had been allowed to fail, some of which might've benefited people who did business with Enron and companies like that. Greenspan said there's a moral hazard in bailing them out, and I agree. I think he underestimated the hazard and overestimated the risk of a failure. The potential for failure is what gives virtue to markets, because that's what keeps people honest. Would it have been better if the major equity firms had stepped in and rescued some of the dot-coms when they failed? Or was it better for some people to take their licks? I'd say the latter.

John Meriwether and his partners paid dearly in the cleanup of Long-Term Capital. They have said that they lost all their holdings in the fund, nearly $2 billion in total. Today, Meriwether and several members of his band of traders are pursuing an encore with a new fund called JWM Partners. They've raised hundreds of millions of dollars, some of it from the same people and institutions that invested in Long-Term Capital. It may be a more low-key effort — without the star power of Scholes and Merton — and the portfolio may be filled with more conservative investments at lower levels of leverage, but the old strategy of looking for mispriced securities in the marketplace remains intact, as always.

CHAPTER 26

THE EMPIRE

In 1999, the U.S. financial system formally tossed aside the last vestiges of the Depression-era regulatory structure that essentially created modern Wall Street when Congress repealed the Glass-Steagall Act of 1933, which had separated commercial and investment banks. But, truth be told, by the late 1990s Glass-Steagall's hold on the country's financial system was tenuous, at best. In 1987, the Federal Reserve reinterpreted Section 20 of the law and allowed commercial banks to derive a small portion of their revenues from securities activities. Then, in 1996, the Fed ruled that bank holding companies could derive 25 percent of their revenues from securities activities. Clearly, the end was near. But if there was a single event that killed Glass-Steagall it was the April 1998 merger of Travelers Group and Citicorp. Finally, there was a concrete example of what a true financial supermarket would look like in the combination of Citibank, the Travelers insurance businesses, and Salomon Smith Barney.

Perhaps not surprisingly, the driving force behind the deal was the man who started his career as Wall Street's ultimate outsider — Sandy Weill. He had rebounded from his disappointing departure from American Express and cobbled together a company that was even more impressive than Shearson. Starting in 1986 with Commercial Credit, a Baltimore consumer-lending outfit, Weill went on an acquisitions tear. He bought the financial-services giant Primerica, which owned the securities broker Smith Barney, from Jerry Tsai. He reacquired Shearson's brokerage and money-management businesses from his old friends at American Express. Then he bought Travelers, the storied 128-year-old insurance firm, based in Hartford, Connecticut, and renamed his newly combined operation Travelers Group. And in 1997, he added Salomon Brothers' trading prowess to Smith Barney's retail brokerage strength and created Salomon Smith Barney. By 1998, he was ready for the "mother of all deals."

KENNETH GUENTHER (former chief executive officer of Independent Community Bankers of America):

The real chipping away at Glass-Steagall started well before Citigroup ever got together. In 1992 [President Bill] Clinton came into office, and he was a great friend of Hugh McCall, at the time the chairman of Nationsbank, and Congressman Steve Neal from the great state of North Carolina. They repealed the McFadden Act and the Douglas Amendment, and that set the stage for the repeal of Glass-Steagall.

BILL SEIDMAN (former chairman of the Federal Deposit Insurance Corporation):

The pressure to get rid of Glass-Steagall had been going on since the act was passed. Numerous academics published studies showing that the separation of financial services had nothing to do with the 1929 crash and the Great Depression. And the truth is, it did create a less efficient financial system. But the goal of the act wasn't efficiency, it was to eliminate conflicts of interest inherent in a situation where banks could loan money to a client and underwrite that same client's stock.

KENNETH GUENTHER:

Actually, this is one of the least-talked-about aspects of Alan Greenspan's legacy. Greenspan is a free-market person. He's a deregulator. He has no use for the Glass-Steagall Act. He has no use for provisions of law separating commercial and investment banking. And Greenspan definitely made the policy decision to do what he could to undo the law through regulation. What he could do via regulation was in the Section 20 actions. Section 20 established the percentage of revenues that commercial banks could generate from investment-banking activities. And he began pushing up the permissible revenue limits in Section 20 to around 25 percent, and at that point there wasn't all that much that a large commercial bank couldn't do in terms of investment banking.

There's a supersecret body in the Federal Reserve System called the Federal Advisory Council. It has one banker from every Federal Reserve district. It goes back to the 1930 act. They meet under law four times a year with the full board of governors of the Federal Reserve System. It's very formal. It's not under the Government in the Sunshine Act; it's not under Freedom of Information. You cannot even get the minutes of these meetings. But now and then I would get briefed on what happened in these meetings. And I remember being briefed on the FAC meeting preparatory to the full board of governors after Greenspan had taken Section 20 up to 25 percent. The big bankers in the room said this allowed them to buy any investment bank they wanted. Meaning, every banker in that room said to himself, "If I wanted to, I could now buy Merrill Lynch."

That was a very key dynamic because Greenspan, through regulatory action, had opened the door for banks to buy Wall Street firms. But those firms — Goldman Sachs, Merrill Lynch, Morgan Stanley — could not buy commercial banks under the existing law. Prior to that, the securities industry for the most part didn't mind having Glass-Steagall in place because it kept the banks out of their backyard. But now Greenspan had said to the banks, "Go ahead. Buy the bastards out." The securities industry saw this and said, "Wait a minute, wait a minute, we want a two-way street." It was only natural. So the securities industry changed its position and got united behind the repeal of the Glass-Steagall Act.

JEFF LANE (former head of asset-management operations at Salomon Smith Barney and former Shearson executive under Sandy Weill):

There were only two countries in the world at that time that had

Glass-Steagall-type requirements — the United States and Japan. The rest of the world's model was universal banking. I think the United States came to the conclusion that the best way to compete was to break down the walls that were put up during the Great Depression.

DAVID ROCKEFELLER (former Chase Manhattan chairman):

I probably was one of the later ones to give in on Glass-Steagall. My uncle had been active in it, and it seemed to me that there probably were merits to keeping the barriers, on the grounds that the reasons the barriers were put up were to stop the abuses that were taking place back in the twenties and thirties. That's what led to the law. So I probably held on longer than others in my advocacy of it. But in retrospect, I think the way the world has evolved, and the way business in the world has evolved, it no longer makes sense.

H. RODGIN COHEN (attorney and banking specialist at Sullivan and Cromwell):

If you go back in time, Glass-Steagall probably was not logically the consequence of what was going on in 1929. There was a lot of inappropriate activity, but it was never demonstrated that banks got into trouble because of their securities activities. There was nothing. There was one bank that reportedly failed because of its securities activities, when in fact it had almost no securities business. It was a heavy investor in real estate. That was probably the cause of the failure. But that was the perception. So I think the model probably didn't make sense in 1933, and it certainly didn't make sense by well before 1999.

JAMIE DIMON (president of JP Morgan Chase and former head of Salomon Smith Barney):

We had been talking about Citi for years. In fact, we owned a piece of Citi in 1990. Remember Prince Alwaleed bought a big stake in Citi? Well, we took $50 million of that. They had collapsed in 1990, and the stock was at 7¾ or something like that.

JEFF LANE:

Let me tell you the story. We are Travelers and we think we're doing great. We have a planning-group meeting — that would be eighteen senior executives — up at our planning-group center, which is up in Armonk, New York. We decide that we're going to put on the board every company that would be a compelling acquisition for us, and two criteria were not important: one, whether they would have any interest, and two, whether it was legal. Just brainstorming what would be the best fit for Travelers. Michael Carpenter led the exercise and he put on the board all the likely names: AIG, J. P. Morgan, American Express. It was everyone you could think of, including Citicorp.

We went through the list and talked about the pluses and minuses. And if you exclude the fact that it was not legal at the time for us to merge with them, and that we didn't have any idea in the world whether [Citicorp chairman] John Reed would have any interest, Citi was clearly the most compelling merger partner for us. If you looked at Travelers and Citi and put all the pieces together, we had a better poker hand than anybody in the world.

JAMIE DIMON:

Sandy and John Reed had known each other for a long time and had served on boards together. One day, Sandy said, "You know, I'm going to see John at this Business Council meeting in Washington and tell him that I've got an idea for him. Maybe we should put these two things together. We can do it."

So he ran into John at the meeting. He said, "Can you come see me in my room?" And John thought Sandy was going to hit him up for some charity. But Sandy kind of gave him his pitch for a merger of Travelers and Citicorp. It wasn't a real detailed thing, more of the broad strokes. "We could put it together . . . it'll be great . . . we'll be huge . . . blah, blah, blah." And John's response was, "You know, that is kind of interesting."

When Sandy came back he was all excited. "John's interested. He's on his way to Singapore, and he's going to write me a letter, by hand, telling me what he thinks the pros and cons are."

I remember Sandy anxiously waiting for this faxed letter. We finally got it after a few days, and John had in fact written it by hand. And you know what? He was interested.

SANDY WEILL (chairman of Citigroup):

The law said that a non-banking company could file to become a bank, and it would have somewhere between two and five years to comply with the law. . . . So we weren't breaking the law by doing [the merger]. We were following the law. What we were very lucky about is that the law changed during that period of time so that we didn't have to divest our insurance assets, which is something that we would have had to do to comply with the law.

JAMIE DIMON:

If you look at the Citi-Travelers deal, we bought Citi. Citi legally could not have bought us. What the rules said was that if a nonbank bought a bank, they would within five years have to sell any insurance underwriting and insurance agency stuff, unless they received permission. You automatically became a bank-holding company, and all the stuff you wanted to do with underwriting securities could fit in a Section 20 sub.

I remember sitting there with [Federal Reserve chairman Alan] Greenspan when Sandy said, "You know, I've got to tell you about this thing we're thinking about doing." We didn't tell him the name the first time. He'd always assumed it was J. P. Morgan. I remember we went down the second time and told him it was Citicorp. Even Greenspan was floored.

KENNETH GUENTHER:

I was somewhat shocked when I heard about the Citigroup deal. It was a huge step. When the announcement was made Greenspan made positive comments about it — I would say even purring comments about it. But what was remarkable to me was, at the press conference to announce the merger Weill said that they had spoken to Greenspan and the president about it. Think about that for a second. This deal was against the law as it stood then, and they'd told the president and the chairman of the Federal Reserve

System about it, implying that they'd given their blessing, which they must've because if they hadn't, there wouldn't have been a press conference. And this was all happening as the repeal of the Glass-Steagall Act was sitting before the House of Representatives. The impact on the members of the House is immeasurable. I think it was the straw that broke the camel's back.

TOM BROWN (founder of Second Curve Capital and former bank-stock analyst at Donaldson, Lufkin and Jenrette):

Sandy is pretty political. He has very good connections down in Washington, and they were going to need to get legislation passed to get the deal done. He's the kind of guy who can get things done on that scale. And the other thing about Sandy is that he's made a career out of creating value through acquisitions. So when you stepped back and took a look at it, it made a lot of sense that he was the guy in the middle of all this.

MICHAEL MAYO (bank-stock analyst at Prudential Securities and former analyst at Credit Suisse First Boston):

I thought it showed a lot of chutzpah — that's the word that came to my mind — on Sandy Weill's part to go ahead and pursue that kind of deal before the law was changed. But I can't say it was a big surprise in light of everything that had gone on before.

JAMIE DIMON:

I guess the next step was, Sandy and I met with John and [Citicorp vice chairman] Paul Collins to talk about the organization, values, and so on. Sandy was very basic about the whole thing, which really is one of his deal-making skills. In the first meeting he told John, "There are three things that will make this so we can actually get it done. One, we need to be cochairmen and co-CEOs. Two, that it be a merger of equals stockwise. And three, that the boards be split evenly, fifty-fifty."

JEFF LANE:

To use the pejorative, Citi was truly a commercial bank. We thought we were a bunch of entrepreneurs. Citi thought that the entrepreneurial spirit we brought to the table was a real plus, or at least John Reed thought so.

JAMIE DIMON:

All firms are different. Remember, Travelers wasn't just an investment bank. Travelers was a lot of different companies, whereas Citibank was a commercial bank. So Citi kind of had one culture, and we had multiple cultures. The culture of Travelers Property and Casualty wasn't the same as Salomon Smith Barney.

The point was, the way Sandy set it up you didn't have to negotiate those big points. The name of the firm would include the word "Citi" so that they knew we understood this was a global brand and that we were willing to drop the name Travelers. But Sandy also knew that if they started arguing over whether John would be chairman for a few years and then Sandy would be chairman for a few years, it would become hard to get it done. This was a risky move for both of them. It was a real gutsy thing.

JOHN REED (former Citicorp chairman):

Say what you want about it, Sandy and I had an idea of why we were doing this, and what it was to do. It was an idea — we didn't have to negotiate it. We both felt it.

Now, personalitywise, I don't think Sandy or I thought we were going to work well together. . . . I'm very much of a process, slow, deliberate guy. Sandy is very much of a personality, immediate-reaction guy. That's a big difference. I'm a builder. He's an acquirer. Just totally different.

JAMIE DIMON:

I thought that they were both taking a very big risk with the co-CEO structure. The most important thing wasn't them, it was going to be the rest of the company, which needed clarity. We all agreed that this was important and we tried to have real clarity in how we organized it beneath them. We didn't end up having that, and I ended up being a casualty of it, too. I knew it was risky and I knew it could hurt if we didn't do it. But when you looked at the thing you had to say that there was enough upside that it was worth taking that risk. And once the big points were behind us, we had a deal. That's really Sandy's strength in all this — he knows what he needs to do to get a deal done.

MICHAEL MAYO:

At first I thought it had amazing potential, but the problem was the organization and execution. I first dubbed the deal "Noah's Ark" because they brought two of everything along. They had loads of coheads of divisions. They had two CEOs. It was just too top-heavy.

JEFF LANE:

Everyone has twenty-twenty hindsight, but I think all of us, including Sandy, thought the co-CEOs could work if both of them played nicely. They each brought unique strengths to the table. Sandy and John Reed are very different kinds of people. And if they could figure out how to work together it probably would be an ideal combination. So I did not assume that Sandy was going to run the company. Maybe I was being naive, but I assumed the two of them were going to work together.

The Citigroup merger was announced on April 6, 1998, and the financial community immediately recognized it as a signal that Glass-Steagall effectively was dead. The Financial Services Modernization Act, which actually finished off the old law, would be passed a year later, but it was merely a formality. Citigroup simply was too big to be stopped.

At the same time, many people in and around Wall Street questioned the new company's executive structure, with John Reed and Sandy Weill sharing responsibilities for the firm as cochairmen and co-CEOs — and they were right to be skeptical. Infighting disrupted the organization almost immediately. The first casualty of the turf wars was Weill's lieutenant, Jamie Dimon. Weill fired Dimon in November 1998, less than a month after the merger closed, after a major falling-out that started when — in a move reminiscent of his battle with

Peter Cohen during the American Express deal a decade earlier — Weill refused to add Dimon to Citigroup's board of directors. But the animosities and rivalries at Citigroup truly were laid bare when Reed announced in February 2000 that he planned to resign after an eighteen-month power struggle. With Reed finally out of the way, Weill once again was in position to dominate his firm by himself — the way he seemed to operate best.

CHAPTER 27

MARKET MESSENGERS

Starting in the mid-1990s, before the World Wide Web exploded, the major driving force in helping Main Street gain access to Wall Street's information was television, specifically CNBC, the business-news channel launched by the NBC network. Of course, this is not to say that CNBC invented financial news. To the contrary; prior to CNBC's arrival on the scene there were a plethora of print-media outlets covering Wall Street, led by the Wall Street Journal. *There also were a few television programs dedicated to discussing business and finance, most notably* Nightly Business Report *on PBS,* Moneyline *hosted by Lou Dobbs on CNN, and* Wall $treet Week with Louis Rukeyser, *which also aired on PBS and long was the highest-rated finance show on television. But what CNBC did differently than the rest was to attack business news full-time. While* Moneyline *was on once a day, and Louis Rukeyser was on once a week, CNBC — regardless of what you thought of its content — was there when you got up in the morning and when you went to sleep at night, with a stock ticker scrolling at the bottom of the screen the entire time.*

CNBC wasn't conceived in some secret laboratory manned by clairvoyant NBC executives. Rather, it was the evolution of an idea started in 1981 on the West Coast at a pioneering outfit called the Financial News Network, or FNN. Short on style and funding, it still was the first television channel dedicated to covering the day's trading on Wall Street from start to finish. Nobody had ever even tried to do it before. And when you take a look at how this concept started, it's amazing it even got off the ground.

BILL GRIFFETH (CNBC anchor and former FNN anchor):

FNN was started by a couple of fellows. One, Glenn Taylor, ran a little production company that did children's programming called Three-Ring Productions. The other gentleman was the general manager of a local UHF station in Los Angeles that did business news. With [Ted] Turner starting CNN only nine months earlier, satellite technology was real hot at the time. And this fellow, Rod Buscher, who was running the local business channel in town, saw the possibility that you could turn a local business channel into a national event, using satellite technology. So they developed this idea.

RON INSANA (CNBC anchor and former FNN anchor):

Being out in California was happenstance. The founders were originally planning to start a children's television network of some sort, but at the very last minute decided that they would do a financial-news network. So they were already out in Santa Monica, at 2525 Ocean Park Boulevard, not terribly far from the beach, in a crappy old building that was two stories, and uncomfortable, and small. And we just had this tiny studio.

BILL GRIFFETH:

We went on the air November 30, 1981. It was a Monday. The production was really crude, and I'm saying that as one of the producers, which is what I had started out doing. We had five anchors, but nobody knew anything about business news. So we took one guy and we said, "You're the main anchor." Then with another guy we said, "You're the stock-market anchor. Go learn about the stock market." To one woman we said, "You're going to be our commodities reporter." She was an orthodox Jew, and here she was talking about pork bellies, so that didn't make a whole lot of sense. Another woman we made the international-news anchor. And then the last fellow was the interviewer. It all took place right in that studio. There was no videotape, none of the remote satellite segments that we all know and love today. It was all right there in the studio.

SUE HERERA (CNBC anchor and former FNN anchor):

We wanted to do market-oriented play-by-play, with issues-oriented shows based on what was going on in the markets. There were some segments that might've gotten their feeling from what Louis Rukeyser was doing, where we'd try to get together a panel and just talk. We had a lot of time to fill.

RON INSANA:

Because we didn't have a lot of money the programming relied on phone-call interviews, where we would put up a full-screen graphic or some old video. We were not a terribly well-resourced place. But we covered the markets all day long.

SUE HERERA:

We didn't have any fancy graphics. We kind of put it together as we went. There were no scripts, so it was ad-libbing and phone interviews. We did format the futures boards and the stock boards, and there were a few over-the-shoulder graphics. But it was very simple.

RON INSANA:

We used to use some generic stock-market video every time we did a stock-market story, and one day some guy calls up and says, "Listen, that tape you're running, the guy in it's been dead for two years." It was a tape called S-1, and it was our generic stock-market footage, you know.

BILL GRIFFETH:

We had a ticker on the bottom of the screen. It was very crude, just the letters and numbers in the style of the old ticker tape, which showed just the stock symbols and the last digit of the stock price. Back then you wouldn't get the full price on the tape because it was assumed that if you were reading the tape you knew where IBM or AT&T had last traded. It was impossible to read, we really should've slowed it down. But none of us understood it anyway, so it didn't matter.

RON INSANA:

None of us had any background in business, so it was immersion therapy. The great part about it is you were kind of on your own. Once you got on the air it was your problem. So you'd call anybody you could call and talk to anybody you could talk to. In the newsroom there were several people who did know what they were doing.

BILL GRIFFETH:

I had no clue about business news when FNN started. We sort of taught each other as we went along.

RON INSANA:

FNN was a twelve-hour network dedicated to business news. The stock market in those days was open from ten to four, there was no before-hours trading or after-hours trading. FNN was a shop that ran the gamut. We covered markets intensively. We covered the economy. A lot of what we do today we did then, but we did it with far fewer resources and a lot less grace and sophistication.

SUE HERERA:

We were pretty intense. We'd get into a lot of the minutiae of Wall Street, arbitrage trading, futures trading, and stock-index futures and technical analysis. So it was more of a tool for the pro.

JAMES CRAMER (CNBC talk-show host, journalist, and former hedge-fund manager):

FNN, the precursor to CNBC, made it so that I could get into it in a way that wasn't geographically possible before. I didn't think that you could stay in touch with the market without a ticker and stuff. Before FNN you would call a broker and get a couple of quotes, but there wasn't really any streaming way to stay in touch, other than those miserable five-minute updates on radio. FNN changed everything for me.

NEAL CAVUTO (Fox News anchor and former CNBC anchor):

There was very little financial news in the 1980s. When I started out in the broadcasting business at *Nightly Business Report* [on PBS], I had some friends in the business, and they would chase political stories; others were into crime. I really was like the nerd on the block. There was nothing sexy about what I was covering — deregulation efforts in Washington, things like that. None of that ever really got the cocktail-party conversation going.

TOM ROGERS (former NBC Cable president):

FNN was out there in not very many cable homes. But they created this notion of stock information being reported during market hours. It had very low viewership. It was part of the package that many cable operators were distributing, but extremely low profile.

RON INSANA:

It was always touch-and-go financially. The guy who ran the joint [Earl Brian] eventually went to jail for financial fraud, which was the undoing of FNN. But we kind of built a business. Sometimes it relied on sponsored programming that was sold in the middle of the market day. We wrapped our newscasts around anything from a five- to a seven- to a twelve- to a thirty-minute infomercial. I wouldn't necessarily say they were about investing — it was all sort of boiler-room kind of stuff, and we were roundly criticized in the financial media for having sold out that way. But it did manage to bring in the revenues they needed to stay alive.

BILL GRIFFETH:

It's a matter of public record now, but basically there were a number of financial shenanigans going on through the years where they would siphon money off from the company. There was just all kinds of stuff going on. Essentially, we went bankrupt, filed for bankruptcy in 1990. But we'd built up such a distribution in cable that NBC, which had started up CNBC in 1989, saw a perfect opportunity to bolster their own distribution by buying us. But it went to an auction between Dow Jones, NBC, and I think another group. Anyway, NBC won the bidding and in May of 1991 shut down FNN as it was put together at the time and shipped five of us back. They bought the five of us, the distribution, which was probably thirty-five million homes at the time, and they incorporated our ticker into CNBC programming.

NEAL CAVUTO:

It wasn't until CNBC merged with FNN in the early 1990s that CNBC was sort of fleshed out to be a more serious financial effort. In the early days it was very much a boring kind of niche product. There was nothing flashy about it. It was a lot of numbers, not a lot of context, and that was it. I think that changed substantially with the merger with FNN, but back then it was, only dullards need apply.

TOM ROGERS:

I had two concepts that derived from the letters CNBC. One was Cable NBC, because this was NBC's first foray into cable and I was going to push the company into a wide number of areas. And the other was the Consumer News and Business Channel, which was intended to cover stock-market and business news, but also give people a broader sense of managing money and pocketbook issues.

BILL GRIFFETH:

I always said that once I got to CNBC, I realized that FNN had been a business-news service that just happened to be on television, while CNBC was a television news network that just happened to be doing business news. There's a very important distinction there. At FNN, while it wasn't stated, we had a reputation of targeting more of a professional audience, or at least those who brought some knowledge to the table to begin with, whereas CNBC was as much an education channel, or at least it tried to be, as it was business news. It would do news that would appeal to a broader audience than FNN did.

NEAL CAVUTO:

I actually think that the 1987 crash, which happened before CNBC even existed, was enormously important for business news. We lost a quarter of the market's value in one day, and suddenly business news was front-page material. I found myself leading broadcasts, general news broadcasts. I was at *Nightly Business Report,* and all of a sudden I was hip and cool? I'd never seen anything like it. That crash changed everyone's perception of investing and the markets. Everyone wanted to investigate what had happened. And once they saw the market coming back, they wanted to be a part of it.

BILL GRIFFETH:

When Roger Ailes was president of CNBC, he brought in a fellow by the name of Jack Reilly, who had been the executive producer at *Good Morning America* for many years. They had worked together on the old *Mike Douglas Show* years ago. And Jack came up with the concept of treating the market day like a sporting event. You had a pregame show, a halftime show and a postgame wrap-up. It really made sense when you thought about it, because the format was so familiar to the same kind of audience we were going after anyway. We've long known that a good piece of our audience is male, and it didn't take a rocket scientist to figure out that it might be a good idea to use that same kind of mentality here and appeal to the same type of demographic that ESPN appeals to with its programming.

TOM ROGERS:

At CNBC what we intended to do was give people a sense that every day you had this huge event, the way a football game is a huge event on

Sundays. We wanted to give people a sense that they're inside, a part of the action, behind the scenes, down on the field, as opposed to kind of a removed, wire-service-copy approach to how it's done.

BILL GRIFFETH:

For years, no one was ever allowed on the floor of the stock exchange other than the traders. It just didn't happen. I know at FNN we had asked to be able to put a reporter there. That was long a dream of ours, to put reporters on the floor of the New York Stock Exchange and at the Board of Trade in Chicago. At CNBC, having NBC and GE as parents, it provided us with deep pockets, in terms of both money and political connections. And that's really how that was able to happen.

MARIA BARTIROMO (CNBC anchor and the first reporter to work on the floor of the New York Stock Exchange):

I got into screaming matches with guys who could have been my father or grandfather. There were people who didn't want me there and they made it known. They tried to intimidate me.

TOM ROGERS:

Putting a reporter on the floor of the stock exchange was all part of making people feel that they were down on the field, part of the game. They know when it begins every day they're getting the inside story. They're in the mix. As a feel on television, it totally transforms the anchor-desk situation into something that becomes, "Hey, there's a live event going on here, and I'm a part of it." That's been a key part of the experience.

NEIL CAVUTO:

I thought then, and think now, that business news is interesting beyond the markets. So if there was a mistake made then and now, it's treating this subject as if it's ESPN *SportsCenter*. I think that while, yes, there is some value to getting sort of a "pregame" look at the markets on a show like *Squawk Box,* continuing it throughout the day and using the market as your focal point is a mistake because the bottom line is that it's very good when the markets are going your way, but as ratings have proven, and as history has proven, people get pissed off when the markets aren't going your way. But then, you're hostage to that programming strategy. I think that was the seminal mistake that we made early on — treating the market like a game, and it's not.

BOB MCCOOEY (chief executive officer of New York Stock Exchange floor brokerage firm and trading house Griswold Company):

CNBC broke down the facade of the New York Stock Exchange. Unfortunately, people only viewed the stock exchange one of two ways in the late eighties and early nineties. One was as the traditional Old Boys' club, where no one really knew what was going on and it was all very mysterious. And the other was as this scandal-tainted thing because Wall Street had such a bad reputation after Milken and all that. The New York Stock Exchange had nothing to do with any of it, of course, but anytime the media did a story about anything in the financial world they showed a shot of the exterior of the exchange or the floor of the stock exchange, and I think the reputation just sort of stuck.

Then, suddenly you had Maria Bartiromo on the floor of the exchange, and you had reporters setting up shots in other parts of the building. And it broke down the place for people. It said, "We're open, come on in. We want you to see and hear what's going on and get a taste of that excitement." That was why I was a huge defender of the idea of having CNBC on the floor of the exchange in the first place, and it's why I continue to be a big defender of it even with a lot of people on the floor bitching to me about it. It was very important for us. It got rid of the mystique. It took the mystery out of the business and let people see what it's all about.

TOM ROGERS:

Whether it was through their 401(k) accounts, or IRAs, the number of individual investors who were making individual decisions about their retirement futures was growing. It wasn't just about stocks going up, it was that the number of people owning stocks and making buy and sell decisions on those stocks just mushroomed. All of a sudden, CNBC became the centerpiece of how people could follow, understand, and comprehend what was going on. It always walked that fine line between being something that professional, hard-core investors would look to as meaningful to what they did, and being something that more generalist consumers could look to for what they did. It found that point in the nineties where it was an important centerpiece for both of those constituencies.

LARRY RAND (financial historian and cofounder of financial public relations firm Kekst and Company):

They did breaking news. They had very good sources. When you go up to Fidelity, you have to see where the eyeballs are. They're on the Bloomberg screen, and they're on CNBC. They're not even looking at the Dow tape anymore, which is a little frightening.

RON INSANA:

You know, in 1996 during the O.J. hearings, business news was not exactly the hottest thing on the planet. We suffered greatly during that period. Then, all of a sudden you hit 1997, when the Asian financial crisis hit, and people started to take notice. I think in the absence of other general news events happening at the time, we had this thing that was going on and it suddenly captured people's attention. It was a two-way street. The market could go down a lot, and it could go up a lot. But the point is, a lot of people were able to watch it happen, unlike 1987, when FNN's distribution wasn't so good. And they tuned in.

We started setting our ratings records in that period. Then, it just took off. You had Dow 5,000, Dow 6,000, Dow 7,000, Dow 8,000 — those were all ratings records for us as we did specials around these millennium marks. The technology boom, the IPO boom, everything that happened required a new set of superlatives every time we talked about it. Wall Street became the stuff of cocktail conversation. We became reasonably well-known. People outside our venue wanted to talk to us.

NEIL CAVUTO:

You don't do this kind of job for the notoriety. You do it because the subject interests you. I was sort of born a nerd, so I like this sort of stuff. But when people started asking for my autograph I thought, "This is weird."

TOM ROGERS:

Watching a business reporter like Maria [Bartiromo] being called the Money Honey and being followed closely in the *New York Post* — clearly this was an indication that it had broken out in terms of the extent to which it was considered hot, mainstream television.

SUE HERERA:

I was in Europe, and people would come up to me, and say, "Oh, I see you on *Business Center* every night." In places that you would not expect it, people were coming up and saying hello. I think that's when I really realized that our reach was far and wide.

IAN WEINBERG (financial adviser and president of Family Wealth and Pension Management):

I think CNBC did a terrible job during the bubble. They led a lot of investors right to the slaughter. CNBC would come on and every day they'd have a nice-looking fellow named Tom Costello reporting from the Nasdaq. And I think they paid him per word — you know, the more he spoke the more he earned — because he spoke in such a frenzied way that he created this sense of urgency. In reality, what he was saying was Dell was up a quarter or down a quarter based on demand for personal computers. It was the same thing with Maria Bartiromo standing on the floor of the exchange. I can remember being at a golf outing in '99, sitting in the men's locker room watching CNBC, and she was screaming about the fact that IBM might move into another business. When she was done, about five guys got up to call their brokers and go buy IBM.

RON INSANA:

Listen, I was one of the cautious people who was roundly criticized for not knowing what I was talking about when I suggested that events like these can end badly or that people had lost a certain sense of rationality. I started saying that in 1996, and I said it for a couple of years, and then kind of backed off because when the market's going up 20 percent a year for five years, and when the Nasdaq goes up 85 percent in a single year, which was not done by any other average in the history of this country, what do you say? You've got to say something. When TheGlobe.com goes up 650 percent in a single day, we didn't make that happen, it just did.

Now, I understand that there's an amplification effect because you get this positive feedback when everybody's involved in the conversation. I get it. But we didn't create the event, nor could we stop it. Believe me, there were plenty of times along the way when I went out with historical analogies that compared — and I'm certain I was the first to do this one — the Internet to RCA in the 1920s during the radio boom. But people told me that I didn't know what I was talking about. The viewers were like, "You're crazy. This is nothing like radio. How could you compare the Internet to radio?" You know you've got a problem when you're looking at one transformational industry compared to another in a different time and people don't get the analogy. The fact that they got angry showed me that we were in the middle of something that we were a part of, but that we certainly couldn't control or change.

NEIL CAVUTO:

When you're at the parade, you have to make a very clear distinction between whether you're covering that parade or in it. I think that the criticism of business journalists during the bubble, and it's a valid one, is that they were in the parade. It made it very difficult for them to cover it. It helped ratings, and it sold *Business Week* magazines and *Fortune* magazines. It sold business sections of newspapers. Advertisers clamored to have a spot in print, broadcast, and cable to be part of that fixation. But I thought it was dangerous then, and it's dangerous now. When you make the markets the be-all and end-all, it's going to end it all for you.

BILL GRIFFETH:

If this had been the very first bubble that had ever occurred in the history of the stock market there might be some credence to blaming us. But there have been so many bubbles in the past where there was no radio or television. They used to call them panics back in the 1800s, and there were some doozies that sent the economy into recession. They caused thousands of people to lose millions of dollars, and amazingly, there was no CNBC at that time. A market bubble is a natural phenomenon that occurs in any free market where you get these extremes of demand for a product when everyone believes they can get rich. In any market like that, if you come late to the game you've already missed the boat. When the bubble starts to pop people all rush to the exits at the same time, and out you go.

My take is, and this is probably controversial and I don't know if the people at CNBC would want me to say this, but there were lots of people watching us in the late nineties who had no business watching CNBC because they didn't understand fully how the market works, or the companies they were investing in, or the investment process. When they lost money — and I'm generalizing here — they were unwilling to take responsibility and looked for a scapegoat. In that case you tend to want to shoot the messenger. Our job was then, and always will be, to put a mirror up to what's going on. If your favorite sports team is in the big game and they lose, do you yell at the announcer?

NORMAN PEARLSTINE (Time Inc. editor in chief):

To me, CNBC has made the biggest difference in the investment psychology. Today you have a very large number of people who have come to appreciate that over the long term, stocks outperform bonds, and the fact that capital gains are taxed at [15 percent] while bonds are taxed as income makes that gap even bigger. So even in a noninflationary period, the idea that the conservative thing to do is own AAA corporates and Treasuries has been severely challenged.

Now, if you have several years of a down market will people feel differently? That's the big question, and I don't know the answer. We'll have to wait and see, won't we?

LOUIS RUKEYSER (former host of *Wall $treet Week with Louis Rukeyser* on PBS):

Television can make Wall Street accessible to the average person, to the extent that you can show someone on Main Street that you don't have to be a bull or a bear, you just have to be a grown-up. Steady, sensible long-term investing is a very good way to prepare for the future. It is today, it was yesterday, and it will be tomorrow. The rich people of 2013 are buying stocks in 2003.

CHAPTER 28

BUBBLE BATH

By the time Wall Street reached the late 1990s, what had started as an enthusiastic response by a few investors to a promising new technology — the Internet — had morphed into an all-out stock-market frenzy. Suddenly, Main Street money was pouring onto Wall Street like never before, as folks who once held their life savings in interest-earning bank accounts and Treasury bonds started looking for instant fortunes among the hot new tech stocks. Average investors were buying stocks on margin, or borrowing to buy stock. With the equity markets continually setting new highs, the Dow Jones Industrial Average raced to, and eventually beyond, the previously unheard-of 10,000-point mark. Getting filthy rich in America had never been easier — or at least that's the way it seemed.

MICHAEL BARONE (head of Nasdaq trading at William Blair and Company in Chicago):

The late nineties was controlled chaos around here. The noise level and energy in this room was something. It's hard to judge even now because today we're all point and click. Just about everything we do now is on a computer, so there isn't much noise. Back then people were still calling on the phones all the time, all the institutions were calling our sales traders. It was just a very loud trading floor — not pandemonium, but extremely busy. Everybody had a smile on his face, though, because that market just kept going up and everyone was making money. I remember one stock that I made a market in was up another five points every five minutes. At one point I looked at my sales trader and said, "I don't know what to tell you. I don't think I can buy this thing."

RODGER RINEY (founder and chief executive officer of Scottrade):

It looked like a bubble. It felt like a bubble. There was no question that it was a bubble. And yet it went on so long that no one could make any money betting against it. Every time people shorted or sold out, they just got themselves into a pickle either with margin calls on their short positions or lost profits because they got out too early. I think a lot of people were saying it couldn't last, but they felt they had to be involved because they couldn't afford to miss it if it went on for another year or two or three.

ROBERT OLSTEIN (chairman of Olstein Financial Alert Fund):

In the late nineties I couldn't get gas and I couldn't get a haircut because the guy at the gas station was outperforming me and my barber was outperforming me. They were making 30 percent a day. That's why the public is just as much at fault in this thing as anyone. They rode it all the way up.

ROBERT POZEN (chairman of MFS Investment Management, former president of Fidelity Management and Research, and author of *The Mutual Fund Business*):

I used to go play tennis at this wonderful club in Boston called Longwood, which has grass courts. I'd always go and talk to the tennis pro, who would ask me for stock tips, and I wouldn't give him any. And I remember going there in 1999 and the guy came up to me and said, "Hey, I'm in this fund, and let me tell you something, you should buy it for yourself!" Suddenly he was giving *me* stock tips. I figured when the tennis pro at Longwood is giving out stock tips the end can't be that far off.

BLAKE DARCY (former chief executive officer of DLJDirect and CSFBDirect):

The problem wasn't that all the construction workers in Jersey City were watching CNBC on their lunch break. It's that they thought the valuations they were watching go across the screen were real and going to last forever. We were doing a focus group in January 2000. And one person was talking about how he was really pleased because he was up 84 percent the year before, and a couple of guys in the group started berating him for his poor performance — that he was pleased with lousy performance and that was unacceptable. It was unbelievable. A good year-over-year performance is 12 percent, 15 percent, and here people were berating the guy for 84 percent. I thought, we are really out of whack here in terms of what people are expecting.

LISE BUYER (Google director of business optimization and former senior equity analyst in Frank Quattrone's technology group at Deutsche Morgan Grenfell and Credit Suisse First Boston):

The other major thing that happened at that time was the chat rooms. These Internet chat rooms started to have big finance sections, and people could talk back and forth to one another about stocks. Sometimes it was useful information; sometimes it was totally made up. But it was a very real phenomenon. These people were using the Internet to pass around information and tips about these Internet stocks, and then they were running out and using the Internet to trade them. If you looked at the ownership of these stocks, a Yahoo or an Excite, at those times, 80, 85 percent of the ownership was individual investors, not the mutual funds and professional investors. They were rightly staying out of the way because it wasn't clear what the business model for any of these companies was.

Peter Lynch, pictured here in his office at Fidelity's Boston headquarters in the 1980s, racked up staggering results while running the Magellan Fund from 1977 to 1990 and became the most well known mutual fund manager in the world.

Sandy Weill (right) was determined to sell Shearson to American Express in 1981, despite his colleagues' advice that he'd be unhappy there and never succeed Jim Robinson (left) as chairman. By June 1985, Weill had resigned from Amex and was looking for another company to run.

Michael Milken's creation of a market for trading junk bonds unleashed a revolution in the financial markets in the 1980s and made him arguably the most powerful man on Wall Street. But it also made him a target for regulators and competitors.

Ivan Boesky was an arbitrage trader with an uncanny sense of timing. As it turned out, much of his market savvy was a result of illegally obtained inside information.

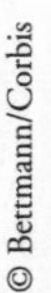

In the 1980s, "raiders" like T. Boone Pickens (above) and Carl Icahn (left) shook up America's corporate establishment. Using cheap capital in the form of Michael Milken's junk bonds, these entrepreneurs took huge stock positions and tried to force changes at various companies. In some cases they ended up with a takeover, and in other cases the companies paid them to go away. Either way, they made money. What a business.

© Bettmann/Corbis

Time Life Pictures/Getty Images

Gary Lynch, head of the Securities and Exchange Commission's enforcement division in the 1980s, brought cases against Ivan Boesky, Michael Milken, and a host of other Wall Street hotshots.

Michael Milken leaves court after pleading not guilty to insider trading charges in April 1989. He eventually received a ten-year sentence for securities violations and served two years in federal prison.

© Michael M. Fairchild

George Roberts (left) and Henry Kravis (right) sign the agreement giving KKR control of RJR Nabisco following the most heated takeover battle of the 1980s. In the end it turned out to be a pretty lousy move, according to Roberts: "Other than not buying the company in the first place, I wouldn't change a thing about the RJR deal."

On October 19, 1987, otherwise known as "Black Monday," the Dow Jones Industrial Average fell more than 500 points and touched off a panic across the country as many people worried about a return to 1929 and the Great Depression. Here a trader in the pits of the Chicago Board Options Exchange frantically signals for attention during the crash.

New York Stock Exchange floor brokers take in the news of the stock market crash from the *New York Post*. In many ways, the day after Black Monday was even more frightening for Wall Street, as the Dow continued to tank and stock exchange officials considered shutting down trading…until the market staged a staggering rebound.

© Ramin Talaie/Corbis

A trader at the Wall Street firm Bear Stearns monitoring the market. By the 1990s, powerful computers had become essential tools for sophisticated traders of increasingly complex securities who need information instantaneously at the press of a button.

© McGoon James/Corbis Sygma

As head of the hedge fund Long-Term Capital Management, John Meriwether put together a band of geniuses who used intricate trading strategies to become a profit-making juggernaut. But when the fund collapsed in 1998, it nearly triggered a global financial crisis.

© Peterson Ezio/Corbis Sygma

Sandy Weill (left), chairman of Travelers Group, and John Reed (right), chairman of Citicorp, are all smiles as co-chairmen of the new behemoth called Citigroup. The happy partnership didn't last long — within eighteen months Reed called it quits, leaving Weill alone at the top.

Henry Blodget, a young equities analyst, emerged as a guru of the Internet era when in December 1998 he said Amazon.com, then selling for less than $250, would be trading for $400 within a year, and the stock proceeded to roar past his target price in just three weeks.

© James Leynse/Corbis

AP/Wide World Photos

"Money Honey" Maria Bartiromo was the first journalist to broadcast from the floor of the New York Stock Exchange. Many individual investors became fascinated with the stock market during the Internet bubble, in part because they were able to follow it for the first time on business news channels like CNBC.

© Chip East/Reuters/Corbis

Frank Quattrone was considered the leading investment banker in Silicon Valley. But he became the most high profile disgrace of the Internet era when he was convicted of obstructing justice in a federal investigation into kickbacks in initial public offerings.

© Erik Freeland/Corbis

After the World Trade Center terrorist attack on September 11, 2001, Wall Street and the entire financial district in lower Manhattan essentially turned into an armed fortress.

© Damon Winter/Dallas Morning News/Corbis

On September 17, 2001, less than a week after the attack, the stock market reopened with a patriotic flourish. Here (left to right), SEC Chairman Harvey Pitt, New York Senator Charles Schumer, New York Governor George Pataki, NYSE Chairman Dick Grasso, Treasury Secretary Paul O'Neill, New York Mayor Rudy Giuliani, and New York Senator Hillary Clinton are among those singing the national anthem before the opening bell at the New York Stock Exchange.

NYSE specialists and floor brokers observe a moment of silence as the stock exchange prepares to reopen after the terrorist attacks.

© Erik Freeland/Corbis

© Reuters/Corbis

In the aftermath of the Internet bubble, New York Attorney General Eliot Spitzer (left) became Wall Street's primary prosecutor, forcing changes in the brokerage and mutual fund industries. Meanwhile, NYSE Chairman Dick Grasso (right) became a poster child for greed when it was discovered that he had a retirement plan worth hundreds of millions of dollars.

© Reuters/Corbis

The New York Stock Exchange trading floor in the twenty-first century is a high-tech haven compared to the days of paper crunch. But its long-term viability is in question because of the efficiency of electronic markets, like Nasdaq.

© Peter Morgan/Reuters/Corbis

When the Google IPO charged out of the gates in August 2004 and nearly doubled in price in just a few months, some Wall Streeters wondered if they were watching a reprise of the Internet bubble. That remains to be seen.

KENNETH PASTERNAK (founder and former chief executive officer of Knight/Trimark):

I used to read our chat room from time to time, and I'd say 98, 99 percent of the information posted there was factually incorrect. They'd say, "We know that Ken Pasternak's in a meeting with Sandy Weill right now talking about a sale." And the truth is I'd be at the beach with my kids. Or someone would say, "I've spoken to three traders and the word is Knight's going to buy an options market maker." And we weren't even considering that.

I have an absolutely true story to tell about this. I have an ongoing fight with my wife because she doesn't think I'm that great a father. And my son was in a kindergarten concert on a day when I was supposed to speak at a Merrill Lynch conference. Now, the day before, Allan Wheat at First Boston had canceled because they were buying DLJ. So I canceled to see my son's play because my wife was making me feel guilty because I always have an important reason to miss these things. And our stock went up 11 points right before the concert. That's $1.5 billion in market value because I was trying to be a good father.

BLAKE DARCY:

We would tell our investors all the time to do their research, do their homework, be careful. And that really is what we wanted our investors to do. But the bottom line is, it was the people who were trading like crazy looking for performance and thinking that the world only goes up that were providing our revenues. It was kind of an odd scenario.

IAN WEINBERG (financial adviser and president of Family Wealth and Pension Management):

As we got into 1996, '97, '98, I remember having conversations with wealthy clients where they were saying, "My friend made 44 percent this year and we made 26 percent. What's going on here?" I think that anybody who was prudent during that time had those kinds of conversations with their clients. You had to help your clients filter out all the noise they were hearing at cocktail parties. Those people seeking 44 percent led to the biggest busts of all.

GUS SAUTER (chief investment officer of Vanguard):

We basically saw a frenzy in our S&P 500 fund. We had a tremendous amount of cash flow into that portfolio in the latter part of the nineties, which propelled it to become the largest fund in the world. We also saw things like capital leaving our Windsor II fund, which is a value fund, going to some of our competitors' momentum funds. There were more and more aggressive funds being offered, feeding the frenzy. In fairness, the frenzy created itself because people wanted these things. But it was fed or accommodated by the mutual fund industry. There were hundreds, if not thousands, of more-aggressive funds being introduced, funds that were so focused they were targeting segments of the Internet industry or segments of biotech. And you had superaggressive momentum funds.

IAN WEINBERG:

The average investor has no idea about the very real risk that's in the stock market. At any given time the S&P 500 could drop 20, 25 percent very quickly — political events, currency issues, wars, you just don't know what will trigger it. But you have to know that it could happen at any time. The average investor also is very late. This is no knock on my clients or anyone who invests on his own, but we like to use individuals as reverse indicators. When someone calls us to put a lot of money into a certain tech stock, that triggers us to think that maybe we should consider a short position in that stock.

GUS SAUTER:

I remember receiving a shareholder letter that included the statement that the person wasn't being greedy, didn't want an aggressive fund; all he wanted was a fund that would return 15 percent a year. And I thought to myself, you may not think you're being greedy, but you are. In the bubble people started thinking that 15 percent was a conservative rate of return.

We were doing surveys and getting back results where 25 percent was the expected rate of return. So you can understand the person who says, "I'm not being greedy. All I want is 15 percent." They really have no idea how difficult it is to sustain 15 percent over a long period of time. It's not at all a reasonable assumption for the average investor. But that's how people thought during the bubble.

PETER LOW (member of the New York Stock Exchange since 1963 and former floor broker):

I'm a tremendous follower of Warren Buffett and his approach. And it's funny, the only time I can really remember anyone saying that Warren Buffett was wrong was during the bubble, when he was avoiding the Internet and everyone was saying, "Warren Buffett doesn't get it." But I knew that Buffett got it perfectly. I read him over and over again in order to make sure that I was on a rational, logical track. It was obvious that it couldn't last.

We would have dinner parties and I'd tell people that I wasn't buying the Internet stocks, and they'd say, "Don't you feel terrible that the market has passed you by?" Even my wife would say to me, "All these people are making a fortune in these Internet stocks and we're not doing anything." I'd tell her, "I don't know the first thing about them; I don't understand their business; and I can't for the life of me figure out how they're going to make any money." I kept saying, "Warren Buffett eventually is going to be proven absolutely correct."

JERRY KENNEY (Merrill Lynch executive vice president of research and corporate strategy):

I remember I visited a bunch of Internet companies just to see what they were like. Everybody was real excited. They had never run a company before. They had all these hot ideas and thought they were working hard. They had a couple of rooms with couches in the back, and that was the standard program.

WILLIAM HAMBRECHT (cofounder of Hambrecht and Quist):

With a lot of Internet companies, these kids were in their twenties. The wisdom was, if you're beyond thirty, you're probably too old to understand what they're doing.

DAVID KAUFMAN (certified public accountant and principal at Rothstein Kass):

I handled at least seventy-five to a hundred technology companies, and very few of them had any revenues whatsoever. All we were reporting were expenditures, capital expenses, technology infrastructure, and then huge marketing costs. As amazing as this may sound, that was all according to plan. There never were supposed to be any outside revenues. The model that I understood a lot of people went for was, if we build a Web site and we get enough hits and have enough content, things that people are interested in, we don't need subscribers and we don't need to charge. People are going to want to advertise on our site, and that's going to bring in the revenue. But that never happened for any of them. I think that was the reason the bubble burst. Everybody assumed that they were going to advertise on each other's site, and it was a big Ponzi scheme.

JERRY KENNEY:

Dot-coms that went public would be more valuable than GM in their first week. The big distortion was a dramatic overvaluation of anything related to the dot-coms or technology that defied any reason. You couldn't even argue against it because people would just say that you didn't understand what was "really" happening. Chuck Clough was a top strategist, and he was saying that the trend is real but the valuations can't be sustained. And he was practically booted out of here. He retired. It turns out he was correct. In fact, all of our macro people thought the whole thing was getting out of control, but people just disregarded them.

BOB MCCOOEY (chief executive officer of New York Stock Exchange floor brokerage firm and trading house Griswold Company):

At one point in the nineties Charles Schwab's market cap [a company's value in the stock market] passed Merrill Lynch's. That as much as anything was symbolic of the times. People were focused on the Internet as the great growth area and chose to make anyone who had anything to do with it a winner. And if you weren't an Internet company you were a loser.

KENNETH PASTERNAK:

We [Knight Trading] rode up to a market value where we were up there with PaineWebber, Lehman, and Bear Stearns in market cap. I thought our value was a little stretched, but we were trading at twenty or twenty-five times pretax income, so it's not as if we were completely out of line. You look at eBay or Yahoo and they were getting valuations that were well beyond anything we had.

ARTHUR LEVITT JR. (former Securities and Exchange Commission chairman):

The culture of our society came to idealize the trader. He was a powerful individual who could move millions of dollars with a keystroke. We saw this in books and movies and on television. So when individuals were given the ability to move significant amounts of money with the stroke of a laptop key, they took advantage of that. They emulated the image of success and strength and power and money, but they lacked the experience or emotional discipline to do what their professional idols were doing with greater levels of success.

MICHAEL LEWIS (journalist and author of *The New New Thing*):

After the boom went on for a few years, and more and more companies were going public and taking off, I thought it almost didn't matter if it was the bubble or if it was real, because the bubble was having real consequences. It was doing things like putting value money managers out of business. Look at Julian Robertson at Tiger. He flamed out because he didn't believe in the Internet. All these people went down because they didn't believe, and all these other people were going up because they did believe. So to think of it as just a bubble is not quite right, because there were lots of real consequences.

DAVID KAUFMAN:

It was a time when if you had an idea and maybe a good management team it was fairly easy to raise capital. The rule of thumb was you could raise $2 million and give up 20 percent of your company. And if you wanted to make even more money, you didn't take that $2 million because everyone was convinced that it was expensive money at 20 percent. So you waited until you had revenues or your idea was on the table, and in the next round of financing your valuation would be better and the appraisals would be higher. Then you could raise $2 million and give up only 10 percent or 5 percent of your company. That really was the problem in the 1990s. Everyone was taking the money and burning through it right away with advertising and promotions and marketing and infrastructure. I had a client that went through $20 million pretty quickly, and when it came time for the second round of financing they thought it was going to be pretty easy again. But it wasn't there.

MICHAEL LEWIS:

If nothing else, it was an exotic time in American financial life. There were all sorts of wonderful side effects, and I can't help admitting I enjoyed many of them thoroughly. I really did like seeing that all of a sudden the Wall Street investment banker was sort of a second-tier character. The most important guy was the guy who started the business. I thought that was neat. The guy who started the business was bossing around these Wall Street characters. That never happened before — it was always the Wall Street guys bossing around the guy who owned the business. In a way, capital became cheap, because everybody was doing IPOs, so the people who controlled access to it were therefore not as important. I thought that was wonderful. It's sort of the way things should work in an ideal world. So a lot of this stuff I was sad to see go, even if it was all a little unreal.

LISE BUYER:

For Wall Street, it meant that there were so many new companies to follow that you needed a whole fleet of new research analysts who hadn't lived through the era when integrity was the only thing an analyst had to sell. The analysts who'd been around for a while understood that you couldn't recommend something you didn't believe in, because all you had was your integrity, and as soon as you screwed that up you were done. But these new guys came into the business at a time when making an outrageous statement got you great publicity. It got you on the front pages of all the business sections of all the newspapers and on CNBC, and that in turn had all the individual investors listening to you, and that in turn became important to investment-banking clients. If they're going to go public, they're going to want to do it with the analyst who they kept reading about. And that turned into huge paydays for the analysts.

I guess one example of that would be — and I don't mean to pick on the guy — but you had Henry Blodget, who was a relatively new analyst at Oppenheimer, saying that Amazon was going to go to $400 a share. There was never any math behind it. But there was so much momentum behind it that he turned out to be right. It did go to $400 a share. Whether or not it should've gone to $400 is irrelevant — it did. So the people who listened to Henry Blodget made money that day. And the people who listened to the more fundamental analysts who said, "I don't think this thing's worth more than $50," well, they missed out — at that time. That became wonderfully lucrative for Henry. And it became wonderfully lucrative for Op Co, and later for Merrill Lynch, after he moved over there. Again, I don't want to pick on him, because he only acted rationally. He understood what people were paying for, that these were momentum-driven stocks. But the flip side of that is, when you don't have the solid underlying analysis going on, it becomes hard to argue with your banker.

JERRY KENNEY:

With Henry, we brought him in and told him that there was no chance that most of these companies were going to succeed. So we really wanted him to have some more balance. But it was hard for him because you've got to be on TV, and everybody wants to know which ones you like. And because he happened to be good-looking and articulate, he got even more attention. It was a tough spot and it was a difficult thing to manage.

FRANK PETRILLI (chief executive officer of TD Waterhouse):

You look at the era of the IPO heyday and show me a sell recommendation on a company that a firm has done business with. It was very, very rare — not a pretty picture if you're looking for unbiased research.

TOM BROWN (former bank-stock analyst at Donaldson, Lufkin and Jenrette):

If you put a sell rating on a company, the company would cut you off from information. This happened to me with First Union. They would then not let you come in and meet with management. They would tell you that they were not going to return your phone calls.

EVELYN Y. DAVIS (well-known shareholder activist):

Don't ever trust the analysts. If an analyst says a company is going to earn $3 a share you better take off a third and assume it's going to be $2 a share. This has been the case for a long time. When I bought my first stock in the 1950s I was a customer of Merrill Lynch, and they recommended Safeway. I had studied business administration at George Washington so I had an idea of how things worked. Right away I found out that the chairman of the board at Safeway, Robert Magowan, was married to the daughter of the chairman of Merrill Lynch. So right away I could see the conflict of interest there. You have to be pretty dumb not to see why they were making that recommendation.

HERBERT ALLEN JR. (head of Allen and Company):

They're not even recommending stocks that they believe in. They're recommending stocks that the parent company wants them to recommend so they can get the investment-banking business.

WILLIAM HAMBRECHT:

In my mind research and investment banking always were intertwined. At Hambrecht and Quist, for the first ten years of our business, we didn't have a corporate finance department. We only had research. My theory was that I needed people who could tell me which semiconductor company to back. There was no financial engineering involved. The financial engineering of taking somebody public through equity is pretty simple.

MICHAEL LEWIS:

The truth is, the endorsement was just a rubber stamp that meant you were giving the investment bank your business. I don't know if there's a case of an Internet company hiring Morgan Stanley, or Goldman Sachs, or whoever, to take them public only to find that the firm's analyst was saying, "Actually, this isn't such a good deal."

JERRY KENNEY:

If you look at the way Frank Quattrone's operation was structured [at Deustche Morgan Grenfell and Credit Suisse First Boston], the analysts reported to him and he got a percent of the spread. So it was very simple — the analyst's job was to support the business, not analyze the company. We learned decades ago that you can't do that.

LISE BUYER:

I don't know the experience of others, but I can honestly say that when I screamed and yelled that this was a crummy company, we didn't do it. I didn't feel pressured to say things about companies that I didn't believe in. I don't think that's what Quattrone's group was about at all. Of course, that's what the perception was because Frank was on the front page of the *Wall Street Journal* having made $100 million in a year. Again, I don't know what went on at other banks. But I know what went on at my bank. And I know that the things I've read, published things, about Quattrone simply weren't true. We need a scapegoat.

Does that mean that everybody behaved well all the time? It does not. Was there a junior analyst at the firm who might've felt different pressures than I did? There may well have been. I wouldn't know because I wasn't in that situation. But I was in meetings with bankers and analysts from all the other banks, and there wasn't a thing different between First Boston and anyone else that you can name.

HERBERT ALLEN JR.:

If you're actually buying the analyst's opinion, isn't that a fundamental corruption of the business? Why is the analyst involved to begin with? It's a level of corruption that's right in front of your face. If we had an SEC that was more aggressive, we'd be looking into this stuff. I'm not a tub-thumper, and I'm not going to run around screaming about injustices. I'm even benefiting from it. But I'm saying it's wrong.

ARTHUR LEVITT JR.:

A firm that is conflicted by representing the interests of both investment-banking clients and their research function is likely to tailor the research in a way that would satisfy their investment-banking clients, often to the detriment of their retail clients. The conflict is a significant one, and one that works against the interests of the individual investor.

MICHAEL LEWIS:

A few of these stocks just popped. And once that happened, investors started buying the stocks, not because they believed the story, but because they knew these stocks popped. So, it didn't require Mary Meeker [of Morgan Stanley] and Henry Blodget to drive the phenomenon. I think investors largely did it to themselves, but analysts were cast in the role of cheerleaders, and when the game was cast as corrupt, all of a sudden the activities of the cheerleaders were regarded in a different light.

LISE BUYER:

The truth is, many of these stocks went through the roof before any analysts were covering them. So, once the Wall Street firms picked them up, these analysts had to come up with a way to explain the valuation. You couldn't do it on earnings, because there were none, so maybe you could use revenues. But I think that's where the eyeballs thing came from — how do we value this thing? Well, Yahoo's got a lot of people staring at it, so it must be that over time somebody's going to be able to translate those eyeballs into dollars.

JAMES CRAMER (CNBC talk-show host, journalist, and former hedge-fund manager):

Maybe these companies shouldn't have been valued on revenues. Maybe they should have been valued on having $150 million in the bank, and as long as that money was in the bank it was worth X, and as soon as the money ran out it should be worth zero. It was very hard to figure out valuations, so we came upon different ratios and formulas: price-to–forward revenues, page metrics, reach. These were all faulty. None of them really produced real valuations. "Planet Rx is the number-one eyeball media metrics play in the category" — that doesn't mean anything at all. A company with one-tenth the reach, Merckmedco.com, is much more profitable. So it turned out we used a lot of flawed methodology and valuations. It became kind of routine to do it wrong.

JENNIFER WILLIAMS (New York Stock Exchange floor broker for Griswold Company):

As time wore on, into 1999 and especially in early 2000, I think the fear started to sink in a little bit. It can't keep going on. The earnings valuations in some of these stocks were 200-to-1, which is absolutely ridiculous historically. Who buys a stock at 200 times its earnings? That's just stupid. But the rah-rah feeling was, I imagine, pretty close to what was going on in 1929. That said, having gone through '29 and through the sixties and the eighties, I think we understood that there was going to be a top and when we hit it, it wasn't going to be pretty.

KENNETH PASTERNAK:

At the end there was a complete abdication of any kind of responsible investment model. And then what happened was what always happens when stock-market bubbles end. Eventually the money flows change and people realize that the musical chairs have stopped and there's kind of a panic. That's basically the pattern with all stocks caught up in a euphoria. I remember during the AIDS scare, when the disease was first discovered, there was a condom stock that was going through the roof. And we figured that if every male in the world screwed three times a day this company was still overvalued. The stock went up 10 points a day for around twenty days. But eventually everybody looked around, realized there were no more chairs, and ran for the exits. That thing came down 100, 150 points fast enough to make your head spin.

IAN WEINBERG:

In February 2000, I remember I was on Presidents' Day weekend vacation with my kids, and I got a call at the hotel I was staying at from a client who was so excited about something that he'd seen on CNBC that he wanted to back up the truck and load up on JDS Uniphase. I remember this goofy fund manager named Eric Gustafson, who managed a fund called Stein Roe Young Investors at the time, and maybe CNBC liked the guy's name, maybe they liked the way he looked, maybe he had a good track record for a year. But this guy had no idea what he was talking about. And he got up on a soapbox and screamed that the greatest stock over the next few years was JDS Uniphase because of their business. I think the call from the client came six minutes after it aired.

JULIAN ROBERTSON (former head of Tiger Management, at one time the largest hedge fund in the world):

The stock market becomes a bubble when you can no longer do an analysis of how you can provide returns to the investor. People just forget that providing returns is the name of the game. Instead, they buy a stock to resell it because they think the next person will want to pay more for it. They're no longer buying because they think it's a good company and they want to hold on to it until it does well. Those are two very different things, see? There's a short-term and a long-term view. I think it's very good to look at investing as a long-term entity, something that you hold on to.

I didn't understand what was going on in the market anymore. My theory of owning the best stocks in the world and shorting the worst stocks in the world was suddenly not only not profit making, it was a recipe for bankruptcy. Looking at these stocks objectively, the Internets were the worst stocks out there, and yet they were going up 500, 600,

1,000 percent per year. You short something like that too often and you'll be killed pretty quickly.

ROBERT OLSTEIN:

By the time we reached 2000 I was ready to retire. I thought I'd lost my marbles. I didn't understand JDS Uniphase or Yahoo and the valuations they were getting. I was up 35 percent in 1999 and didn't even come in in the top 25 percent of all funds. I was buying "old economy" stocks because they were so damn cheap. We have a hard-core bunch of investors who have been with me forever, and even some of our hard-core people were taking some of their money out of my fund to give it to the Internet funds and everyone else that was exploding.

LISE BUYER:

There used to be rules — well, not technical rules, but sort of internal beliefs — about when a company should go public. Basically, it was if the company didn't have at least $10 million in trailing twelve-month revenue, then you wouldn't take them public. These weren't official rules, but that's basically the way it was for the better firms — the smaller firms would act differently. Part of the thinking on that was, give the company a chance to coalesce. Make sure everyone knows where the staplers are and where the copy room is before you take the thing public. By the time you've amassed $10 million of revenue everybody basically knows what's going on at the company.

But the market had such an appetite for these new emerging companies that it became unrealistic to wait that long to take something public. Somebody, somewhere would get it done, so you might as well do it. It was going to happen. It was not the investment bankers foisting these things on the public. This was about investors in general, institutional investors and individual investors, who were upset that only the high-net-worth venture guys had the chance to make money on these emerging start-ups. They said, "That's not fair, just because we're the little guy. We should have a chance at it, too."

WILLIAM HAMBRECHT:

Traditionally, an IPO was priced at a small discount to the market to make the first-time buyer feel good. To me, that was perfectly logical because most institutional buyers hold the winners and sell the losers. So when I would go out in the sixties, seventies, and eighties, when I was doing some of these small deals, I'd tell the companies, "Look, if we think it'll sell at $12 or $13, let's do it at $11 or $12. Because the Fidelity guy will buy it and he'll hold it. It gives him bragging rights, and it shows that he's a winner. Then, if you need money the next year, he'll come back and happily average out. Whereas, if you come at $14 and it goes to $11 he'll sell it and you won't hear from him again because he doesn't want to apologize for the losers." So I felt there was a very valid reason for this discount.

Now, what happened in the nineties is, the markets are very smart, and people figured out that there was a guaranteed profit here. So the big-commission-generator guys figured it out and said, "Hey, I should capture some of that value for my shareholders." So the big funds that generated a lot of mutual fund commissions and therefore were the best customers for the underwriters, they would come in and put in orders for 10 percent of each deal, knowing it was going to be discounted. The academics will tell you that what you're doing here is creating an economic rent. This is effectively a guaranteed profit. And people will bid for it. So hedge funds started bidding for it, small guys started bidding for it.

LISE BUYER:

As of March of 2003, 1,705 technology companies had gone public in the last 22 years. They created approximately $1.6 trillion in public market wealth, up 275 percent from their IPO valuation of $614 billion. So that's the good news. Now, of those 1,705 companies, 65 were up more than 1,000 percent from their IPO valuation, and just 5 percent of the 1,705 accounted for 100 percent of the net-wealth creation.

JACK BOGLE (founder of Vanguard Group, president of Bogle Markets Research Center, and former chairman of Wellington Management):

The bubble really was a happy conspiracy. You had directors who were not supervising management the way they were supposed to. You had management focusing on the price of the stock rather than the value of the corporation. You had the onset of quarterly earnings guidance, where companies were giving Wall Street constant guidance on their quarterly earnings. It makes no sense at all to do that — you just get pressure to meet those goals. You had executives paid on the price of the stock rather than the value of the business they'd built — that is to say, paid on illusion rather than reality. So what you get is executives hyping their stock. You had the Wall Street hype machine, the analysts, out in full force. You had accountants providing more consulting services than auditing services, so they were conflicted. You had lawyers getting pieces of underwritings and all that. You saw regulation, through political pressure, being relaxed. In short, you saw every single factor that could make things worse join in this happy conspiracy.

So it was a bubble, and in the end these kinds of things eventually break from the amount of air that gets into them. It's like a balloon. It gets bigger and bigger and then it bursts. In this case it was mostly hot air.

Hot air indeed. On January 14, 2000, the Dow Jones Industrial Average reached its all-time high of 11,723. Two months later, on March 10, the Nasdaq stock market peaked at 5,048. By the end of the year that number would be cut in half. It would take a little longer for the Dow stocks to crack, but eventually the entire stock market would be dragged down by the burst bubble.

As is so often the case, the market decline would expose the real seamy side of the Street and result in some serious consequences for a few key players. But before reality could truly set in, the financial community—and the rest of the country—would have to face a terror more frightening than a stock market crash.

CHAPTER 29

MORE THAN JUST BUSINESS

On September 11, 2001, radical Islamic terrorists hijacked four commercial jet airliners on the East Coast of the United States with the intent of attacking the very heart of America. Their targets: the White House and Pentagon in Washington, and the World Trade Center towers in New York City, just a few blocks north of Wall Street. The symbolism of the targets was lost on no one.

At 8:46 that morning, the first plane struck the north tower of the World Trade Center, followed seventeen minutes later by a second plane hitting the south tower. Within an hour, a third plane would dive into the Pentagon, while a fourth would crash in a field in Pennsylvania before reaching its presumed destination, the White House. At one minute to ten in the morning on September 11, 2001, the south tower of the World Trade Center collapsed to the ground. A half hour later, the north tower came down as well.

For Wall Street, the disaster brought very real consequences. The bond-trading house Cantor Fitzgerald, which was headquartered on the top floors of the north tower, lost 658 of its 1,800 employees. The investment-banking and re-

search firm Keefe, Bruyette and Woods, which was based on the 89th floor of the south tower, lost 67 of its 224 employees. The investment bank Sandler O'Neill, which was on the 104th floor of the south tower, lost 66 of its 171 employees. And those are just a few of the firms that suffered losses among the nearly 3,000 people who died that day. The combined loss of Wall Street brainpower on that single morning was staggering.

From a practical standpoint, the immediate response from the nation's two largest stock markets — the New York Stock Exchange, which is a few blocks away from the site of the World Trade Center, and the Nasdaq Stock Market, which was headquartered across the street — was first to delay trading before the markets opened at nine thirty that morning, and then to shut it down altogether. The disaster had destroyed the telecommunications system in lower Manhattan, so it would have been pointless to do anything else. Major Wall Street firms Merrill Lynch and Lehman Brothers, which were based across the street in the World Financial Center, were displaced. Morgan Stanley had to relocate 2,700 employees who had worked at the World Trade Center. As the days ahead unfolded, it truly wasn't clear when Wall Street would be able to get back up on its feet and start trading again.

WICK SIMMONS (former Nasdaq chairman):

I was on the fiftieth floor of 1 Liberty Plaza, which was right across the street from the World Trade Center. So I was right there looking at it. I was at my desk at about twenty of nine when I heard this incredible roar, and I thought my building had been hit with something. It was just so loud. Now, if you know Liberty Plaza, you know that the fiftieth floor equates to about the seventy-fifth floor of the Trade Center because we were on a hill looking down on it. I remember I looked up from my desk, and right there in my window was this huge fireball coming at me. There was nothing between us. Then, from underneath this fireball, came an enormous plume of paper, and it blew right up into the air over the top of us.

MICHAEL LABRANCHE (chairman of New York Stock Exchange specialist firm LaBranche and Company):

I was at my desk that morning and the day before, September 10, our firm had issued a profit warning. So I was sitting there watching CNBC, and Maria Bartiromo was giving an update on the market and what the movers were going to be that day. And she started talking about how LaBranche was going to be heading down because of the profit warning. So I flipped off the TV and went down in the elevator to walk over to the stock exchange, which is a two-block walk from my office, because I had a meeting there with a few executives from Denver. I got out of the elevator and walked out on the street and all this paper was floating in the air. I saw some guy running down the street and I said, "Is there a ticker-tape parade today or something?" And he said, "No, I think a plane flew into the Trade Center." I asked what kind of plane, and he said, "I think it was a Cessna."

WICK SIMMONS:

I really thought it was one of those small planes that normally fly up and down the Hudson River. I thought, "Oh my God, what a horrible accident." I didn't put two and two together that the fireball was much bigger than anything a plane like that could cause. But then, you didn't expect anything like this to ever happen. So, to me it was this gigantic accident. Then everything started to fall out of the building.

MICHAEL LABRANCHE:

I walked up to the World Trade Center, which was another two blocks up, and the fire was wrapped around the building and it was huge. But I couldn't see the hole because I was on the east side of the building and the hole was on the north side. So I went to my appointment at the stock exchange, but I told them I had to leave because I wanted to check our systems because something was happening at the Trade Center.

JENNIFER WILLIAMS (New York Stock Exchange floor broker for Griswold Company):

After the first plane hit the Trade Center, a bunch of us were watching the news on the TV in the stock-exchange luncheon club, and everyone was commenting on the plane crash. They had a live picture of the World Trade Center and you could see it burning. All of a sudden the TV went snowy, no reception, and we heard the loudest *bang* in the entire world. The whole building shook. The pressure on the windows in the luncheon club — which is this old gentlemen's smoking club, there wasn't even a ladies' room in there until about ten years ago — was so extreme that I thought they would just explode. And then all this shit started flying past the windows, paper, debris, just crap. We all stopped and our jaws dropped. About three seconds later — and these were the longest three seconds of my life — the TV came back on and — remember, TV runs on a delay — you could see the second plane slamming into the building. That's what we had felt. So we felt it, and then we saw it. And that's when somebody came running into the room and said, "Get out! We're evacuating the building!"

JERRY GENTILELLA (barber at the New York Stock Exchange since 1963):

On September 11 I had my first customer at eight thirty, and as soon as I finished with my customer we saw people running all over the place. We thought, what's going on? People aren't supposed to be running around here. But my barbershop is in the basement of the exchange so we didn't hear the crash or feel anything. We just saw all the people running everywhere.

ROBERT NEWBURGER (executive director of the New York Stock Exchange Alliance of Floor Brokers and member of the exchange since 1940):

The whole stock exchange shook. People started running every which way. People were crying, particularly women, saying that they wanted to go home and be with their babies. It was a kind of pandemonium in here with nobody really knowing where to go. I remember looking outside and just seeing this cloud of debris. Little pieces of burnt paper were piled a foot high on the ledges of the buildings across the street.

WICK SIMMONS:

So we got everybody on our floor away from the window side of the building and back in the alcoves where the elevators are. I went back into my office to get the stuff I needed, and I saw the second plane hit the building. Then you knew exactly what was happening. See, I'd been in that building many times before. I spent eight years of my life [while at Shearson] on the 106th floor of that south tower. I remember the instructions we got at that time of what to do in case of fire. On that floor, fire, by definition, had to happen below you because there was nothing above you. So our escape was to the roof, and we'd be picked up off the roof by helicopters.

Looking out the window of my office I could see the building burning in the middle, and I saw some people. When the second building started to burn we got everybody down those fifty flights. People were remarkably orderly. I went around and swept everybody up off the floor, making sure nobody was there. I missed one person, Lillian, who came back and was looking for her boss, who'd already gone down. But eventually we got everybody down and out.

JENNIFER WILLIAMS:

We all left the building. There were like three thousand people in their trading jackets standing around on Broad Street in front of the stock exchange. Nobody's cell phone worked because the primary cellular tower for downtown Manhattan was the World Trade Center. So everybody was frantically trying to get a signal but it was impossible. I wanted to call my mother just to say I was alive and okay, but the line at the pay phone on the corner was about twenty-five people long. I stood there, praying that I had a quarter. Luckily I did.

MICHAEL LABRANCHE:

Our building had been evacuated so all our employees were out on the street, on Broadway. One of our employees came running up from the exchange, shouting that the Pentagon had been attacked. We all said, "Calm down. People are starting to get a little carried away." But there was a bank nearby with a TV monitor on, and it was showing the Pentagon on fire. We couldn't believe it.

JENNIFER WILLIAMS:

So we were all milling around in front of the exchange wondering what we were supposed to do. Then the word came that it was safer to be inside than outside; but it was just mass confusion. And here's the sick part, we were all still under the impression that we might be opening for business that day. We knew that we wouldn't open on time, but we were fairly confident that the market was going to open. That's why we were all standing around; that's why I went back after I spoke to my mom. I ran into my boss's brother, Tim McCooey, who also works for the firm. He said, "Everybody at the firm has left. Go home." I said, "Timmy, what if we open and there's nobody here?" He said, "Bob says if you don't leave you're fired."

I went back in the building to change because I was still in my trading jacket. I put my suit jacket back on and called my mom again because everything in the stock exchange was working. We have a separate generator and communications system in case of an emergency, so our phones and electricity still were on. So I told my mom that I was going to try to get home. And she said that from her rooftop — she lives at UN Plaza, right next to the United Nations — they could see the buildings on fire. She told me that they were watching TV and that the police were shutting down the city below Fourteenth Street. And then she said, "Whatever you do, don't get on the subway because you don't want to get stuck in a tunnel." So I left my Doc Martens on because I figured I was in for a hike, took my purse, and walked out of the building.

I headed east toward Water Street, just to get as far away from the World Trade Center as I could. And as I turned up Water Street I heard the loudest crash I'd ever heard in my entire life. People started screaming and running and looking over their shoulders. I swear to God, it looked like something out of a B-grade horror movie. But this was real. So I looked down the street and all of a sudden this rolling cloud of gray smoke, it looked like a wave, started coming for us. At that point everyone started running.

MICHAEL LABRANCHE:

We just had no idea what was going on. No one knew. We were just standing there, waiting. So when the buildings fell we had no idea what was happening. That cloud of smoke and dust and debris just came rolling down Broadway and you couldn't see anything, you couldn't see up into the sky. We just started running to get away from the cloud, but there was no way to avoid it. It just overtook us.

FRANK PETRILLI (chief executive officer of TD Waterhouse):

The day was so eerie and weird. Time stood still. We just sat there and watched the clouds of dust roll in.

WICK SIMMONS:

I had to call off business at the Nasdaq market. Somehow I had to make contact with somebody, so I grabbed a cell phone and it was useless. The towers were gone, I didn't even think about that. So I had to find a landline. I walked down to Prudential, where I'd been [the CEO] for ten years. When we were about two-thirds of the way over there, the north tower came down. We heard this rush and then a huge cloud of crap came and smothered us. So we were covered with shit by the time we got over there. They'd all evacuated the building, and I found a fellow by the name of Hank DiGenest, who was the director of security over there, and he let me up onto the twentieth floor. And it was there that I called the SEC and the treasury, and we had a conference call with [then NYSE chairman] Dick Grasso at the stock exchange, so we could call off all the markets. I spent the next hour at Prudential, trying to locate things and make sure that we were shut down properly. Then we commandeered a car and got out of the city.

JENNIFER WILLIAMS:

I made my way to Fourteenth Street, running and walking as briskly as I could, and when I got there I started looking for a cab. I was exhausted, I'd gone about four miles, and I just wanted to get home to my dog and my cat. I spotted an empty cab and said to the driver that I needed to go uptown, and he said, "Screw you, I'm going home." I looked at him and said, "I'll give you a hundred bucks to drive me home." And he goes, "Okay, get in." It took us an hour and a half to get to the Upper East Side. I even picked up a lady on the way who also was trying to get uptown.

MICHAEL LABRANCHE:

I had to find out where people were and from our systems guys what was working and what wasn't. Mostly I was worried about the people. I remember one of our assistants had a sister who worked in the World Trade Center, and she had run up there to find her sister. That was the kind of thing that was on my mind.

JERRY GENTILELLA:

That night I stayed at the exchange and slept in my barbershop. I live on Staten Island and the ferry wasn't running. There were no restaurants open or anything. I ate a couple of bananas that I had left lying around, and I went to sleep. The next day I went home.

JENNIFER WILLIAMS:

After I got home and calmed down, that night I took my dog out for a walk. And I remember there were all these people out in the cafés enjoying themselves. The only word I could think of for that was surreal. These people were sitting out having their glass of wine and spinach salad, like nothing had happened that day. I remember thinking, how nice it would be to be you right now.

HARVEY PITT (former chairman of the Securities and Exchange Commission):

For the financial markets, the immediate impact of the attack was it took out the communications network that the exchanges and Nasdaq relied upon. We immediately called together the President's Working Group on Financial Markets — the chairman of the SEC, the chairman of the Federal Reserve Board, the secretary of the treasury, and the chairman of the Commodity Futures Trading Commission. We began communicating with everyone. We were talking to the self-regulatory bodies and all the various markets. I had senior staff in the building that basically ended up camping out in my office. We did not evacuate. People went home, but my reaction was that we had to be at a place that was reachable.

PETER FISHER (former undersecretary of the treasury for domestic finance):

The equity markets didn't open and bond markets were open but then with the loss, tragically, of Cantor Fitzgerald key pieces of the infrastructure of the bond market suddenly were not there. The Federal Reserve kept operating to keep the core function of banking going.

WICK SIMMONS:

The Manhattan infrastructure went down. For Nasdaq, our infrastructure wasn't in Manhattan, so we could've traded that day, right then and there. Nasdaq is really just a big electronic network. It has no fixed assets on the ground like the stock exchange, except in its plants in Connecticut and Maryland. But what happened was all the connectivity of the New York firms was lost.

HARVEY PITT:

I was in touch with [Dick] Grasso, and Wick Simmons, and [National Association of Securities Dealers CEO] Rob Glauber, and others. The first decision was to delay the opening. I was concerned about the credibility of trading. What I didn't want was trading activity that might take place when there was no ability to verify, when professionals couldn't basically ensure that their customers were treated fairly, and the like. This was sort of a constant discussion.

WICK SIMMONS:

On that day, it was suggested by some, what I'll call "voices" in Washington, that Nasdaq should maybe open for trading. That was kind of the hubris of Washington, that we should have something open, to show that nothing can take us down. But there was no way we could do that. With the New York Stock Exchange down, which it had to be because of its location, the only stocks that would be trading would be Nasdaq stocks. If people want to sell stocks you can't just tell them, you can sell this, but not that. So we all decided to shut down.

HARVEY PITT:

It became clear that with the knockout of power there was going to be a real problem. So after the initial decision was made to delay the opening, and after consulting with us, the markets decided not to open. I thought that was important because once the markets were going to shut down I wanted investors to have a sense that this was only a temporary glitch and the markets would reopen just as quickly as we could ensure that the process would go as smoothly as everybody had a right to expect.

PETER FISHER:

Even that first day I was very focused on the idea that we didn't want to keep the markets closed for very long. We don't like closing markets. We think it's better for anxieties to express themselves in asset prices than to bottle it up.

HARVEY PITT:

I went up to New York the very next day, on September 12, and convened a meeting of the heads of all the major firms, together with Verizon, Con Ed, the mayor's office, the governor's office, the self-regulators. All of that was designed to satisfy us that everybody was on the same page and that we were all going to proceed together on this, which I thought was important, and that nobody was going to be out of step.

PETER FISHER:

The next morning, Thursday the thirteenth, Dick Grasso led a meeting at the stock exchange for all the infrastructure people. I'm talking about infrastructure people of all types: banking infrastructure, the Fed, Verizon, the city, water, electricity, police, all the different moving parts. If you think about it, it's all the stuff we take for granted every day, all the stuff that you just assume is going to work, and then we can run this extraordinary machine known as our modern economy. And if you don't know that it's going to be there, you have to re-create the confidence that it will be.

HARVEY PITT:

Getting the New York Stock Exchange running was critical because it was the marketplace that not only had the largest trading volume in the largest U.S. listed companies, but also effectively was the pricing mechanism for the rest of the financial markets. All derivative instruments, in one way or another, trade off the prices that get set on the New York Stock Exchange.

WICK SIMMONS:

We were going to open together — Nasdaq and New York — whenever that happened. We were going to make sure that the rules of trading, the time of trading, were uniform. In a sense, what we wanted to do was get the country's financial markets back on their feet at once, as opposed to opening one here, one there. It had to be a cooperative effort.

BOB MCCOOEY (chief executive officer of New York Stock Exchange floor brokerage firm and trading house Griswold Company):

The main problem with opening the stock exchange was an infrastructure issue. Literally, how do you get people downtown? There was soot and dust and debris everywhere. Basically, all of downtown was completely nuts. The whole area was cordoned off, so trying to get people in immediately afterward would've been impossible. And some of our major customers were hit. In addition to the firms that were in the Trade Center, over in the World Financial Center you had Merrill, Lehman, Oppenheimer, and they were out of commission, too.

JERRY CORRIGAN (Goldman Sachs managing director and former Federal Reserve Bank of New York president):

September 11 was a huge problem for the entire financial system. We had hundreds of billions of dollars of failed deliveries of securities. It was a communications problem at the stock exchange, but parts of the system functioned throughout that week, and there were huge problems. They were all technical problems and eventually were settled. But the reason it didn't become a financial crisis is there were no credit scares.

One of the messages of the past is, when we have market events without credit scares, the market sorts them out by itself pretty well. It's the credit scare that really makes the difference. If you compare what happened in 1987 and 1998 — with Russia and Long-Term Capital — in both those periods there were real credit issues on the table, almost from day one. Certainly that was true in '87. But that was not the case in 2001, after September 11.

HARVEY PITT:

There's always the possibility of people becoming alarmed and concerned about the state of the financial markets when something like this happens. And then panic can set in — and people, of course, have panicked over less.

JERRY CORRIGAN:

Billions of dollars of liquidity were pumped into the market on September 11 and several days after. There was no statement from the Fed — as there was in 1987 — but everyone knew it. It was no secret. You can't keep that a secret anyway. But there was no real financial crisis. There was a human crisis, of course. But there was no real financial crisis. No one was afraid that people weren't going to get paid, or that their securities ultimately wouldn't be returned to them, that their collateral wouldn't be returned to them. They didn't know when it was going to happen. They knew it might take a few days. And everyone knew it might be messy. But they didn't have any serious doubt that they would be kept whole, in terms of cash, securities, or collateral.

As long as that's what people feel, then they're not going to get themselves too worked up. They're not going to radically alter their behavior. They're not going to try to do things out of self-interest to protect themselves. They're not going to say, "I won't deliver a security to him, because I don't know if he's going to deliver a security to me." It's when fear produces changes in behavior that things get dicey. Markets are all about behavior. It's not some laboratory experiment. Markets are real people responding to real things as they see them.

PETER FISHER:

On Thursday, the bond markets had opened, and that afternoon we determined that we would test the equity markets over the weekend, and if that went well we'd reopen on Monday. The important thing there was to give everyone a chance to do tests over the weekend to make sure they were ready for Monday.

JENNIFER WILLIAMS:

When we came to work that Monday, as soon as we got off the subway we had to show our driver's licenses and our New York Stock Exchange IDs because lower Manhattan was closed off except for people who worked at the stock exchange. The train didn't stop at Wall Street, so I got out at Bowling Green, and as I was walking up Broadway it was completely deserted and there were army tanks in the middle of the street. It was the weirdest experience. Here I was, all dolled up and ready to go to work on Wall Street, and it looked like a war zone. And that stench! Now I know what the smell of burning flesh is like — and it's not pretty. That smell pervaded the entire area. And it lasted down here for five months because they didn't even put the fires out until January. It stank down here for almost half a year.

WICK SIMMONS:

When we did finally open up the next week, I went down to Dick's opening at the NYSE and Dick came up to our closing ceremony. It was important to symbolically show that we were all acting together and nobody looked to take advantage of anyone else during this period of time. I think it was important for the country to know that its financial markets could rally, coordinate, and come back.

JENNIFER WILLIAMS:

I have never given or received as many hugs as I did that morning. We had lost two of our members. Two New York Stock Exchange members had been having breakfast at Windows on the World [in the north tower] that morning. The membership down here is tighter than most families. If something happens to one person everyone feels it. That was really hard. It was like having a member of your family perish.

MICHAEL LABRANCHE:

It was very emotional. On Monday the seventeenth people were happy that the market was opening, but it also was very, very emotional. Our neighborhood had been attacked.

JENNIFER WILLIAMS:

And then we went back to work, because the market doesn't stop for anyone. I've never been busier than I was September 17, 2001. The market was down something like 800 points at one point, it was bad. But I wasn't concerned about anything. I was grateful to be alive and that most everyone I knew had survived.

PETER FISHER:

Markets are trying to predict the future; it's all about the future. And the future was much more uncertain all of a sudden — values are down, investment horizons are shrinking, risk premiums are going up, asset values are coming down. So the losses didn't concern me at all. I was just ecstatic that things were working.

WICK SIMMONS:

Wall Street's a funny place. It's got its sharks and everybody takes advantage of everybody else. It's very much the nexus of capitalism. But at various times, particularly under pressure, Wall Street can work marvelously well together. Everybody knows one another. It's a tiny community in many ways. There are ten firms that account for 65 percent of its business. So if they can work together, everybody can.

PETER FISHER:

The attacks were against the bastion of capitalism. So the bastion of capitalism picked itself up, dusted itself off, and got on with business. I think that's what we all were looking for — because after that, then maybe we could try to move on, too.

When the markets reopened on September 17, 2001, it had been the longest shutdown of trading since the national banking holiday from March 4 to 14, 1933, during the Great Depression. The first day of trading was orderly, but the sentiment was decidedly negative. The Dow Jones Industrial Average fell 684 points to 8,920. It was the biggest one-day point decline in the history of the index, but in terms of percentage declines it wasn't in the top ten of all time. And when you consider the volume of shares that pumped through the system, it's remarkable it happened at all. On September 17, the New York Stock Exchange traded 2.37 billion shares, which at the time was a record. The week of September 17 to 21 was, at the time, the busiest week in the history of the exchange, as more than 10.5 billion shares, worth nearly $314 billion, were traded, all on a platform that had been decimated less than a week earlier.

For Wall Street, the disaster has led to an even further dispersal of the securities business from its traditional home on the southern tip of Manhattan. Lehman Brothers has left the area for good and set up shop in midtown, and Morgan Stanley hasn't returned its employees to lower Manhattan. But Merrill Lynch is back in its offices at the World Financial Center. And regardless of where they're located, all Wall Street firms have developed concrete contingency plans for backup operations and alternate trading sites in case something like that happens again.

CHAPTER 30

MUST COME DOWN

Although placing a specific time frame on a bubble isn't an exact science, most experts agree that the eye of the hurricane lasted from sometime in 1998 until early 2000, when the values of many Nasdaq technology stocks started to fall. In time, the entire market would be dragged down along with them, particularly as the downturn was exacerbated by the chaos, confusion, and depression that followed September 11, 2001. Terrorism didn't break the bubble, but it certainly didn't help with the recovery.

In the aftermath of the burst bubble there was plenty of finger-pointing and blame spread around. But as law enforcement started wading into Wall Street's business, examining exactly what went wrong and why, the findings were startling. First, New York State attorney general Eliot Spitzer uncovered egregious practices by Wall Street's analysts. As it turns out, Merrill Lynch's Henry Blodget was saying things to investors that he himself did not believe and Salomon Smith Barney's Jack Grubman was wearing two hats — one as an investment banker and the other as an analyst.

Then, Spitzer found that mutual fund companies were allowing certain wealthy portfolio managers to trade in and out of their funds after the trading day ended. This put ordinary investors at a disadvantage, which was distinctly contrary to the mutual fund industry's image as prudent fiduciaries. But perhaps the most staggering discoveries were in the level of greed that Wall Street and corporate America enjoyed in the 1990s. The scandals that dogged onetime stock-market darlings like Enron, WorldCom, and Tyco exposed a layer of corruption that was inconceivable. Eventually anger over excess in the executive suite would claim the New York Stock Exchange's longtime chairman Dick Grasso in a dispute over hundreds of millions of dollars in pay that the exchange's board awarded him.

As the numbers continued to total up, ordinary Americans were left to wonder if they ever should have trusted Wall Street in the first place.

JAMES CRAMER (CNBC talk-show host, journalist, and former hedge-fund manager):

The bubble's over now. The period started in November 1998 when TheGlobe.com went public, the first nonexistent company to go public. Most of them didn't really have a valid reason for being, or had customer-acquisition costs that would always be too high. I can always open a business where you give me a dollar and then I give you a dollar and at the end of the day nothing's happened.

MICHAEL LABRANCHE (chairman of New York Stock Exchange specialist firm LaBranche and Company):

If you look at the history of markets, what happens in bubbles is that toward the end, their leadership gets much narrower, meaning there are fewer and fewer stocks driving it. The breadth of the market really narrowed to what you'd call in retrospect the bubble stocks. But the rest of the market had started to go down a year earlier.

JOHN CALAMOS (chairman and chief executive officer of Calamos Investments):

You could see the hype in the valuations. When a stock is priced at 30 percent growth per quarter — *per quarter* — things are getting a little out of hand. And by the way, the stock is priced as if it's going to go on forever, so where's the upside? That's what we saw in the nineties—all that hype eventually took away the upside from these stocks and the whole thing imploded.

WILLIAM HAMBRECHT (cofounder of Hambrecht and Quist):

Barron's went and did a survey, and they found that all these companies were going to run out of money soon. That was like the guy biting the tulip bulb. It was right there in a *Barron's* article. All these companies that you love are going to be broke in a year. The attitude in the marketplace, I think, changed overnight with that article.

ALAN PATRICOF (venture capitalist and head of Patricof and Company):

I think [the *Barron's* article] was the seminal event, when people started looking at those Internet companies and saying, if it doesn't have enough cash, where's it going to get the cash?

ROBERT OLSTEIN (chairman of Olstein Financial Alert Fund):

To me, the top was put on by Barry Diller. I even wrote about it to my shareholders at the time. Diller turned down a deal for Lycos in March 2000. He'd made a tender offer and Lycos stock went from $50 to $100. So Lycos wanted $150, and he just said no. That's when I knew the prices had reached a top. Diller really wanted it, wanted the Internet, but he wasn't just going to pay any price. So he turned them down. I said to myself, "Are these guys from Lycos out of their minds? He's taking them out at a ridiculous price, and they want more?" When you're looking for signs of a top, that's what you're looking for.

BLAKE DARCY (former chief executive officer of DLJDirect and CSFBDirect):

I figured that we'd reached a top when AOL merged with Time Warner. Steve Case was probably the best negotiator of timing and strategy and deals through this whole period, and despite the fact that he's much maligned now, the fact is he wouldn't sell. And here he was selling to Time Warner, which was a good-quality company, but it sort of represented the big, slow, old economy. The message was that this is all going to come to an end, and Steve Case is getting out while he can.

LISE BUYER (Google director of business optimization and former senior equity analyst in Frank Quattrone's technology group at Deutsche Morgan Grenfell and Credit Suisse First Boston):

As we rolled into 2000, there was more and more evidence that things had peaked. There were still lots of companies going public, but we'd already burned through the ones that had real promise, and now everything that was going public was just lower and lower quality. Eventually it just imploded of its own weight.

FRANK PETRILLI (chief executive officer of TD Waterhouse):

We had a false sense of confidence. People had made so much money on paper that they didn't even notice when things started to slide. They just kept buying every IPO that came out until April of 2000. In April of 2000 it was so scary. The Nasdaq just kept going down over a period of about five to ten days around April 14. But we on Wall Street, it took us a year to realize that it wasn't coming back — a year. In February of 2001 when the market went down another 25 percent we said, "This baby is dead." Then we all started scrambling and restructuring and doing everything we could to survive.

BLAKE DARCY:

I remember being in Dubai on the day that the Nasdaq took its first big tumble. We were about to open up our first Middle East office. Of course, I was watching CNBC in Dubai, and I started thinking, "Oh, this probably wasn't such a great idea." But then listening to all the analysts come on and say, "No, no, no, this is just a blip," I can see why some people didn't see the end until it was too late.

DAVID KAUFMAN (certified public accountant and principal at Rothstein Kass):

I had a client who had a substantial amount of profits on paper from his stock portfolio. He was one of the founders of a Latin American Web site that had seen substantial growth and appreciation in the stock market. He was a very young guy who was in public relations and marketing, did some early work on the Web site, and left the company. He never actually sold his stock and eventually it was worth $15 million. But he recorded his transactions in such a way that he had a substantial amount of income that he had to pay tax on. At the time he came to me his stock was worth only $10 million, and he still had capital-gains taxes to pay on the $15 million.

This guy held on to his stock and waited and waited and waited, because he didn't want to believe that it wouldn't come back up. And he rode it to the point where the tax that he owed was greater than the amount of the proceeds he would receive when he sold his stock. Is that because of greed? Is that because of a lack of understanding of how the game is played? I don't know. If he had gotten out at the beginning instead of looking for the last dollar, he'd have $7 million or $8 million in his pocket. But at the end of the day he had to make a deal with the IRS because he couldn't afford to make his payments.

ARTHUR LEVITT JR. (former Securities and Exchange Commission chairman):

All bubbles are pricked by changes in the economy, overcapacity. These are economic issues, business issues. And once the public and the institutions see that they've been buying on hopes that may not be realized for more years than they had contemplated, it triggers selling. I think the aftermath of all bubbles is a period of economic Darwinism. The best and the strongest will make it and the rest will not. That's what markets are for.

WILLIAM HAMBRECHT:

What's interesting is that the boom in underwriting was not done by a bunch of rogue underwriters. These were the best underwriters in the business. It was the guys with the good reputations. The good underwriters, just seeing the economic benefit, it was hard for them to ignore. So they would do a $50 million deal that doubled, even if it was for a couple of kids with no experience and an idea that might or might not work. It just got them so much money.

If you looked at the 1999 underwritings, the average deal was $50 million and it went to $100 million. It doubled. The $50 million of underwriting became $100 million in market value. So that $50 million was basically guaranteed profit, which the underwriter would parcel out to his customers. He would basically get $15 million in commission-business flow back. That's why there was enormous incentive to underprice these IPOs at the start and then really support them in the aftermarket, to make sure they got this flip. So what you need is, you need a "greater fool."

IAN WEINBERG (financial adviser and president of Family Wealth and Pension Management):

I think a lot of people were thinking about making enough money to retire in five years. With the multiples continually expanding, a lot of people were thinking that they'd make a pile of money over a few years and never have to work again. And if you looked at how prices were going up, and if you thought that it would last forever, it really seemed possible. That was the greed; and it was the greed that convinced people that it was going to last forever — even when it clearly wasn't.

ROY SMITH (finance professor at New York University and former partner at Goldman Sachs):

Before we criticize greed too much, we have to remember that greed is only a motivation for business. Without greed business wouldn't exist. Call it avarice or incentives or whatever you want, but that's what it is.

LISE BUYER:

The investment banks faced the question of, are we the arbiters of taste? Or are we the enablers of the market? The market was saying, "We want to take the risk, let us at it." The banks could either say, "No, you aren't fit to own these things. You don't know enough, so you're not entitled to buy them." Or it could be, "It's a risk-reward system. We'll facilitate this transaction, but then you have to make your own decisions." The banks were being put in the position of telling their customers that they couldn't buy these stocks that were going through the roof, and that wasn't going to happen.

So, I think if it just ended there, then people really couldn't complain about Wall Street's behavior in the nineties. But of course it didn't end there. Then, you had analysts writing and saying things they didn't believe. Then the system became corrupted. Nobody ever forced an investor to buy these things, but the investors did believe that because an investment bank took something public it was a real tangible business. And banks took some businesses public that should not have become public, but they felt that they were fulfilling their role in a capitalist society. Everybody forgot to exercise judgment and now everybody's trying to blame the other guy.

STANLEY O'NEAL (Merrill Lynch chairman):

I read this book called *The New New Thing,* which I enjoyed immensely, and it uses a particular person and a series of deals to illustrate a few points about the Internet. One of those points is that the leverage and dynamics of the world of corporate finance have changed forever. As I was reading, I remember thinking to myself that while it was a highly entertaining book, the thesis was true only as long as the valuations held up and investors continued to fall all over themselves to invest in ideas. But the moment that stopped being the case, this thesis sort of started to break down. Like everything else, each new innovation and idea gets a little overwrought. There has to be a bringing back into balance at some point.

The first challenge Wall Street faced was Eliot Spitzer's investigation into the conflicts of interest in research at investment banks. And the poster child for the investigation became Merrill Lynch's Internet star Henry Blodget, who was telling people privately what he wouldn't say publicly — that many of these hot Internet stocks were dogs.

MICHAEL MAYO (bank-stock analyst at Prudential Securities and former bank-stock analyst at Credit Suisse First Boston):

I'm amazed at what Eliot Spitzer uncovered. I mean, you never expect to hear those comments in the first place, but some of the smoking guns they found were just ridiculous. What Henry Blodget said, what Jack Grubman did, is just beyond my understanding of what was possible in this business. What bothered me during the bubble were things that I thought were egregious practices, but that didn't approach what we found out later on. For example, I saw an analyst go on CNBC to talk about a bank merger that was announced that morning and in which his firm was representing one of the banks in the deal. I thought that was incredible. It's not illegal, just wrong. And analysts found different ways to curry favor with CEOs, like Phua Young at Merrill Lynch, who sent that $4,500 case of wine to Dennis Kozlowski [of Tyco]. It seemed more important for analysts at the time to be close to CEOs than to do good research for investors.

TOM BROWN (founder of Second Curve Capital and former bank-stock analyst at Donaldson, Lufkin and Jenrette):

A "Chinese wall" is designed to prevent the passing of inside information from the investment-banking side of a brokerage firm to the research side. In the 1990s the Chinese walls got eroded because Wall Street realized that the analysts had a greater value in promoting their investment-banking clients than they did in coming up with investment ideas and trying to make money for their investing clients. Brokerage firms have two sets of clients: people who invest and people who raise money. In the eighties there was more of a balancing of those interests. In the nineties the attitude wasn't openly stated but it basically was, "We'll screw the investing clients." The reason for this was that the most profitable thing a Wall Street firm could do was collect fees from its investment-banking clients. So they didn't really care about their investing clients. And the reason it could go on for so long was that you had a bull market in stocks where even shit floated, so nobody really complained.

JULIAN ROBERTSON (former head of Tiger Management, at one time the largest hedge fund in the world):

I think Henry Blodget got a little bit of a bad rap. Let's face it, Henry Blodget was relatively new to the game. He was a big hero and was in an area promoting a bubble along with a lot of other people. He was really in the mainstream of American thought at the time. There should've been some senior people in there who were looking at it from a no-nonsense basis, and who should've said, let's stop this.

MICHAEL MAYO:

The common theme in the 1990s is that people were paid to do different things than they were supposed to be doing. The auditors were getting paid to be consultants instead of examining the books. The analysts were getting paid to be investment bankers instead of looking at the companies critically. And the investment bankers were getting paid to create quick flipping transactions for rich executives instead of advising companies on the best course of action. They all were getting paid in such ways that they didn't have the financial incentive to serve their true client.

In May 1999 I basically put a sell rating on the banking industry. I knew this was a very difficult call to make. It was a major, professional, life-changing event. The reason was, sell ratings were basically obsolete, especially at the major brokerage firms. The market was in a period of euphoria and the investment banks were supporting that attitude, so there was a general bias against saying anything negative. But through our bottom-up work we saw that the quality of earnings was becoming weak, which was a sign of potential earnings shortfalls down the road. So we put sell ratings on the largest banks — J. P. Morgan, Chase, Citi, Bank One, and the industry overall.

I spoke at the morning meeting at CS First Boston and they were so shocked that they had me come back a half hour later just to make sure they'd heard me properly, particularly because this was after five years of me being quite bullish. To some degree people didn't believe it. But that day the entire stock market declined because of the call. Throughout the rest of the year I got a lot of backlash from all types. Some of the companies I covered reduced the investment business they gave us. I got some hostile phone calls from CEOs talking about the amount of investment-banking business they'd just given us. Then they wouldn't return my calls, wouldn't set up meetings, and wouldn't take my questions on conference calls. They would go out and literally make negative comments about me personally to investors and the press and top officials at my firm. The broad theme here is using power to achieve your goals. These companies were going to do everything they could to shut me up and put me out.

I eventually got fired from CS First Boston due to the merger with DLJ. I was the second analyst in two decades to be ranked in the top two in two different bank categories, and the analyst who replaced me, the analyst at DLJ, was ranked below me before the merger, and by the way, has remained below me in every year since. But of course I never got an actual answer as to why I was the one who they let go.

JERRY KENNEY (Merrill Lynch executive vice president of research and corporate strategy):

In retrospect, we could've managed this whole thing better because we'd seen it before and aren't surprised with the way everything's turned out. If anything, we're surprised because things actually are worse than we thought they'd be. So hopefully, the analysts now are chastened. Remember, most of the portfolio managers and analysts hadn't been through an equity bear market. Our equity business went straight up through the nineties. In fact, we didn't have a single down year in equities in the nineties. We never had a down year from the 1990 dip. And there were so many young portfolio managers and analysts that their attitudes became hard to manage. We were actually trying to manage them, but I would say that we didn't do it well enough. Since we could see what the outcome would be, we should've insisted that we were right no matter what anyone said. But the people in the marketplace didn't want to hear what we had to say.

On April 28, 2003, Spitzer, along with SEC chairman William Donaldson and other state securities regulators, announced a $1.4 billion agreement where *ten of Wall Street's largest investment banks accepted fines and reforms to settle allegations that they put out biased stock research during the stock-market bubble of the late 1990s. In effect, the banks admitted that they had put their own interests in luring investment-banking clients ahead of the interests of ordinary investors. Among the key points in the settlement, Wall Street was required to put together an independent research fund that would provide unbiased analysis of the financial markets, to set up an investor-education program, to tally the performance of analysts each quarter, and to end the practice of using hot IPOs to curry favor with executives and board members of prospective investment-banking clients.*

ROY SMITH:

I think if you got together serious, well-meaning professionals from all the Wall Street firms and asked them to evaluate the Spitzer reforms, they'd say, here's a guy who's reforming things and he doesn't know what he's talking about. So we've had a lot of wasted motion that costs money and is a big burden. Therefore, it increased the costs of research or providing access to capital, and in the end this cost is borne by the market users, not by the manufacturers of the products.

So Eliot Spitzer's essentially made the markets more expensive for investors. There is room for some flagellation because of the revelations of various abuses, but I don't think we've got a very good picture of what the abuses were or where the flagellations have been applied. We had something like ten thousand analysts employed during the time that Spitzer was investigating, and as far as I know only two of them have been named as people who were deserving of punishment, Henry Blodget and Jack Grubman. They didn't even name Mary Meeker or a lot of other people. So if it was such a terrible thing, where are the guilty parties? So the only way you can gain satisfaction out of this is to bludgeon firms into an agreement in which they pay a large amount of money, but one that they can afford in order to get it behind them and avoid any future prosecutions. I don't think they're going to improve markets much by what they've done.

TOM BROWN:

Spitzer's all about change as opposed to prosecution. He needed to have a couple of people be prosecuted in order to get change. He needed the Grubmans of the world to be banned from the industry, but he doesn't have the resources to prosecute all the wrongdoers, and that's not what he's interested in personally. He wants to make sure that his legacy is that he created constructive change. But this settlement hasn't changed enough.

A few years later, Spitzer uncovered even more evidence of how the public was wronged during the bubble with his investigation into the mutual fund industry. Essentially, what the attorney general found here was that some mutual funds had allowed certain hedge funds to trade their shares illegally after the market had closed. Spitzer's investigation was triggered by Noreen Harrington, an executive at Stern Asset Management, which owned the hedge fund Canary Partners. Harrington was brought in to build a wealth-management business for Canary, and when she noticed the suspicious trading and asked her boss about it, she was told that it was simply an arbitrage opportunity for the fund. She swallowed that explanation for a little while, but eventually decided that she no longer could keep quiet about what she saw.

NOREEN HARRINGTON (former executive of Stern Asset Management whose testimony initiated New York attorney general Eliot Spitzer's investigation into the mutual fund industry):

I understand arbitrage in many sectors of the markets, pricing discrepancies and so on, and that you're supposed to take advantage of those opportunities. If you grow up in trading, that's what you do. So I didn't think that there was anything wrong.

ROBERT POZEN (chairman of MFS Investment Management, former president of Fidelity Management and Research, and author of *The Mutual Fund Business*):

The Spitzer investigation found two things, and they're very different. One is late trading, which is when people are placing orders after 4:00 p.m. Say it's six or seven o'clock and they're getting the four o'clock price. That, in my view, has always been illegal. It looks as if there were two classes of mutual fund companies that were involved in this. There were companies, like Bank of America, where there were agreements to allow these hedge funds to do this kind of thing — and Bank of America has moved swiftly to kick those people out. There also were situations where it was being done and the mutual fund company didn't know about it. That can happen because of the technological access that people have now online. MFS was a company that had late trading unknown to management.

The other thing was market timing, which means that people moved in and out of funds very quickly. There's no doubt that this can be perfectly legal. So the issue is what was disclosed to investors and what was the language of the prospectus. But the late trading is illegal, always was illegal, and needed to be stopped.

NOREEN HARRINGTON:

I was working in New Jersey on something and it was quite late, like nine o'clock or so. Suddenly there was all this activity. Then one of the guys shouted, "Oh my God, we just picked off these funds!" When people brag they're often not conscious of what they're saying. The enthusiasm of the moment takes you away. But as someone who's been on Wall Street for twenty years I must've sounded rather stupid, because I said, "The market's closed. Are you doing Japan?" And they said, "Oh no, we're doing the four o'clock price." So I said, "How?" But the more I started to dig the more the wall came closing down. I could see people didn't want to answer my questions.

Ultimately I confronted Eddie [Stern, head of Canary Capital] with it. I said, "Eddie, do you know the securities laws? Do you read these prospectuses?" And his answer was completely unnerving. He could've lied to me and said it was perfectly legal, and I would've had to do a lot more homework. But what he said was, "If the regulators ever look at this, Noreen, they're not going to want me. They're going to want the mutual fund companies." In other words, he told me straight out that he knew what was going to happen. In trading, that's what you call having an exit strategy. He knew that if anyone ever caught up with him, he would just cut a deal.

Well, I guess I didn't make myself too popular with those questions because a little while later they said, "We're not going to build that wealth-management business we said we were after all. We're just going to run the family's money." They knew that I never would've come in the first place if that was the deal. So at that point I had to leave. I stayed for another four months to help with transition and then I left. It was amicable. I made no noise about doing anything or saying anything about what I'd seen and how wrong I thought it was. The truth is, had it been confined to just one family I don't know if I would've taken such a dramatic step.

After I left I went on a fact-finding mission because I wanted to find out more about mutual fund timing. I learned that it was so blatant that on Bloomberg "timing" was listed as a strategy with different funds underneath. But it wasn't until I saw it from [the perspective of] who it was hurting that I understood what I had to do.

A lot of times on Wall Street you do transactions and you don't really think about the human toll things take. You think about the math and a lot of other things, but the human element kind of gets lost. And particularly when you grow up in trading, you're operating in open warfare. My job was to get more money for Goldman than someone else was getting for Merrill Lynch. But that's all well and good because everyone's eyes are open and the rules are clear. Here, I saw my family as a victim in what was happening, and that hammered it home to me. It was a crime, larceny. If you saw someone being murdered, would you not report it? At that point the only reason I wouldn't was because it might hurt me, and I couldn't live with that.

RODGER RINEY (founder and chief executive officer of Scottrade):

I've been in the business since 1965 part-time, and I'm embarrassed to say that I had no idea what was going on in the mutual fund industry. I was really caught flat-footed on much of that. And I think there are a lot of people around who feel the same way. That one surprised us.

GUS SAUTER (chief investment officer of Vanguard):

The whole after-hours-trading thing was very troublesome. Allowing certain investors to trade after the fund is closed for the day, potentially on news that comes out after the fund price has been determined, puts the existing investors in the fund at a very distinct disadvantage. The second huge issue was allowing market timers into a fund, and I think the differences between the two have really been blurred.

We were totally shocked when we came in on the Tuesday after Labor Day in 2003 — which is when Eliot Spitzer's investigation broke — and heard about this. There was no one in our senior management that had suspected any of that. I remember we had a senior-staff meeting that Tuesday, and of course the topic of conversation was what we were reading in the paper and what was unfolding, and we were all just shocked by it, had never even heard of anything like it.

JOHN CALAMOS:

It's funny, the hedge funds caused all the problems for the mutual fund industry, and it's the mutual funds that everyone's looking at. Like what those guys at Canary were doing, trading after hours, that's not a hedge, that's cheating. I'd love to trade on yesterday's prices. It seems that today the definition of a hedge fund is a guy who can do anything.

MICHAEL BARONE (head of Nasdaq trading at William Blair and Company in Chicago):

I think the fund scandals shook up people, individuals, more than anything else that's happened since the bubble broke. For all the talk about the individual investor, mutual funds are the way most people invest in the market. That's where the rubber hits the road.

Some of the problems the financial markets faced after the bubble burst actually had little to do with the business of Wall Street. As the pressure for companies to meet Wall Street's quarterly expectations rose during the bubble, many corporations resorted to accounting gimmicks and outright fraud to make their numbers work. But in the sober light of day these companies — like Enron, Tyco, and WorldCom — were being exposed. And in the echo chamber of the financial community, the effects were rebounding onto Wall Street.

ROBERT OLSTEIN:

We saw the problems at Enron and WorldCom and Tyco, all of them, from a mile away. Now, I didn't know there was fraud. But their accounting was out of control. With Enron, I read the proxy statement in 2000 and saw that that CFO was in joint ventures in conflict with the company. I couldn't believe what I was reading. I'd never seen it before in my life. And because of that I was probably the only fund not in Enron as it was doubling every day. And Tyco, c'mon, that was easy to see. They were buying good companies, but they weren't growing at 30 percent a year the way they were saying. They were buying a security business or a business that made staples for surgery — these things don't grow 30 percent a year. What they were doing was using overpriced stock to buy good companies at inflated values, and then using purchase accounting to show huge growth. If you want to, you can make the numbers show anything. But if you look carefully and know what you're looking for, you can see through these things. Really, it's not hard when it's right in front of your face.

But nobody wanted to hear it. Everyone was too busy making money. All the investment bankers were getting rich. All the analysts were out of control, making $5 million a year, $10 million a year. Everybody was in a utopian society. I heard housewives were staying home from the country club, watching CNBC and trading on E-Trade.

HOWARD SCHILIT (founder of the Center for Financial Research and Analysis and author of *Financial Shenanigans*):

I remember a conference call Enron gave around August 2001, a few months before they declared bankruptcy. A guy on the call asked a very simple question: Why are you only disclosing partial results on your balance sheet? Why aren't you giving the whole thing? Now [Enron CEO Jeff] Skilling thought his microphone was off, and his answer was, "You asshole!" Everyone laughed and it became a joke. The company was selectively deciding what to disclose, to whom, and when.

SHERRON WATKINS (former vice president and accountant at Enron):

I've changed the way I look at business because of Enron. I've changed the way I invest because of Enron. You have to be aware of the problems that are right in front of your eyes. For example, Ken Lay always had us use his sister's travel agency. It was not low cost; it was not good service. It was always disclosed in Enron's financial statements in a "related party" footnote, but it was couched differently each time. One year they'd talk about revenues to the business, another year they'd talk about profits. But what Ken Lay really was doing was moving company assets to his sister's business. And that sent a clear message to people like [former Enron CFO] Andy Fastow that once you get to the executive suite it's perfectly fine to move company assets to you or your family because Ken Lay's been doing it for all these years.

DAVID KAUFMAN:

I have attended seminars where I was given specific information on some of the things that Enron did and you're just talking about out-and-out fraud. Setting up new companies, flowing revenues from one company to another, basically stealing money — it's the same thing that happened at Adelphia, where they decided to buy the Buffalo Sabres with the shareholders' money.

HOWARD SCHILIT:

The trickery during the 1990s was more common and more serious than in most other periods you can study. But that being said, underlying the surface there is always a certain amount of gimmickry in how companies present information to investors. You particularly see this in periods where you have a bubbling stock market. So in the 1960s you saw it in some of the go-go stocks. In the 1980s you saw it. And then you saw it in the 1990s. We really shouldn't be surprised.

JOHN CALAMOS:

I could live with all the hype in the markets in the nineties — that's something that you expect if you've been around long enough. What I didn't expect was the fraud, like Enron and WorldCom. That level of financial shenanigans, where people were basically liars, that's not something the market can afford to stomach.

MICHAEL LABRANCHE:

When you talk about something like Enron it's different from most situations because it isn't just the people who lost money on the stock, which was a lot of people. There was a lot of market cap lost, just gone. At its peak Enron's market cap was $80 billion and two years after that it was worth zero. That means more money was lost in that one stock than the entire stock market was worth at its peak in '29. That just gives you an idea of how much bigger and far-reaching the markets are today. And then beyond all of that, it's also how many Enron employees lost their jobs, and how many families were affected by that. How many pensions were lost. It's a cascading thing.

For the most part, the corporate scandals of the late 1990s could be classified under the heading of executive greed. For some time, pay for CEOs and other executives had been drifting upward, but in the late 1990s it exploded, causing some companies to make decisions that were not in their shareholders' best interests in order to feather the nests of seemingly valuable employees. As the numbers became public, the anger in the financial community was palpable. And when the problem floated to the chairman's office at the New York Stock Exchange, where Dick Grasso was racking up an incredible retirement package, he didn't stand a chance.

BOB MONKS (cofounder of the Corporate Library and the Lens Funds):

In the 1990s, the symptom was chief executive pay and the problem was chief executive power. CEOs ended up with the power to pick directors, the power to pick auditors, the power to pick the head of the compensation committee and other committees, the power to pick outside advisers, and the power to set merger strategy. That combination meant there was no countervailing force to restrain CEOs. And through the Business Roundtable, CEOs became corrupt. The Business Roundtable organized the U.S. Senate to pass a resolution directing the Financial Accounting Standards Board not to require that options be expensed.

NELL MINOW (cofounder of the Corporate Library and the Lens Funds):

Congress stepped in and — in a move that will occupy an entire room in the Museum of Unintended Consequences — produced a tax-code change that had the exact opposite effect of what it was intended to do. The new law said that executive pay over $1 million could not be deducted as a business expense unless it was tied to performance. And stock options were tied to performance. So the first thing that happened was everyone's base pay went up to $1 million. And second, everyone started getting these whopping loads of stock options, which were tied to the performance of the stock, not the performance of the individual within the company. So we started going from pay plans that were $5 million or $6 million, to seeing $100 million pay plans.

SHERRON WATKINS:

There also was a demand for increased disclosure from the companies on how much executives were making, which had an unintended consequence. The idea was to shine a spotlight on CEO pay in the hopes that it would embarrass CEOs into not paying themselves so much money. But the unintended consequence happened because the stock market was rising and no one was paying attention to the fine print in all the disclosures. The only ones who were reading the fine print were the CEOs, who started saying, "Wait a minute, do you see what this guy is making? I'm running this large company and I'm only making $5 million, while he's running a small company and making $7 million. I deserve $8 million, if not more." CEOs would go to their boards with all this peer analysis to show that they were being underpaid. And the boards would up their pay by issuing more stock options, which just meant that the next guy was going to ask for even more.

EVELYN Y. DAVIS (well-known shareholder activist):

They always would say, "My competitor is getting so much, so I should, too." It was never about the need for money exactly. It was about status. But then that backfired when you had Enron, WorldCom, Tyco, and so on. Now it's getting more sensible, but in many cases they're still getting paid too much.

BOB MONKS:

In the nineties, CEO pay went up about 1,000 percent. That's really what it's all about. It sounds paranoid and ugly, but those are the facts. And that's just part of it, because they're legally required to disclose some of the compensation, but by no means all of it. So we can only guess at what they're really getting.

And I think this is the issue that really spilled over with Dick Grasso at the New York Stock Exchange.

DICK GRASSO (former New York Stock Exchange chairman):

I was forced from the exchange last September [2003] by the very board that had voted for my compensation — with eyes open to every dollar I had earned and been awarded — just weeks earlier. After Chairman McCall announced in August 2003 that I had agreed to extend my contract and receive my already earned deferred compensation and benefits over my last four years, certain political candidates and others with their own agendas attacked the board decision. The exchange board was unwilling to stand by its own earlier action in the wake of a media firestorm, and turned around and fired me for receiving the compensation that the same board had awarded.

ROBERT NEWBURGER (executive director of the New York Stock Exchange Alliance of Floor Brokers and member of the exchange since 1940):

If you can believe it, we had no idea what Grasso was making. No idea. A not-for-profit corporation does not have to publish compensation. So, Dick would say, "I've been treated very handsomely this year. The board told me what I got and I said four words: 'Thank you. I'm blessed.'" At every meeting he said this. So we had no real idea of how much he'd been blessed. Dick Grasso made his bones in the listing department. He went around the country and met captains of industry and convinced them to list their stock with us. He increased our listings many, many times over. Who was going to ask him questions about what he was making? We loved the guy.

There were other problems with the way Dick was running the place. I once went to him and said, "Dick, you're doing a great job here. But if you get hit by a bus, what are we going to do? You don't have any successor in place." I've seen it in the army and in business; it's a big responsibility for top executives to establish succession. It's a small man who's afraid to bring in somebody good below him because he's threatened. But Dick didn't have any plans in place for what would happen after he left. He just said, "I'm working on it, Bob."

I also said to Dick, "You're a director of Computer Associates. You shouldn't be a director there unless you're a director of every listed company. I trust you. But the appearance of this — it stinks!" He said, "I'm working on it, Bob." But he never did anything about any of that, and I'd already said more than most people would ever say to him because they were afraid of what he might do. So we were really powerless to do anything about what was happening.

JOHN JAKOBSON (member of the New York Stock Exchange since 1955):

It was a modern-day version of the Great Train Robbery. Hundreds of millions of dollars were taken from the exchange to pay people who should have been making good salaries, but not the amount of money you would get if you were in a risk-taking, entrepreneurial, for-profit business. Some guys got together and decided that Dick Grasso was the greatest thing since sliced bread and that he should be compensated the same way that the guys at Goldman and Morgan and Lehman are, even though Grasso just runs a stock exchange and those guys risk billions of dollars in the market every day, are at the mercy of shareholders, and basically are wide open and transparent in what they're making.

He took out $139.5 million in the dead of night, two days before Labor Day, when it was earning 8 percent free of tax. Why would he do that out of the blue? Maybe he was afraid that somebody was going to say he shouldn't have it in the first place. I spent a lot of time with him on this and, well, he disagreed.

It's no different from what was going on at Enron or Tyco or any of those other places. He's a poster child for greed. He saw the others taking out tons of dough and he decided to take it out, too. He had his own personal IPO, free of risk.

ROBERT NEWBURGER:

People were terribly upset when the whole thing came to light. And then, people started to remember how Dick had denied certain requests or made certain rulings that went against them, and the atmosphere just became really negative. When everyone was making money all these antipathies were buried. But after the bubble popped and the business wasn't so good, these feelings boiled to the surface.

This whole story about Dick's salary reminds me of the story about the teller at the bank who one week is short on money so on Friday he decides to take five dollars from the drawer and put it back on Monday. But Monday comes and nobody notices, so this time on Friday he takes ten dollars. Ten years later he's half a million bucks into the bank and they don't even know it because it happened behind their backs. It's the same thing here. If his compensation had been reported and we'd known from the beginning what he was getting, someone might've raised a stink and we might've stopped it there. Maybe because he was so successful, people would've said, "Fine, he deserves it." At least we would've had the opportunity to say something. But we didn't know, and over time the numbers accrued to such a ridiculous level. If we'd known, it would've been public and people wouldn't feel as if the wool had been pulled over their eyes.

My personal feeling about this whole thing is, say what you want about Dick Grasso, he's done a lot of wonderful things for this place and has caused a lot of heartache, but if there's blame for what happened it lies with the board of directors of the New York Stock Exchange. I'm talking about Hank Paulson, who's the head of Goldman Sachs, and Carl McCall, who was the comptroller of New York State, and the rest. These are very smart people, captains of industry. Do you think they didn't know what they were doing? Can they be led by the nose? Of course not.

DICK GRASSO:

Reasonable people can disagree about what an executive should be paid, but the directors who evaluated my performance were well aware of the market for executive compensation on Wall Street, because that is where many of them worked and earned their own substantial income.

ROY SMITH:

The argument is, "We paid you more than we intended to, so please give some of it back." But the question is, why did they pay him so much? You could say it was because they wanted to keep him, that he was being lured away by someone who could offer him stock options. I know Grasso. I never thought he was a particularly great head of the exchange, but everybody I know at the exchange said he's been great.

BERNARD HEROLD (fifty-year Wall Street veteran and founder of Bernard Herold and Company):

I called for the resignation of Grasso and the whole board. My reason for wanting to get rid of Grasso has nothing to do with how much he made. Yes, he was overpaid and all that horseshit. But I think he was a lousy chairman. People are running around saying he was a great chairman? Eliot Spitzer is saying it? Bullshit. In the old days if you had a company that wanted to go public it might list over-the-counter first, then they'd move it to the American Exchange, and then they'd go to the New York Stock Exchange. That was the sequence. All of a sudden, some of the great companies in America aren't on the Big Board, and Grasso was the chairman all through that period. Microsoft, Intel, Sun Microsystems — he couldn't get any of them to jump from Nasdaq because he was a lousy chairman. The exchange has always been secretive. I once tried to find out how much money [former NYSE chairman] John Phelan was making, and I never was able to do it. That's not what concerns me. It's that he did a lousy job and should have been fired.

DICK GRASSO:

My record at the NYSE speaks for itself. The value of a membership seat nearly tripled during my tenure as chairman, soaring to more than $2 million from $700,000; the income to seat owners leasing their seats to others likewise jumped to $300,000 from $100,000. Under my leadership, the NYSE significantly increased its market share. It nearly doubled the number of listed companies, and the great majority of the near 500 non-U.S. companies now in the NYSE were listed during my tenure.

JENNIFER WILLIAMS (New York Stock Exchange floor broker for Griswold Company):

I don't personally care what you pay Dick Grasso. The man brought the exchange into the new millennium. So whatever you think of him, the fact is that we are here today, thriving, because he was the leader. I don't care if you think he was an egomaniac.

BOB MCCOOEY (chief executive officer of New York Stock Exchange floor brokerage firm and trading house Griswold Company):

Frankly, I feel misled by Dick. As this first broke I was very worried because I never knew life at the stock exchange without Dick. And I think there were a lot of people in that camp. But over time, as more and more has come out, as you look back and think about some of the things that went on, it wasn't handled appropriately by the board or Dick. There's a lot of blame to go around.

JERRY KENNEY:

So that's what happened in the mania. And now we have to go about fixing it. We have to make some changes in the way we do business. In a way we, meaning Merrill Lynch, are sort of relieved that this exogenous pressure is behind us and that the industry can get back to doing business the way it's supposed to be done. To us, restoring credibility is our top priority now. It has to be.

JOHN JAKOBSON:

The game never changes, just the players. The more there is to steal, the more it will be stolen. This isn't just at the New York Stock Exchange or on Wall Street; it's in the entire financial world. It's a gene flaw, I think. You know, whenever they say it's not the money — it's the money.

Epilogue

It's the money, indeed. Just two weeks before Christmas 2006, Goldman Sachs released its earnings figures for the year, and the numbers were eye-popping. Goldman took in $9.5 billion in profits on revenues of $37.7 billion, both of which were records for the firm. But those weren't the figures Wall Street was drooling over. No, the number on everyone's lips was $16.5 billion, which is how much Goldman paid its employees in 2006. To put the sum in perspective, two weeks earlier Bank of New York bought Mellon Financial, the parent company of Pittsburgh's venerable Mellon Bank, and created one of the largest financial institutions in the country. The price tag for that deal? $16.5 billion.

The total compensation figures for Goldman Sachs in 2006 amounted to more than $600,000 for each of its 26,000 full-time workers. But in reality the firm was far more generous to some employees than others. Take Lloyd Blankfein, Goldman's chairman and chief executive, for instance. Blankfein, a fifty-two-year-old former tax attorney, received a salary of exactly $600,000 in 2006. His year-end bonus, on the other hand, was

$53.4 million in cash, stock, and stock options — the largest ever given to a Wall Street CEO — bringing his total paycheck to the tidy round sum of $54 million. Combined with the $40 million Morgan Stanley forked over to its chairman and chief executive John Mack, and the equally gaudy profits posted by trading titans like Lehman Brothers and Bear Stearns, 2006 likely will be remembered as the year that Wall Street officially rebounded from the economic meltdown triggered by the financial scandals of the late twentieth century and the September 11 terrorist attacks.

Still, despite a surging Dow Jones Industrial Average, which crossed the 12,000-point mark on October 18 and ended the year up more than 16 percent, much of Main Street continued to struggle through tough times in 2006. So in many ways the whopping bonuses paid to Wall Street leaders like Blankfein and Mack were merely symbols of a suddenly widening gulf between average Americans and the financial world. The Federal Reserve recently reported that the percentage of U.S. families owning stocks directly or through mutual funds or retirement plans such as IRAs and 401(k)s fell to 48.6 percent in 2004 from 51.9 percent in 2001. This was the first dip of any kind since the Fed started its triennial Survey of Consumer Finances in 1989.

The findings represent a potentially troubling reversal for Wall Street's long-term growth plans. In 1995, roughly 40 percent of American households owned stocks. Then, as the market took off in the late nineties, stock ownership surged to more than half of all U.S. families. At the dawn of the new millennium, many Wall Street firms were envisioning themselves as Main Street's bankers of the future. That's hard to imagine now. Clearly, the decline in equity ownership can be explained in part by the overall downturn in the financial markets that followed the booming nineties. But the securities industry also has to be concerned that some of its customers appear to be questioning whether the risks of investing are worth the rewards over the long haul.

Beyond that, Wall Street also has to wonder whether its historical model of fostering strong independent companies based in downtown New York City can remain a viable strategy in the future. The financial community's physical footprint in lower Manhattan has been shrinking for some time, as firms like Morgan Stanley, Bear Stearns, and Donaldson, Lufkin & Jenrette all moved a few miles uptown to be closer to the suburban commuter trains at Grand Central and Pennsylvania stations. And since the September 11 terrorist attacks, the industry's presence in and around Wall Street has grown even smaller. Today, the only major investment banks based in New York's financial district are Goldman Sachs, which remains at 85 Broad Street, down the block from the New York Stock Exchange, and Merrill Lynch, which has reoccupied its old offices in the World Financial Center overlooking the site of the World Trade Center.

Obviously, this Wall Street diaspora is only symbolic. But it's also true that in some very real ways the securities industry has ceded power to other parts of the financial services business. With the demise of the Glass-Steagall banking structure, the culture of the business is being diluted by large, deep-pocketed banks that are waiting to pick off any weakening securities franchises. In an era where trading and investment banking deals require cavernous pools of capital, it's an open question whether even traditional powerhouses such as Merrill Lynch, Morgan Stanley, and Goldman Sachs can continue to last on their own. Or will they too be forced to sell out to bigger international finance companies to remain competitive?

Of course, on Wall Street, mergers and acquisitions are just another fact of life. And few people felt like weeping for investment bankers after the bonanza of 2006. In the wake of the stock market slump that started in 2001, corporate America was forced to renew its focus on the bottom line. Many companies were afraid to spend their precious capital, and as a result nationwide job growth stalled and the overall economy suffered. Meanwhile, corporate war chests grew fatter and fatter, and, with the U.S. foundering economically, the Federal Reserve was forced to keep interest rates at historically low levels to provide corporations with access to money if they wanted or needed it. At the same time, well-heeled investors, frustrated with the stock market's anemic returns, began to seek more profitable venues for their cash. As Jerome Kohlberg, Henry Kravis, and George Roberts proved with the staggering success of Kohlberg Kravis Roberts & Co. in the seventies, leveraged buyouts are a business that thrives in depressed market environments. So, not surprisingly, buyout firms like KKR and Blackstone Group, the outfit launched by Pete Peterson and Stephen Schwarzman after they left Lehman Brothers, started raking in investment capital.

As a result, by the middle of the decade, as the financial markets began to rebound and the economy slowly improved, the climate was ripe for an old-fashioned M&A frenzy. Once corporate America got over its fear of spending, companies started looking for growth again. To a corporate executive sitting on a pile of cash, secure in the knowledge that there's more where that came from through inexpensive bank loans, the quickest way to increase the size of your company is to buy someone else. And that's what they did. At the same time, "private equity" firms — the LBO business's less pernicious-sounding, "new millennium" name for itself — had ample investment opportunities just picking and choosing among the scads of good companies with depressed stock prices. In other words, the predators were out in force.

Not surprisingly, 2006 was the best year in the history of the mergers and acquisitions business. Nearly $3.8 trillion worth of corporate assets were bought and sold across the globe, topping the previous record of $3.4 trillion established in 2000, at the peak of the dot-com bubble. Eight of the ten biggest buyouts in history also took place in 2006, the largest being Blackstone Group's $36 billion purchase of Equity Office Trust. Hostile takeovers became particularly popular, even in Europe, where the once gentlemanly business world has been transformed into another capitalist jungle. Consider the nasty $33.6 billion takeover of Luxembourg steelmaker Arcelor SA by its Netherlands rival Mittal Steel. The nasty fight started with an unsolicited offer by Mittal, the industrial conglomerate controlled by Lakshmi Mittal, India-born, London-living billionaire, and lasted longer than six months. With venom spewing from both sides, the Continent had never seen anything quite like it — and the press and the public ate it up.

In truth, much of the frenetic merger activity was provoked by the highly competitive private equity business. By 2006, "private equity" had become *the* buzz phrase on Wall Street, and private equity shops had supplanted hedge funds as the preferred moneymaking status game for billionaires. The industry exploded to the point where Henry Kravis and George Roberts at mighty KKR no longer were the biggest kids on the block. In July 2006, the *Wall Street Journal* estimated that the Carlyle Group, the Washington firm headed by former IBM chief Louis Gerstner, which has a bevy of well-connected partners including former President George H. W. Bush, was sitting on $44.3 billion in assets under management. Blackstone was just behind with $43 billion, dwarfing KKR at $27 billion. And the competition keeps on coming, as increasing numbers of corporate leaders seek to jump ship and join a buyout shop or start one of their own. This trend shows no sign of slowing, considering that at the beginning of 2007 LBO firms controlled roughly $750 billion in capital — a sizable chunk of change in search of something to buy.

One unexpected outgrowth of the recent round of merger mania was the dramatic reshaping of the business of trading stocks, bonds, and commodities. In late 2003, the New York Stock Exchange hired John Reed, Sandy's Weill's old partner at Citigroup, to be its interim chairman, replacing the ousted Dick Grasso. A respected figure in the financial world, Reed was given the primary responsibility of steadying the institution in the wake of the Grasso fiasco. So he convinced John Thain, the highly regarded president of Goldman Sachs, to take a pay cut and join him as the NYSE's new chief executive officer. Both Reed and Thain had well-known fascinations with technology, and their goal was to automate the exchange's labor-intensive floor trading system.

Meanwhile, the New York Stock Exchange trading floor was in complete turmoil. An SEC investigation found that from 1999 to 2003 some floor brokers had traded illegally and unethically, at times jumping in front of their customers' orders to get better prices for themselves. Several people lost their jobs and the specialist firms themselves paid $240 million in fines to settle the charges. For the stock exchange's vocal critics, which included the mutual fund giant Fidelity, the SEC's findings and the subsequent settlement were the most glaring examples yet of the inefficiencies in the NYSE's floor trading system. And in Reed and Thain, they finally had friends in the executive suite who agreed with them.

In February 2004, Thain and Reed rocked the floor of the exchange with a plan to allow institutional investors to do more electronic trading than ever before. The idea behind the new proposal was to keep the NYSE ahead of Nasdaq, which was actively promoting the efficiency of its electronic platform and eating away at the NYSE's market share. But to the brokers on the trading floor, the plan meant two things: fewer orders and reduced commissions. At around the same time, Thain and Reed also began to recruit a new team of executives to join the exchange. These new leaders gave everyone the responsibility of eliminating all signs of waste within the organization.

But cutting costs meant that some of the institution's longtime traditions would have to go — traditions like Jerry Gentilella's basement barbershop. It turns out that Gentilella's barbershop received $80,000 a year from the exchange as a subsidy. To Reed and Thain, the subsidized barbershop was emblematic of everything wrong with a public organization that behaves like a private club. But to many of the men and women who'd spent their lives on the floor of the exchange — making million-dollar deals in packed crowds based on nothing more than a nod or a wave — the closing of the barbershop was just one more sign of how the close-knit business culture they once knew was changing before their eyes.

A year later, the last remaining vestiges of old club culture finally were obliterated. In April 2005, the New York Stock Exchange announced that it was buying the electronic trading firm Archipelago and creating a new publicly traded company. In that one move, Thain permanently smashed the exchange floor and replaced its human face with a machine. Life on Broad Street would never be the same again. Supporters of the "old guard" protested the move and tried to fight. But eventually they too gave up and accepted that the future had arrived.

On March 8, 2006, shares of NYSE Group Inc. started trading on the New York Stock Exchange under the symbol "NYX." The stock ended the day up 25 percent at $80, giving the company a market capitalization of $10.2 billion. Suddenly Thain had a publicly traded currency and a pile of cash to use in building the company. That June, the NYSE Group agreed to pay $20 billion for Euronext — the parent company of the Paris, Amsterdam, Brussels, and Lisbon bourses — creating the world's first transatlantic stock market.

Meanwhile, Nasdaq was in the middle of its own hostile takeover bid for the London Stock Exchange. But unlike Euronext, LSE executives were less enthralled with the entreaties from their American competitors, repeatedly belittling the Nasdaq offer as too small and vowing to remain independent. Nasdaq, for its part, promised to fight on. Then, in July, the Chicago Mercantile Exchange merged with the Chicago Board of Trade, creating a Midwestern derivatives dynamo. The two exchanges had discussed a combination for years, but with the pressure to grow mounting the time finally was right for a deal. And finally, in January 2007, word started circulating through the financial markets that the New York Stock Exchange and Tokyo Stock Exchange were entering into a cooperative alliance that would bring the Japanese market into the NYSE Group fold.

Considering the amount of money that's flowing through worldwide financial markets each day and the fact that technology is making consolidation increasingly profitable, we should expect to see more of these mergers of financial markets in the coming years. As a result, it's highly likely that in the near future most of the world's financial markets will be controlled by just a few multinational companies, the largest of which probably will be the New York Stock Exchange. And to think it all started so humbly in 1792 with a collusive contract signed under a buttonwood tree near the southern tip of Manhattan Island.

As for Dick Grasso, the once gallant leader of the New York Stock Exchange, his reputation lies in tatters among the wreckage of the nineties stock market bubble. After Grasso's resignation in September 2003, the exchange's new leadership asked New York State Attorney General Eliot Spitzer to launch an investigation into the former leader's pay. Spitzer demanded that Grasso return more than half of the $190 million he received as compensation. Grasso refused. So Spitzer sued him. The case dragged on for more than two years until finally, in October 2006, New York State Supreme Court Justice Charles Ramos ruled that Grasso had violated his fiduciary duty as an executive and should have more fully disclosed his soaring compensation to the exchange's board. He then ordered Grasso to return as much as $100 million to the NYSE. Not surprisingly, Grasso disagreed and appealed. So the case goes on and likely will for many more years to come. But at least Grasso won't have to face off against his chief tormentor anymore. Eliot Spitzer was elected governor of New York in November 2006.

Of course, Grasso was hardly the only figure of nineties excess to spend much of the next decade lingering around various courthouses. In reality, the coda for the era ultimately was written in the courts. With investors seething over revelations of outright corporate fraud, regulators and prosecutors tried to extract a pound of flesh from the people they felt were most responsible for taking advantage of the frenzied atmosphere. The major Wall Street figure to stand trial was Silicon Valley investment banker Frank Quattrone. While analysts Henry Blodgett and Jack Grubman were banished from the securities industry and scorched by the press, Quattrone actually was found guilty of obstructing justice and sentenced to a year and a half in prison. But he appealed the decision and won a full reversal. In August 2006, prosecutors worked out a deal that dismissed Quattrone's charges and allowed him to return to work in the industry. After three years of pure hell, he was back in the game.

Things didn't turn out quite so well for many of the poster children of nineties corporate greed, however. In the wake of the burst stock market bubble, numerous executives were sent to prison for committing fraud or participating in the looting of their companies. Ken Lay and Jeff Skilling, the chairman and chief executive of Enron during the company's heyday, were found guilty of lying to analysts and investors in May 2006. Lay died of heart problems before he could receive his sentence, but Skilling is serving twenty-four years on nineteen counts of conspiracy, fraud, and insider trading at a low-security federal prison in Waseca, Minnesota. Still, Skilling's sentence wasn't the longest ever handed down for a corporate scandal. That honor belongs to Bernie Ebbers, the disgraced former head of WorldCom. In September 2006, at sixty-five years of age, Ebbers began serving a twenty-five-year term at a federal prison in Oakdale, Louisiana, for his role in the $11 billion fraud that led to his company's collapse. By comparison, former Tyco chief Dennis Kozlowski got off relatively easy for bilking the company out of more than $400 million. Kozlowski was sentenced to just eight to twenty-five years in prison in September 2005, and he could be out in as few as seven years if he behaves himself. He would be just shy of sixty-six years old.

Certainly the most publicly entertaining episode to emerge from the aftermath of the stock market frenzy was Martha Stewart's insider trading trial. Stewart, the well-known entrepreneur who turned an obsession with home economics into a billion-dollar multimedia enterprise, was a stockbroker before launching her company, Martha Stewart Living Omnimedia. As an executive, she continued to be a savvy and aggressive Wall Street investor. But when she sold her stake in the biotechnology firm Imclone, which was founded by her friend Sam Waksal, right before the Food and Drug Administration declined to review the company's cancer drug Erbitux, regulators were curious about her eerily prescient sense of timing. The trades were particularly suspicious because Waksal and his family also had sold their stock ahead of the news. Suddenly, the "diva of domesticity" found herself unwittingly ensnared in an FBI investigation into an insider trading conspiracy involving Sam Waksal and his family and friends.

The prosecution never could nail Stewart on the insider trading charges, though. In the end, she pleaded guilty to obstructing justice and was sentenced to five months at a minimum security prison and five months of home confinement. As it turned out, her company probably received the harshest punishment, since its market value plummeted as the scandal unfolded. In the end the fiasco offered yet another painful lesson for Main Street about the vagaries of investing on Wall Street: ethical misconduct by executives at the companies you buy can have very real ramifications on the value of your investments.

But perhaps the most surprising turnaround for a hero of the nineties executive culture was Sandy Weill, Wall Street's master builder, whose legacy sank along with the fortunes of the company he built — Citigroup. After forcing out his merger partner and former cochairman John Reed in 2000, Weill continued to tinker with the company. But calls from shareholders and corporate governance activists forced him to name a successor. Weill flirted with several underlings before ultimately picking his replacement. On October 1, 2003, he named Citigroup's legal counsel Chuck Prince to be the firm's next chief executive officer and gave President Robert Willumstad the additional title of chief operating officer. Weill, who would remain chairman until April 2006, offered his protégés a single piece of advice: "They better not screw it up."

So what did they do? Screw it up. Though, in fairness, it also turns out that the company they inherited from Weill wasn't all that it was cracked up to be.

For a chief executive in today's business world, success or failure ultimately is judged by your stock price. Using that yardstick, Sandy Weill constructed a juggernaut for himself and his investors. From 1986 to 2004, as Weill built Commercial Credit into Citigroup through merger after merger, the value of his company's stock gained an average of 22 percent each year. Then he handed the reins to Prince, and the growth stalled. For the next three years the stock went nowhere as the company repeatedly posted disappointing results. Particularly dismaying to investors was Citigroup's continued failure to keep its expenses down, which always was a hallmark of Weill's operations.

By all appearances, it seemed as if Prince and Willumstad weren't up to the standard set by their former boss. But taking a closer look at the overall company, it's clear that there were real problems with the business Weill built. In cobbling together all those mergers, Citigroup executives had spent a lot of time cutting costs and meeting bottom-line projections. But they didn't put the same emphasis on successfully integrating their different operations. So by the time Prince took over, the company had become an unwieldy mix of disparate parts that didn't fit together particularly well.

To get his arms around the problems, Prince was forced to completely rework the corporate strategy. He changed Citigroup's focus from spotting new merger targets to linking all of the company's different subsidiaries together and building a unified culture from within. For example, in late 2005 Prince and his lieutenants decided that Citigroup needed to bulk up its Citibank consumer banking operation. In the past, the company's solution would've been to look for another bank to buy. But Prince didn't feel that Citigroup could prudently burn the capital, or take on the debt, necessary to complete a major deal. So he decided to open more than five hundred new bank branches during the first half of 2006 and offer a new high-yielding online bank account. It wasn't a sexy decision, and it certainly wasn't a dramatic Weill-esqe move. But it was a less costly option.

Prince's real challenge, however, was reestablishing trust with Citigroup's customers, not to mention the markets as a whole, following a series of withering regulatory investigations that started in 2002 and lasted for the next four years. The most significant punishment came from the Federal Reserve Board. In May 2004, the Fed slammed Citigroup with the largest fine in its history, $70 million, for a variety of violations at the company's subsidiary that specializes in lending money to people with sketchy credit histories. Essentially the Fed found that in 2000 and 2001 Citi employees had tried to mislead customers and had lied to regulators. The findings were especially devastating because two years earlier Citi had been forced to pay $215 million to settle charges of deceptive and abusive lending practices from the Federal Trade Commission. From the outside, it appeared that the company Sandy Weill had built into Citigroup was rotting from within.

With events spiraling out of control, an internal shake-up at Citigroup probably was inevitable. The first to go was Willumstad, who was supposed to be running the company with Prince. But Willumstad left in July 2005 with thoughts of heading his own outfit. He eventually became chairman of the embattled insurance giant American International Group. Then, a few weeks later, rumors started circulating around Wall Street that Weill himself was trying to get out of his responsibilities as Citigroup chairman and start his own leveraged buyout shop. Though the plans never came to fruition, the gossip further rattled the company. Finally, less than a month after the talk of Weill leaving died down, Citigroup's global consumer banking chief, Marjorie Magner, announced that she too was stepping aside. The word on the street was that Weill, Willumstad, and Magner all felt frustrated because their CEO was ignoring their advice. So perhaps Prince did learn a thing or two from his old boss after all.

On April 18, 2006, Sandy Weill formally retired as Citigroup chairman, just as he'd long said he would, and by the close of the year, Chuck Prince was ensconced in the corner office with both the chairman and chief executive titles firmly in his grasp. But he could hardly be described as comfortable. The company's stockholders were becoming increasingly restless. In December, Prince reshuffled his lieutenants again. This time he named Robert Druskin, the head of Citigroup's corporate and investment bank, to be the new chief operating officer and his clear second-in-command, a move designed to send a message to the financial community that the company was focused on cutting costs and getting its businesses in line. But all that was forgotten a month later when Prince was forced to fire Todd S. Thomson, head of Citigroup's wealth management business. Thomson had become closely linked to CNBC's "Money Honey" anchor, Maria Bartiromo, and his sins included booting several Citigroup bankers off of a corporate jet in Hong Kong so he could ride home with Bartiromo, and spending $5 million to have Citigroup sponsor a planned television program on the Sundance Channel that Bartiromo would cohost with Robert Redford. In the eyes of the investing public, the episodes provided further proof that Prince, Weill's handpicked successor, couldn't handle the out-of-control culture he inherited from his mentor. For Wall Street's master architect, it was a sad close to a storied run and one that offers a sobering lesson for all executives who believe bigger is better.

Yet, it remains to be seen whether any of the lessons from the past actually have registered with anyone on Wall Street. Once again, many stock market experts are wondering whether investors recognize the risks inherent in the stratospheric prices of the latest Wall Street darlings, like the search engine Google, which went public at $85 in August 2004 and by November 2006 was trading for more than $500. A recent study by Merrill Lynch showed that most mutual fund managers expect the economy and corporate earnings to grow as fast in 2007 as they did in 2006 — if not faster. But an annual survey of economists conducted by the *Wall Street Journal* predicted slower growth in 2007 and 2008. Once again, many bulls seem blinded by the market's ability to print money and are forgetting that stock prices can move in two directions.

So for the folks who today are calling around the Street in a desperate search for the next Google or some other hot stock, a sobering reminder from the late author and Harvard University economist John Kenneth Galbraith seems appropriate:

"Don't listen to anything these people say. Just be guided by history."

Cast of Characters

PETER ACKERMAN: Former Drexel Burnham Lambert executive vice president and deputy to Michael Milken in the high-yield bond department.

FRED ALGER: Chairman of Fred Alger Management and one of the leading mutual fund managers of the go-go era.

HERBERT ALLEN JR.: Billionaire financier and senior partner at the investment bank Allen and Company. Son of legendary investor and merchant banker Herbert Allen Sr. His annual Sun Valley, Idaho, retreat is a deal-making haven for media and technology titans.

HERBERT (HERB) ALLISON: Chairman, president, and chief executive officer of TIAA-CREF and former president and chief operating officer of Merrill Lynch.

ROBERT BALDWIN: Former chairman of Morgan Stanley.

MICHAEL BARONE: Head of Nasdaq trading at William Blair and Company in Chicago.

MARIA BARTIROMO: CNBC anchor and the first reporter to broadcast from the floor of the New York Stock Exchange. She became known as the Money Honey during the 1990s.

JAMES BENHAM: Former chairman of Benham Capital Management and founder of Capital Preservation Fund, an early money-market mutual fund.

BRUCE BENT: Chairman of the Reserve Funds and cofounder of the Reserve Fund, which is formally considered to be the first money-market mutual fund.

ALFRED R. BERKELEY III: Former president and vice chairman of Nasdaq Stock Market.

ROGER BERLIND: Founding partner of Carter, Berlind and Weill with Sandy Weill and Arthur Carter. He retired from Wall Street in 1975, and has since produced numerous Broadway shows including *Amadeus, City of Angels,* and *Guys and Dolls.*

ROBERT BERNHARD: Former partner at Lehman Brothers and Salomon Brothers. He also is a well-connected member of the Lehman family.

PETER BERNSTEIN: Investment adviser and author of several important financial books including *Capital Ideas* and *Against the Gods.* In 1967 he sold his asset-management firm, Bernstein-Macaulay, to Carter, Berlind and Weill. It was Sandy Weill's first deal.

JESSICA BIBLIOWICZ: Sandy Weill's daughter, who has run mutual fund operations at Prudential and Smith Barney, her father's firm. She left Smith Barney after a falling out with Weill's protégé, Jamie Dimon. Today she is CEO of National Financial Partners.

ROGER BIRK: Former chairman of Merrill Lynch and president under chairman Donald Regan.

STEPHEN BIRMINGHAM: Author of many books, including *"Our Crowd."*

JOHN C. (JACK) BOGLE: Founder of Vanguard Group, president of Bogle Markets Research Center, and former chairman of Wellington Management. He is responsible for the introduction of the first index fund.

CHARLES BRANDES: Founder of the value-investing firm Brandes Investment Partners, who got to know Ben Graham after he retired from Wall Street.

TOM BROWN: Founder of Second Curve Capital and former bank-stock analyst for Donaldson, Lufkin and Jenrette.

HARRIS BRUMFIELD: Chief executive officer of Trading Technologies International and former trader in the futures pits at the Chicago Board of Trade.

WARREN BUFFETT: Berkshire Hathaway chairman.

I. W. (TUBBY) BURNHAM: Founder of Burnham and Company. In 1971, he merged the firm with Drexel Firestone to form Drexel Burnham.

BRYAN BURROUGH: Journalist, former reporter for the *Wall Street Journal,* and coauthor of *Barbarians at the Gate.*

LISE BUYER: Director of business optimization at Google and former senior equity analyst in Frank Quattrone's technology group at Deutsche Morgan Grenfell and Credit Suisse First Boston.

JOHN CALAMOS: Chairman and chief executive officer of Calamos Investments.

ARTHUR CARTER: Founding partner of Carter, Berlind and Weill with Sandy Weill and Roger Berlind. He left the firm in 1970 and pursued a series of leveraged buyouts. Today he is publisher of the *New York Observer.*

ARTHUR CASHIN: Director of New York Stock Exchange floor operations for UBS Financial Services.

NEAL CAVUTO: Fox News anchor and former CNBC anchor.

ALGER (DUKE) CHAPMAN: Former Shearson Loeb Rhoades cochairman, he was the head of Shearson and sold the firm to Sandy Weill in 1973.

ROGER CLINTON: Former Fidelity mutual fund manager.

MARSHALL COGAN: Joined Carter, Berlind and Weill in 1965 and emerged as the firm's driving force through the late 1960s and early 1970s. After leaving the firm in 1973 when Sandy Weill became CEO, he was an early investor in junk bonds with Michael Milken and owned the Manhattan restaurant "21" Club.

H. RODGIN COHEN: Partner and banking expert at the law firm Sullivan and Cromwell.

PETER COHEN: Joined Cogan, Berlind, Weill and Levitt as an analyst and became Sandy Weill's right-hand man. After Weill sold Shearson to American Express and became president of the parent company, Cohen took over at Shearson/American Express.

SAUL COHEN: Former Lehman Brothers in-house legal counsel and the former SEC-approved in-house counsel for Drexel Burnham Lambert.

E. GERALD (JERRY) CORRIGAN: Managing director at Goldman Sachs and the former president of the Federal Reserve Bank of New York. He ran the New York Fed during the 1987 stock-market crash.

DAN CORWIN: Former partner at Burnham and Company.

JAMES CRAMER: Financial journalist, broadcaster, and former Wall Street trader and cofounder of the hedge fund Cramer Berkowitz.

BLAKE DARCY: Former chief executive officer of DLJDirect and CSFBDirect.

EVELYN Y. DAVIS: Private investor and shareholder activist. She is a survivor of the Holocaust.

THOMAS E. DEWEY JR.: Former partner at Kuhn Loeb and Company and son of former New York governor Thomas E. Dewey.

JAMIE DIMON: President of JP Morgan Chase, former head of Salomon Smith Barney, and assistant to Sandy Weill at American Express.

WILLIAM DONALDSON: Chairman of the Securities and Exchange Commission, former New York Stock Exchange chairman, and cofounder of Donaldson, Lufkin and Jenrette.

JUDITH RAMSEY EHRLICH: Coauthor of *The New Crowd,* which provides an in-depth profile of Sandy Weill's career through the late 1980s. It is considered by most of his former partners to be the most accurate public account of Weill's early life.

LOUIS ENGEL: Former partner at Merrill Lynch and the first head of the firm's advertising and marketing operation.

ROBERT FARRELL: Merrill Lynch senior investment adviser and one of Wall Street's most popular market strategists in the 1970s and 1980s. *Institutional Investor* named him the top market timer in every year except one from 1975 to 1992, when he stepped down as an active analyst.

PETER FISHER: Managing director of BlackRock, former head of the Federal Reserve Bank of New York's markets group, and former undersecretary of the treasury for domestic finance.

RICHARD FISHER: Former chairman of Morgan Stanley.

JOSEPH FLOM: Partner and cofounder of the New York law firm Skadden, Arps, Slate, Meagher and Flom. He is considered the dean of mergers-and-acquisitions legal strategy and is a specialist in corporate- and securities-law issues.

JOHN KENNETH GALBRAITH: Famed economist, Harvard University professor, and author of numerous important financial books.

ELAINE GARZARELLI: Head of Garzarelli Management and former Lehman Brothers strategist who became famous for calling the 1987 stock-market crash a week before it happened.

JERRY GENTILELLA: Barber at the New York Stock Exchange since 1963.

RUDY GIULIANI: Former New York City mayor and former U.S. attorney for the Southern District of New York.

LEWIS GLUCKSMAN: Former chairman of Lehman Brothers. He took charge of the firm after leading traders in a corporate coup that toppled Lehman's then leader, Pete Peterson.

JACK GOLSEN: Oklahoma chemical-manufacturing entrepreneur. In the late 1960s he invested in the failing brokerage Hayden Stone just a few months before it was set to collapse. He was the final investor to accept the terms of the firm's bailout by CBWL.

JOSEPH GRANO: Chairman of UBS Financial Services, chairman of the Homeland Security Advisory Council, and former head of retail brokerage operations at Merrill Lynch.

JAMES GRANT: Author, journalist, and publisher of *Grant's Interest Rate Observer.*

RICHARD (DICK) GRASSO: Former chairman of the New York Stock Exchange.

ALAN GREENSPAN: Chairman of the Federal Reserve Board since August 1987. He arrived two months before the stock-market crash.

BILL GRIFFETH: CNBC news anchor and former anchor and producer at Financial News Network.

KENNETH GUENTHER: Former chief executive officer of Independent Community Bankers of America and former assistant to the Federal Reserve Board.

JOHN GUTFREUND: Joined Salomon Brothers in 1953, became senior partner in 1978 and chairman in 1980. He lost his job in 1991 after a bond-trading scandal crushed the firm.

ROBERT HAACK: Former president of the New York Stock Exchange, and the first exchange executive to publicly support the idea of unfixing trading commissions on Wall Street.

WILLIAM HAMBRECHT: Chairman of WR Hambrecht and Company and cofounder of the Silicon Valley investment bank Hambrecht and Quist.

NOREEN HARRINGTON: A twenty-year Wall Street veteran and former executive of Stern Asset Management whose testimony initiated New York attorney general Eliot Spitzer's investigation into the mutual fund industry.

WARREN HELLMAN: Chairman of the San Francisco investment firm Hellman and Friedman and former president of Lehman Brothers.

SUE HERERA: CNBC news anchor and former anchor and reporter at Financial News Network.

BERNARD HEROLD: Founder of Bernard Herold and Company.

DANIEL HERTZBERG: Deputy managing editor of the *Wall Street Journal* and former reporter for the newspaper who won a Pulitzer prize with James B. Stewart for their coverage of the 1987 stock-market crash and Wall Street's insider-trading investigations.

J. TOMILSON (TOM) HILL: Former Lehman Brothers partner and investment banking chief at Shearson Lehman Brothers, partner at Blackstone Group, M&A adviser and deal maker. He supposedly was the physical model for the character Gordon Gekko in the movie *Wall Street.*

RICHARD HOLLAND: Retired advertising executive in Omaha, Nebraska, and longtime friend of and investor with Warren Buffett.

JACK HYLAND: Former partner at Morgan Stanley.

RON INSANA: CNBC news anchor and former anchor and producer at Financial News Network.

JOHN JAKOBSON: Member of the New York Stock Exchange since 1955.

RICHARD JENRETTE: Cofounder and former chairman of Donaldson, Lufkin and Jenrette, the first New York Stock Exchange member firm to go public.

EDWARD C. JOHNSON II: Former lawyer who bought Fidelity Fund in 1943 and turned it into the company Fidelity Investments. He also is credited with changing the investment psychology of the mutual fund industry.

EDWARD C. (NED) JOHNSON III: Chairman of Fidelity Investments, former manager of Fidelity Trend Fund, and son of Edward C. Johnson II.

F. ROSS JOHNSON: Former chief executive of RJR Nabisco who failed in his bid to lead a leveraged buyout of the company in 1988.

FRED JOSEPH: Former chief executive of Drexel Burnham Lambert. He was Michael Milken's boss in the 1970s and 1980s.

IRVING KAHN: Chairman of the value-investing firm Kahn Brothers and Company, former analyst at Graham-Newman, and longtime friend and colleague of Benjamin Graham.

DAVID KAUFMAN: Certified public accountant and principal at Rothstein Kass.

HENRY KAUFMAN: Former Salomon Brothers senior partner, economist, and Fed watcher.

JERRY KENNEY: Executive vice president of research and corporate strategy at Merrill Lynch. He was Internet analyst Henry Blodget's boss in the late 1990s.

ANDY KILPATRICK: Stockbroker in Birmingham, Alabama, and longtime investor in Berkshire Hathaway. He also is the author of *Of Permanent Value,* his self-published biography of Warren Buffett. The 2004 edition of the book runs more than 1,500 pages.

TOM KNAPP: Well-known value investor, former head of Tweedy Browne Company, and former analyst at Graham-Newman.

JEROME KOHLBERG: Cofounder and former partner of the leveraged-buyout firm Kohlberg Kravis Roberts and Company.

DAVID KOMANSKY: Former chairman of Merrill Lynch.

HENRY KRAVIS: Cofounder and partner of the leveraged-buyout firm Kohlberg Kravis Roberts and Company.

MICHAEL LABRANCHE: Joined his family's NYSE specialist firm in 1977 as a floor trader. Today he is chairman of LaBranche and Company, the exchange's largest specialist firm.

DAVID LANDES: Chief executive officer of Bondsonline.com.

JEFF LANE: Chairman of Neuberger Berman, former head of asset-management operations at Salomon Smith Barney, and former Shearson executive under Sandy Weill.

ARTHUR LEVITT JR.: Former chairman of the Securities and Exchange Commission. He joined Carter, Berlind and Weill as a broker, eventually became a partner, and stayed with Sandy Weill through a series of mergers before stepping down to become chairman of the American Stock Exchange.

MICHAEL LEWIS: Former Salomon Brothers bond salesman for John Meriwether's risk-arbitrage department, journalist, and author of *Liar's Poker* and *The New New Thing*.

RICHARD R. LINDSEY: Former director of market regulation at the Securities and Exchange Commission.

ROBERT LINTON: Former chairman of Drexel Burnham Lambert and partner at Burnham and Company.

MARTIN LIPTON: Partner and founder of New York law firm Wachtell, Lipton, Rosen and Katz. He's an expert M&A strategist and a specialist in corporate and securities law.

PETER LOW: Member of the New York Stock Exchange since 1963, managing director of Griswold Company, and former independent floor broker. He is the third generation of his family to work at the exchange — both his father and grandfather were members.

ROGER LOWENSTEIN: Journalist and author of several books, including *When Genius Failed: The Rise and Fall of Long-Term Capital Management* and *Buffett: The Making of an American Capitalist*.

DAN LUFKIN: Cofounder of Donaldson, Lufkin and Jenrette, the first New York Stock Exchange member firm to go public.

GARY LYNCH: Executive vice chairman of Credit Suisse First Boston and former director of the Securities and Exchange Commission's enforcement division during the insider-trading investigations of the 1980s.

PETER LYNCH: Vice chairman of Fidelity Management and Research, Fidelity's mutual fund arm, executive vice president of Fidelity Investments, and former manager of Magellan Fund.

GORDON MACKLIN: The first president of the Nasdaq Stock Market and former chairman of Hambrecht and Quist.

BERNARD MADOFF: Founder and chairman of Bernard L. Madoff Investment Securities.

ROBERT MAGOWAN: Former Merrill Lynch executive and Safeway chairman, and Charlie Merrill's son-in-law.

DONALD MARRON: Former chairman of PaineWebber.

MICHAEL MAYO: Bank-stock analyst at Prudential Securities and former analyst at Credit Suisse First Boston.

BOB MCCOOEY: Chief executive officer of trading and brokerage firm Griswold Company.

WILLIAM MCDONOUGH: Former president of the Federal Reserve Bank of New York.

LEO MELAMED: Highly respected trader, former head of the Chicago Mercantile Exchange, and the creator of financial futures contracts.

JOHN MERIWETHER: Founder of Long-Term Capital Management and former Salomon Brothers vice chairman.

CHARLIE MERRILL: Cofounder and former chairman of Merrill Lynch and Company. His innovations in the brokerage business helped bring Americans back into the stock market in the 1950s.

JAMES MERRILL: Poet and son of Charlie Merrill.

TIM METZ: Former reporter for the *Wall Street Journal* and author of *Black Monday*.

MICHAEL MILKEN: Former head of Drexel Burnham Lambert's high-yield bond department, who is credited with leading a revolution in finance in the 1970s with his development of the junk-bond market. He was sent to prison for violations of securities laws and now is a cancer activist.

NELL MINOW: Cofounder of the Corporate Library and the Lens Funds.

ROBERT A. G. (BOB) MONKS: Cofounder of the Corporate Library and the Lens Funds.

JOHN NEFF: Legendary value investor and manager of the Windsor Fund from 1964 to 1995.

ROBERT NEWBURGER: Executive director of the New York Stock Exchange Alliance of Floor Brokers and member of the exchange since 1940. He has worked on Wall Street since 1933.

JOSEPH (JOE) NOCERA: Journalist and author of *A Piece of the Action*.

LELAND OLSON: Retired doctor in Omaha, Nebraska, and longtime friend of and investor with Warren Buffett.

ROBERT OLSTEIN: Chairman of Olstein Financial Alert Fund and former high-net-worth broker for Smith Barney.

STANLEY O'NEAL: Chairman and chief executive of Merrill Lynch.

KENNETH PASTERNAK: Founder and former chief executive officer of Knight/Trimark.

ALAN PATRICOF: New York City venture capitalist and chairman of the investment and finance firm Patricof and Company Ventures.

NORMAN PEARLSTINE: Editor in chief of Time Inc. and former managing editor of the *Wall Street Journal*.

EDWIN PERKINS: Financial historian, professor at the University of Southern California, and author of *Wall Street to Main Street.*

PETER (PETE) PETERSON: Cofounder of the buyout firm Blackstone Group with investment banker Stephen Schwarzman. Former chairman of Lehman Brothers and U.S. Secretary of Commerce under President Richard Nixon in 1972 and 1973.

FRANK PETRILLI: Former chief executive officer of TD Waterhouse.

JOHN PHELAN: Chairman of the New York Stock Exchange from 1984 to 1991. He was the leader of the exchange during the 1987 stock-market crash.

T. BOONE PICKENS: Former chairman of Mesa Petroleum. He is considered one of the most feared "corporate raiders" of the 1980s. Today he runs the investment firm BP Capital.

HARVEY PITT: Former chairman of the Securities and Exchange Commission.

HARRY POULAKAKOS: Former owner of Harry's of Hanover Square bar and restaurant.

ROBERT POZEN: Chairman of MFS Investment Management, former president of Fidelity Management and Research, and author of *The Mutual Fund Business.*

JERRY PUTNAM: Chief executive officer of Archipelago Holdings.

LARRY RAND: Financial historian with a PhD in U.S. economic history from New York University and cofounder of the financial public relations firm Kekst and Company.

JOHN REED: Former Citigroup cochairman and former Citicorp chairman. He became the interim chairman of the New York Stock Exchange after the resignation of former chairman Dick Grasso in September 2003.

DONALD REGAN: Former chairman of Merrill Lynch, treasury secretary, and White House chief of staff under President Ronald Reagan.

RODGER RINEY: Founder and chief executive officer of Scottrade.

GEORGE ROBERTS: Cofounder and partner of the leveraged-buyout firm Kohlberg Kravis Roberts and Company.

JULIAN ROBERTSON: Former head of the hedge fund Tiger Management.

LINDA ROBINSON: CEO of New York public relations firm Robinson, Lerer and Montgomery, and wife of former American Express chairman Jim Robinson.

DAVID ROCKEFELLER: Former chairman of Chase Manhattan Bank and grandson of John D. Rockefeller. He is considered the banker-diplomat of his time.

TOM ROGERS: Former president of NBC Cable.

ROBERT E. RUBIN: Senior executive and director of Citigroup, former treasury secretary, former director of the White House National Economic Council, and former co-senior partner at Goldman Sachs.

ROBERT S. (BOB) RUBIN: Former Lehman Brothers partner.

LOUIS RUKEYSER: Host of *Louis Rukeyser's Wall Street* on CNBC and former host of *Wall $treet Week with Louis Rukeyser* on PBS.

ANDREW G. C. (ANDY) SAGE: Former Lehman Brothers partner. He also served as an adviser to F. Ross Johnson during his bid to buy RJR Nabisco.

WILLIAM (BILLY) SALOMON: Son of Salomon Brothers founder Percy Salomon and former Salomon Brothers senior partner.

GEORGE (GUS) SAUTER: Chief investment officer of Vanguard.

DAVID SCHIFF: Former partner at Kuhn Loeb and Lehman Brothers, son of former Kuhn Loeb senior partner John Schiff, and great-grandson of legendary financier and Kuhn Loeb founder Jacob Schiff.

HOWARD SCHILIT: Founder of the Center for Financial Research and Analysis and author of *Financial Shenanigans.*

WALTER SCHLOSS: Well-known value investor, founder and former chairman of Walter and Edwin Schloss Associates, and former analyst at Graham-Newman.

MYRON SCHOLES: Nobel Prize–winning economist and former Long-Term Capital Management partner.

WILLIAM SCHREYER: Chairman of Merrill Lynch from 1984 to 1992.

CHARLES SCHWAB: Founder and chairman of the pioneering discount brokerage firm Charles Schwab and Company.

STEPHEN SCHWARZMAN: Former Lehman Brothers partner and cofounder of the buyout firm Blackstone Group with former Lehman Brothers chairman Peter Peterson.

BILL SEIDMAN: Former chairman of the Federal Deposit Insurance Corporation and first-ever chairman of the Resolution Trust Corporation.

ROGER SERVISON: Longtime marketing executive at Fidelity Investments and president of Fidelity Strategic New Business Development.

MURIEL (MICKIE) SIEBERT: Founder of Muriel Siebert and Company and Siebert Financial, and the first woman member of the New York Stock Exchange.

HARDWICK (WICK) SIMMONS: Former chairman of the Nasdaq Stock Market, former executive at Shearson, former partner at Hayden Stone, and great-grandson of Hayden Stone cofounder Galen Stone.

ROY SMITH: Finance professor at New York University and former partner at Goldman Sachs.

WINTHROP (WIN) SMITH JR.: Former executive vice president for international operations at Merrill Lynch. He also is the son of former Merrill Lynch chairman Win Smith Sr.

WINTHROP (WIN) SMITH SR.: Former chairman of Merrill Lynch and the man credited with bringing Charlie Merrill back into the brokerage business in the late 1930s.

ROBERT SOENER: Retired stockbroker in Omaha, Nebraska, and longtime friend of and investor with Warren Buffett.

PETER SOLOMON: Former Lehman Brothers partner.

LARRY SONSINI: Chairman and chief executive officer of the law firm Wilson Sonsini Goodrich and Rosati and one of the leading legal advisers in Silicon Valley.

JOHN L. (LAUNNY) STEFFENS: Former head of Merrill Lynch's brokerage operations.

PAUL STEIGER: Managing editor of the *Wall Street Journal.*

SAUL STEINBERG: Former chairman of Reliance Insurance and financial entrepreneur who amassed a fortune through aggressive investing tactics. He also was an early player in Michael Milken's junk-bond syndicates. In the 1980s he developed a reputation as a greenmailer because of his profitable failed takeover bids for companies like Disney.

ROBERT (BOBBY) STILLWELL: Legal counsel to T. Boone Pickens and partner at BP Capital.

TOM STRAUSS: President of Salomon Brothers from 1986 to 1991.

PAUL TIERNEY: Former partner at Coniston Partners.

JERRY TSAI: Legendary former manager of Fidelity Capital Fund and Manhattan Fund, who flamed out in the late 1960s. In the 1980s, he transformed American Can into the financial-services firm Primerica, and then sold it to Sandy Weill for $1.5 billion.

DANIEL TULLY: Chairman of Merrill Lynch from 1992 to 1997 and an early investor in Long-Term Capital Management.

JUDE WANNISKI: Chairman of Polyconomics and former associate editor of the *Wall Street Journal.* He was a vocal defender of Michael Milken and is the father of supply-side economics.

SHERRON WATKINS: Former vice president and accountant at Enron who tried to alert chairman Ken Lay to problems at the company and eventually testified before Congress.

DONALD WEEDEN: Chairman of institutional trading firm Weeden and Company.

SANFORD I. (SANDY) WEILL: Chairman of Citigroup. He was a founding partner of Carter, Berlind and Weill who survived power struggles to become the firm's leader in the 1970s. He sold the company to American Express in 1984, disappeared for a while, and then reemerged as a power player on Wall Street by putting together Citigroup through a series of mergers.

IAN WEINBERG: Financial adviser and president of Family Wealth and Pension Management.

JOHN WEINBERG: Former cochairman of Goldman Sachs with John Whitehead as well as former senior partner. He is the son of Wall Street legend Sidney Weinberg.

JOHN WHITEHEAD: Former cochairman of Goldman Sachs with John Weinberg. Currently he is the head of the Lower Manhattan Development Corporation, and he served as deputy secretary of state during the Ford administration.

FRED WHITTEMORE: Morgan Stanley partner known throughout Wall Street as "Father Fred," he ran the firm's underwriting syndicate during the 1960s and 1970s.

JENNIFER WILLIAMS: New York Stock Exchange floor broker for Griswold Company.

FRANK ZARB: Former chairman of Nasdaq. He joined Cogan, Berlind, Weill and Levitt in 1968 and has worked for Sandy Weill in various capacities since then. He also was a partner at Lazard Frères and served as White House energy czar in the mid-1970s.

ARTHUR ZEIKEL: Wall Street mutual fund expert who is credited with building the Merrill Lynch asset-management business.

Acknowledgments

I conducted hundreds of interviews for this book. So many people were extremely generous with their time and patient as I asked hours of questions that I couldn't list them all here. Some didn't want their names to appear in the story but were eager to provide assistance and insight behind the scenes. And others unfortunately ended up on the cutting-room floor in the process of editing the final version of the book. Regardless of the situation, every conversation I had with the people who participated in this project was helpful in some way. Thank you all.

I also need to acknowledge the contributions of numerous Wall Street professionals and others who believed in this project and offered me special assistance in completing it. They are: Eric Berman, Bobbie Collins, Paul Critchlow, Bob Dilenschneider, Gayle Dragity, Judith Ehrlich, Burt Fabricand, Stephanie Cohen Glass, Bernie Herold, Russell Horwitz, Tom Kelly, Dick Kosmicki, Peter Low, Andy MacMillan, Larry Mark, Barbara Martz, Dan McCooey, Jean Marie McFadden, Selena Morris, Leo Murray, Ed Novotny, Ruth Pachman, Frank Petrilli, Betsy Pohl, Peter Rose, Jay Rosser, Alison Rudnick, Ian Weinberg, and Adam Weiner.

Professionally, I owe a major debt of gratitude to *Dow Jones Newswires,* where I was an editor, Wall Street reporter, and columnist for more than six years. Rick Stine gave me the chance to cover Wall Street and helped me learn everything I needed to know to tell this story, while Paul Ingrassia provided constant personal encouragement and inspiration. And I also have to thank all of my wonderful Dow Jones friends and colleagues who put up with me over the years.

Truth be told, this book most likely never would've gotten off the ground if not for my agent, Andrew Wylie, who read a ten-page outline and saw exactly what this story could be. At the Wylie Agency, Jeff Posternak was a constant encouraging voice and ferocious advocate, while occasionally providing the necessary kick in the butt. At Little, Brown, I was lucky to have three outstanding editors. Rick Kot signed this project and helped me organize the broad themes this story addressed. Bill Phillips shepherded the project and offered knowledgeable advice on how best to structure the story. And Geoff Shandler was a master at prodding the best out of me. This is a far superior book because of his shrewd editorial guidance. Behind the curtain, Michael Pietsch was constantly supportive of this project, giving me all the room I needed to tell the story I wanted to tell. And then there's the entire team at Little, Brown, which has to be the best in the business. I specifically want to thank Junie Dahn, Peggy Freudenthal, Melissa Clemence, Chris Nolan, and Heather Fain for all of their effort on my behalf.

On a personal level, two of my best friends in the world — Andrew Albanese and Chris Nagi — provided invaluable editorial insight and support from start to finish. My parents, Carol and Carl, always encouraged me to pursue a career as a writer and most understood how much finishing this book meant to me. My brother, Glen, was my most loyal reader and objective critic, offering "surprisingly" valuable advice. And finally, there's my wife, Paige. There are so many different words I could use to describe her contributions to my life, but the bottom line is I'm pretty sure none of this would have happened without her.

—ERIC J. WEINER, *May 26, 2005*

Notes

The following notes reflect, for the most part, direct quotes and comments that appear in this book but did not come from my first-person interviews. In many cases, the reason these people could not be interviewed is that they no longer are alive or could not be located. Other sources included here were not available to be interviewed because they refused my requests. But in all instances, everyone who appears in this book, is still alive, and could be located, was contacted and given the opportunity to participate.

CHAPTER I: GOOD TIME CHARLIE

The quote from Charlie Merrill on page 12, in a letter to clients dated March 31, 1928, came from an in-house history of Merrill Lynch called *A Legacy of Leadership: Merrill Lynch, 1885–1985,* edited by Henry R. Hecht (New York: Merrill Lynch, 1985), page 41. Robert Magowan's comment on page 14 about Charlie Merrill came from the biography of Charlie Merrill *Wall Street to Main Street* by Edwin Perkins (Cambridge: Cambridge University Press, 1999), page 11. James Merrill's comment on page 15 about his father came from his memoir *A Different Person* (New York: Knopf, 1993), page 34. Charlie Merrill's comment on page 17 about "mass education" came from *A Piece of the Action: How the Middle Class Joined the Money Class* by Joe Nocera (New York: Simon and Schuster, 1994), page 43. Louis Engel's comment on page 19 about Win Smith came from *Co-Leaders: The Power of Great Partnerships* by David A. Heenan and Warren Bennis (New York: John Wiley, 1999), page 76. Winthrop Smith Sr.'s comment on page 19 about Charlie Merrill's absence is also from Heenan and Bennis, page 73. Numbers of individual investors given on page 25 are from Nocera, page 44.

CHAPTER 2: WHITE SHOES

Robert Baldwin's lengthy description of a hypothetical bond offering by General Motors that begins on page 33 came from *The Seven Fat Years* by John Brooks (New York: Harper and Brothers, 1958), pages 43–44.

CHAPTER 4: INTRINSIC VALUE

Warren Buffett's comment on page 60 about *The Intelligent Investor* being the best book about investing ever written came from the preface to *The Intelligent Investor,* revised edition, by Benjamin Graham and Jason Zweig (New York: HarperBusiness, 2003), page ix.

CHAPTER 5: BLACKBALLED

Sandy Weill's comments on pages 72 and 74 are from *The New Crowd: The Changing of the Jewish Guard on Wall Street* by Judith Ramsey Ehrlich and Barry J. Rehfeld (Boston: Little, Brown, 1989), page 51 ("It was a turning point . . ." and "I think they realized . . ."). Sandy Weill's comment on page 73 about first peering into the Bache office in Times Square came from "Sandy Weill Roars Back" by Jon Friedman, *Business Week,* December 4, 1989. Dan Corwin's comment on pages 73–74 about Weill's sartorial selections came from Ehrlich and Rehfeld, page 53.

CHAPTER 6: GO-GO BOYS

The comments by Edward C. Johnson II on pages 89–90 and 97 came from *The Go-Go Years* by John Brooks (New York: John Wiley, 1999), page 131 ("We didn't want to feel . . .") and page 135 ("It was a beautiful thing . . ."). The comments by Edward C. Johnson II on pages 94, 95, and 103 came from *The Money Managers,* edited by Gilbert Edmund Kaplan and Chris Welles (New York: Random House, 1969), page 98 ("We want a man . . ." and "You want an environment . . .") and pages 98–99 ("We start off with . . ."). Roger Clinton's comment on page 95 about the atmosphere at Fidelity came from Kaplan and Welles, page 103. Fred Alger's comment on page 99 about the impact of Jerry Tsai on mutual fund managers came from Kaplan and Welles, page 79. Ned Johnson's comment on page 102 about Jerry Tsai came from *The Way It Was: An Oral History of Finance, 1967–1987,* by the editors of *Institutional Investor* (New York: Morrow, 1988), page 203.

CHAPTER 7: POWER TO THE PEOPLE

William Donaldson's comment on page 122 about the idea for starting Donaldson, Lufkin and Jenrette came from "The Pioneers" by Justin Schack, *Institutional Investor,* October 1, 2001.

CHAPTER 8: CORNED BEEF WITH LETTUCE

Sandy Weill's comment on page 132 about Arthur Carter leaving came from *The New Crowd: The Changing of the Jewish Guard on Wall Street* by Judith Ramsey Ehrlich and Barry J. Rehfeld (Boston: Little, Brown, 1989), page 60. Sandy Weill's comment on page 134 describing the firm after Carter left came from "Sandy Weill Roars Back" by Jon Friedman, *Business Week,* December 4, 1989. Sandy Weill's comments on pages 136–137 and 138 came from *The Way It Was: An Oral History of Finance, 1967–1987,* by the editors of *Institutional Investor* (New York: Morrow, 1988), page 366 ("When we started . . ." and "So we hired . . ."). I. W. "Tubby" Burnham's comment on page 137 describing Sandy Weill is from "Sandy Weill" by Robert Lenzer, *New York Times Magazine,* November 7, 1993.

CHAPTER 9: THE PAPER CRUNCH

Sandy Weill's comments on pages 142 and 143 about the Hayden Stone deal are from *The Way It Was: An Oral History of Finance, 1967–1987,* by the editors of *Institutional Investor* (New York: Morrow, 1988), page 368.

CHAPTER 10: KISMET FUNDS

Although I interviewed Peter Lynch, his comment on pages 151–152 about money-market mutual funds came from *One Up on Wall Street: How to Use What You Already Know to Make Money in the Market* by Peter Lynch with John Rothchild (New York: Simon and Schuster, 1989), page 69.

CHAPTER 11: MAYDAY

Robert Haack's comments about the deregulation of trading commissions on pages 164–165, 165–166, and 166 came from *The Way It Was: An Oral History of Finance, 1967–1987,* by the editors of *Institutional Investor* (New York: Morrow, 1988), pages 286–287 ("Toward the end of my tenure . . .") and page 287 ("I was not for abolishing . . ." and "I said in the introduction . . ."). Joe Nocera's comment on page 169 about Charles Schwab picking up Charlie Merrill's legacy came from *A Piece of the Action: How the Middle Class Joined the Money Class* by Joe Nocera (New York: Simon and Schuster, 1994), pages 107–108.

CHAPTER 13: THE THUNDERING HERD

The statement on page 183 that Merrill Lynch brokers were adding three thousand new CMA accounts a week in 1979 came from an in-house history of Merrill Lynch called *A Legacy of Leadership: Merrill Lynch, 1885–1985,* edited by Henry R. Hecht (New York: Merrill Lynch, 1985), page 138. The statement on page 183 that Merrill Lynch brokers were adding six thousand new CMA accounts a week by the early 1980s came from *The Year They Sold Wall Street* by Tim Carrington (Boston: Houghton Mifflin, 1985), page 216.

CHAPTER 15: HAVE YOUR CAKE AND EAT IT, TOO

The statistic on page 200 about KKR being the top client for Deloitte and Touche in 1989 came from *Merchants of Debt: KKR and the Mortgaging of American Business* by George Anders (New York: Basic Books, 1992), page xiv.

CHAPTER 16: A LICENSE TO PRINT MONEY

I. W. "Tubby" Burnham's comment on page 214 about why he named the firm Drexel Burnham came from *The Predators' Ball: The Junk-Bond Raiders and the Man Who Staked Them* by Connie Bruck (New York: American Lawyer/Simon and Schuster, 1988), pages 30–31. Michael Milken's comments on page 215 about the scope of the junk-bond market before he started trading junk bonds and on page 226 about the changes at Disney in the 1980s came from "My Story — Michael Milken" by James W. Michaels and Phyllis Berman, *Forbes,* March 16, 1992. Michael Milken's comments on pages 216 and 217 about the development of the junk-bond market came from "Prosperity and Social Capital" by Michael Milken, *Wall Street Journal,* June 23, 1999.

CHAPTER 17: TRADING UP

Sandy Weill's comments on pages 234, 234–235, and 237 about the origins of the Shearson–American Express deal and on pages 243 and 245 about why he left American Express came from *The Way It Was: An Oral History of Finance, 1967–1987,* by the editors of *Institutional Investor* (New York: Morrow, 1988), pages 372 and 373. Sandy Weill's comment on page 241 about his relationship with Peter Cohen is from "Sandy Weill Roars Back" by Jon Friedman, *Business Week,* December 4, 1989. Sandy Weill's comment on page 242 about why he ultimately decided to sell Shearson to American Express came from *The New Crowd: The Changing of the Jewish Guard on Wall Street* by Judith Ramsey Ehrlich and Barry J. Rehfeld (Boston: Little, Brown, 1989), page 369.

CHAPTER 18: CULTURE CLASH

Lewis Glucksman's comments on page 249 about the stature of Lehman Brothers, on page 255 about his relationship with Pete Peterson, and on page 258 about his plans for the firm after he took over for Peterson came from *Greed and Glory on Wall Street: The Fall of the House of Lehman* by Ken Auletta (New York: Random House, 1986), pages 46, 7, and 93, respectively. Lewis Glucksman's comments on pages 260 and 263 about the partners at Lehman Brothers came from "After the Lehman Mutiny — Lew Glucksman's Story" by Geoffrey Smith, *Forbes,* June 18, 1984.

CHAPTER 20: BLACK MONDAY

Although I interviewed Henry Kaufman, his comment on pages 282–283 about the days leading up to the 1987 stock-market crash came from *On Money and Markets: A Wall Street Memoir* by Henry Kaufman (New York: McGraw-Hill, 2000), page 271.

CHAPTER 21: KILLING THE GOLDEN GOOSE

F. Ross Johnson's comments on pages 301 and 317 about his attempt to buy out RJR Nabisco came from "They Cleaned Our Clock" by Bill Saporito, *Fortune,* January 2, 1989. Linda Robinson's comment on page 314 about whether she thought KKR had dropped out of the bidding for RJR Nabisco came from *Barbarians at the Gate: The Fall of RJR Nabisco* by Bryan Burrough and John Helyar (New York: Harper and Row, 1990), page 432.

CHAPTER 22: GREED IS BAD

Rudy Giuliani's comments on pages 320, 325, and 330 about the prosecution of Michael Milken came from the first-person question-and-answer interview "From Milken to the Mafia," *Barron's,* November 26, 1990. Michael Milken's comment on page 324 about trading with Ivan Boesky came from "My Story — Michael Milken" by James W. Michaels and Phyllis Berman, *Forbes,* March 16, 1992.

CHAPTER 24: DIGITAL BABYLON

Robert E. Rubin's comment on page 350 about Alan Greenspan's Irrational Exuberance speech came from *In an Uncertain World: Tough Choices from Wall Street to Washington* by Robert E. Rubin and Jacob Weisberg (New York: Random House, 2003), page 189.

CHAPTER 25: A RISKLESS TRANSACTION

Arthur Cashin's description of the origins of hedge funds on pages 362–363 came from his comments on the CNBC television program *Business Center* on July 15, 2003. William McDonough's comments on pages 364–365, 365–366, 368, and 373 about Long-Term Capital Management's trading strategies and the events that eventually brought the fund down came from his testimony before the House Committee on Banking and Financial Services on October 1, 1998. Mr. McDonough declined to be interviewed, but referred the author to this specific testimony for his perspective on these events. The comment by Myron Scholes on page 370 about what happened to LTCM after the Russian default came from the PBS documentary "The Trillion Dollar Bet" produced for the program *Nova.* John Meriwether's comment on page 371 about LTCM's miscalculations came from "Long-Term Capital Chief Acknowledges Flawed Tactics" by Gregory Zuckerman, *Wall Street Journal,* August 21, 2000. Richard R. Lindsey's comment on page 371–372 about the level of LTCM's losses came from his testimony before the House Committee on Banking and Financial Services on October 1, 1998. Robert E. Rubin's comment on page 372 about the public-policy questions raised by the LTCM crisis came from *In an Uncertain World: Tough Choices from Wall Street to Washington* by Robert E. Rubin and Jacob Weisberg (New York: Random House, 2003), page 286. Alan Greenspan's comment on page 379 about the rescue of LTCM came from his testimony before the House Committee on Banking and Financial Services on October 1, 1998.

CHAPTER 26: THE EMPIRE

Sandy Weill's comment on page 387 about specific stipulations in the laws regulating the financial-services industry came from his interview on the CNBC television program "Special Report with Maria Bartiromo" on July 21, 2003. John Reed's comment on page 389 about the cochairman structure at Citigroup came from "Lifetime Achievement: John Reed Looks Back" by Barbara A. Rehm, *American Banker,* February 1, 2001.

CHAPTER 27: MARKET MESSENGERS

Maria Bartiromo's comment on page 399 about what it was like to first broadcast from the floor of the New York Stock Exchange came from "CNBC's Maria Bartiromo Stepping Away from the New York Stock Exchange" by David Bauder, *Associated Press,* May 12, 2004.

CHAPTER 30: MUST COME DOWN

Dick Grasso's comments on pages 458, 460, and 461 about his ouster as chairman of the New York Stock Exchange came from "My Vindication Will Come in a Courtroom," by Richard A. Grasso, *Wall Street Journal,* May 25, 2004.

EPILOGUE

Sandy Weill's comment on page 464 about the leadership change at Citigroup comes from a conference call with investors ("Citigroup Announces New Senior Leadership Conference Call"), July 16, 2003.

Bibliography

This bibliography is divided into two parts. The first part is a list of books I used in my research. A few are quoted in the text, but most aren't. The second part is a list of news articles and transcripts of interviews and congressional testimony that are directly quoted in the text. Obviously, in working on a project of this magnitude I also read countless other articles and transcripts that don't appear in the book, but listing all of them here would be impractical.

BOOKS

Anders, George. *Merchants of Debt: KKR and the Mortgaging of American Business.* New York: Basic Books, 1992.

Auletta, Ken. *Greed and Glory on Wall Street: The Fall of the House of Lehman.* New York: Random House, 1986.

———. *The Highwaymen: Warriors of the Information Superhighway.* New York: Random House, 1997.

Baker, George P., and George David Smith. *The New Financial Capitalists: Kohlberg Kravis Roberts and the Creation of Corporate Value.* Cambridge, UK: Cambridge University Press, 1998.

Bernstein, Peter L. *Against the Gods: The Remarkable Story of Risk.* 1996. New York: John Wiley and Sons, 1998.

———. *Capital Ideas: The Improbable Origins of Modern Wall Street.* 1992. New York: The Free Press, 1993.

Birmingham, Stephen. *"Our Crowd": The Great Jewish Families of New York.* 1967. New York: Dell, 1968.

Brooks, John. *The Go-Go Years: The Drama and Crashing Finale of Wall Street's Bullish '60s.* 1973. New York: John Wiley and Sons, 1999.

———. *The Seven Fat Years: Chronicles of Wall Street.* New York: Harper and Brothers Publishers, 1958.

Bruck, Connie. *The Predators' Ball: The Junk-Bond Raiders and the Man Who Staked Them.* New York: American Lawyer/Simon and Schuster, 1988.

Burrough, Bryan, and John Helyar. *Barbarians at the Gate: The Fall of RJR Nabisco.* 1990. New York: Harper and Row, 1991.

Carrington, Tim. *The Year They Sold Wall Street: The Inside Story of the Shearson/American Express Merger, and How It Changed Wall Street Forever.* Boston: Houghton Mifflin, 1985.

Cassidy, John. *dot.con: How America Lost Its Mind and Money in the Internet Era.* New York: HarperCollins, 2002.

Chancellor, Edward. *Devil Take the Hindmost: A History of Financial Speculation.* New York: Farrar, Straus and Giroux, 1999.

Chernow, Ron. *The Death of the Banker: The Decline and Fall of the Great Financial Dynasties and the Triumph of the Small Investor.* New York: Vintage, 1997.

———. *The House of Morgan: An American Banking Dynasty and the Rise of Modern Finance.* 1990. New York: Touchstone, 1991.

Cramer, James J. *Confessions of a Street Addict.* 2002. New York: Simon and Schuster, 2003.

Ehrlich, Judith Ramsey, and Barry J. Rehfeld. *The New Crowd: The Changing of the Jewish Guard on Wall Street.* 1989. New York: HarperPerennial, 1990.

Endlich, Lisa. *Goldman Sachs: The Culture of Success.* New York: Alfred A. Knopf, 1999.

Fischel, Daniel. *Payback: The Conspiracy to Destroy Michael Milken and His Financial Revolution.* 1995. New York: HarperBusiness, 1996.

Fischer, David Hackett. *The Great Wave: Price Revolutions and the Rhythm of History.* New York: Oxford University Press, 1996.

Fromson, Brett Duval, ed. *The Gaga Years: The Rise and Fall of the Money Game, 1981–1991.* New York: Citadel Press, 1992.

Galbraith, John Kenneth. *The Great Crash 1929.* 1954. Boston: Houghton Mifflin, 1997.

———. *A Short History of Financial Euphoria.* 1990. New York: Penguin Books, 1994.

Geisst, Charles R. *The Last Partnerships: Inside the Great Wall Street Money Dynasties.* New York: McGraw Hill, 2001.

———. *Wall Street: A History.* New York: Oxford University Press, 1997.

Graham, Benjamin, and Jason Zweig (with preface and appendix by Warren Buffett). *The Intelligent Investor: The Definitive Book on Value Investing, Revised Edition.* New York: HarperBusiness, 2003.

Grant, James. *The Trouble with Prosperity: A Contrarian's Tale of Boom, Bust and Speculation.* New York: Times Books, 1996.

Hecht, Henry R., ed. *A Legacy of Leadership: Merrill Lynch, 1885–1985.* New York: Merrill Lynch, 1985.

Heenan, David A., and Warren Bennis. *Co-Leaders: The Power of Great Partnerships.* New York: John Wiley and Sons, 1999.

Henriques, Diana B. *Fidelity's World: The Secret Life and Public Power of the Mutual Fund Giant.* 1995. New York: Touchstone, 1997.

Ingebretsen, Mark. *Nasdaq: A History of the Market That Changed the World.* Roseville, California: Prima Publishing, 2002.

Institutional Investor, editors of. *The Way It Was: An Oral History of Finance, 1967–1987.* New York: William Morrow, 1988.

Jenrette, Richard H. *Jenrette: The Contrarian Manager.* New York: McGraw-Hill, 1997.

Kaplan, David A. *The Silicon Boys: And Their Valley of Dreams.* New York: William Morrow, 1999.

Kaplan, Gilbert Edmund, and Chris Welles, eds. *The Money Managers.* New York: Random House, 1969.

Kaufman, Henry. *On Money and Markets: A Wall Street Memoir.* New York: McGraw-Hill, 2000.

Kornbluth, Jesse. *Highly Confident: The Crime and Punishment of Michael Milken.* New York: William Morrow, 1992.

Kilpatrick, Andrew. *Of Permanent Value: The Story of Warren Buffett, More in '04 California Edition.* Birmingham, Alabama: AKPE, 2004.

Kurtz, Howard. *The Fortune Tellers: Inside Wall Street's Game of Money, Media and Manipulation.* New York: The Free Press, 2000.

Langley, Monica. *Tearing Down the Walls: How Sandy Weill Fought His Way to the Top of the Financial World . . . and Then Nearly Lost It All.* New York: Wall Street Journal Books, 2003.

Lefevre, Edwin. *Reminiscences of a Stock Operator.* 1923. Burlington, Vermont: Fraser Publishing, 1980.

Levine, Dennis (with William Hoffer). *Inside Out: An Insider's Account of Wall Street.* New York: G. P. Putnam's Sons, 1991.

Levitt, Arthur (with Paula Dwyer). *Take On the Street: What Wall Street and Corporate America Don't Want You to Know.* New York: Pantheon Books, 2002.

Lewis, Michael. *Liar's Poker: Rising Through the Wreckage on Wall Street.* 1989. New York: Penguin Books, 1990.

———. *The New New Thing: A Silicon Valley Story.* New York: W. W. Norton, 2000.

Lowe, Janet. *Benjamin Graham on Value Investing: Lessons from the Dean of Wall Street.* Chicago: Dearborn Financial Publishing, 1994.

Lowenstein, Roger. *Buffett: The Making of an American Capitalist.* 1995. New York: Main Street Books, 1996.

———. *When Genius Failed: The Rise and Fall of Long-Term Capital Management.* New York: Random House, 2000.

Lynch, Peter (with John Rothchild). *One Up On Wall Street: How to Use What You Already Know to Make Money in the Market.* 1989. New York: Fireside, 2000.

Mayer, Martin. *The Bankers, the Next Generation: The New Worlds of Money, Credit and Banking in an Electronic Age.* 1997. New York: Truman Talley Books/Plume, 1998.

———. *The Fed: The Inside Story of How the World's Most Powerful Financial Institution Drives the Markets.* New York: The Free Press, 2001.

———. *Nightmare on Wall Street: Salomon Brothers and the Corruption of the Marketplace.* New York: Simon and Schuster, 1993.

Melamed, Leo (with Bob Tamarkin). *Escape to the Futures.* New York: John Wiley and Sons, 1996.

Merrill, James. *A Different Person: A Memoir.* New York: Alfred A. Knopf, 1993.

Metz, Tim. *Black Monday: The Catastrophe of October 19, 1987 . . . and Beyond.* New York: William Morrow, 1988.

Niederhoffer, Victor. *The Education of a Speculator.* New York: John Wiley and Sons, 1997.

Nocera, Joseph. *A Piece of the Action: How the Middle Class Joined the Money Class.* New York: Simon and Schuster, 1994.

Partnoy, Frank. *Infectious Greed: How Deceit and Risk Corrupted the Financial Markets.* New York: Times Books, 2003.

Perkins, Edwin J. *Wall Street to Main Street: Charles Merrill and Middle-Class Investors.* Cambridge, UK: Cambridge University Press, 1999.

Pickens, Boone. *The Luckiest Guy in the World: An Autobiography.* Washington: Beard Books, 2000.

Regan, Donald T. *For the Record: From Wall Street to Washington.* New York: Harcourt Brace Jovanovich, 1988.

———. *A View from the Street.* New York: New American Library, 1972.

Reich, Cary. *Financier: The Biography of Andre Mayer.* New York: William Morrow, 1983.

Rubin, Robert E., and Jacob Weisberg. *In an Uncertain World: Tough Choices from Wall Street to Washington.* New York: Random House, 2003.

Schiller, Robert J. *Irrational Exuberance.* Princeton, New Jersey: Princeton University Press, 2000.

Slater, Robert. *The Titans of Takeover.* Englewood Cliffs, New Jersey: Prentice-Hall, 1987.

Soros, George (with Byron Wien and Krisztina Koenen). *Soros on Soros: Staying Ahead of the Curve.* New York: John Wiley and Sons, 1995.

Stewart, James B. *Den of Thieves.* 1991. New York: Touchstone, 1992.

Tanous, Peter J. *Investment Gurus: A Roadmap to Wealth from the World's Best Money Managers.* New York: New York Institute of Finance, 1997.

Wasserstein, Bruce. *Big Deal: The Battle for Control of America's Leading Corporations.* New York: Warner Books, 1998.

Weeden, Donald E. *Weeden and Co.: The New York Stock Exchange and the Struggle over a National Securities Market.* Greenwich, Connecticut: Donald E. Weeden, 2002.

Welles, Chris. *The Last Days of the Club: The Passing of the Old Wall Street Monopoly and the Rise of New Institutions and Men Who Will Soon Dominate Financial Power in America.* New York: Dutton, 1975.

Winans, Foster R. *Trading Secrets: Seduction and Scandal at The Wall Street Journal.* New York: St. Martin's Press, 1984.

Wolff, Michael. *Burn Rate: How I Survived the Gold Rush Years on the Internet.* New York: Simon and Schuster, 1998.

Articles, Transcripts, and Testimony Quoted in the Text

Bauder, David. "CNBC's Maria Bartiromo Stepping Away from the New York Stock Exchange." Associated Press. May 12, 2004.

Cashin, Arthur. Interview on CNBC *Business Center*. July 15, 2003.

Friedman, Jon. "Sandy Weill Roars Back." *Business Week.* December 4, 1989.

Giuliani, Rudy. "From Milken to the Mafia." Interview in *Barron's.* November 26, 1990.

Grasso, Richard A. "My Vindication Will Come in a Courtroom." *Wall Street Journal,* May 25, 2004.

Greenspan, Alan. Testimony before the House Committee on Banking and Financial Services. October 1, 1998.

Lenzer, Robert. "Sandy Weill." *New York Times Magazine.* November 7, 1993.

Lindsey, Richard. Testimony before the House Committee on Banking and Financial Services. October 1, 1998.

McDonough, William. Testimony before the House Committee on Banking and Financial Services. October 1, 1998.

Michaels, James W., and Phyllis Berman. "My Story — Michael Milken." *Forbes.* March 16, 1992.

Milken, Michael. "Prosperity and Social Capital." *Wall Street Journal.* June 23, 1999.

Rehm, Barbara A. "Lifetime Achievement: John Reed Looks Back." *American Banker.* February 1, 2001.

Saporito, Bill. "They Cleaned Our Clock: RJR Nabisco's CEO Describes How the 'Country Boys' Were Outfoxed, How KKR Put Air in Its Offer, and How Charges of Greed Were Shrewdly Shifted from Wall Street to Ross Johnson." *Fortune,* January 2, 1989.

Schack, Justin. "The Pioneers: The Three Founders of Donaldson, Lufkin and Jenrette." *Institutional Investor.* October 1, 2001.

Smith, Geoffrey. "After the Lehman Mutiny — Lew Glucksman's Story." *Forbes.* June 18, 1984.

"The Trillion Dollar Bet." PBS Documentary for *Nova.* Original air date: February 8, 2000.

Weill, Sandy. Interview on CNBC *Special Report with Maria Bartiromo.* July 21, 2003.

Zuckerman, Gregory. "Long-Term Capital Chief Acknowledges Flawed Tactics." *IDX.* August 21, 2000.

Index

About the Author

Eric J. Weiner is a financial journalist and former Wall Street reporter for the Dow Jones News Service. His stories have appeared in countless publications, including the *Wall Street Journal,* the *Los Angeles Times,* the *Boston Globe,* and the *Village Voice*. He lives in Great Barrington, Massachusetts, with his wife, Paige.

ALSO AVAILABLE IN PAPERBACK

The Faber Report

How Wall Street Really *Works —*
and How You Can Make It Work for You

by David Faber
CNBC's Wall Street correspondent
with Ken Kurson

"An invaluable tool to navigate through the booms and busts."
— Mario J. Gabelli, Gabelli Asset Management, Inc.

The Tipping Point

How Little Things Can Make a Big Difference

by Malcolm Gladwell

"As a business how-to, *The Tipping Point* is truly superior, brimming with new theories on the science of manipulation."
— Aaron Gell, TimeOut.com

Natural Capitalism

Creating the Next Industrial Revolution

by Paul Hawken, Amory Lovins, and L. Hunter Lovins

"Hugely important. . . . *Natural Capitalism* ought to be on the nightstand of every CEO."
— Thomas Petzinger Jr., former "Front Lines" columnist, *Wall Street Journal*

Back Bay Books • Available wherever books are sold